My
iPad®

ELEVENTH EDITION

D0067239

Gary Rosenzweig

My iPad®, Eleventh Edition

Copyright © 2019 by Pearson Education, Inc.

ISBN-13: 978-0-7897-6044-9
ISBN-10: 0-7897-6044-4

Library of Congress Control Number: 2018959185

01 18

Trademarks

All terms mentioned in this book that are known to be trademarks or service marks have been appropriately capitalized. Pearson Education cannot attest to the accuracy of this information. Use of a term in this book should not be regarded as affecting the validity of any trademark or service mark.

Warning and Disclaimer

Unless otherwise indicated herein, any third-party trademarks that may appear in this work are the property of their respective owners, and any references to third-party trademarks, logos, or other trade dress are for demonstrative or descriptive purposes only. Such references are not intended to imply any sponsorship, endorsement, authorization, or promotion of Pearson Education products by the owners of such marks, or any relationship between the owner and Pearson Education or its affiliates, authors, licensees, or distributors.

Special Sales

For information about buying this title in bulk quantities, or for special sales opportunities (which may include electronic versions; custom cover designs; and content particular to your business, training goals, marketing focus, or branding interests), please contact our corporate sales department at corpsales@pearsoned.com or (800) 382-3419.

For government sales inquiries, please contact governmentsales@pearsoned.com.

For questions about sales outside the U.S., please contact intlcs@pearsoned.com.

Editor-in-Chief
Mark Taub

Senior Acquisitions Editor
Laura Norman

Development Editor
Charlotte Kughen

Marketing Manager
Stephane Nakib

Managing Editor
Sandra Schroeder

Senior Project Editor
Lori Lyons

Indexer
Erika Millen

Proofreader
Debbie Williams

Technical Editor
Paul Sihvonen-Binder

Cover Designer
Chuti Prasertsith

Compositor
Kim Scott,
Bumpy Design

Contents at a Glance

Chapter 1   Getting Started 3

Chapter 2   Customizing Your iPad 39

Chapter 3   Networking and Syncing 63

Chapter 4   Playing Music and Video 89

Chapter 5   Reading Books 119

Chapter 6   Organizing Your Life 135

Chapter 7   Surfing the Web 165

Chapter 8   Communicating with Email and Messaging 191

Chapter 9   Taking and Editing Photos 223

Chapter 10   Recording Video 261

Chapter 11   Writing with Pages 285

Chapter 12   Spreadsheets with Numbers 303

Chapter 13   Presentations with Keynote 323

Chapter 14   Navigating with Maps 343

Chapter 15   The World of Apps 355

Chapter 16   Must-Have Apps 409

Chapter 17   Games and Entertainment 447

Chapter 18   iPad Accessories 467

Chapter 19   Maintaining Your iPad and Solving Problems 493

Index 514

Table of Contents

1 **Getting Started** **3**

  Generations of iPads...3

    iPad Models over the Years.................................3

    iOS 12 **New!**..5

  The iPad Buttons and Switches...........................5

    The Home Button **New!**...............................5

    The Wake/Sleep Button.....................................6

    The Volume Control..8

    Orientation and Movement................................8

  Screen Gestures..9

  Learning Your Way Around.................................10

    The Lock Screen..11

    The Home Screen...12

    The Search Screen..13

    Today View...15

    The Notifications Screen.................................17

  Virtual Buttons and Switches............................18

    Switches and Option Lists...............................18

    Toolbars..19

    Menus...19

    Tab Bars..20

  Entering Text...20

    Using the On-Screen Keyboard.....................20

    Keyboard Modes..20

    Undocking and Splitting the Keyboard.......22

    Using the Keyboard Shortcut Bar..................24

    Using Predictive Text.......................................26

    Dictating Text..27

    Editing Text..28

    Copying and Pasting..29

  Talking to Your iPad with Siri.............................31

    Asking Siri Questions......................................31

  Using Control Center **New for iOS 12!**.......33

2 **Customizing Your iPad** **39**

  Changing Your Wallpaper...................................40

  Setting Alert Sounds..43

Password-Protecting Your iPad 44

    Making Access Easier with Touch ID 48

Modifying Keyboard Settings 50

Adjusting Do Not Disturb Settings 52

Setting Parental Restrictions 53

Making Text Easier to Read 56

Controlling Automatic Downloads 57

Customizing the Control Center 58

Working with Other Useful Settings 60

3   **Networking and Syncing**   **63**

Setting Up Your Wi-Fi Network Connection 63

Connecting to Your Apple ID and iCloud Account 66

    Signing In with Your Apple ID 67

Syncing with iTunes 72

    Syncing Options 73

    Syncing Music 74

    Syncing Photos 77

    Syncing Everything Else 79

Sharing with AirDrop 80

    Using AirDrop 80

Storing, Organizing, and Viewing Files 83

    Accessing Your iCloud Drive Files 83

    Accessing Files in Other Cloud Services 86

4   **Playing Music and Video**   **89**

Playing a Song 90

Building a Playlist 93

    Creating Playlists 93

Making iTunes Purchases 95

    Buying on Your iPad 96

Sharing Purchases with Your Family 98

    Setting Up Family Sharing 98

Having It All with Apple Music 100

    Signing Up for Apple Music 101

    Playing Songs with Apple Music 102

    Discovering New Music with Apple Music 105

    Discovering Music with Apple Music Radio Stations .. 106

Listening to Podcasts 108
   Subscribing to Podcasts 109
Playing Video 111
   Adding Your TV Networks to the TV App 111
   Watch Videos on Your iPad 113
Using AirPlay to Play Music and Video on
   Other Devices 115
   Accessing AirPlay 116
   Mirror Your Screen with AirPlay 117

5 Reading Books 119

Buying a Book from Apple 119
Reading a Book 122
Using Reading Aids 123
Adding Notes and Highlights 125
Adding Bookmarks 127
Organizing Your Books 127
Using Books App Alternatives 130

6 Organizing Your Life 135

Using the Contacts App 135
   Adding a Contact 136
Searching for a Contact 138
Working with Contacts 140
Using the Calendar App 141
   Creating a Calendar Event 141
Using Calendar Views 143
   Exploring Day View 143
   Exploring Week View 145
   Exploring Month View 146
Creating a Calendar 147
Using the Notes App 149
   Creating a Note 149
   Creating Checklists in Notes 151
   Adding Photos and Sketches to Notes 152
   Scanning Documents with Notes 154
   Signing and Sending Documents with Notes 156

Using the Reminders App 158

    Setting a Reminder 159

Using the Clock App 161

    Setting Clock Alarms 161

7   Surfing the Web   165

Getting Started with Safari 165

    Browsing to a URL and Searching 166

    Viewing Web Pages 169

    Opening Multiple Web Pages with Tabs 171

    Viewing Articles with Safari Reader 173

Bookmarks, History, and Reading List 174

    Using Bookmarks and Favorites 174

    Using History 176

    Creating Home Screen Bookmarks 178

    Building a Reading List 179

Working with Web Forms 181

    Filling in Web Forms 182

    Saving Time with AutoFill 183

    Setting Up AutoFill 184

    Using AutoFill 186

8   Communicating with Email and Messaging   191

Configuring Your iPad for Email 192

    Set Up Your Email Account 192

Reading Your Email 195

Composing a New Email 198

Deleting and Moving Emails 199

Searching Email 201

Customizing Your Email 202

    Configuring How You Receive Email 202

    Creating a Signature 204

    More Email Settings 205

Communicating with Messages 207

    Setting Up Messages 207

    Conversing with Messages 209

    Using Emojis in Text Messages 212

Expressing Yourself Through Messages 213

Responding with Tapback Quick Replies 213

Sending Messages with Bubble Effects 214

Sending Messages with Animations 216

Sending Handwritten Notes 217

Sending Digital Touch Messages 218

Send Animated GIFs and Other Special Messages 219

9 Taking and Editing Photos   223

Working with Photos 223

Taking Photos 224

Editing and Adjusting Photos 226

Taking Panoramic Photos 230

Using Photo Booth 232

Understanding Photo Sources 234

Browsing Your Photos 235

Searching Your Photos 240

Viewing Your Photos 242

Sharing Your Photos 244

Working with Albums 246

Viewing Albums 247

Creating Albums 249

Creating a Slideshow 250

For You and Memories 252

Marking Up Photos 255

Capturing the Screen 257

10 Recording Video   261

Shooting Video 262

Trimming Video Clips 265

Editing in iMovie 267

Editing Transitions 271

Adding Photos to Your Video 273

Adding Video Titles 275

Making Video Calls with FaceTime 277

Setting Up FaceTime 277

Placing Video Calls with FaceTime 279

Receiving Video Calls with FaceTime 282

11 Writing with Pages   **285**

    Creating a New Document 286

    Styling and Formatting Text 288

    Creating Lists 292

    Inserting Images 295

    Document Setup 298

    Sharing and Printing Documents 300

12 Spreadsheets with Numbers   **303**

    Creating a New Spreadsheet 303

    Calculating Totals and Averages 307

    Styling Tables and Cells 311

    Creating Forms 313

    Using Multiple Tables 315

    Creating Charts 318

13 Presentations with Keynote   **323**

    Building a Simple Presentation 323

    Building Your Own Slide 327

    Adding Transitions 331

        Magic Move 332

        Object Transitions 334

    Organizing Slides 336

    Playing Your Presentation 338

14 Navigating with Maps   **343**

    Finding a Location 344

    Searching for Places and Things 346

    Getting Directions 347

    Getting a Better View with Maps Settings ... 349

        Using Satellite View 350

        Using 3D View 351

    Getting Traffic Reports 352

15 The World of Apps   **355**

    Purchasing an App 356

        Finding Good Apps 362

Organizing Apps on Your iPad 364

    Arranging Apps on the Home Screen 364

    Moving Apps to and From the Dock 366

    Using the Dock While in Apps 367

    Creating App Folders 368

Working with Apps 369

    Viewing Currently Running Apps 370

    Using More Than One App at a Time 371

    Viewing Video with Picture-in-Picture 374

    Using iPhone/iPod touch Apps 375

Dragging and Dropping Between Apps 376

    Inserting Photos into an Email Message 376

    Dragging Text from a Web Page to Notes 378

    Exporting Photos to Files 379

Getting Help with Apps 381

Monitoring and Managing Your Apps 383

    Viewing App Storage Information 383

    Viewing Battery Usage 385

    Viewing Location Usage 386

    Viewing Information Sharing Permissions 388

    Modifying Notifications Settings 389

Watching Your iPad Usage with Screen Time **New!** 391

    Checking How You Spend Your Time 391

    Limiting Your iPad Time 394

Controlling Apps with Siri Shortcuts **New!** 398

    Using Pre-Built and Suggested Siri Shortcuts 398

    Creating Your Own Siri Shortcuts 401

16 Must-Have Apps   **409**

Connecting with Friends on Facebook 410

Reading the News 413

Checking Your Stocks **New!** 419

Recording Voice Memos **New!** 421

Adding a Dictionary 423

Making Phone Calls with Skype 425

Handwriting Notes with WritePad 427

Sketching Ideas with Paper 430

Adding a Calculator with PCalc Lite 432

Finding Recipes with Epicurious 434

Checking the Weather 437

Learning New Things with iTunes U 440

Other Useful Apps 443

17 Games and Entertainment   **447**

Composing Music with GarageBand 447

Watching Videos with YouTube 450

Watching Movies and TV Shows with Netflix 453

iPad Games and Entertainment 456

    Monument Valley and Monument Valley 2 457

    Minecraft: Pocket Edition 457

    Prune 458

    Superbrothers: Sword & Sworcery EP 458

    Kingdom Rush 459

    Where's My Water 459

    Cut the Rope 460

    Harbor Master HD 460

    Angry Birds HD 461

    Plants vs. Zombies HD 461

    Scrabble for iPad 462

    Temple Run 2 462

    The Room, The Room Two, The Room Three 463

    Gold Strike 463

    Just Mah Jongg Solitaire 464

18 iPad Accessories   **467**

Printing from Your iPad 467

    Printing from the Notes App 468

AirPlay Mirroring with Apple TV 470

    Setting Up AirPlay 470

Video Output Adapters 472

Using Wireless Keyboards 474

Importing Photos with an SD Card and USB Adapters 477

Charging Your iPad with Power Accessories 479

Listening with EarPods.. 481

Protecting Your iPad... 482

    iPad Smart Cover... 483

    Third-Party Protective Covers and Cases 484

Apple Pencil.. 485

Controlling Your Home with Your iPad...................... 485

    Controlling an Appliance with the Home App.......... 486

    Automating Appliances..................................... 488

19 Maintaining Your iPad and Solving Problems   493

Getting Help on Your iPad..................................... 494

    Using the Tips App... 494

    Getting Help Inside Apps................................... 495

Getting Help from Apple 497

    Using the Apple Support App............................. 497

    Using the Apple Support Website........................ 500

    Asking a Question Online 503

Keeping Your iPad Up to Date 505

    Updating iOS.. 505

    Updating Apps 506

Securing Your iPad... 508

    Basic Security Measures 508

    Using Find My iPad 509

    Setting Up Find My iPad.................................... 509

    Locating a Lost iPad 510

Index   514

Figure Credits

Cover Images	©echo3005 | Shutterstock
	Products, Chuti Prasertsith
Amazon screenshots	Courtesy of Amazon (pgs 34-35)
Instagram screenshots	Courtesy of Instagram (pgs 31-32)
Logos shown in Chapter 16:	
twitter	Courtesy of twitter
LinkedIn	Courtesy of LinkedIn
pinterest	Courtesy of pinterest
Google+	Courtesy of Google+
Snapchat	Courtesy of Snapchat
USA Today	Courtesy of USA Today
Flipboard	Courtesy of Flipboard
Feedly	Courtesy of Feedly app used in iPad Apple Inc
Zinio	Courtesy of Zinio
Oxford English Dictionary	Courtesy of Oxford English Dictionary
Urban Dictionary	Courtesy of Urban Dictionary
Wikipedia	Courtesy of Wikipedia
MyScript Nebo	Courtesy of MyScript
Dragon Anywhere	Courtesy of Dragon Anywhere, Nuance
Communications	
Autodesk SketchBook	Courtesy of Alias Systems Corporation
Adobe Illustrator Draw	Screenshots of Adobe Systems
MyScript Calculator	Courtesy of MyScript
Food Network In the Kitchen	Courtesy of Television Food Network
Yummly	Courtesy of Whirlpool Corporation
Allrecipes Dinner Spinner	Courtesy of Allrecipes.com
The Weather Channel	Courtesy of TWC Product and Technology LLC
Weather Underground	Courtesy of TWC Product and Technology LLC
WeatherBug	Courtesy of Groundtruth
Living Earth	Courtesy of Living Earth
Craftsy	Courtesy of NBCUniversal Media, LLC
TED	Courtesy of TED Conferences, LLC
1Password	Courtesy of AgileBits Inc
MindNode	Courtesy of IdeasOnCanvas
WordPress	Courtesy of WordPress Foundation
Day One Journal	Courtesy of Bloom Built, LLC
StarWalk 2	Courtesy of Vito Technology, Inc.
WolframAlpha	Courtesy of Wolfram Alpha LLC
Bloomberg	Courtesy of Bloomberg
VNC Viewer	Courtesy of RealVNC Ltd
Mocha VNC Lite	Courtesy of mochasoft app
Figures 11.119-11.132	Morphart Creation/Shutterstock

About the Author

Gary Rosenzweig is an Internet entrepreneur, software developer, and technology writer. He runs CleverMedia, Inc., which produces websites, computer games, apps, and podcasts.

CleverMedia's largest site, MacMost.com, features video tutorials for Apple enthusiasts. It includes many videos on using Macs, iPhones, and iPads.

Gary has written numerous computer books, including *ActionScript 3.0 Game Programming University*, *MacMost.com Guide to Switching to the Mac*, and *Special Edition Using Director MX*.

Gary lives in Denver, Colorado, with his wife, Debby, and daughter, Luna. He has a computer science degree from Drexel University and a master's degree in journalism from the University of North Carolina at Chapel Hill.

Website: http://garyrosenzweig.com

Twitter: http://twitter.com/rosenz

More iPad Tutorials and Book Updates: http://macmost.com/ipadguide/

Acknowledgments

Thanks, as always, to my wife, Debby, and my daughter, Luna, and the rest of my family.

Thanks to all the people who watch the show and participate at the MacMost website.

Thanks to everyone else at Pearson who worked on this book: Charlotte Kughen, Paul Sihvonen-Binder, Lori Lyons, Kim Scott, and Debbie Williams.

We Want to Hear from You!

As the reader of this book, *you* are our most important critic and commentator. We value your opinion and want to know what we're doing right, what we could do better, what areas you'd like to see us publish in, and any other words of wisdom you're willing to pass our way.

We welcome your comments. You can email to let us know what you did or didn't like about this book—as well as what we can do to make our books better.

Please note that we cannot help you with technical problems related to the topic of this book.

When you write, please be sure to include this book's title and author as well as your name and email address. We will carefully review your comments and share them with the author and editors who worked on the book.

Email: informit.com/myipad11

Reader Services

Register your copy of *My iPad* at quepublishing.com for convenient access to downloads, updates, and corrections as they become available. To start the registration process, go to quepublishing.com/register and log in or create an account*. Enter the product ISBN, 9780789760449, and click Submit. Once the process is complete, you will find any available bonus content under Registered Products.

*Be sure to check the box that you would like to hear from us in order to receive exclusive discounts on future editions of this product.

Learn to tap, swipe, flick, and pinch to use your iPad

Learn to use the iPad's physical switches

In this chapter, you learn how to perform specific tasks on your iPad to become familiar with the interface.

→ Generations of iPads

→ The iPad Buttons and Switches

→ Screen Gestures

→ Learning Your Way Around

→ Virtual Buttons and Switches

→ Entering Text

→ Talking to Your iPad with Siri

→ Using Control Center

Getting Started

Before you learn how to perform specific tasks on your iPad, you should become familiar with some basic concepts. If you have used an iPhone or a similar gadget before, you already know how to use a touchscreen device. But if the iPad is your first such device, you need to take time to become accustomed to interacting with it.

Generations of iPads

The first thing you may want to do is identify which iPad you have and what features are available to you. There have been many versions of the iPad since the original appeared in 2010.

iPad Models over the Years

The first iPad had a 9.7-inch screen and today's basic iPad model has a screen that's the same size, although it comes in a thinner, lighter package. There are also iPad mini models with smaller 7.9-inch screens, and iPad Pro models that come with 9.7-, 10.5- and 12.9-inch screens. All these screens are the same 3×4 screen ratio, so everything looks pretty much the same between models; it's just the scale that is different.

iPad displays vary not only in size, with the iPad mini models being smaller than the other iPads, but also in pixel density. The retina display has four pixels for every one of a regular display. Whereas a non-retina display is 768x1024 pixels, a retina display is 1536x2048 pixels. This means photographs and text are crisper and clearer on the retina display. In fact, you can't even distinguish the individual pixels with your eye unless you hold the iPad very close to your face. The iPad Pro 12.9-inch has even more pixels at 2048x2732.

Time for a New iPad?

Most earlier model iPads are not compatible with iOS 12, the version of iOS discussed in this book. Because these models can't run iOS 12, some of the latest third-party apps might not work, or won't work very well. Every iOS 12-compatible iPad has a Lightning connector, retina display, and an A7 or better processor.

Another difference between iPad models is the camera. Since the first model in 2010, the cameras on the iPad have improved, with higher quality and picture resolution.

Each iPad has also become a little more powerful with a faster processor at its heart. Other parts have picked up speed and power as well, processing graphics and accessing memory faster. Early models aren't powerful enough to use features like voice dictation and advanced 3D game graphics.

>>>Go Further
THE NEED FOR SPEED

With each generation of iPad, the processor changes. Each iPad is faster and more powerful than its predecessor. It is hard to quantify, but by some metrics the iPad Pro has more processing power than many desktop computers. This also helps apps to run smoother, games to display faster with more detailed graphics, and makes performing taxing tasks like editing video or flipping through hundreds of high-resolution photos work faster.

iOS 12 New!

The primary piece of software on the iPad is the operating system, known as iOS. This is what you see when you flip through the screens of icons on your iPad and access default apps such as Mail, Safari, Photos, and iTunes.

This book covers iOS 12, the version released in September 2018. There have been 12 generations of the software that runs iPhones and iPads. The original iPhone OS was developed for the first iPhone. The third version, iOS 3, worked on iPhones and the iPad. This latest version, iOS 12, works on iPads introduced around 2014 and later. If you have an older version of the iPad, you will not be able to install iOS 12 and will be stuck with an earlier version. Many of the things you see on your older iPad will look different than what you see in this book, and some features will be missing entirely.

Some features and tasks in this book work the same in iOS 5 through 11, but you won't be able to use the latest features. To find out which version you are using and to learn how to update, go to the Settings app, and under General settings, tap the About item. The About screen shows information about your iPad, including its model number, serial number, version of iOS currently running, and available memory. You learn how to use the Settings app when you get to Chapter 2.

New to iOS 12 New!

There are some changes in iOS 12 you will notice. For features that have changed significantly, or are completely new, we have added **New!** to the text and table of contents to help you easily locate them. Be sure to check out those tasks to get up to speed on what's new in iOS 12.

The iPad Buttons and Switches

The iPad features a Home button, a Wake/Sleep button, and a volume control.

The Home Button New!

The iPad, iPad mini, and older iPad Pros have a Home button. The new iPad Pro models released in November 2018 don't. If you have an iPad with a Home button, pressing the Home button returns you to the Home screen when you are inside an application, such as Safari or Mail, and you want to launch another app. You can also double-press the Home button to switch between apps.

If your iPad does not have a Home button, you will see a thin bar at the bottom the screen when you are inside an app. Swipe that bar up quickly to return to the Home screen. Drag it up slowly to switch between apps. If you have used an iPad before with a Home button, you can now simply swipe this bar up instead of pressing the Home button.

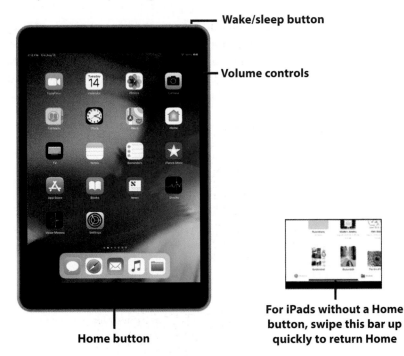

Wake/sleep button

Volume controls

For iPads without a Home button, swipe this bar up quickly to return Home

Home button

Where's the Quit Button?

Few, if any, apps on the iPad have a way to quit. Instead, pressing the Home button hides the current app and returns you to your Home screen. The app is paused and hidden in the background. It is usually unnecessary to truly "quit" an app. If you really want to quit an app completely, see "Quitting Apps" in Chapter 15.

The Wake/Sleep Button

The primary function of the Wake/Sleep button (sometimes called the On/Off or Power button) at the top of your iPad is to quickly put it to sleep. Sleeping is different than shutting down. When your iPad is in sleep mode, you can instantly wake it to use it. You can wake the iPad from sleep by pressing the Wake/Sleep button again or by pressing the Home button.

Peek a Boo!

If you are using the Apple iPad Smart Cover, Smart Case, or the iPad Pro Smart Keyboard (see Chapter 18, "iPad Accessories"), your iPad goes to sleep when you close it and wakes up when you open it, as long as you use the default settings. Many third-party cases and covers also do this.

You can also use the Wake/Sleep button to shut down your iPad, which you might want to do if you leave your iPad for a long time and want to preserve the battery life. Press and hold the Wake/Sleep button for a few seconds, and the iPad begins to shut down and turn off. Confirm your decision to shut down your iPad using the Slide to Power Off button on the screen.

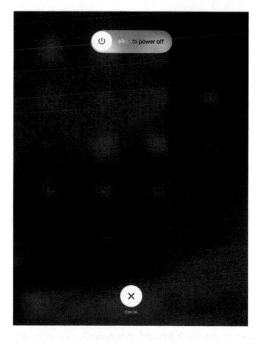

To start up your iPad, press and hold the Wake/Sleep button for a few seconds until you see the Apple logo appear on the screen.

When Should I Turn Off My iPad?

It's normal to never turn off your iPad. In sleep mode, with the screen off, it uses little power. If you plug it in to power at night or during longer periods when you aren't carrying it with you, you don't need to ever shut it down.

The Volume Control

The volume control on the side of your iPad is actually two buttons: one to turn the volume up, and the other to turn it down.

Your iPad keeps two separate volume settings in memory: one for headphones and one for the internal speakers. If you turn down the volume when using headphones and then unplug the headphones, the volume changes to reflect the last settings used when the headphones were not plugged in, and vice versa. A speaker icon and a series of rectangles appear on the screen to indicate the current level of volume.

Orientation and Movement

In addition to the physical switches you see on your iPad, the entire iPad is a physical control.

Your iPad knows which way it's oriented, and it knows if it is being moved. The simplest indication of this is that it knows whether you hold it vertically with the Home button at the bottom or horizontally with the Home button to one of the sides. Some apps, especially games, use the screen orientation of the iPad to guide screen elements and views.

Shake It Up!

One interesting physical gesture you might perform is the "shake." Because your iPad can sense movement, it can sense when you shake it. Many apps take advantage of this feature and use it to set off an action, such as shuffling songs in the Music app, erasing a drawing canvas, or as an "undo" function.

Screen Gestures

Any way to tap, swipe, drag, or otherwise interact with the screen with one or more fingers is a possible gesture that you can use to control your iPad's main screens and any apps you use. Here is a list of some of the most common gestures and some examples of their use.

 Tap: Use one finger to quickly touch the screen in one location. You use this gesture to launch apps on the Home screen.

Double-Tap: With one finger, tap two times quickly in the same location. You use this gesture to zoom in on maps.

Tap-and-Hold: Sometimes you get a different reaction if you tap and hold a spot as opposed to quickly tapping and releasing. For instance, if you tap a link on a web page you will go to that link. But if you tap and hold the link, you get a list of options such as Open in New Tab, Add to Reading List, and Copy.

 Drag: Touch the screen with one finger, keep it pressed against the screen, and move it to another location. Use this gesture to reposition elements in apps like Keynote or to draw in graphics apps. Drag vertically to scroll documents and web pages.

Double-Drag: Touch the screen with two fingers close together, keep them pressed against the screen, and move them to another location. Use this gesture in apps to reposition an entire document or image.

Swipe: Touch the screen with one finger and move it quickly left, right, up, or down. Use this gesture to move between pages of the Home screen.

 Pinch Close: Place two fingers, usually your thumb and index finger, far apart on the screen and move them together. Use this gesture to zoom out on maps and images.

Pinch Open: The opposite of a pinch, where you start with two fingers close together and move them apart. Use this gesture to zoom in on maps and images.

Rotate: Touch the screen with two fingers far apart, and rotate them both around a point in between. Use this gesture to rotate maps and objects in graphics apps.

Swipe from Edge: Start with your finger outside of the screen, either above, below, to the left, or to the right. Drag your finger onto the screen and toward the middle. Use this gesture to bring notifications down from the top center of the screen, the Control Center down from the top-right corner, and the app Dock up from the bottom.

Four-Finger Swipe: Place four fingers together and close to the middle of the screen and swipe in one direction. In most apps, a four-finger swipe to the right switches you back to the previous app.

Five-Finger Pinch Close: Place all fingers on the screen and pinch in to the center to go from your current app to the App Switcher (covered in Chapter 15).

This list isn't complete. There's really no limit to the types of gestures that apps can use. The Files app, for instance, allows you to drag a file, and then while you're dragging, you can tap a second file with another finger to group the two files and drag them together.

Learning Your Way Around

When you pick up your iPad and touch either the Wake/Sleep button or the Home button to activate the screen, you see what is called the Lock screen. From there, you unlock your iPad and return to the last screen you were using—either the Home screen or an app's screen.

Let's look at the different types of screens you see every day on your iPad, and how to navigate between them.

The Lock Screen

When you first wake up your iPad, you're on the Lock screen. The background is a colorful picture, called the wallpaper. Some very basic information displays on top of the wallpaper. The largest element is the time. Under that is either the battery level or the date. It alternates between them every few seconds. The Wi-Fi and battery status are at the top right.

From the Lock screen there are three places you can go. You can swipe left to right to go to the Today View, which I cover in more detail shortly. You can also swipe right to left to bring up the Camera app to take a quick picture. Read about the Camera app in Chapter 9, "Taking and Editing Photos."

You can also press the Home button to exit the Lock screen and go to the Home screen. When you do this, you are prompted to enter your passcode or rest your thumb or other finger on the Home button to verify your identity using Touch ID. See "Make Access Easier with Touch ID" in Chapter 2.

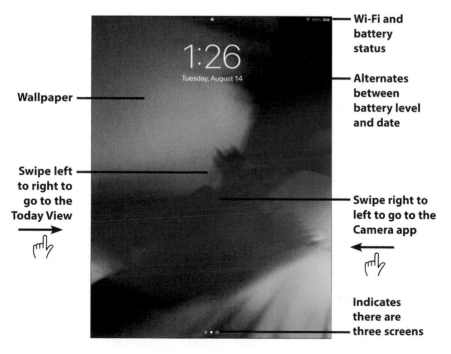

Wi-Fi and battery status

Alternates between battery level and date

Wallpaper

Swipe left to right to go to the Today View

Swipe right to left to go to the Camera app

Indicates there are three screens

The Home Screen

Think of the Home screen as a single screen but with multiple pages that feature different app icons. The background image is your Home screen wallpaper. At the bottom of the Home screen are app icons in the App Dock that do not change from page to page. Find out how to add more apps to your iPad in the tasks in Chapter 15.

The number of pages on your Home screen depends on how many apps you have. The number of pages you have is indicated by the white dots near the bottom of the screen, just above the Dock. The brightest dot represents the page you are currently viewing. You can move between pages on your Home screen by dragging or flicking left or right.

Date and time ——

Wi-Fi and battery status

App icons

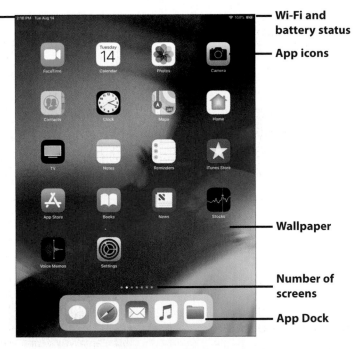

Wallpaper

Number of screens

App Dock

In addition to jumping into an app by tapping the app icon, there are three other screens you can get to from the Home screen. If you swipe left to right from the initial Home screen, you go to the Today View. If you swipe down from the very top of the screen, you go to the Notifications screen. If you swipe down from the center of the screen, you go to the Search screen.

The Search Screen

If you are on your Home screen looking at page one of your app icons, you can drag from the center of the screen downward to bring up a Spotlight Search field at the top and a keyboard at the bottom. This allows you to search your iPad for apps, contacts, events, and other information.

You can type in anything to search for a contact, app, email message, photo, and so on. You don't have to define what type of thing you want to search for.

1. From the Home screen, tap in the center of the screen and drag down. If you've been using your iPad for a while and have Siri enabled, you will see suggestions for apps, contacts, and other content on this screen even before you type a search term.

Drag from the Center, Not the Top

Don't start at the very top of the screen, as dragging from there brings up Notifications Center. Correct placement of your finger can be a bit tricky; if you do accidentally open Notifications Center, just tap the Home button to go back to the Home screen and try again.

2. The onscreen keyboard, also called the virtual keyboard, displays for you to type your search term.

3. As you type, the characters appear here, in the Search field.

4. You see suggested search terms based on the letters you have typed so far. You can tap one of these to fill in the Search field.

5. You see a list of items on your iPad that match the search term. The search results show apps, calendar events, email messages, reminders, or even web search results.

6. Tap the Search button on the keyboard to dismiss the keyboard and complete the search.

7. Tap the X in the Search field to clear the search and start again.

8. Tap any of the items to go to the appropriate app and view the content.

How Do I Get Out of Here?

To exit the Search screen instead of completing a search, just tap outside of the search results or press the Home button. This takes you back to the Home screen.

Today View

You can get to the Today View, also called the Widgets screen, one of three ways: swipe left to right on the Lock screen, swipe left to right on the Notifications screen, or swipe left to right on the first page of the Home screen. When you use the first two methods, you see the time and date at the top; when you use the third method, you see only the widgets themselves.

The Today View is filled with useful widgets or modules that present information and allow you to take simple actions.

1. Swipe from the left to the right from the left-most page of apps on the Home screen.

What Are Widgets?

Underneath the weather and date, the rest of the screen is filled with widgets. You can completely customize these, removing ones you don't need and adding new ones. The four shown in this task are four default widgets. The default widgets may vary in future updates to iOS.

2. The Calendar widget shows you your next scheduled event.

3. Tap an event to open the Calendar app and go right to it.

4. The Siri App Suggestions widget usually shows your recently used apps. Tap any of the icons to go directly to that app.

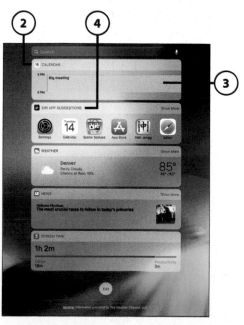

5. A variety of other widgets are shown, depending on which ones you have chosen to appear. You can usually tap most widgets to jump to the corresponding app for more information.

6. If you have more widgets than can fit on the screen, swipe up to see them.

7. At the top of the Widgets screen is a Search field that you can use to search for anything on your iPad. It is another way to access the Search screen mentioned earlier in this chapter.

8. At the bottom of the list is an Edit button that enables you to customize what you see on the Widgets screen. Tap it.

9. Tap the red – buttons next to any item to remove that widget from the Widgets screen.

10. Tap the green + buttons next to items to add them to the Widgets screen.

11. Tap the handles to the right of any item and drag up or down to rearrange the order of items on the Widgets screen.

12. Tap Done to save your changes and return to the Widgets screen.

Results May Vary

You might find that some widgets work differently, or show different information, depending on whether you accessed the Widgets screen from the Lock screen or Home screen. From the Lock screen you haven't entered your passcode or used Touch ID to log in to your iPad so that might restrict what is allowed.

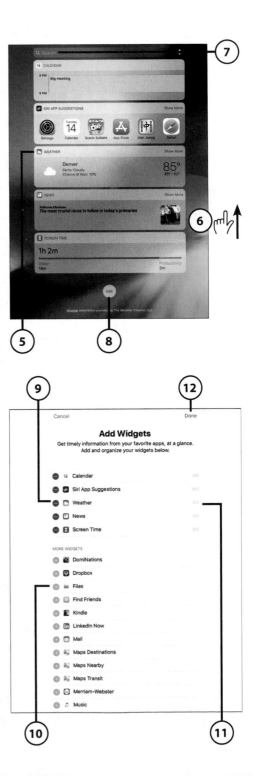

The Notifications Screen

If you swipe down from the very top of the Lock screen or Home screen, you go to the Notifications screen, which is a list of recent notifications, such as calls, messages, emails, or app alerts.

For Your Eyes Only

If you don't like the idea of your notifications being shown on the Lock screen, before you need to enter a passcode to get into your iPad, you can turn off Lock screen notifications in Settings, Notifications, Show Previews. Using the Settings app is covered later in this chapter.

In most cases you can tap the notification to take appropriate action. For instance, tapping a notification that you have a text message takes you into the Messages app and right to that conversation so you can respond.

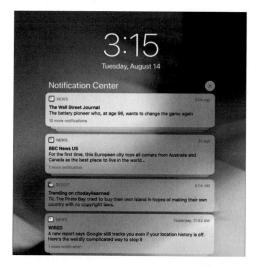

Notifications are grouped by default, so if you get multiple notifications from the same app or source, they appear as a single item, with one on top. When you tap the stack, it expands to show all the items.

From the Notifications screen, you can press the Home button to return to either the Lock screen or the Home screen, depending on where you came from originally.

If you happen to be using your iPad when a notification arrives, you also see the notification pop up as an overlay on part of your screen. You can tap the notification to take action, drag it up to dismiss it, or ignore it so it goes away after a few seconds.

If your iPad is nearby but you aren't using it and it's locked, you might notice notifications appearing on the screen as they happen. When the iPad is locked, the screen turns on and you see the notification on the Lock screen.

For notifications on the Lock screen, you can swipe right to left across it to see View, Clear, and Manage buttons. The Manage option, new in iOS 12, allows you to turn off notifications from this source.

You can also swipe left to right to see an Open button. Or, you can tap and hold the notification to perform a relevant action, such as a quick reply to a message. If you do nothing, the screen simply turns off again after a few seconds. When you go to wake up your iPad later, you see the notification on the Lock screen again.

Virtual Buttons and Switches

Several interface elements are more complex than a simple button. In typical Apple style, these elements are often self-explanatory, but if you have never used an iPad before, you might find some that give you pause.

Switches and Option Lists

A switch is a simple button that enables you to turn something on or off. You just tap the switch to change it—no need to slide it. The background of a switch turns green when the switch is "on."

For example, the switch in the figure indicates whether labels in the Maps app are displayed in English. Tapping the switch changes the position of the switch.

But the Distances setting above that offers another way to switch between options that works better when the setting isn't as simple as on or off/yes or no. In that case, you tap the option you want, which then displays a check mark like the one next to In Miles.

DISTANCES	
In Miles	✓
In Kilometers	
MAP LABELS	
Always in English	⬤

Toolbars

Some apps have a set of controls in a toolbar at the top of the screen. Buttons shown there are sometimes nothing more than a word or two that you can tap to trigger an action. The toolbar might disappear or the buttons might vary depending on the mode of the app. If a toolbar disappears, a tap on the screen brings it up again.

The iTunes Store app includes an example of a toolbar. When you are viewing the music section of the iTunes Store, it has a button to access Genres, a title in the middle, a button that brings up more controls, and a Search field. However, this toolbar can change. For instance, if you switch from viewing the Music screen to viewing Top Charts, you see buttons that let you switch between Music, Movies, TV, or Audiobook charts.

Genres	**Music**	≔	Q Search

Menus

Often tapping a single button in a toolbar brings up more buttons or a list of choices, which are like menus on your computer. The choices in the list are usually related. For example, a button in Safari gives you many different ways to share a web page.

Tab Bars

At the bottom of the screen, you sometimes see a row of buttons that function similarly to toolbars, but each button represents a different mode for the app. For instance, at the bottom of the iTunes Store app, you see a tab bar that you use to switch between various screens: Music, Movies, TV Shows, Top Charts, Genius, and Purchased.

Entering Text

Entering text on your iPad means interacting with an on-screen keyboard or speaking to your iPad. Even if you are not a writer, you need to enter text quite often to input addresses in the web browser or to compose messages and emails.

Using the On-Screen Keyboard

The on-screen element you might interact with the most is the keyboard. It pops up from the bottom of the screen automatically whenever you are doing something that requires entering some text.

Keyboard Modes

An on-screen keyboard can have many different modes. With the default keyboard, the first mode shows letters and a few punctuation marks. There are two Shift keys that enable you to enter uppercase letters. You also have a Backspace key and a Return key.

The standard on-screen keyboard

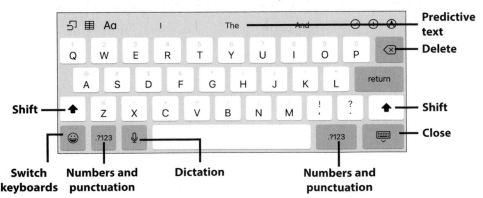

Is There a Quicker Way to Capitalize?

To capitalize a word, you tap the Shift key, and then type the letter, right? You can. But a faster way is to tap the Shift key; then, without letting your finger off the screen, drag it to the letter and release in a single tap-slide-release action.

You can do the same with numbers and punctuation by tapping the .?123 key and sliding and releasing over the key you want.

Notice that there are secondary characters above the letters on the keyboard. To type those, tap a key, drag down slightly, and then release. For instance, tapping the Y key, dragging down, and releasing results in the number 6 instead of a Y.

Another way to get to special characters is to tap the .?123 key to switch your keyboard into a second mode for numbers and punctuation. To return to the letters, just tap the ABC key.

Numbers and punctuation mode

Symbols mode

Symbols mode

Letter mode

Letter mode

From the numbers and punctuation mode, you can tap the #+= key to go to a third keyboard mode that includes less frequently used punctuation and symbols.

Punctuation and symbols mode

Numbers and punctuation mode — Letter mode — Letter mode — Numbers and punctuation mode

There are other keyboard variations. For instance, in some cases if you type in a location that needs a web address, a keyboard that doesn't have a spacebar appears. Instead it has commonly used symbols such as colons, slashes, underscores, and even a .com button.

Not only are there other keyboard variations, but there are completely different keyboards you can use. The iPad has many non-English language keyboards, and even a keyboard composed of little images (smiley faces and other pictures) called Emoji. Plus, you can add third-party keyboards from developers. Adding new keyboards is covered in the task "Modifying Keyboard Settings" in Chapter 2. Find out more about typing emoji characters when you read about the Messages app in Chapter 8, "Communicating with Email and Messaging."

Undocking and Splitting the Keyboard

You can also split the keyboard and/or move it away from the bottom of the screen to make it easier to type if you're holding your iPad with two hands. Grasp with your hands on either side of the iPad, and type with your thumbs.

1. Undock or split your keyboard by tapping and holding the keyboard button at the bottom-right corner.

2. Select Undock to move the keyboard up from the bottom of the screen and have control of its vertical position.

3. Select Split to undock the keyboard and also split it in half so you can reach all the keys from either side with your thumbs. You can also do this by tapping the keyboard button and dragging up.

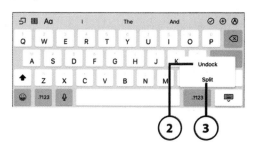

4. When the keyboard is undocked or split, you can tap and hold the keyboard button to drag it vertically to find the best position for you. If you tap and hold but do not drag, then you get the option to Merge, or Dock and Merge.

5. Tap Merge to merge the two halves of the keyboard into one. You can also do this by tapping in the middle of the keyboard and pinching inward.

6. Tap Dock and Merge to merge the halves and also lock the keyboard to the bottom of the screen. You can also do this by dragging the keyboard all the way down to the bottom of the screen.

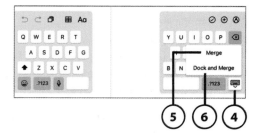

Using the Keyboard Shortcut Bar

Above the letter and number keys on the on-screen keyboard is the shortcut bar. This narrow horizontal strip can contain a variety of buttons and some predictive text shortcuts. We look at predictive text in the next section.

The buttons in the shortcut bar vary depending on which app you are using and even what type of text you are typing within the app.

If you don't see the shortcut bar, but instead see a narrow line with a smaller white line in the center, then tap and drag that small white line up to reveal the shortcut bar.

So far, we've been looking at the keyboard as it appears in the Notes app. Let's take a tour of the shortcut bar as it appears as you type in Notes.

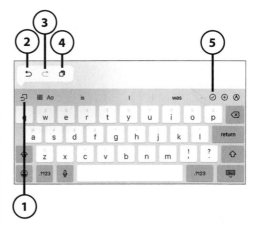

1. Tapping this button brings up Undo and Paste from the clipboard buttons. If you have text selected, it instead brings up Cut, Copy, and Paste buttons.

2. This undoes the last insertion or edit.

3. This redoes the last undo.

4. You can paste text you have previously copied into the clipboard. This is similar to using Command+v or Control+v on a desktop computer.

5. In Notes, you get a button to begin writing a checklist.

6. You can also choose from a variety of other text styles such as Title, Heading, Body, and so on.

7. You can tap this button to take a picture with your iPad's camera or insert a photo from your library.

8. Notes includes a special sketch function that lets you add a drawing to your note. We take a closer look at that in Chapter 6, "Organizing Your Life."

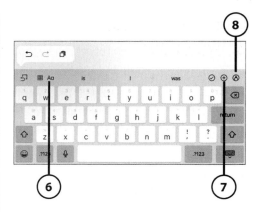

>>>Go Further
MORE KEYBOARD VARIATIONS

If you bring up the on-screen keyboard in the Mail app while composing a message, you get a slightly different set of buttons. Instead of the Undo, Redo, and Paste buttons being combined into one button on the left, you get each as its own button. In addition, you get a style button on the right that lets you choose bold, italic, or underline and an attach button that lets you choose a file to attach to your message.

Another example of a shortcut bar is the one you get when typing a URL or search term in the address field in the Safari web browser. Here, you only get Cut, Copy, and Paste buttons.

Using Predictive Text

You might have noticed that while you are typing, three buttons with words in them appear on top of the keyboard in the shortcut bar. This is the predictive text feature of the keyboard, also sometimes referred to by Apple as QuickType.

As you're typing, you can use these three buttons to complete a word with just one tap. For instance, you might be typing the word "Clever." As you type, the three buttons change to represent what comes closest to the letters you have typed so far. When you have typed "Cle," you might get "Clearer" and "Clear" as suggestions. But when you get to "Clev," you will probably see "Clever" as one of the buttons. Simply tap that button and the word is completed without you needing to type "r." Notice that a space is automatically inserted as well. If the word you inserted was the end of your sentence, simply tap the spacebar two times to insert a period. The app is ready to start a new sentence.

Predictive text does more than look at the letters in the word you are typing; it also considers the context of the whole sentence. For instance, if you type "pur," you might get "put" and "pure" as suggestions. But if you type "color pur," you get "purple" as a suggestion.

Also note that the leftmost button of the three usually displays the text exactly as you have typed it, but with quotes around it. This allows you to type a name or unusual word without having autocorrect get in the way.

Predictive text also looks at which app you are using and what the situation involves. For instance, it might suggest different words based on the person whom you are emailing, whether it's a work colleague or friend. When you respond to text messages in the Messages app, you might see "Yes" and "No" appear automatically when you are responding to a question. If someone messages you to ask whether you want to meet at 6:00, 7:00, or 8:00, those three options are offered before you even type the first letter of your response.

Dictating Text

You can also dictate text using your voice rather than typing on the keyboard. Almost any time you see a keyboard, you should also see a small microphone button to the left of the spacebar. Tap that and you are prompted to speak to your iPad. You need to be connected to the Internet through a Wi-Fi or cellular connection for this to work.

1. Tap the microphone button on the keyboard to begin dictating. If this is the first time you are doing it, you might be asked for permission to enable the feature.

2. The keyboard is replaced with a waveform line that vibrates as you speak. Speak a few words or a sentence or two. As you speak, the text appears in your document or text field, though it may lag behind by a few seconds.

3. Tap the keyboard button when you are finished speaking. You can now edit the dictated text as needed before sending it.

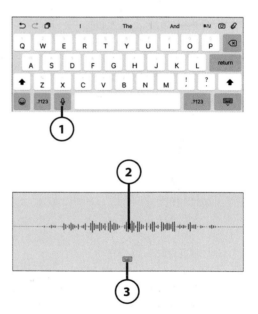

Speak Clearly

Speak somewhat slowly and clearly, and in segments about the length of a sentence for best results. Of course, this feature isn't perfect. Pay careful attention to what is transcribed and correct any mistakes using the keyboard. Over time you will get better at speaking in a way that minimizes mistakes.

>>>Go Further
DICTATION TIPS

The dictation button appears any time a standard keyboard is present in any app. You can use it in Notes, Pages, or any writing app. You can use it in search fields and text entry fields on the Web. You cannot use it when there are specialty keyboards, like the ones used to enter email addresses, web URLs, and telephone numbers. So, for instance, you can use it in the Contacts app to speak a name or address but not to enter an email address.

You need to be connected to the Internet for dictation to work. Your iPad sends the audio to Apple's servers, which handle the transcription and send the text back to your iPad. If you are not connected, it does not work.

Dictation works according to your language set in Settings, General, Language & Region. Not all languages are supported, but Apple is adding more all the time.

You can indicate the end of a sentence by saying "period" or "question mark." You can also speak other punctuation like "comma" or "quote."

You can speak commands like "new line," or "cap" to capitalize the next word. There is no official list of what the dictation feature supports, and because the transcription takes place on Apple's servers, it can change how it handles commands at any time.

Editing Text

Editing text has its challenges on a touchscreen device. Even though you can touch any portion of your text on screen, your fingertip is too large for the level of precision you usually get with a computer mouse and cursor. To compensate, Apple developed an editing technique using a magnifying glass area of the screen that you get when you touch and hold over a piece of text.

For example, if you want to enter some text into a field in Safari, touch and hold on the field. A circle of magnification appears with a cursor placed at the exact location you selected.

The quick brown fox jumps over the lazy dog.

When you find the exact location that you want to indicate, release your finger from the screen. A variety of options then display, depending on what kind of text you selected, such as Select, Select All, and Paste. You can ignore the options presented and start typing again to insert text at this location.

Copying and Pasting

You can copy and paste text inside an app, and between apps, on your iPad. Here's how you might copy a piece of text from one place in a document to another in the Notes app.

1. Launch Notes. If you don't have any notes yet, create one by typing some sample text.

2. Touch and hold over a word in your note. The Select/Select All pop-up menu appears.

3. Choose Select.

4. Some text appears highlighted surrounded by dots connected to lines. Tap and drag the dots so the highlighted area is exactly what you want.

5. Tap Copy.

6. Alternatively, you can tap this icon on the keyboard shortcut bar to bring up Cut, Copy, and Paste icons, and then choose the Copy icon.

Variations

In other apps, you might find the Cut, Copy, and Paste icons already visible on the keyboard shortcut bar; and in still other apps, you might not find this alternative at all.

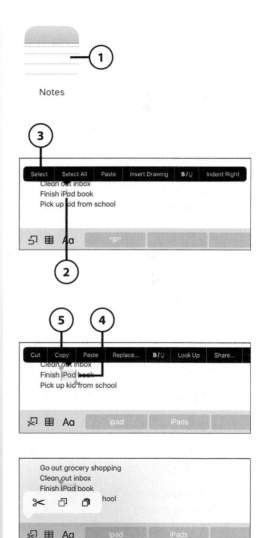

7. Tap one time at the bottom of the document to bring up a pop-up menu with the Paste command.

8. Tap Paste to insert the copied text. Alternatively, you can use the same method as in step 6 to paste.

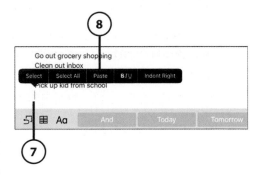

>>>Go Further
YOUR KEYBOARD AS A TRACKPAD

You can use the keyboard to precisely position the text cursor in apps where you work with text, such as Notes, Pages, Mail, and so on. With the on-screen keyboard visible, tap it with two fingers and keep your fingers pressed to your iPad. Or, you can tap and hold the spacebar with just one finger. Then drag your fingers around, and you can move the cursor as if you were using a trackpad or mouse on a computer. Notice that the keyboard letters disappear when you are doing this to indicate that you are in trackpad mode.

You can also tap quickly with two fingers to simply select the word that currently contains the text cursor. Two taps with two fingers selects the whole paragraph. Then you can tap and drag with two fingers to expand the selection.

This takes some getting used to. If you plan to use this feature, you might want to practice with a sample document first.

Talking to Your iPad with Siri

Siri is another way to communicate with your iPad. You can use your voice and speak commands to your iPad, and Siri responds. It either gives you information or takes action using one of the apps on the iPad.

To use Siri, you need to make sure you have Siri turned on in the Settings app. Then, you use the Home button to activate Siri. Chapter 2 explains how to work with the Settings app.

Asking Siri Questions

1. Press and hold the Home button for about a second. The Siri interface pops up, showing a waveform line at the bottom of the screen that reacts to the sound of your voice.

   If you hesitate for a few seconds, the iPad displays a list of examples of things you can ask Siri.

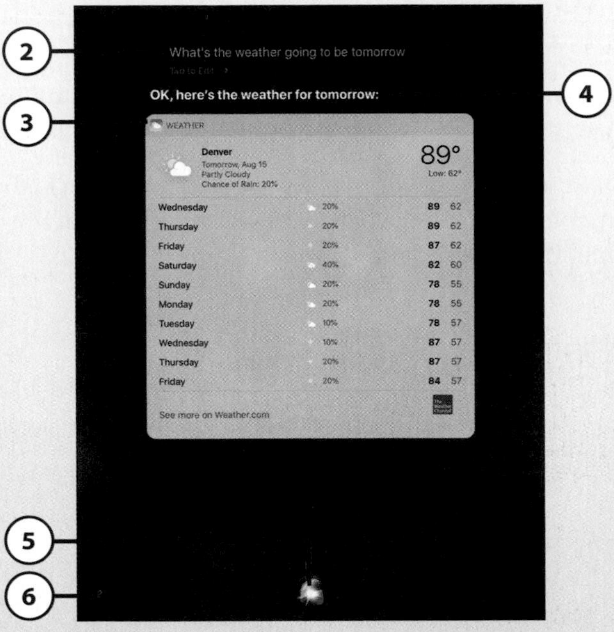

2.   Speak clearly at a normal pace and say, "What's the weather going to be like tomorrow?" As you speak, the words appear near the top of the screen. When you stop speaking, Siri attempts to perform an action based on those words.

3.   In this case, a short weather forecast appears.

4.   Siri also responds with a statement and speaks it audibly. The text of the response typically appears above the screen content.

5.   You can ask Siri another question by tapping the colorful button at the bottom of the screen.

6.   If you wait for the list of suggestions to appear, you also see a question mark appear at the bottom left. Tap it to get a detailed list of apps that Siri can interact with, and things you can say for each app.

Siri Tips

To use Siri, you must have a connection to the Internet. It can be a Wi-Fi connection or a mobile connection. When you speak text, the audio is transmitted to Apple's servers to convert it to text and interpret the command. The results are sent back to your iPad.

It is best to speak clearly and to limit background noise. Using Siri in a quiet room works better than in a crowded outdoor space or in a car with the radio on, for instance.

Because Apple's servers control Siri, they can update Siri's capabilities at any time. For example, originally Siri did not understand a request for local sports scores, but after an update this functionality was added.

You can use Siri to perform many tasks on your iPad without typing. For example, you can search the Web, set reminders, send messages, and play music. Throughout the rest of this book, look for the Siri icon for tips on how to use Siri to perform a task related to that section of the book.

>>>Go Further

HEY SIRI!

You can activate Siri without pressing the Home button. In the Settings app, under Siri & Search, is a switch labeled Allow Listen for Hey Siri. Turn that on so that any time you utter the words "Hey Siri" followed by a question, Siri will respond.

There's an initial setup sequence when you first turn Siri on. You need to speak a few phrases so Siri can distinguish your voice from other people and react only to you. Because having the Hey Siri feature turned on means your iPad needs to leave your microphone on to constantly monitor input, it works only when your iPad is plugged into AC power. Otherwise, it would drain your battery very quickly.

Using Control Center New for iOS 12!

The Control Center is a set of buttons and switches that you can bring up from the bottom of your screen in almost any mode and in almost any app while using your iPad. It has been redesigned for iOS 12.

The exact controls shown depend on which iPad model you own, which capabilities you have enabled or disabled in Settings, and even what other devices you have available on your network.

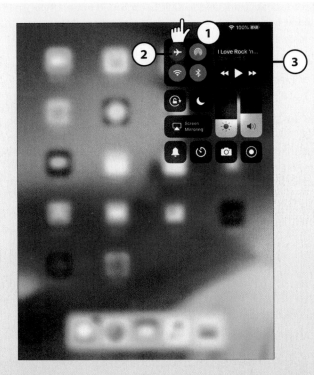

1. To bring up the Control Center, swipe down from the top of the screen, on the right side. If you are having trouble, try starting above the screen in the top-right corner and swiping down onto the screen area.

2. The top of the Control Center features a set of switches. The first one allows you to quickly switch into Airplane Mode, which turns off Wi-Fi and Bluetooth (as you might be asked to do during takeoff and landing on an airplane). The other three switches in this group are individual switches for AirDrop, Wi-Fi, and Bluetooth. You can turn on Airplane Mode and then re-enable Wi-Fi only if your flight has Wi-Fi service. AirDrop is covered in Chapter 3, "Networking and Syncing."

3. This section gives you control over whichever app is currently, or most recently, playing audio. The main button toggles between play and pause, and the upper-right corner brings up output options for switching to Bluetooth or AirPlay speakers. If you tap and hold this whole section, it brings up a larger control area.

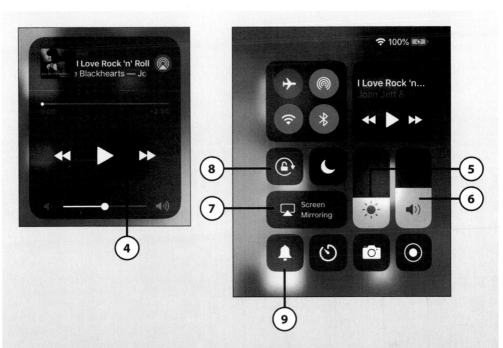

4. The larger area shows album artwork, a playback timeline, volume controls, and more depending on the app.

5. You can tap and drag vertically in this area to adjust your screen brightness.

6. You can tap and drag vertically in this area to adjust the volume.

7. Tap here to access AirPlay controls, so you can mirror your screen to an Apple TV connected to the same network. AirPlay is discussed in Chapter 4, "Playing Music and Video."

Customizable Buttons

The next section contains buttons you can customize. You look at picking the buttons that appear here in Chapter 2, in the section "Customizing the Control Center." Here is a look at some of the buttons you might find there.

8. This button locks your iPad's orientation, so when you turn your iPad 90 degrees, the screen does not rotate.

9. This button puts your iPad into silent mode, muting all sound.

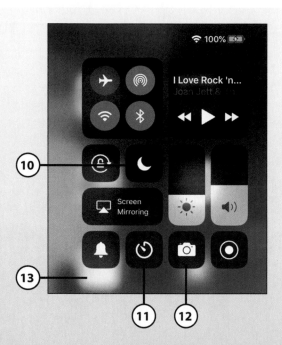

10. You can quickly switch to Do Not Disturb mode, which silences all notifications.

11. This is a shortcut button to jump to the Clock app and set a timer.

12. Another shortcut button to jump to the Camera app so you can quickly take a photo.

13. Dismiss Control Center by tapping the screen outside of the Control Center or simply pressing the Home button.

More Than One Route

There's not much that Control Center does that cannot be done in the Settings app or the Home screen. Control Center simply provides quick access to a variety of functions.

Enlarge the size of
text in apps

Customize how your iPad
looks and works through
the Settings app

Change your
wallpaper image

In this chapter, you learn how to change some of the settings on your iPad, such as your background images, sounds, passcode, and the way some apps behave.

2

→ Changing Your Wallpaper

→ Setting Alert Sounds

→ Password-Protecting Your iPad

→ Modifying Keyboard Settings

→ Adjusting Do Not Disturb Settings

→ Setting Parental Restrictions

→ Making Text Easier to Read

→ Controlling Automatic Downloads

→ Customizing the Control Center

→ Working with Other Useful Settings

Customizing Your iPad

As with any relationship, you fall in love with your iPad for what it is. And then, almost immediately, you try to change it. It's easier, though, to customize your iPad than it is to customize your significant other because you can modify various settings and controls in the Settings app.

Changing Your Wallpaper

The wallpaper is the image behind the icons on the Home screen and on the Lock screen. You'll see it often, so make sure it's something you like.

Settings

1. Tap the Settings icon on your Home screen.

2. Choose Wallpaper from the Settings app on the left side of the screen.

3. Tap Choose a New Wallpaper.

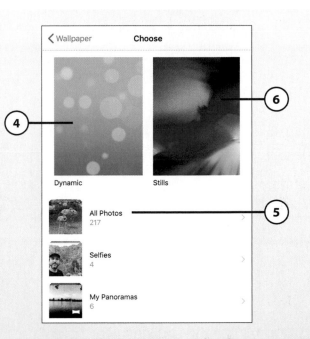

4. Now you have three choices. The first, Dynamic, is if you want to use one of Apple's dynamic wallpapers. Dynamic wallpapers have patterns that slowly animate.

5. A second choice is to use a photo from your photo library—either a photo you took with your iPad or one you synced from your computer. Tap one of the groups of photos listed.

6. A third choice is Stills, which is a collection of Apple's default wallpaper images.

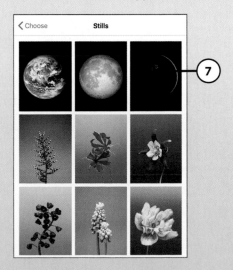

7. Choose an image from the category you selected in step 4, 5, or 6.

8. You see the full image in a preview covering the entire screen.

9. Choose Set Lock Screen to set this image as the background of your Lock screen.

10. Choose Set Home Screen to set this image as the background for your Home screen.

11. Choose Set Both to make the image the background for both the Lock screen and the Home screen.

12. Perspective Zoom is an option that appears when you choose one of Apple's stills or your own photo. When it is on, the image is slightly enlarged and seems to sit in a 3D space below your Lock screen text or Home screen icons. As you move your iPad, you see the image move slightly behind the other elements. You can turn this off by tapping the Perspective Zoom: On button.

13. Tap Cancel at the bottom-left corner of the screen to go back to the wallpaper icons.

Adjusting the Wallpaper Image
When you select one of your own photos as a wallpaper, you can touch and drag in a photo to move to other areas of the image so you can choose the part of the image you want as your wallpaper. You can also pinch to zoom in and out on your photographs.

Setting Alert Sounds

Your iPad can be a noisy device with various events that trigger alert sounds. Just typing on the on-screen keyboard can produce a series of clicks. Here's how to adjust your iPad's sound settings.

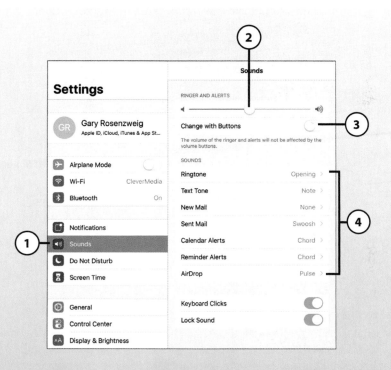

1. Tap the Settings icon on your Home screen (not shown) to launch the Settings app. Then, tap Sounds from the list of settings on the left.

2. Adjust the volume of system sounds, like FaceTime ringtones and notification alerts. This does not affect the volume of music or video.

3. When this is turned on, the volume in step 2 can be changed by using the buttons on the side of the iPad. If you turn this off, you can still use the buttons to adjust the volume of music and video when those are playing; otherwise, the side volume controls won't affect the system sound volume.

4. Tap any of these settings to set the sound that plays when an event occurs. You can choose ringtones, alert tones, or custom tones for any of the events. Ringtone refers to FaceTime calls and Text Tone refers to the Messages app.

Settings	Sounds
	RINGER AND ALERTS
Gary Rosenzweig Apple ID, iCloud, iTunes & App St...	Change with Buttons
	The volume of the ringer and alerts will not be affected by the volume buttons.
✈ Airplane Mode	SOUNDS
📶 Wi-Fi CleverMedia	Ringtone Opening >
⚫ Bluetooth On	Text Tone Note >
	New Mail None >
🔔 Notifications	Sent Mail Swoosh >
🔊 Sounds	Calendar Alerts Chord >
🌙 Do Not Disturb	Reminder Alerts Chord >
⏳ Screen Time	AirDrop Pulse >
⚙ General	Keyboard Clicks ⟶ 5
🎛 Control Center	Lock Sound ⟶ 6
AA Display & Brightness	

5. Switch Keyboard Clicks on or off.

6. Switch the Lock Sound on or off. When this setting is on, a sound plays when you unlock the Lock screen.

How About Custom Sounds?

Any sound event can play a ringtone rather than a plain alert sound. You're offered a list of alert tones that are built into iOS, as well as a list of ringtones, which include the built-in ringtones and any custom ringtones. You can add your own custom ringtones in iTunes on your Mac or PC and then sync them with your iPad. After the sync, you see them listed when you select an alert sound. See "Syncing with iTunes" in Chapter 3, "Networking and Syncing." By obtaining or creating your own custom ringtones, you can set your alert sounds to anything you want.

Password-Protecting Your iPad

Password-protecting your iPad is very important. By using a passcode, you can make sure that someone else can't access your information or use your iPad. It is so important, in fact, that Apple includes setting up a passcode as part of the welcome screens you go through when you first use your new iPad. If you skipped that, you should set it up now.

Settings	Touch ID & Passcode

Settings

- Airplane Mode
- Wi-Fi   CleverMedia
- Bluetooth   On
- Notifications
- Sounds
- Do Not Disturb
- Screen Time
- General
- Control Center
- Display & Brightness
- Wallpaper
- Siri & Search
- Touch ID & Passcode
- Battery
- Privacy

Touch ID & Passcode

USE TOUCH ID FOR:

iPad Unlock

iTunes & App Store

Apple Pay

Password AutoFill

FINGERPRINTS

Finger 1   >

Add a Fingerprint...

Turn Passcode On

Change Passcode

Require Passcode   Immediately >

ALLOW ACCESS WHEN LOCKED:

Today View

1. Open the Settings app and tap Touch ID & Passcode from the list of settings on the left. If you have previously set a passcode, you are required to enter it before moving into the Passcode settings. If you have an older iPad without Touch ID, the button on the left is labeled Passcode instead of Touch ID & Passcode. See the "Make Access Easier with Touch ID" section later in this chapter to learn more about Touch ID.

2. Tap Turn Passcode On to activate this feature. You then are prompted to enter a passcode.

Set Passcode   Cancel

Enter a passcode

○ ○ ○ ○ ○ ○

Passcode Options

1	2 ABC	3 DEF
4 GHI	5 JKL	6 MNO
7 PQRS	8 TUV	9 WXYZ
	0	⊗

Changing a Passcode

If you already had a passcode set and you want to change it, tap Change
Passcode in step 2 instead of tapping Turn Passcode On.

3. Type in a six-digit passcode that you can easily remember. Write it down and store it
   in a safe place. You can run into a lot of trouble if you forget the passcode—which will
   most likely require that you erase your iPad and restore it from your last backup.

4. Re-enter your passcode when prompted.

5. Tap Passcode Options to switch from the default six digits to something else, like four
   digits or a longer alphanumeric passcode.

6. Tap Require Passcode and choose the delay before a passcode is required after you
   lock your iPad. Often, Immediately is your only option, especially if you use features
   like Apple Pay.

7. Some features of your iPad's Lock screen can be accessed even without a passcode.
   You can allow viewing of today's calendar events and reminders, notifications, and
   ask Siri questions without your passcode. Turn off any options you don't want to be
   accessible from the Lock screen.

8. Turn on Erase Data if you want to erase the iPad data after 10 failed passcode
   attempts. This is a good idea from a security standpoint, but not so good if you think a
   mischievous child might grab your iPad and try guessing the passcode. If you use the
   Erase Data feature, be very sure you back up your iPad very often.

9. Press the Wake/Sleep button to confirm your new settings work. Then press the Home button and slide to unlock the iPad. The Enter Passcode screen displays.

Use a Real Password

Would you rather use a real password with letters and numbers instead of a set of digits? If so, good for you! That's much more secure. And you can set one easily. Just follow steps 1 and 2 in the preceding task. In step 3 tap Passcode Options. You can set an alphanumeric code, a custom numeric code that can be as many digits as you like, or a four-digit numeric code.

It's Not All Good

You Forgot Your Passcode?

Well, it wouldn't be secure if there were a way to get around the passcode. So, you're out of luck until you can connect your iPad to your Mac or PC and use iTunes to restore it or erase the iPad using your Apple ID. Hopefully, this never happens to you. For the gory details on what to do in this dire situation, see https://support.apple .com/en-us/HT204306. The one ray of hope is that if you have backed up your iPad recently, you'll be able to restore your data from that backup after you reset the iPad.

Making Access Easier with Touch ID

After you set a passcode for your iPad, you can make it easier to get access to your iPad by using Touch ID on newer iPads. Touch ID allows you to touch your fingertips to your Home button instead of typing the passcode.

1. Tap Touch ID & Passcode on the left side of the Settings app. If you see only Passcode instead of Touch ID & Passcode, then your iPad doesn't have a Touch ID sensor.

2. Tap Add a Fingerprint.

3. You are instructed by your iPad to repeatedly place a finger on the Home button and then lift it off. Follow the instructions carefully as your iPad continues to ask until it has enough information from your fingerprint. Remember to use only one finger while doing this. You will have the opportunity to add more fingers later.

4. When you are done, you see your first fingerprint listed as Finger 1. You can tap here to change the name of this fingerprint or delete it.

5. Tap Add a Fingerprint to add other fingerprints. You might want to add both thumbs and both index fingers so you can use Touch ID while holding your iPad in different ways.

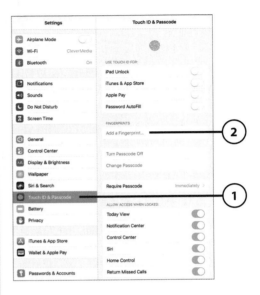

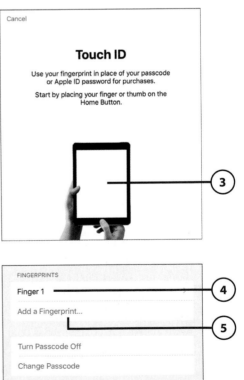

Face ID on the New iPad Pro New!

The new iPad Pro models released in November 2018 do not have a Home button, so you can't use Touch ID. Instead, these models use Face ID, just like the iPhone. Face ID uses cameras at the top of your iPad to verify your identity by looking at your face.

You are prompted to set up Face ID the first time you use your new iPad Pro. You simply look at your iPad as it records your face. Instead of Touch ID & Passcode in the Settings app, you see Face ID & Passcode as the category name. You can go into this section in Settings if you ever want to modify or reset Face ID. You can even scan your face another time for an alternate appearance if you notice that Face ID doesn't always recognize you, or if you want to add another person's face.

To unlock your iPad Pro with Face ID, hold the iPad so the camera at the top can see your face. It should recognize you and unlock automatically after a second. Face ID can sometimes be used to unlock information or functionality in apps. However, just as with Touch ID, you will sometimes be asked for your passcode instead. For instance, if you restart your iPad, you need to use your passcode the first time you unlock it.

Buy with Touch ID or Face ID

Touch ID and Face ID not only make it quicker and easier to unlock your iPad, you also can use them in some third-party apps and the App Store. Instead of needing to confirm your identity in those places, you might be asked to place your finger on the Home button or look at your iPad to data or purchase an item.

>>>Go Further
MAKING TOUCH ID WORK FOR YOU

If your iPad supports Touch ID, you are prompted to set it up while going through the welcome screens. You can always add more fingerprints, or redo the one you entered, in the Settings app. It can be useful to have both your thumbs and perhaps your index fingers recorded in the Touch ID settings. This makes it easier to unlock your iPad in different situations, depending on how you are holding it at the moment. Also, if it seems that Touch ID is often having trouble with one finger or another, you can erase that finger and re-record it.

Modifying Keyboard Settings

If you use your iPad for email or word processing, you will use the on-screen keyboard often. The keyboard does several things to make it easier for you to type, but some of these might get in the way of your typing style. Use the following steps to modify the keyboard settings to your preferences.

1. Open the Settings app and tap General.

2. Scroll through the General Settings list and tap Keyboard.

3. Tap Keyboards to choose a different keyboard layout. In addition to keyboards commonly used in other countries, you can switch to a Dvorak keyboard or one of several other alternatives to the traditional QWERTY keyboard. You can also select a keyboard installed by a third-party app.

4. Tap to add your own text shortcuts. For instance, you can set it so "omw" is instantly expanded to "On my way!" Add your own replacements for things you commonly type.

5. Turn Auto-Capitalization on to automatically make the first character of a name or a sentence a capital letter.

6. Turn Auto-Correction on to have mistyped words automatically corrected.

7. Turn Check Spelling on to have incorrectly spelled words underlined in red.

8. Turn Enable Caps Lock on. When Caps Lock is turned on, you can double-tap the Shift key to lock it.

9. Disable the shortcut bar by switching the button to off. (Read more about the shortcut bar in Chapter 1, "Getting Started.")

---

①

⚙ General	Date & Time >
Control Center	Keyboard >
AA Display & Brightness	Language & Region >
Wallpaper	Dictionary >
Siri & Search	

②

< General **Keyboards**

Keyboards	2 >	③
Text Replacement	>	④
Auto-Capitalization	⬤	⑤
Auto-Correction	⬤	⑥
Check Spelling	⬤	⑦
Enable Caps Lock	⬤	⑧
Shortcuts	⬤	⑨
Predictive	◯	
Smart Punctuation	◯	
Split Keyboard	◯	
Enable Key Flicks	◯	
"." Shortcut	⬤	

Double tapping the space bar will insert a period followed by a space.

Enable Dictation ⬤

About Dictation and Privacy...

10. Turn on or off Predictive Text. See "Using Predictive Text" in Chapter 1 for more about this time-saving feature.

11. Smart Punctuation automatically replaces straight quotes and apostrophes with curly ones that point in the right direction. This is good for writers, but could be problematic for programmers.

12. Switch this button to off if you want to lock the keyboard so it can never be split and moved up vertically. See "Using the On-Screen Keyboard" in Chapter 1 for more details on using a split keyboard.

13. Switch this button to On to enable Key Flicks, which allow you to tap and drag downward on keys to access other characters, such as numbers and punctuation.

14. Turn on the "." shortcut if you want a double-tap of the spacebar to insert a period followed by a space.

15. Tap the key to the left of the spacebar to change keyboards. Note that this key sometimes looks like a globe, sometimes an emoji smile, and sometimes other things. It depends on which keyboard is currently showing. Tap it to move to the next keyboard in your list, or tap and hold to get a list of keyboards so you can select one. You can go directly to the Keyboard settings portion of the Settings app.

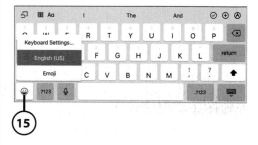

>>>*Go Further*
KEYBOARDS GALORE

You can add all sorts of keyboards created by third-party developers to your iPad. Doing this is just a matter of installing the developer's app on your iPad. Keyboards you add appear in the list in step 3 of the "Modifying Keyboard Settings" task.

Some third-party keyboards allow you to type in different ways. For instance, the Gboard, Swype, and TouchPal apps give you keyboards that allow you to tap the first letter of a word, and then swipe with your finger across the keyboard to the other letters to form the word instead of tapping for each letter. The TextExpander 3 app gives you advanced capabilities for creating shortcuts to type long pieces of text. See Chapter 15, "The World of Apps," to learn how to search for and install apps.

Adjusting Do Not Disturb Settings

Your iPad is trying to get your attention. It beeps and rings with notifications, FaceTime calls, messages, and event alarms. In fact, it might be hard to have it nearby when you're trying to sleep, attending a meeting, or enjoying some time "offline."

Do Not Disturb is a mode where your iPad quiets down. Most audible alerts are silenced. You can set your iPad to enter this mode manually with the Do Not Disturb settings, or set a predefined block of time each day.

1. Launch the Settings app and tap Do Not Disturb.

2. You can turn on Do Not Disturb mode manually with this switch. (You can also turn Do Not Disturb on and off from the Control Center.)

3. Tap Scheduled for Do Not Disturb mode to automatically start and end at specific times. For instance, you can set it to start at 10:00 p.m. and end at 7:00 a.m. so you aren't disturbed while you sleep.

4. Tap here to use time and date controls to set the start and end times.

5. You can choose to have Do Not Disturb only affect sounds when your iPad is locked, instead of at all times, including when you are actively using your iPad.

6. Tap Allow Calls From to allow FaceTime calls and messages from specific people by selecting a group in your contacts list.

7. Turn on Repeated Calls so that someone can reach you in an emergency by calling twice within three minutes.

Setting Parental Restrictions

If you plan to let your kids or grandkids play with your iPad, you might want to set some restrictions on what they can do. In iOS 12, these settings are under the new Screen Time feature, which allows you to monitor and restrict use of your iPad. I give more details of the other features of Screen Time in Chapter 15. Here is how you use it to restrict the use of an iPad for a younger user.

1. Open the Settings app and tap Screen Time. You might be asked right away if this is your iPad, or one that will be used by a child.

2. Tap Content & Privacy Restrictions.

3. Tap Enable Content & Privacy Restrictions.

4. The Restrictions settings are a long list of categories, each with multiple settings. Tap each category to reveal all the options. If you want to prevent new apps from being installed and apps from being deleted, tap iTunes & App Store Purchases.

5. Tap Allowed Apps to prevent access to apps such as Mail, Safari, Camera, News, and so on.

6. Tap Content Restrictions.

7. You can use standard movie and TV ratings systems for your country to restrict video playback. This applies only to content in the TV app. You would need to examine settings for third-party apps and services like Netflix if you want to restrict content in those apps.

8. Tap Web Content to restrict access to websites in Safari. You can choose to disallow a preset list of "adult websites" or specify your own list of allowed sites.

9. Tap Back to return to the previous menu.

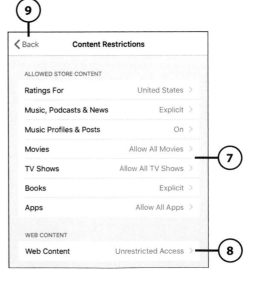

10. Adjust the many other services in the Privacy section. Most of these aren't that important for preparing your iPad for use by a child—they're personal preferences concerning how your iPad and apps handle privacy issues.

11. Tap Back to return to the main Screen Time menu.

12. Tap Use Screen Time Passcode.

13. Set a passcode to prevent a child from simply going to the Settings app and switching off the content restrictions you have set. Remember this passcode because you'll need to change these settings or disable them when you want to use your iPad again.

⑪

‹ Back	Content & Privacy Restrictions	
iTunes & App Store Purchases		›
Allowed Apps		›
Content Restrictions		›
PRIVACY		
Location Services	Allow	›
Contacts	Allow	›
Calendars	Allow	›
Reminders	Allow	›
Photos	Allow	›
Share My Location	Allow	›
Bluetooth Sharing	Allow	›
Microphone	Allow	›
Speech Recognition	Allow	›
Advertising	Allow	›
Media & Apple Music	Allow	›
ALLOW CHANGES:		
Passcode Changes	Allow	›
Account Changes	Allow	›
Cellular Data Changes	Allow	›
Volume Limit	Allow	›
Do Not Disturb While Driving	Allow	›

⑩

⑫

⬛ Wallpaper	Use Screen Time Passcode
⬛ Siri & Search	Use a passcode to secure Screen Time settings, and to allow for more time when limits expire.

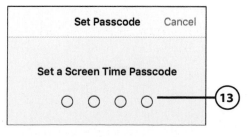

Set Passcode   Cancel

Set a Screen Time Passcode

○   ○   ○   ○

⑬

It's Not All Good

Settings Not Remembered

It would be nice if you could just switch restrictions on and off so that you could hand your iPad to Junior after quickly turning them on. But the settings are reset each time you switch Restrictions to off. So you need to set the switches again each time after turning Restrictions back on. Once they are on, however, you can go back any time and adjust the individual settings.

Making Text Easier to Read

If you find that text in standard apps like Calendar, Reminders, and Notes is difficult to read because it is too small or the letters are too thin, you can change that in the Display & Brightness settings.

1. Open the Settings app and tap Display & Brightness.

2. You can make the letters of standard text thicker and easier to read. Changing this setting requires your iPad to restart.

3. Tap Text Size to make the default text larger or smaller.

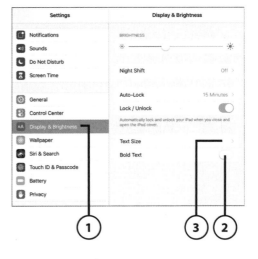

4. Tap and drag the dot along the line to change the size of text. Because the Settings app is one of the apps affected by this, you see the changes in most of the text on the screen as you drag.

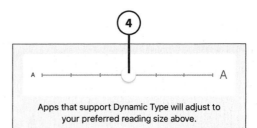

Apps that support Dynamic Type will adjust to your preferred reading size above.

Text Size Isn't Universal

Changing the text size doesn't affect all apps. It works on some of the Apple preinstalled apps, but even in those, it works only in some places. With the Calendar app, you can see the change in Week and Day view but not Month view.

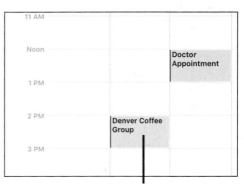

Smaller text

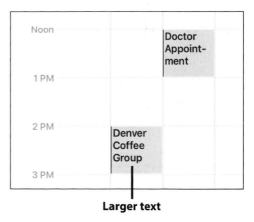

Larger text

Controlling Automatic Downloads

Your iPad can automatically download app updates when they become available. This saves you from missing an update to your favorite apps. You can also set your iPad to download new content that you purchase from iTunes on another device.

1. Open the Settings app and tap iTunes & App Store on the left.

2. There are three switches that control automatic content downloads. Turn these on if you want your iPad to automatically get music, apps, or books when you purchase them on another device, such as your computer or an iPhone.

3. Turn on Updates if you want updates to Apple and third-party apps to automatically download and install.

4. Your iPad can automatically offload apps if you haven't used them in a while. This means the app is uninstalled to save space, but a placeholder icon is still in the same location on your Home screen, and your data connected to the app remains. You can tap the placeholder icon at any time to have the app redownloaded and restored, provided you are connected to the Internet.

Cellular Data

Note that if you have an iPad with mobile wireless capability, you see another setting here for Use Cellular Data. Turn this off to prevent these automatic downloads from happening while you are away from a Wi-Fi connection.

Customizing the Control Center

The Control Center is a set of switches that you can quickly access by swiping down from the upper-right corner of the screen (see Chapter 1). The Control Center can be customized so it's more useful to you. You can use the Settings app to add and remove some buttons, and change their order.

1. In the Settings app, tap Control Center.

2. Tap Customize Controls.

3. Tap the red – button next to any item in the Include list to remove it from the Control Center.

4. Tap the green + button next to any item in the More Controls list to add it to the Control Center.

5. Tap and drag these handles up and down to change the order of appearance for the included buttons.

6. Some buttons, like Notes, are just shortcuts to take you quickly to that app.

7. Tap Text Size in the Control Center to display a slider for adjusting the system text size. This is the same setting covered earlier in this chapter in "Making Text Easier to Read."

8. The Magnifier button launches a camera-like app that enables you to use your iPad's camera as a magnifying glass.

Settings	Control Center
General	Swipe down from the top-right edge to open Control Center.
Control Center	**Access Within Apps**
Display & Brightness	Allow access to Control Center within apps. When disabled, you can still access Control Center from the Home Screen.
Wallpaper	
Siri & Search	**Customize Controls**
Touch ID & Passcode	
Battery	
Privacy	

① ②

‹ Control Center   **Customize**

Add and organize additional controls to appear in Control Center.

③

INCLUDE

— ⏱ Timer ≡

— 📷 Camera ≡ ⑤

— ⦿ Screen Recording ≡

④

MORE CONTROLS

+ Accessibility Shortcuts

+ Alarm

+ Apple TV Remote

+ Guided Access

+ Hearing

+ Home

+ Magnifier ⑧

+ Notes ⑥

+ Scan QR Code

+ Stopwatch

+ Text Size ⑦

+ Voice Memos

Working with Other Useful Settings

The Settings app contains too many controls to go into detail on each one. It is worth taking the time to explore each section of the Settings app to see what is possible. The item to tap on the left side of the Settings app screen is listed first in each of the following bullets, followed by the items you tap on the right side. For example, in the first bullet you open the Settings app, tap General on the left side, and then tap iPad Storage on the right side. When the settings appear, tap Available to see your available storage.

- **General, iPad Storage:** See the remaining amount of storage space you have on your iPad.

- **General, About, Version:** Quickly find out which version of iOS you are using.

- **General, About, Model:** Get the model number of your iPad. This could come in handy if you ever need to figure out if an accessory will work with your specific model.

- **Wi-Fi, Ask to Join Networks:** Regardless of whether this switch is on, your iPad looks for and connects to any Wi-Fi network you have previously signed on to. If you switch this setting on and the iPad can't find any familiar network, you see a dialog asking if you want to join the strongest network it can find. Because you don't want to join networks you don't know or trust, leave this setting off and simply go to the Wi-Fi settings to join a new network.

- **Siri & Search:** Here you can turn on and off different types of content you see when you search the contents of your iPad. You can also set the order by dragging the items in the list up or down.

- **General, Reset**: Here is a set of potentially dangerous switches that allow you to erase your settings and content. If you ever decide that your iPad's Home screens are too disorganized, you can use the Reset Home Screen Layout to move the Apple default apps back to their original positions and your other apps out of folders into alphabetical order starting on screen two. The other reset options should be used only if you understand their end result.

- **General, Shut Down:** You rarely need to do it, but you can shut down your iPad. If you plan to be away from your iPad for a long period of time—such as several weeks, for example—then you might want to shut down to preserve the battery for when you return.

More Apps, More Settings

The Settings app adds new items as you add new apps to your iPad. Some apps have settings inside the app, whereas others have all their settings as an item along the left side of the Settings app. Still others put some settings in the app and some in Settings. It is a good idea to periodically check the Settings app to see what new items have appeared, and then look to see which settings are available for that app.

Search Your Settings

You can also search at the top of the left sidebar in the Settings app. Drag the list all the way down to see the Search field at the top above Airplane Mode. Then type into that field the name of an app to find its settings, if there are any. You can also type the name of subcategories, such as "Storage" to find the Storage & iCloud Usage settings inside the General category.

Put your favorite
photos on your iPad

View your
files

Sync your music and other
content with your Mac or PC

In this chapter, you find out how to connect your iPad to your local Wi-Fi network. You also see how to sync your iPad with your Mac or Windows computer and with Apple's iCloud service.

→ Setting Up Your Wi-Fi Network Connection

→ Connecting to Your Apple ID and iCloud Account

→ Syncing with iTunes

→ Sharing with AirDrop

→ Storing, Organizing, and Viewing Files

Networking and Syncing

Your iPad connects you to the world. You can surf the Web, view all sorts of information, communicate with friends, and share photos. But first, you must connect your iPad to the Internet. You can do that using a Wi-Fi connection. Some iPads also have the capability to connect to a cellular network.

Setting Up Your Wi-Fi Network Connection

One of the first things you need to do with your iPad is to establish an Internet connection.

Chances are that you did this when you started your iPad for the first time. It should have prompted you to choose from a list of nearby Wi-Fi networks. You might need to do this again if you first used your iPad away from home, or if you need to switch to another Wi-Fi network.

To connect your iPad to a wireless network, follow these steps.

Settings

1. Tap the Settings icon on the Home screen.

2. Choose Wi-Fi from the list of settings on the left.

3. Make sure that Wi-Fi is turned on.

4. Tap the item that represents your network. (Tap the blue-circled i button next to each network to customize your network settings.)

I Don't Have a Wireless Network

If you don't have a Wi-Fi network but do have high-speed Internet through a telephone or cable provider, you have several options. The first is to call your provider and ask for a new network modem that enables wireless connections. Some providers might upgrade your box for free or a small cost.

Another option is to keep your current box and add a wireless base station of your own, such as the Apple AirPort Extreme base station.

5. If the network is protected by a password, you're asked to enter the password.

6. Tap Join. After you enter the password, your iPad remembers it. If you switch between two locations, like work and home, you are asked to enter the password the first time you use that connection. From that point on, your iPad automatically logs on to each connection as you move around.

>>>Go Further

SECURITY? YES!

Your wireless network at home should have security turned on. This means that you should see a padlock next to it in the list of Wi-Fi networks on your iPad. When you select it for the first time, you should be asked to supply a password.

If you don't require a password, seriously consider changing your Wi-Fi network box's settings to add security. The issue isn't simply about requiring a password to use your Internet connection. It is about the fact that a secure network sends encrypted data through the air. Otherwise, anyone can simply "sniff" your wireless connection and see what you are doing online—such as using credit cards and logging on to websites and services. See your network equipment's documentation to set up security.

>>>Go Further

SETTING UP YOUR CELLULAR DATA CONNECTION

If you have an iPad with cellular data capabilities, you can set it up to use AT&T, Verizon, or any other compatible network. You can purchase a monthly data plan, or purchase service in shorter increments. If you have previously set up a plan, you cannot complete these steps again. You need to contact your service provider directly to change or cancel your plan.

1. Open the Settings app and tap Cellular Data on the left.

2. Turn on Cellular Data. In addition, go into Cellular Data Options and turn on Enable LTE for a faster connection. You can also decide on that screen whether you want to allow data roaming, which could cost more depending on your data plan.

3. Tap the Manage button to sign up for and manage your account, or change your plan.

4. Look for the Cellular Data Usage section. The usage numbers are shown here, which helps you keep tabs on your costs.

5. Depending on your plan, you might also have the option to turn on Personal Hotspot, which turns your iPad into a mobile Wi-Fi network with which other devices can connect.

Working with Wi-Fi and Cellular Data

After you establish a cellular data plan, your iPad should still connect to your Wi-Fi networks when it is in range and use cellular data only when it cannot find a Wi-Fi network. You can also return to Settings and turn on or off Cellular Data to specifically prevent your iPad from using the cellular data network. This is handy when you are completely out of mobile data range but have local Wi-Fi; for instance, you might be on an airplane flight.

Looking at the top-left corner of your iPad's screen, you can tell which sort of connection you are currently using. You see the Wi-Fi symbol, a fan of four curves, when you are connected to Wi-Fi. If you have a cellular data plan, you see the name of your network next to it, such as "AT&T," plus a series of bars that show your connection strength. You are using that connection only if the characters "3G," "4G," or "LTE" are shown instead of the Wi-Fi symbol.

It's Not All Good

Watch for Data Roaming

In the Cellular Data settings, you can turn Data Roaming on or off. This is what enables your iPad to connect to wireless data networks that are outside of your data plan, such as networks in other countries. If you leave Data Roaming on and your iPad connects to such a network, you might find a surprise bill in the mail. You can avoid extra charges by leaving Data Roaming off or by purchasing a plan from AT&T for International Data Roaming.

Connecting to Your Apple ID and iCloud Account

When you think of your contacts, calendar events, and email messages, you might be tempted to think of that information as being "on your iPad" or "on your computer." But today this information is usually in both places, and more. This is referred to as "the cloud"—when the actual location of the information isn't important as long as it is where you need it, when you need it.

As an iPad user, you have access to several different cloud services, most notably Apple's system called iCloud. It is a free service that offers email, contacts, calendar, documents, and other types of data stored on Apple's servers and is automatically synced to your iPad and the other Apple devices you may own.

In addition, you could choose to use other cloud services, such as Gmail, for mail and calendar events. There's no reason to pick just one. You can use both iCloud and Gmail on your iPad.

When you use cloud services, you get automatic syncing as long as you have a connection to the Internet. For example, add a contact to your iPad and your iPhone automatically updates to show that new contact.

First, let's look at how you sign in to your Apple ID on your iPad. This connects you to your iCloud account. Perhaps you already did this when prompted when you first turned on your iPad. If not, you can do it in the Settings app.

Signing In with Your Apple ID

1. Open the Settings app and tap here to sign into iCloud. If you instead see your name here, that means you have already signed in with your Apple ID.

2. If you have never set up an account with Apple before, then tap Don't Have an Apple ID or Forgot It? to set one up. You can also use this if you don't remember your Apple ID. Any account you have with Apple, such as an iTunes account, would be an Apple ID, and you should use that instead of starting a new account.

3. If you already have an Apple ID, even if you have never used iCloud before, enter your ID and password. Apple IDs can be any email address, not just an @icloud.com email address.

4. Tap Next to access your account (not shown). If your account has been used only for things like iTunes in the past, you are prompted to set up the new iCloud part of your account.

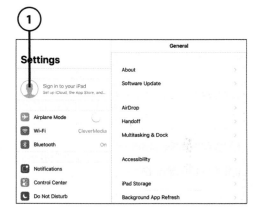

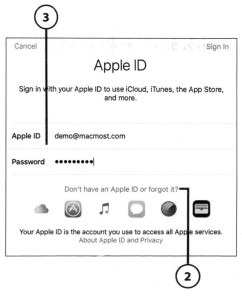

It's Not All Good

Don't Confuse ID with Email

An Apple ID is a unique identifier that allows you to log in to your iCloud account. It can be an Apple email address, like myipadbook@icloud.com, but it can also be a non-Apple email address, like myipadbook@gmail.com. In the former case, the ID is the same as your iCloud email address. In the latter case, the ID is just an ID. Your email account would be a Gmail account and have nothing to do with your iCloud account.

5. After signing in, the top entry in the Settings app changes to show your name. Your name also appears on the top of the section on the right side.

6. You can tap in the Name, Phone Numbers, Email section to check your Apple ID settings.

7. Use the Password & Security section to change your Apple ID password directly from your iPad.

8. Use the Payment & Shipping section to change which payment method is used for music, movie, app, and other purchases.

9. In the iCloud section, you can find the settings related to iCloud Drive and other iCloud services.

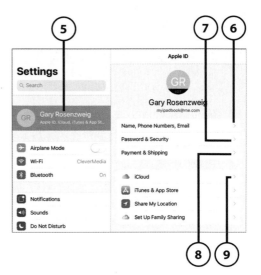

10. The top section shows you your iCloud storage space and which services are using it. Apple gives you 5GB of space for free, but you can purchase more by tapping Manage Storage. You see a button that lets you Upgrade to a monthly paid plan that gives you more storage.

11. The rest of the settings allow you to turn off and on various services and types of storage. You can turn photo-related iCloud services, such as Photo Stream and iCloud Photo Library, on or off here. See Chapter 9, "Taking and Editing Photos," to learn about how photos are stored.

12. You can use your iCloud email on your iPad. This would typically be an @icloud.com email address. These addresses are part of the free iCloud service. If you happen to be using a non-Apple email address as an Apple ID, note that this setting has nothing to do with that email account.

13. If Contacts is on, iCloud stores all your contacts so they automatically sync with the iCloud servers and then to your other Apple devices.

14. Likewise, iCloud can store your calendar events when the Calendars switch is on.

15. Turn on Reminders to have the Reminders app use iCloud to store reminders and automatically sync them with your other devices.

16. Turn the Notes switch on so that Notes can also sync over iCloud.

17. Safari can sync over iCloud as well. Things like your bookmarks, tabs, and reading list sync across devices when the Safari switch is on.

18. You can have your News app preferences sync across your devices. The News app is covered in Chapter 16, "Must-Have Apps."

19. iOS allows you to store passwords while using Safari so you don't need to enter them each time. Syncing these over iCloud means that you can also access these passwords on other Apple devices. Tap Keychain to configure this setting. See "Saving Time with AutoFill" in Chapter 7, "Surfing the Web," for more details on working with the Keychain.

20. iCloud Backup backs up your settings, documents, photos, and other data to iCloud wirelessly. If your iPad is lost or breaks, you are able to restore your data to a repaired or new iPad. You should use iCloud Backup unless you prefer to back up to your computer via iTunes and do so on a regular basis.

21. Find My iPad is an option that lets you locate your iPad on a map using another Apple device or the iCloud.com website. Be aware that if your Location Services are not on, this feature does not work. See "Using Find My iPad" in Chapter 19, "Maintaining Your iPad and Solving Problems."

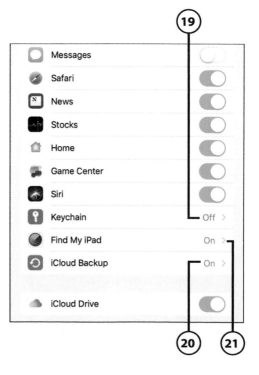

22. iCloud Drive is for general file storage and allows you to see files you have stored in iCloud Drive across all your devices: Macs, iPhones, and iPads. Further down the list are individual apps that can use iCloud Drive to store files, such as Pages, Numbers, Keynote, GarageBand, and so on. Leave these on if you plan on sharing these kinds of files between your iPad and other devices.

Notes		⬤
Messages		◯
Safari		⬤
News		⬤
Stocks		⬤
Home		⬤
Game Center		⬤
Siri		⬤
Keychain		Off >
Find My iPad		On >
iCloud Backup		On >
iCloud Drive		⬤

(22)

>>>Go Further

iCLOUD.COM

In addition to syncing between devices, much of your iCloud information is available if you go to iCloud.com and log in using your Apple ID. You can do this on any computer. So even if you are using your iPad as your only computing device, there still is another way to get to your data when you need it.

Syncing with iTunes

With iCloud, the iPad can be a truly stand-alone device, no desktop computer needed. iCloud is also great for keeping your iPad and your Mac in sync, sharing settings, music, photos, and so on. For most users today, syncing via iCloud is all you need. The days of syncing with a cable to your Mac or PC are gone, and it is no longer necessary. That said, there are still some minor advantages to syncing to your computer:

- Using iTunes, you can back up your iPad to your computer. You can restore all your data from these backups if you lose your iPad. You can do the same with iCloud backup, but it can take a lot longer to restore an iPad because it has to transfer the data across the Internet.

- Syncing with a computer is a good way to get a large number of photos from your collection on your iPad if you aren't using iCloud Photo Library.

- Syncing is how you get your music stored on your computer onto your iPad if you aren't using iTunes Match or Apple Music. If you have a large collection of music, you can opt to copy only a selection of it to your iPad at any one time.

You might get a message asking if you trust this computer and whether it is okay to sync your iPad to this computer the first time you connect your iPad and open iTunes. The message won't reappear after you have connected the iPad to the computer.

After connecting the first time, iTunes should automatically open when you connect your iPad. While connected to your computer, you can always click the Sync button in iTunes to re-sync and apply any changes to the iPad.

You can also choose Sync over Wi-Fi connection in your iPad's options in iTunes. This allows you to sync when your iPad isn't connected to the computer by the USB cable. It only needs to be on the same network as your Mac or PC that is running iTunes.

As we look at some of the syncing options for the iPad, the Mac version of iTunes is used as an example. The Windows version of iTunes is similar but not exactly the same.

Syncing Options

After your device is in sync, you can change some general options for your iPad from the Summary screen in iTunes. Most of the options are self-explanatory, such as Open iTunes When This iPad Is Connected.

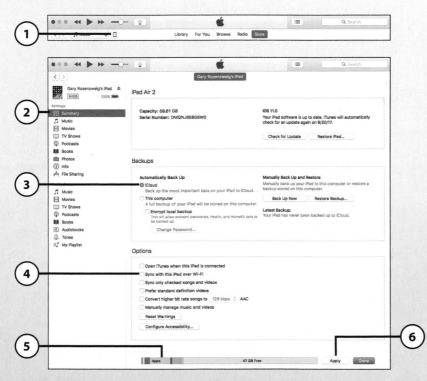

1. Using iTunes 12.8 or newer, look for a button representing your iPad at the top of iTunes. After you select it, the items in the rest of the iTunes window pertain to your iPad, with settings and content categories listed on the left.

2. You are now viewing the sync settings for your iPad. Tap Summary to view some general settings.

3. You can configure your backups. iCloud backups are convenient for those without regular access to a computer, but this uses Internet bandwidth and can be a problem if you have a slow connection. Backing up to your computer is a good option if you regularly sync to your computer anyway.

4. You can set your iPad to connect via Wi-Fi. From then on, you only need to be on the same network as your computer to sync with iTunes.

5. A handy chart of your iPad's storage is shown.

6. Any changes you make on this screen, or any other iTunes sync screen, require that you click Apply to re-sync with the new settings.

The Manually Manage Music and Videos Option

One option that dramatically changes how your iPad syncs is Manually Manage Music and Videos. This option turns off automatic syncing of music and videos and enables you to simply drag and drop songs and movies from your iTunes library onto the iPad icon on the left. (You might need to scroll down the Summary page to locate this check box if your screen size is too small to show the entire page at once.)

>>>Go Further

BACK IT UP!

Perhaps the most important part of syncing with your computer is backing up your data. Everything you create with apps, every preference you carefully set, and every photo you take could be gone in a second if you drop your iPad or someone swipes it. Even a hardware failure is possible—the iPad isn't perfect.

Choosing This Computer saves all your data on your computer in a backup file. Try to do it once per day. With a good backup, you can replace a lost iPad and restore all your data from the backup. It works incredibly well.

You can always plug your iPad into your Mac or PC, launch iTunes, and click the Back Up Now button in the Backup section. Backup also happens automatically, once per day, if you connect your iPad to your computer and click Sync.

Your other option is iCloud. This backs up your data wirelessly to iCloud. It is your only option if you are not going to sync your iPad with a computer. It does use up your data storage allotment in your iCloud account, so you might need to upgrade your iCloud account to allow for more data.

Even so, backing up to iCloud is a great alternative, especially if you travel often and use your iPad for critical tasks. You can always do both types of backups by selecting iCloud in step 3 and also connecting your iPad to your computer on a regular basis and clicking the Back Up Now button in iTunes.

Syncing Music

There are now many ways to listen to music on your iPad. For many people, a streaming service like Apple Music or Spotify has completely replaced the old technique of building a music file library on your computer and then syncing it to your iPad. Chapter 4, "Playing Music and Video," discusses streaming music in more detail.

If you still want to sync music to your iPad from your computer, then the simple way to do it is to select Entire Music Library in iTunes on your computer. If you have more music than can fit on your iPad, though, you must make some choices. Syncing Movies, TV Shows, Podcasts, Tones (ringtones for messaging and FaceTime), iTunes U, and Books all work in a similar way to syncing music, so you can apply what you learn in these steps to those items as well.

1. If you are not already viewing your iPad settings in iTunes, select your iPad at the top of the iTunes window.

2. Click Music under Settings.

3. Select Sync Music, if it isn't already turned on.

4. Click the Selected Playlists, Artists, Albums, and Genres button.

5. Check off any playlists in the Playlists section that you want to include.

6. Check off any artists for which you want to include every song by that artist.

7. Check off any genres to include in their entirety.

8. Check off any albums you want to include.

9. Use the Search box to quickly find specific artists.

10. Click the Apply button if you want to apply the changes now.

One Copy Only

Note that songs are never duplicated on your iPad. For instance, if the same song appears in two playlists and is also by an artist that you have selected to sync, the song only has one copy on your iPad. But it appears in both playlists and under that artist, album, and alphabetical list of all songs.

>>>Go Further
MORE WAYS TO SYNC

iTunes Match is a service from Apple. For an annual fee, you can sync your music collection with Apple's servers. Then you can access all your music on your iPad by turning on iTunes Match in the Music settings in the Settings app. When you do this, you no longer need to sync your music. Instead, you see all your music on your iPad, and it downloads from Apple's servers when you want to listen to a particular song.

Visit www.apple.com/itunes/itunes-match/ to find out more about Apple's iTunes Match service.

Apple Music is a service from Apple where you pay a monthly subscription fee in return for access to a huge library of music from iTunes. You can add any songs in the Apple Music catalog to your collection and they will appear on your iPad and other Apple devices for as long as you remain a subscriber. See "Having It All with Apple Music" in Chapter 4.

You can also sync your music and videos manually. This sounds like a lot of work, but for many people it can be an easier way to sync your music. If you check off Manually Manage Music and Videos on the iTunes Summary screen for your iPad, you can then drag and drop music from your iTunes music library to your iPad. It requires a bit of knowledge about how the iTunes interface works, however. You need to choose View, Show Sidebar so you can see your iPad in the left sidebar. Then you can look at the Music item listed to see which songs are there. Switch to your iTunes Music library to see what songs you have on your computer and simply drag and drop songs, albums, or artists from the iTunes Music library to your iPad in the left sidebar.

Syncing Photos

With Apple's iCloud Photo Library, your iPad automatically shows all your photos without requiring you to do any syncing. iCloud Photo Library is covered in Chapter 9. But if you are not using iCloud Photo Library, then you need to use the older technique of manually syncing photos to your iPad.

The process for syncing photos from your computer to your iPad is very similar to how you move music, videos, and other data to your iPad. So let's use photos as an example. The steps here are very similar if you want to sync something else, like movies, to your iPad. You would just choose the Movies tab in iTunes instead of the Photos tab.

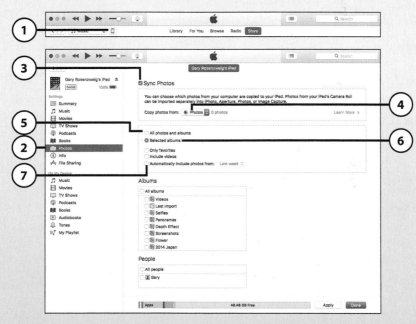

1. Select your iPad.

2. Choose Photos.

3. Click the check box to indicate that you want to sync photos.

4. You can choose from any applications that are compatible with iTunes and store photos. For instance, on the Mac you can choose the new Photos app or the old iPhoto or Aperture apps, if you have them. You can also simply select a folder to use as the location for your photos. The rest of the steps here assume you are using Photos.

5. Click All Photos and Albums to sync all your photos. Only do this if you have a fairly small collection.

6. Choose Selected Albums to select which albums to sync.

7. You can also have photos taken over a recent period of time automatically sync. For instance, you can have it sync all photos from the past 6 months.

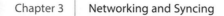

8. Choose which albums you want to sync. Albums are collections of photos, like music playlists, that allow you to compile your favorite or related photos into a group.

9. When you are satisfied with your selections, click Apply to begin the transfer.

No Duplicates

When you sync photos, you get only one copy of each photo, no matter how many times the photo appears in albums, events, and faces. The photos appear in all the right places but take up only one spot in memory on your iPad.

It's Not All Good

One Direction

Syncing photos can be a confusing concept: You sync photos from your photo collection to your iPad using iTunes, but you sync photos from your iPad to your computer using Photos or a similar app.

Think of it this way. Syncing to your iPad works the same for music, videos, and photos. These are all media stored on your computer, and iTunes lets you copy them from your computer to your iPad. But when you take photos with your iPad, your iPad is acting just like a digital camera. You want to copy those to your photo-handling app on your computer as you would if you were using a digital camera.

When you sync photos from your computer to your iPad, the original is on your computer, and there is merely a copy on your iPad. Your iPad is just a viewing device for these photos. It is important that you maintain your real photo library on your computer and remember to back it up.

Syncing Everything Else

Music and photos are two out of many types of items you might want to sync between your computer and your iPad. In most cases, if you use iCloud for that type of item, there is no need to ever sync it via iTunes.

If you look in iTunes, you have the ability to sync Info, Music, Movies, TV Shows, Podcasts, Books, and Photos. Each has a similar screen to the Music and Photos syncing settings screens. Let's take a look at each and see why you may or may not want to sync them using iTunes.

- **Info:** This means syncing Contacts and Calendars. If you use iCloud, this happens automatically as you make changes. There is no need to sync.

- **Music:** If you are using Apple Music or iTunes Match, you don't need to use iTunes to sync your music. If you don't have much music, and want to save a few dollars, you can simply sync your music with iTunes on your computer.

- **Movies and TV Shows:** These two categories are used mainly to sync videos you have purchased in the iTunes Store. However, this also works for other videos you store in iTunes. Videos that are part of your photo collection are synced under Photos.

  One thing to keep in mind is that once you purchase a movie or TV show episode, you can always redownload it from Apple later. So if you buy 22 episodes of a TV season and watch them all, you don't need to keep them on either your iPad or your computer. You can remove those items from iTunes to save some storage space, and then download them again from Apple if you want to watch them again later.

- **Podcasts:** Thanks to the standalone Podcasts app that comes with your iPad, there's not much of a need to sync podcasts from your computer to your iPad. You can simply download episodes directly to your iPad. See "Listening to Podcasts" in Chapter 4.

- **Books:** Books work in much the same way as Movies. When you buy a book from Apple, you can redownload it later. If a book is just text, it's a quick download. If you buy a book on your computer in iBooks, you can easily find it and download it in the iBooks app on your iPad, too. Syncing is useful for those who import other types of books into the iBooks library on a Mac, and then want to get them to their iPad later on.

- **Photos:** As noted earlier, the main reason to sync photos is if you aren't using iCloud Photo Library and you want to take some recent or favorite albums from your computer and put them on your iPad for viewing.

Sharing with AirDrop

A quick way to get data from your iPad to another iOS device or Mac is using AirDrop. This technique uses Wi-Fi, but instead of going through a Wi-Fi network, it uses your iPad's Wi-Fi hardware and goes directly from device to device. The devices don't need to be on the same network—they don't need to be on any Wi-Fi network at all. They just need to be nearby.

With AirDrop you can share things like photos, contacts, documents, and other kinds of files. If an app has a Share button, then most likely it has a way to send some data to another device using AirDrop.

AirDrop requires the latest Wi-Fi hardware in your iPad, but any iPad capable of running iOS 10 should be able to use AirDrop. On a Mac, it requires a recent model as well, running at least Mac OS X Yosemite. Using AirDrop is pretty straightforward.

Using AirDrop

To use AirDrop, follow these steps:

1. To use AirDrop, make sure you have turned it on. Do this by accessing Control Center. See "Using Control Center" in Chapter 1, "Getting Started." Tap the AirDrop button.

2. Make sure that it is set to Everyone. Another option is to set it to Contacts Only, which means you can use AirDrop only with devices that have Apple ID email addresses that are in your Contacts.

3. This example uses the Contacts app. You can share any contact. Just go into that contact and tap Share Contact.

4. In addition to sharing options such as Message and Mail, you see a list of AirDrop-compatible devices that are within range. You see whatever image the user has chosen as a user icon, plus their name. If you do not see your other device, it could be asleep, or have AirDrop disabled, or possibly is not a model that has AirDrop available. Tap the device you want to share with. You see a Waiting message below the icon.

5. The recipient receives an alert asking them to accept the transfer. This example shows what the user sees if they are using a Mac.

Friends Share

The real power of AirDrop is sending between friends. For instance, if you are standing with your iPad next to a friend with an iPhone, you can send her a picture without both of you needing to share a common Wi-Fi network or exchanging email addresses. You just Share, select her for the AirDrop, and she accepts.

>>>Go Further

HANDOFF

Handoff is a feature of iOS and macOS that allows you to put down one device and pick up another to continue what you are doing. There are no settings for this; it just works as long as both devices are signed into the same iCloud account, and they are nearby.

Suppose you start composing an email on a Mac. Then you decide that it would be easier to type the message on your iPad. All you need to do is look at the dock at the bottom of the Home screen of your iPad. You see a Mail app icon at the right, with a desktop screen icon attached to it, telling you that you can pick up your work on the iPad. Tap the icon, and the Mail app opens and your half-completed message appears, ready for you to finish.

There are a lot of things that need to be just right for Handoff to work. Both devices need to not only use the same iCloud account, but also need to see each other using Bluetooth and Wi-Fi systems. A little radio interference is all it takes for this to not work one time, but work other times.

Handoff indicator

Storing, Organizing, and Viewing Files

Computer users are familiar with the idea of files. When you work in apps, you create and edit files, such as word processor documents, spreadsheets, images, audio, and any other type of computer data. You store the files in folders on your computer.

Your iPad uses files, too. When you create a document in the Pages app, for instance, you create a file. But until recent versions of iOS, you could only see Pages files in Pages. iOS 10 provided the capability to use the iCloud Drive app to see Pages files, and files created by other apps as well, as long as those files were stored in iCloud Drive.

Staring with iOS 11, the iCloud Drive app evolved into the Files app. The Files app shows you all the files on your iPad, whether they are local documents, stored on iCloud Drive, or even stored on third-party services like Dropbox or Google Drive. If you're using iCloud Drive on a Mac and use the same Apple ID on your iPad, you can see your Mac files on your iPad. You can view text files, images, and PDFs inside the Files app. Other file types can be opened in specific apps, such as Pages documents in Pages.

Freely Move Between Machines

If your Mac is running macOS Sierra or newer, you can even see your Desktop and Documents folders and their contents in the iCloud Drive app on your iPad. You can easily move between these devices with iCloud Drive and work on the same files. You don't need to take any manual steps to keep these files in sync; as long as you are connected to the Internet, iCloud takes care of it for you. Just move between your Mac and iPad as you're working. And if you have an iPhone with at least iOS 10, then you can bring that into the mix as well.

Accessing Your iCloud Drive Files

Here is how to access your iCloud Drive files. First, refer to "Connecting to Your Apple ID and iCloud Account" earlier in this chapter and check the final step to see where to enable iCloud Drive.

1. Launch the Files app. It is easier to use the Files app in horizontal orientation, so you can see the left sidebar at all times.

Files

2. Tap Browse to make sure you are browsing all files, not just looking at recently accessed files.

3. Tap iCloud Drive on the left.

4. Tap Name to sort by filename. You can also sort by date, size, and tags.

5. Tap to switch to a list view instead of an icon view.

6. Tap a folder to view that folder's contents.

7. If the folder contains subfolders, you can tap them to dig further down in the folder structure.

8. Many types of files, such as PDFs, text documents, and images, can be viewed directly in the Files app. Just tap to open the document for viewing. Tap the Done button at the top left to return to the file list. If the file is handled by an app, such as Pages, then that app launches and loads that document.

9. Tap to create a new folder. If you don't see the New Folder button or the sorting buttons to the right of it, tap and drag down to reveal them.

10. Tap Select for more file organization functions.

11. In Selection mode, you can tap files and folders to select them. A blue circle with a check mark indicates which items are selected.

12. Tap to duplicate the selected items to make new files that are identical to the originals.

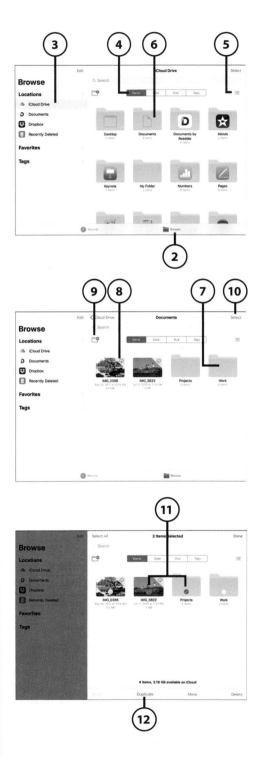

13. Tap to move the selected files. You're prompted to select a new location either in your iCloud Drive or another storage location that the Files app has access to.

14. Tap to delete the selected files.

15. Tap Select All to select all files and folders in the current folder.

16. Tap the Share button to send the selected files via AirDrop, email, Messages, and many other methods. This button is inactive in the figure because a folder is selected in addition to a file.

17. Tap Done to return to the normal file view.

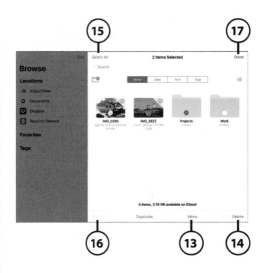

>>>Go Further

YOU STILL MAY NEED AN APP

Just because you can see the file in iCloud Drive doesn't mean you can work with it on your iPad. The iCloud Drive app acts as a simple viewer for many file types. But, as with desktop computers, you need the right app to work with the file.

For instance, if you get a Photoshop file on your desktop computer, you wouldn't expect to edit it unless you had Photoshop installed. The same is true on the iPad. You need the right app to work with the file. Sometimes, the app doesn't exist as an iPad app and there is nothing you can do to work with the file.

Creating documents and then saving them to iCloud Drive also requires the appropriate app. An app developer needs to build iCloud Drive compatibility into the app to allow you to save the file to iCloud Drive.

Accessing Files in Other Cloud Services

The big difference between the new Files app and the former iCloud Drive app is its ability to access files stored locally on your iPad and also access files on services like Dropbox and Google Drive. To even have the possibility of using Dropbox and Google Drive in Files, you need to have the apps from those services installed. You can find them in the App Store. After the app is installed, you should see it appear as an option in Files.

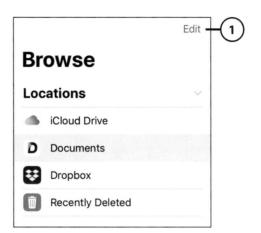

1. Launch the Files app. In horizontal orientation, you should see the left sidebar with the Edit button at the top. Tap it.

2. Here you see a list of different file storage services you can use in iCloud Drive. If you don't see a service you need, it is either because you have not installed the relevant app, or that service is not yet compatible with the Files app.

3. Switch on a service to add it.

4. Tap Done. You see the service in the left sidebar.

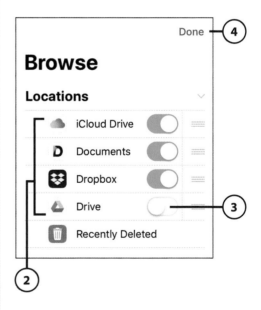

5. Tap the app to find out if the app is connected to the Files app.

6. If you haven't signed into the service on this iPad before, such as in the dedicated app for that service, then you get a sign-in request. Complete the information to sign in.

After you have added your favorite cloud storage services, you can browse your files in those services just like you did in the previous task with iCloud Drive.

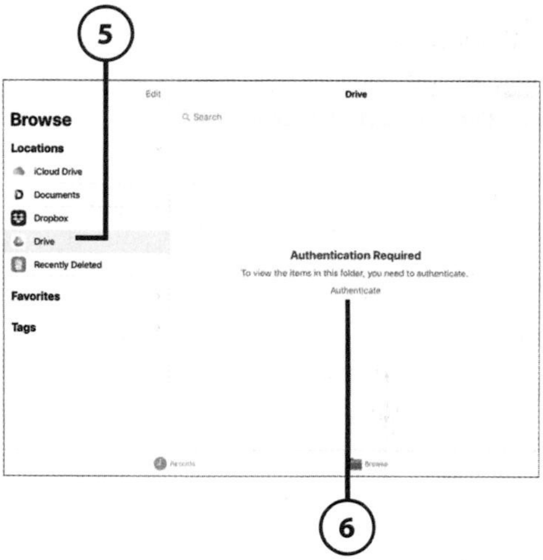

⑤

Edit   Drive

Browse   Q Search

Locations
☁ iCloud Drive
D Documents
📦 Dropbox
☁ Drive   **Authentication Required**
📋 Recently Deleted   To view the items in this folder, you need to authenticate.

Favorites   Authenticate

Tags

⑥

Watch purchased,
rented, or
synced videos

Purchase
music
and buy or
rent videos

Listen to
podcasts

Play music from
your collection
or subscribe to
Apple Music

In this chapter, you learn how to use the Music and Video apps to play music and watch video. You also learn how to use Apple Music.

→ Playing a Song
→ Building a Playlist
→ Making iTunes Purchases
→ Sharing Purchases with Your Family
→ Having It All with Apple Music
→ Listening to Podcasts
→ Playing Video
→ Using AirPlay to Play Music and Video on Other Devices

Playing Music and Video

The iPad handles playing music as well as any iPod or iPhone ever has, plus it has a large, beautiful screen for you to use to browse your collection. Chapter 3, "Networking and Syncing," explains how to sync music to your iPad from your computer. That's one way to get music onto your iPad. You can also use the iTunes app to purchase music. Families can share purchases using the Family Sharing feature. Apple's streaming music service, Apple Music, gives you unlimited access to nearly all the songs on iTunes.

No matter how you put music on your iPad, you play your music using the Music app. You can also listen to podcasts with the Podcasts app, and you can watch movies and TV shows with the Videos app.

Playing a Song

So let's start by simply selecting and playing a song synced to your iPad from your computer or purchased from iTunes. Skip ahead to the "Having It All with Apple Music" section if you are using Apple Music.

Music

1. Tap the Music icon along the bottom of your Home screen, unless you've customized your toolbar and moved it elsewhere.

2. Tap the Library icon at the bottom of the screen, if it isn't already selected.

3. At the top of the screen, tap the Library menu and then choose how you want to view the songs in your library. You can view a list of recently added songs, your custom playlists, songs by artist or album, a full list of all songs, or just your downloaded music.

4. Choose Artists.

5. Tap an artist on the left. A list of albums by that artist displays on the right. It doesn't matter if you own all the songs from that album or just some of the songs; you'll see the album artwork listed on the right.

6. Tap the album to view the songs in that album.

7. Some information about the album (such as the genre and the year it was published) is displayed.

8. The songs on the album are listed. Tap any song to play it. Or, tap the Play button to play them all in order.

9. At the bottom of the screen the currently playing song is shown. The Play button changes to a Pause button. You can tap this button to pause the song. If you let the song play out, the Music app continues with the next song.

10. Use the Shuffle button to play the songs in a random order. That probably isn't what you want to do when listening to an album. But this interface is the same for playlists, which are often nice to shuffle.

11. Tap the song artwork to see a more detailed set of controls.

12. Tap and drag the dot along the slider to jump to a specific part of the song.

13. Adjust the volume by dragging the dot along the volume slider.

14. The list of songs shows you what song will play next. You can drag the three-line handles on the right side of each item up or down to change the order. You can swipe left to remove a song.

15. You can also tap here to set the whole list to repeat once, or repeat over and over.

16. Tap the left side of the screen to return to the album view.

17. Tap and hold any song to see a small menu on the left.

18. Tap to add a song to the top of the playlist so the song plays next. This enables you to browse through your artists and albums and decide what you want to listen to, song by song. (Instead of tapping once to start playing back the album as described in step 8, you can add a variety of songs.)

19. Tap to add a song to the end of the list.

20. Tap the Love button to indicate that this is one of your favorite songs. iTunes and Apple Music use this information to make suggestions for new music you might like.

21. Tap Artists to return to the screen showing your artists. You can also tap and drag anywhere on the screen from left to right.

22. At any time, tap the Search button to search for songs, albums, or artists in your library.

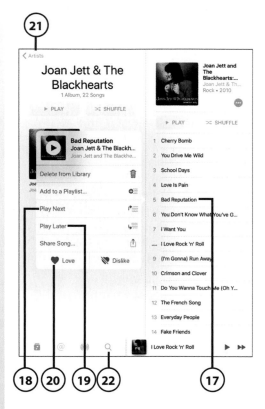

Siri: Playing Music

You can use Siri to play music. Here are some examples:

"Play The Beatles."

"Play 'Georgia On My Mind.'"

"Play some blues."

"Play my driving music" (plays the playlist named "driving music").

"Shuffle all songs."

"Skip."

"Pause."

Building a Playlist

Playlists are a way to take the songs you have on your iPad and arrange them in ordered groups. For instance, you can create one to listen to while working, while working out, while trying to go to sleep, or you can make a party mix for your next get-together.

Creating Playlists

You can create playlists in iTunes on your Mac or PC, but you can also build playlists on your iPad.

1. In the Music app, tap the Library button.

2. Tap the Library menu.

3. Tap Playlists.

4. You see a list of current playlists.

5. Tap New to create a new playlist.

6. Give the new playlist a name, such as *My Playlist*, by tapping here and typing a name.

7. Tap here and type a description for this playlist.

8. After you start to add songs, the Music app creates a piece of art for this playlist based on the art for those songs. But you can tap here and take a picture or use a photo from your Photos library instead.

9. Tap Add Music.

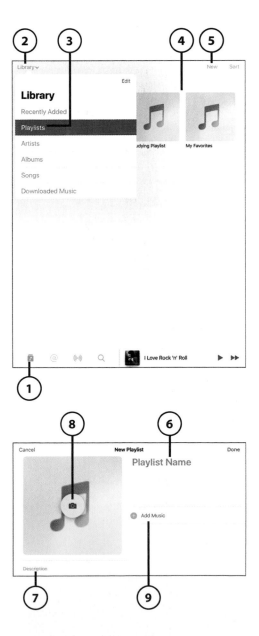

10. Search for music by artist, album, or song by typing the term you're looking for.

11. Tap Artists, Albums, Songs, Genres, and so on to dig into your library to find songs to add.

12. Tap the + button next to a song to add it to the playlist. The + button changes to a check mark.

13. Tap Library to go back up a level to continue to search for songs.

14. Tap Done when you are done adding songs to the playlist.

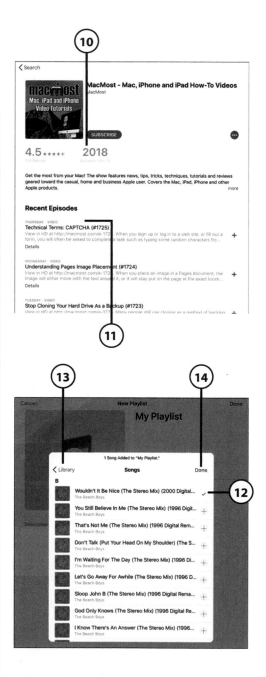

15. Tap and drag the three-line handles to the right of a song to move it up and down in the list.

16. Tap the red – buttons to remove a song from the list.

17. Tap Add Music to add more songs.

18. Tap Done when you are finished editing the playlist. You see the same list from step 4, but your new playlist is included. Tap it to view the playlist.

19. The playlist is now just like an album. You can tap a song in the list to start playing it.

20. Tap Edit to remove, add, or reorder the songs in the playlist.

21. Tap the Play button to play the whole playlist in order.

22. Tap to shuffle the playlist to listen to it in a random order.

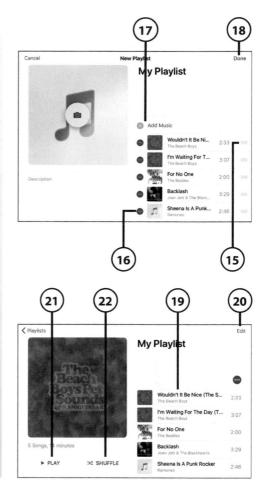

Making iTunes Purchases

You have lots of options when it comes to adding more music to your iPad. You can simply add more music to your iTunes collection on your computer and then sync those songs to your iPad. In that case, you can buy them from iTunes or another online source, or you can import them from music CDs.

How Else Can I Get Music?

You can purchase music on your iPad only through the iTunes app. But through your computer you can sync music that you get from any source that doesn't use special copy protection, like CDs you import into iTunes. You can buy online from places such as Amazon.com, eMusic.com, cdbaby.com, or even directly from the websites of some artists.

Buying on Your iPad

In addition to syncing music to your iPad from your computer, you can purchase music, movies, TV shows, and audio books directly on your iPad using the iTunes app and using the same account that you use in iTunes on your computer.

1. Tap the iTunes Store app icon on your Home screen to go to the iTunes Store. If this is the first time you have used the iTunes Store, you might be asked about setting up Family Sharing. See the next task for more information about this.

2. Tap Music at the bottom of the screen.

3. Initially, you see a screen showing featured albums and songs from all genres. But you can select a specific genre of music instead.

4. Swipe left and right to browse more featured albums.

5. Drag the screen up to reveal more lists, such as top albums, top songs, and music videos.

6. Use the Search field to search for an artist, album, or song by name.

7. Select a suggestion from the list, or tap the Search button on the keyboard to complete the search.

iTunes Store

8. Find a song or album you want to buy, and tap its artwork to view more information.

9. Swipe up to move down the page and see ringtones, music videos, movies, and even books that match your search.

10. Tap a song name to listen to a sample of the song.

11. Tap outside the album window to close it and return to the previous view.

12. To buy a song, album, or any item in the iTunes Music store, tap the price of that item, and then tap again on the Buy button.

Syncing Devices

After you make an iTunes purchase, the music, TV show, or movie you downloaded should transfer to your computer the next time you sync your iPad. From your computer, you can sync your new purchase to any of your other devices that use your iTunes account.

You can also set iTunes on your computer and your other devices to automatically download new purchases. So when you buy on your iPad, you get the new music everywhere. On your iPad, that setting is in Settings, iTunes & App Store, Automatic Downloads. In iTunes on your computer, the setting is in iTunes, Preferences, Store, Automatic Downloads.

Apple Music—No Purchase Required

If you use Apple Music, you don't need to use the iTunes app to purchase music. There's no need to use the iTunes Music store except for rare cases where some music may be available for purchase in iTunes, but it isn't available for streaming in Apple Music.

Sharing Purchases with Your Family

Family Sharing lets you share items you purchase from iTunes with other members of your household. One family member is set up as the organizer, and his or her iTunes account is the one that will be charged for all purchases.

Each member of the family sharing group can have their own Apple ID and iCloud account, which will be used for email, calendars, and other purposes. Purchases are made through the iTunes account of the organizer's Apple ID.

In addition, those who are part of your Family Sharing group also have a shared photo stream in the Photos app, a special shared calendar in the Calendar app, a shared Reminder list in the Reminders app, and they can see one another's location with the Find My Friends app.

Setting Up Family Sharing

1. Tap Settings to open the Settings app, and then tap Apple ID and iCloud settings.

2. Tap Set Up Family Sharing.

3. Read through the screens telling you more about Family Sharing and asking you to read the legal agreement and confirm your Apple ID and payment information. Tap Get Started to begin working with Family Sharing.

Family Sharing

Share music, movies, apps, storage and more with up to six members of your family.

You'll also get a family photo album, family calendar, and access to family devices in Find My iPhone.

Get Started

Learn more about Family Sharing

4. You see some of the different services you can share using Family Sharing. This example shows how to share iTunes purchases. Tap iTunes & App Store Purchases.

5. Check to make sure you are using the right Apple ID, in case you have more than one. Then tap Continue.

6. Confirm that the payment for your iTunes account looks right. Then tap Continue.

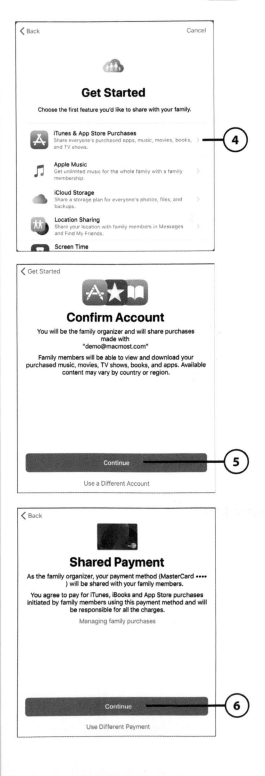

7. Invite a family member to share your purchases. Tap Invite via iMessage to go to the Messages app where you can address a message to the family member's Apple ID. The message includes a link that enables the person to complete the connection to your iTunes account.

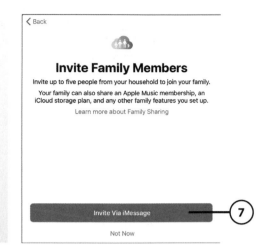

> ‹ Back
>
> **Invite Family Members**
>
> Invite up to five people from your household to join your family.
>
> Your family can also share an Apple Music membership, an iCloud storage plan, and any other family features you set up.
>
> Learn more about Family Sharing
>
> Invite Via iMessage ⑦
>
> Not Now

>>>*Go Further*
PARENTAL GUIDANCE

If a family member younger than 13 years old is added to your group, every time they try to make a purchase, the Family Sharing organizer receives a notification and has to approve that purchase before it goes through. Also, children ages 13–17 can have this option turned on when they are added to Family Sharing.

The organizer can also tap any adult family member's name in the Family Sharing settings and then flip the switch labeled Parent/Guardian to enable that adult to approve purchases made by children.

Having It All with Apple Music

A popular option for music lovers today is to subscribe to an unlimited music service. Apple offers such a service, called Apple Music, which is built into the Music app on your iPad.

For a monthly fee, you can play music from a huge collection of millions of songs—nearly everything that is available in iTunes, with only a few notable exceptions, like The Beatles. You can listen to what you want, when you want, on your iPad, iPhone, and Mac. For a modest increase in the monthly fee, you can also share your music access with your family members.

Signing up for Apple Music is fairly easy, and Apple even allows you to try it for a while before you start paying for your subscription. After you are signed up, you can browse Apple Music and pick songs or whole albums to add to your collection in the Music app, and then play those songs any time you want.

Apple Music also includes a For You section that offers specially curated playlists and listening ideas based on your listening preferences and history.

Signing Up for Apple Music

You sign up for Apple Music in the Settings app.

1. In the Settings app, tap Music.

2. Tap Join Apple Music.

3. Tap the button to begin your trial period.

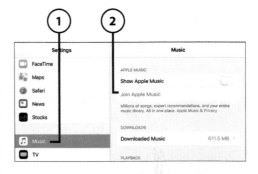

4. Select your plan. The Individual plan is just for you and works on all of the devices and Macs you have set up with your Apple ID. The Family plan also includes others you have set up with Family Sharing. Continue to follow the prompt to complete setup.

Cancelling

Signing up for the trial is low risk because you can always cancel your subscription before the trial period ends. Just tap the ID button at the top of the Music app (it looks like a circle with a head in it), select View Apple ID, and then tap Manage under Subscriptions.

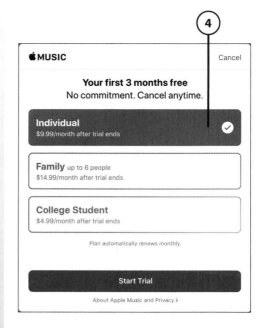

Playing Songs with Apple Music

Think of Apple Music as an all-you-can-eat music buffet. You can search the entire Apple Music library and play any song you like. Let's start off by searching for and playing a song. You can also add songs to your library just as if you had purchased them.

1. In the Music app, tap the Browse button to go to the New Music page of Apple music.

2. You see featured new artists, albums, and songs. Tap a song to start listening to it.

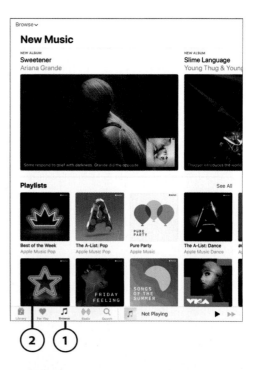

3. Alternatively, tap the For You button to see music that you might like based on your previous behavior.

4. Another alternative is to tap the Search button to look for a specific song, artist, or album.

5. Tap the Search field and start typing your search term.

6. Make sure that you select Apple Music as the search type. If you have Your Library selected instead, you get search results for only music that's already in your library.

7. Tap a result that best matches what you are looking for. Alternatively, you can tap the Search key on the keyboard to get all search results that match what you are typing.

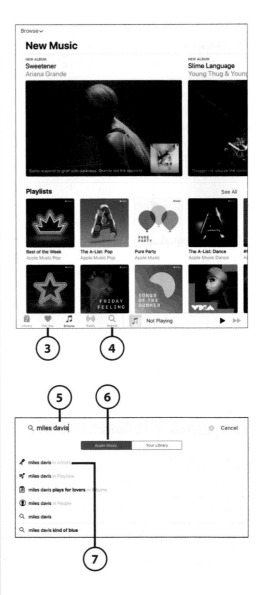

8. If you see the song you want to hear, tap it, and it starts playing.

9. Tap the + button next to any song to add the song to your library, which makes it easier to play the song again later. Adding songs to your library mimics "purchasing" the music, and the song is listed in your library next to others you have imported or purchased from iTunes. You don't pay anything extra for the song, though, because it is part of your Apple Music subscription.

10. If you find an album rather than a single song, you can tap it to go to that album.

11. Tap + Add to add the entire album to your library. When you do, you're asked if you want to have this album downloaded to your iPad. Doing so means that you can play the album even if you are not connected to the Internet at that moment.

12. You can also add a single song with the + button next to it, or tap the song name to simply play that song.

13. Tap Play to listen to the whole album.

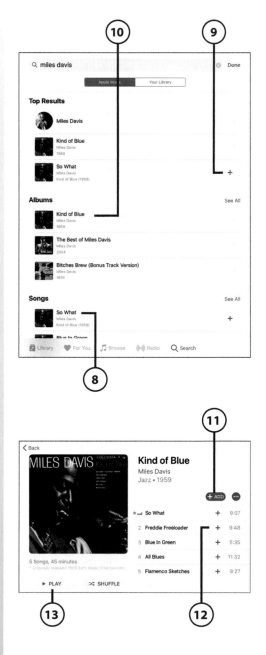

Playing Offline

The problem with streaming music services like Apple Music is that you need to be connected to the Internet to use them. However, you can decide to keep some of your music library on your iPad for offline listening. Step 11 explains how the Music app sometimes does this for you automatically. You can also tap the three-dot (…) button in Apple Music when viewing albums or playlists and tap Download to indicate that you want that album or playlist to be available offline.

>>>Go Further
TRY NEW THINGS

One big advantage to a subscription service like Apple Music is you can try new songs as much as you like. If you hear of a new artist, or catch a song on the radio, or hear something in a TV show, you can go to Apple Music and play the album just to see if you like it. That's not easy to do otherwise, as you would end up buying lots of albums that you only listen to once.

Discovering New Music with Apple Music

Because you have so much music available to you with Apple Music, you might not want to just listen to specific songs. Instead, you might want to explore new artists or entire genres of music. Apple creates special playlists for this. You can also create a custom streaming radio station based on an artist or song.

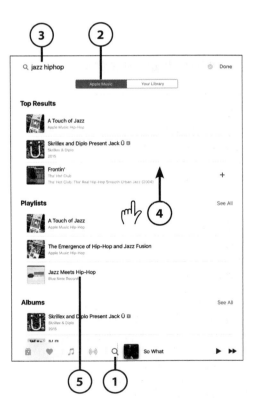

1. In the Music app, tap the Search icon.

2. Make sure you are searching Apple Music, not Your Library.

3. Type a search term and tap the Search key to get results. You can type an artist name, a genre of music, a mood, decade, or anything that can be used to describe music.

4. Tap and drag to scroll down to see playlists.

5. Tap a playlist to go to it.

6. Tap a song to listen to it, or tap + to add the song to your library.

7. Tap Shuffle to play the playlist in a random order.

8. Tap Play to play the list in order.

9. Tap the More (…) button to download the playlist for offline listening, add it to your library, and other functions.

Discovering Music with Apple Music Radio Stations

Another way to explore is to listen to Apple Music radio stations. Apple has a professionally run streaming radio station called Beats 1 that has programming 24 hours a day. In addition, Apple curates special genre-based stations that are simply infinite playlists of music. You can also create your own streaming station based on a song or artist.

1. In the Music app, tap the Radio button.

2. Tap the Beats 1 logo to listen to the radio station. Beats 1 is usually the first item in the main list on this screen.

3. Other stations are listed on the front page of the Radio section. Browse this page and tap any one to go to it.

4. Tap Radio Stations to see even more featured stations.

5. Tap the Search button to search for stations by title or keyword.

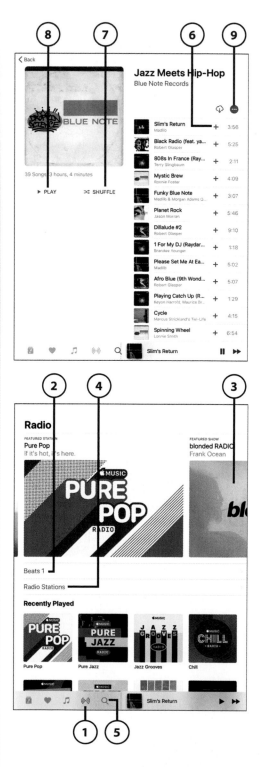

6. Type a search term, just as if you were searching for a song or album, and tap the Search button on the keyboard when done.

7. If necessary, scroll down the page to get to the Radio Stations section.

8. Sometimes there are more stations that meet your search criteria. Look for the See All button to go to a complete list.

9. Tap a radio station.

10. That station starts playing.

11. Tap the More (…) button to bring up more options while a song is playing.

12. Use the Love and Dislike buttons to tell Apple Music whether you'd like more or less of this kind of song on this station, which continues to customize itself for you this way.

13. You can add a song to your library so it appears in your Library section on the Music app, as it would if you had purchased the song.

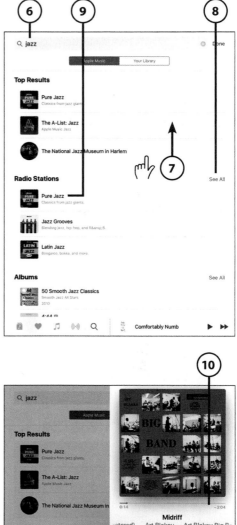

14. The Create Station button starts a new station based on this one song. This button is also present when playing any song in Apple Music in any way. For instance, if you are listening to an album from your favorite artist, you can start a station based on a song in that album. Then you can continue to adjust the music on that station with the Love and Dislike buttons.

15. You can share a radio station with a friend who is also on Apple Music using Messages, Email, Facebook, and other methods.

How Do I Get Back to This Station?

After you listen to or create a radio station, you can find it again by tapping the radio station button at the bottom of the Music app, and looking under Recently Played.

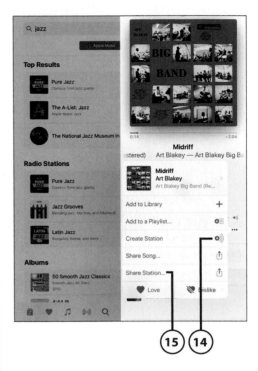

Listening to Podcasts

Podcasts are episodic shows, either audio or video, produced by major networks, small companies, and individuals. You'll find news, information, tutorials, music, comedy, drama, talk shows, and more. There is something covering almost any topic you can think of.

Subscribing to Podcasts

To subscribe to and listen to or watch podcasts, you use the Podcasts app from Apple.

1. Tap the Podcasts app icon on your Home screen.

2. Tap the Library button to look at the podcasts you've already downloaded.

3. Tap Browse to go to a screen with Apple's currently featured podcasts. Alternatively, if you know what you are looking for, you can tap the Search button at the bottom of the screen to search for a podcast by name or topic.

4. Tap Featured to see more featured podcasts.

5. Tap Top Charts to see the most popular podcasts.

6. Tap All Categories to see a list of categories and featured podcasts in each category.

7. From any of the screens you see in steps 3 through 6, tap a podcast to view more information and episodes.

8. Swipe up to view more episode descriptions, reviews, and other similar podcasts.

9. Tap Subscribe to add this podcast to your library. New episodes of this podcast automatically appear in your library.

10. Tap any episode to listen to it or view it.

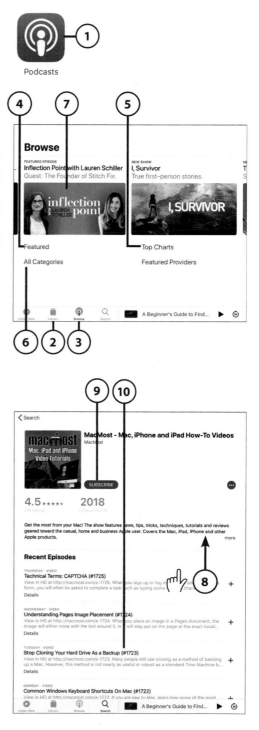

Podcasts

11. Tap More (…) to access more settings, such as the order in which episodes are played.

12. Tap Library to view the podcasts you have added to your library.

13. On the Library screen, tap Episodes to see the most recent episodes from all the shows you have added to your library.

14. Tap any episode for more information and to play it.

15. Use the Edit button for additional functions, such as the ability to add a podcast that is not listed in iTunes by using the show's podcast URL address.

Playing Video

After you have movies, TV shows, and home videos on your iPad, you need to play them using the TV app.

The TV app enables you to play video from a variety of sources, such as movies and TV shows you have purchased in the iTunes app, shows from your cable or satellite provider, and shows directly from television networks.

Adding Your TV Networks to the TV App

If you are paying for a subscription to a TV network, either through a cable or satellite vendor, or directly to that network, you can see those shows listed in the TV app. First, though, you need to add the app for that network.

1. Launch the TV app.

2. Tap Store to see a list of movies and TV shows available for purchase or rent on iTunes and apps that connect to the TV app. You might need to scroll down to see the Start Watching Now section with the list of apps.

3. Some apps are stand-alone services like HBO Now, where you use an in-app purchase to access all of that network's shows.

4. Online networks like Netflix and Hulu charge a monthly subscription and offer a variety of shows.

5. You might already be paying for some networks through your cable or satellite TV provider. In these apps, you're asked to log on using your cable or satellite TV user ID and password, and then you have access to the shows in the network-specific app and in the TV app.

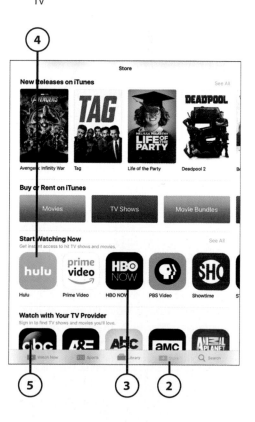

TV

6. In the Settings app, you can go to the TV app screen to see more settings.

7. You can see which TV networks and apps you have added and will be available in the TV app. You can turn off networks you do not want to see in the TV app.

8. While here, you can adjust the video playback quality settings for videos you've purchased and rented from iTunes.

How About My Home Videos?

If you shoot a home video with a video camera, or iPod touch or iPhone, you can bring that into iTunes on your Mac or PC and sync it to your iPad. They appear as Home Movies in the menu along the top of the Videos app.

Changing the Orientation

For most video content, you can rotate your iPad to view in a horizontal orientation and use the Zoom button at the upper right to crop the left and right sides of the video so that it fits vertically on the screen. This is similar to watching a movie on a standard TV.

What About My DVDs?

If you can import CD music content into iTunes, you'd think you'd be able to import video content from your DVDs. Well, technically it is possible (although not necessarily legal) by using programs like Handbrake (http://handbrake.fr/) for your Mac or PC to import DVD content and then drag the resulting file into iTunes. You can then sync it with your iPad. These might also show up as Home Movies because your iPad doesn't recognize them as official movie content.

Watch Videos on Your iPad

When you play video from the TV app, one of two things can happen. In most cases, the appropriate app for watching the video launches, and the video automatically starts. So if you choose a Hulu video, the Hulu app launches, and the video plays. However, some videos play inside the TV app. Video playback controls vary depending on which app is playing the video.

1. In the TV app, on the Watch Now screen, you can tap any video to start it. In many cases the related app launches, and you start watching the video in that app.

2. Tap Library to view purchased and rented videos you have already downloaded and that are ready to watch.

3. Tap the Library button at the top to see a list of categories, which includes Home Videos and any Macs on your network that are using Home Sharing to allow other devices on the network to view iTunes Library content.

4. Tap a video to play it.

5. Tap the middle of the screen to bring up playback controls.

6. Use the Play/Pause button to pause.

7. Drag the dot along the line to jump to another part of the video.

8. Tap to switch to a picture-in-picture mode to keep watching the video while you go to other apps. This enables you to check your email or look up something online while watching.

9. Tap Done to exit the video and return to the previous screen.

>>>Go Further
BUYING AND RENTING VIDEO

Although buying video is similar to buying music, some significant details are different and worth taking a look at.

Copy Protection: Although music in the iTunes Store is copy-protection free, videos are a different story altogether. Purchased videos can be played back only on the Apple devices you own that use your iTunes account. You can't burn videos to a DVD, for instance, or watch them on a TV unless it is hooked up to an Apple device. Rentals are even more strict because you can watch them only on the device you rent them on.

Collecting Movies: Thinking of starting a collection of videos by purchasing them from Apple? These videos take up a lot of space on your hard drive. An iPad, even a

128GB version, quickly fills up if you start adding dozens of movies. Fortunately, once you purchase a movie with iTunes, you can download it again. So you can purchase many movies over time, but only put the ones you want to watch on your iPad. Movies you own appear in your Videos app as well, even if they are not actually on your iPad. You see a little iCloud Download button next to them. You can tap that icon to start downloading that movie to your iPad from Apple's servers.

Time-Delayed Rentals: Rentals have some strict playback restrictions. After you download a rental, you have 30 days to watch it. After you start watching it, you have only 24 hours to finish it. This means you can load up your iPad in advance with a few movies to watch while you're on an airplane or away on vacation.

TV Show Season Passes: You can purchase seasons of TV shows that aren't complete yet. When you do this, you are basically pre-ordering each episode. You get the existing episodes immediately but have to wait for the future episodes. They usually appear the day after they've aired on network television.

Multi-Pass: In addition to season passes, you can also get a Multi-Pass, which is for TV shows that broadcast daily. When you purchase a Multi-Pass, you get the most recent episode plus the next 15 episodes when they become available.

Using AirPlay to Play Music and Video on Other Devices

In iTunes, with the TV app and many other apps that play music or video, you have the option to send the audio or video stream from your iPad to another device that is connected to the same Wi-Fi network, such as an Apple TV.

You need to enable AirPlay on those devices first. For instance, using the Apple TV (2nd generation models or newer), you need to go into settings on the device and turn on AirPlay. You also need to make sure that the device is using the same Wi-Fi network as your iPad.

Accessing AirPlay

AirPlay is an option in many cases when you are viewing video in an app.

1. Look for the AirPlay button and tap it.

2. A control appears in the middle of the screen, and any AirPlay-compatible devices, such as Apple TVs, are listed. Tap any device to stream the video to that device.

3. You can tap Done to exit, or just tap outside of the control.

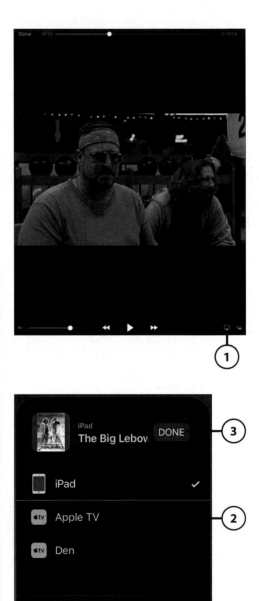

Mirror Your Screen with AirPlay

You can also use AirPlay to show whatever is on your iPad's screen at almost any time. The iPad screen is simply shown on both your iPad and the AirPlay device at the same time. This is called "mirroring," and you access it from the Control Center.

1. Swipe down from the upper-right corner of the screen to bring up the Control Center.

2. Tap the Screen Mirroring button.

3. You see a control with a list of AirPlay devices, such as Apple TVs. Tap one to start mirroring your screen to that device.

4. After mirroring has started, you can return to this control by repeating steps 1 and 2 and then tapping Stop Mirroring.

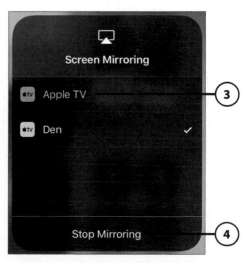

Purchase and read
books with the iPad's
ebook reader

In this chapter, find out how to purchase books from the Apple Books Store and how to read them on your iPad.

→ Buying a Book from Apple
→ Reading a Book
→ Using Reading Aids
→ Adding Notes and Highlights
→ Adding Bookmarks
→ Organizing Your Books
→ Using Books App Alternatives

Reading Books

As an ebook reader, your iPad gives you access to novels, textbooks, and more, storing hundreds inside.

A single app, the Books app, allows you to both read and purchase new books. You can also download and add books from other sources, including via the Kindle app.

Buying a Book from Apple

The first thing to do with the Books app is to get some books! You can buy books using the store in the app. You can also find some free books there.

Books or iBooks? (New for iOS 12)

Prior to iOS 12, the Books app was called iBooks, and the store inside it was the iBooks store. Apple has simplified the name to just Books, and the store is referred to as the Book Store or Apple Book Store.

1. Tap the Books app icon to launch Books.

2. If you have previously purchased and downloaded books, you see those when the Books app opens. You can swipe through the horizontal Reading Now list or tap Library to see all your books.

3. Tap Book Store to go to the Apple Books Store to purchase books or download free ones.

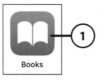

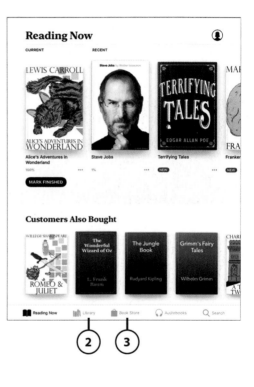

Don't Want to Purchase from Apple?

You don't necessarily need to buy books from Apple. You can buy from any seller that sends you an ePub or PDF formatted file with no copy protection. If you receive the file on a computer, just drag and drop it into Books. It shows up in your books collection there, ready to be synced to your iPad.

You can also add PDFs you find on the web or receive in email to your Books library. While viewing a PDF on your iPad in Safari, tap once in the middle of the screen, and an Open in Books option appears at the top. While viewing a PDF attached to an email message, you can use the Share button to open it in Books. Many other third-party apps also allow sharing PDFs to Books this way. Text and ePub-formatted documents often work as well. When you open a document in Books, a copy is placed in your Books library.

4. At the top of the page, you can tap Browse Sections to reveal a sidebar with genres such as Biographies, Fiction, Education, History, and Mysteries.

5. Tap one of the collections to see a list of recommended books by Apple's editors.

6. Swipe right to left to move through horizontal lists of books.

7. Swipe up to reveal more sections including bestseller charts.

8. Tap the Search button to search for book titles and authors.

9. Tap any book cover to view more information about the book.

10. Scroll through this page to read a summary and reviews and to see a list of related and similar titles.

11. Tap the Sample button to download a sample of the book.

12. Tap the Buy button to purchase the book.

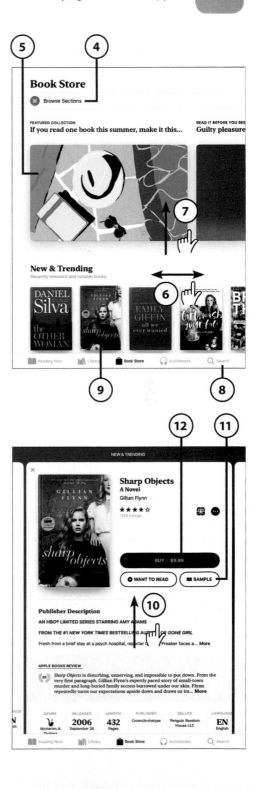

Reading a Book

Reading books is a simple process. Following are the basics of reading your downloaded books.

1. Tap the Books app icon to launch the Books app.

2. If you are still in the store section of the app, tap Library at the bottom to see all your books. Then, tap a book to open it.

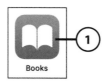

Can't Find Your Book?

Did you download a book only to discover that you can't see it in your Library? Try tapping the All Books button at the top of the screen and switching to a different collection. For instance, by default, PDF documents are put in the PDF collection, not in the Books collection.

3. To turn a page, tap and hold anywhere along the right side of the page, and then drag to the left. A virtual page turns. You can also tap the right side of the page.

4. Tap and drag from the left to the right or simply tap the left side of the page to turn the page back.

5. Move quickly through pages by tapping and dragging the small marker at the bottom of the page along the dotted line. Release to jump to a page.

6. Tap the Table of Contents button at the top to view a table of contents.

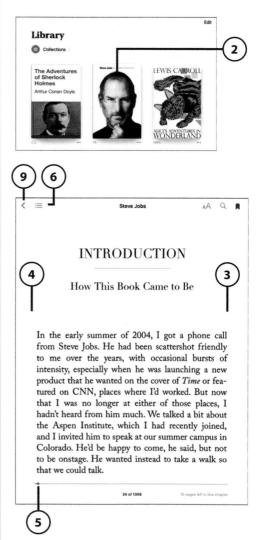

7. Tap anywhere in the table of contents to jump to that part of the book.

8. Tap the Resume button to return to the page you were previously viewing.

9. Tap the arrow to return to your books. If you return to the book later, you return to the last page you viewed. No need to stick a bookmark or piece of scrap paper into your iPad.

⑦ ⑧

	Steve Jobs		Resume
	Contents	Bookmarks	Notes
Epigraph			16
Characters			17
Introduction: How This Book Came to Be			24
Chapter One: Childhood: Abandoned and Chosen			35
Chapter Two: Odd Couple: The Two Steves			81
Chapter Three: The Dropout: Turn On, Tune In . . .			101
Chapter Four: Atari and India: Zen and the Art of Game Design			124
Chapter Five: The Apple I: Turn On, Boot Up, Jack In . . .			161
Chapter Six: The Apple II: Dawn of a New Age			182
Chapter Seven: Chrisann and Lisa: He Who is Abandoned . . .			212
Chapter Eight: Xerox and Lisa: Graphical User Interfaces			225

Using Reading Aids

The Books app has a variety of ways you can customize your reading experience. You can change the font size or the font itself, and you can even turn your iPad on its side to see two pages at one time.

1. While viewing a page in Books, tap the display adjustment controls at the top of the screen. If you don't see the controls, tap once in the middle of the screen to bring them up.

2. Drag the brightness control left or right. Dragging to the left makes the screen dim, which you might use if you're reading in a dark room. Dragging to the right makes it bright, which could make reading easier while outdoors.

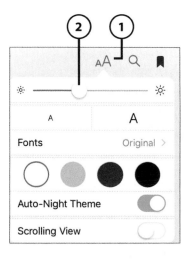

3. Tap the smaller A button to reduce the size of the text.

4. Tap the larger A button to increase the size of the text.

5. Tap Fonts to choose from a few font options.

6. Tap to select one of four color themes.

7. The Auto-Night Theme switch monitors the light around your iPad and switches to Night mode when it's dark.

8. Turn on Scrolling View to read your book as one long scrolling page.

9. Turn your iPad on its side to change to a two-page view. (Make sure your orientation lock is not on.)

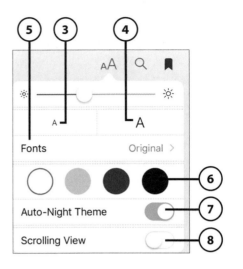

Where Did the Buttons Go?

If you tap in the middle of the screen, the buttons at the top and the dotted line at the bottom disappear. You can still turn the pages; you just don't have access to these buttons. To see the buttons again, tap in the middle of the screen.

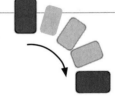

Adding Notes and Highlights

Each time you launch the Books app, your iPad returns you to the page you were last reading. However, you might want to mark a favorite passage or a bit of key information.

1. Go to a page in a book in Books. (See the previous tasks in this chapter to find out how to access a book.)

2. Tap a word and hold your finger there for about a second.

3. Release your finger and you see six choices: Copy, Look Up, Highlight, Note, Search, and Share.

Look Up, Search, and Share
Tapping Look Up brings up a definition of the word. Tapping Search brings up a list of the locations of the word throughout the text. When you tap Share, you can send the excerpt you have selected to someone else using email, a text message, Twitter, or Facebook.

4. Drag the blue dots to enlarge the section of text that is highlighted.

5. Tap Highlight. Alternatively, you can tap a word and hold for a second and then immediately start dragging to highlight text.

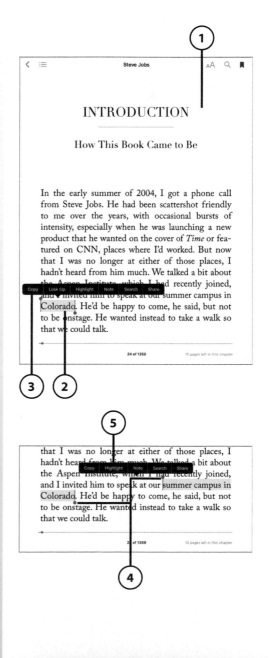

6. The text is highlighted.

7. Tap the first button to change the type of highlighting. You can choose from various colors or a simple red underline.

8. Tap the second button to remove the highlight completely.

9. Tap Note instead of Highlight to bring up a pad of paper and add a note.

10. Tap in the note to bring up the keyboard and start typing.

11. Tap outside the paper to finish the note. It appears as a small sticky note to the right side of the page. Tap it any time you want to view or edit the note. You can delete a note by removing all text in the note.

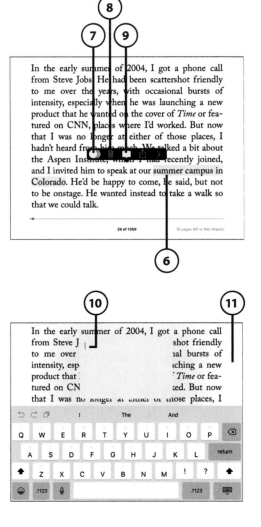

Adding Bookmarks

You can also bookmark a page to easily find it later.

1. Tap the Bookmark button at the top of a page to bookmark the page. You can bookmark as many pages as you want in a book. If you don't see the Bookmark button, tap once in the center of the screen to bring up the controls.

2. Tap the Bookmark button again to remove the bookmark from the page.

3. Tap the Table of Contents button to go to the table of contents.

4. Tap Bookmarks at the top of the table of contents to see a list of all the bookmarks, highlights, and notes you have added to the book.

5. Tap any bookmark, note, or highlight to jump to it.

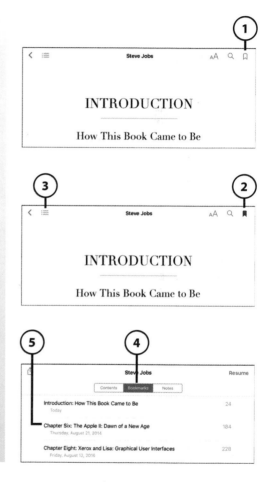

Organizing Your Books

Like to read a lot? You aren't alone. Many people gather massive collections of ebooks on their iPads. Fortunately, the Books app includes a few great ways to organize your ebooks.

1. Tap Library to view your library if you are not already there. If you are viewing a book, tap the small left-facing arrow in the upper-left corner to return to the book library.

2. Tap Collections at the top of the page to reveal a sidebar.

3. The sidebar shows you several default categories of books, including those you have marked in the Book Store as "Want to Read," but haven't purchased.

4. Any Audiobooks you have purchased appear in a special category.

5. PDFs you have manually added to your Library are in this section.

6. Pretty much everything else appears under Books.

7. In addition to those default categories, you can create your own. These custom collections appear at the bottom of the list. They are like playlists in Music, in that a book can appear in several collections. For instance, you can have a For School collection and a Reread Later collection, and you can place a book in both. Tap any collection you have created to view the books in it.

8. Tap New Collection to create a new collection and type in its name.

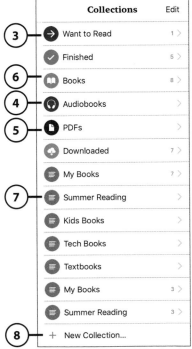

9. Tap Edit to reorder your custom collections and delete ones you no longer need. Like with music playlists, deleting a collection deletes only the collection, not the books inside it, which might still be in other collections and default categories like Books, Audiobooks, and so on.

10. After you have created a collection, you can add books to it by tapping the Edit button at the top-right corner of the Books app.

11. Tap books to select them. A check mark appears on selected books.

12. Tap Add To to add the selected books to a collection.

13. Select the collection and the books will be added to it.

14. You can also remove books from your Books library. Note that books you have purchased from Apple remain available to re-download if you ever want them back, but books you have added manually are deleted.

15. Tap Done to exit the book selection screen.

16. Tap a collection name in the sidebar to view that collection.

17. Tap the List View icon to switch to a list view of the books in your collection.

18. Tap the Sort indicator to change the order of the books in the list. You can sort by time, title, or author.

19. Tap Edit to change the manual sort order of the books in the collection or to remove books from the collection.

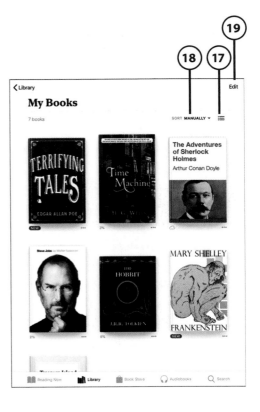

Books in the Cloud

When you view your Purchased Books collection, you see all the books you have bought in the past, even if that book is no longer on your iPad because you removed it. Books not currently on your iPad have a little iCloud icon in the lower-left corner; tap the icon to download the book. If you later delete the book, you can always re-download it by tapping the Purchased button at the bottom of the Collections screens, selecting Not on This iPad from the top, and tapping the download button next to that book.

Using Books App Alternatives

You can purchase and read books from sources other than Apple. The Kindle app enables you to buy books from Amazon.com, or read books you have already purchased on a previous device. You can also find many small independent publishers and authors in Amazon's catalog that aren't available in the Apple Book Store.

You can use the App Store app to search for and install the free Kindle app. See "Purchasing an App" in Chapter 15 to learn how to get third-party apps.

1. Tap the Kindle icon to launch the Kindle app (not shown). Then tap Library to view the books in your library.

2. Tap a book to open it.

3. Tap the middle of the page to bring up controls at the top and bottom.

4. Tap the Font button to change the font size, brightness, and background.

5. Tap the right side to flip to the next page.

6. Use the slider at the bottom to quickly move to other pages in the book.

7. The button at the top left allows you to jump to chapters or sections.

8. You can add your own bookmarks just like in the Books app.

9. Tap the Search button to search text in the book.

Cloud Versus Device

The Kindle app has a Cloud/Device control at the bottom of the screen. You can tap a book on the Cloud screen to download it to your device. After it has been downloaded, you can tap it again to read it.

More eBook Alternatives

If you like to buy your books from Barnes & Noble, you can also get the Nook app. This lets you read books you have purchased in the Nook store. If you own a Nook and have already bought books, you can access those books and load them onto your iPad.

Another app you can get is the Google Play Books app. This works with books purchased in the Google Play Store, which is similar to the Amazon Kindle store or the Apple Book Store. You can choose whether you want to buy from Apple, Amazon, Barnes & Noble, or Google.

Store and
search all your
contacts

Track your
appointments

Take notes and
sign documents

Set reminders

In this chapter, you learn how to add and look up contacts and calendar events. You're also introduced to the Notes and Reminders apps.

→ Using the Contacts App
→ Searching for a Contact
→ Working with Contacts
→ Using the Calendar App
→ Using Calendar Views
→ Creating a Calendar
→ Using the Notes App
→ Using the Reminders App
→ Using the Clock App

6

Organizing Your Life

Whether you are a well-connected businessperson or just someone who has lots of friends, you can use the iPad to organize your life with the default Contacts, Calendar, Notes, and Reminders apps. Let's take a close look at some of the things you can do with these apps.

Using the Contacts App

The primary way iPad users store their contacts is to use Apple's iCloud service. This places your contacts database on Apple's servers, making them available to you on any iOS device or Mac you use. You can even access them from a PC with Apple's iCloud.com website. It also keeps all these devices in sync; so any time you add or edit a contact, the change will show up everywhere. The Contacts app on your iPad is how you access and modify your contacts.

Adding a Contact

Let's start by adding a new contact from scratch.

1. Tap the Contacts app icon to launch the app.

2. Tap the + button near the top of the screen. A New Contact form and keyboard appear.

3. Type the first name of the contact. No need to use Shift to capitalize the name because that happens automatically. Tap the Return key on the keyboard to advance to the next field.

4. Type the last name for the contact. If you are adding a company instead of a person, skip the first and last name fields and use only the company field. The contact will be listed under the company name.

5. To add more information, like a phone number, tap the green + button next to the field name.

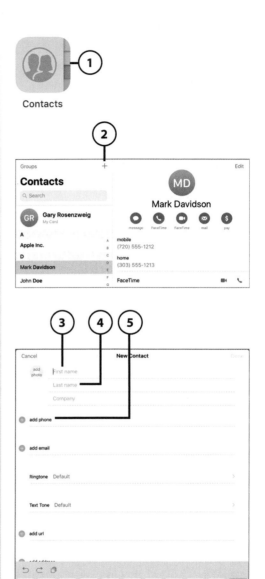

Contacts

6. Type the phone number.

No-Worry Formatting
You don't need to type phone numbers with parentheses or dashes. The iPad formats the number for you.

7. If you ever want to remove some information from the contact, you can use the red – buttons.

8. You can add more than one phone number per contact. When you add a new number, it's assigned a label such as "work." You can tap that label and choose another, such as "mobile" or "iPhone," and so on.

9. Tap Add Photo to add a photo from one of your photo albums or take one right now using your iPad's camera.

10. You can add one or more email addresses to the contact as well. These will be used in your Mail app when you compose a new message. When writing an email, you only need to type the person's name, or choose them from a list, instead of typing the full email address.

11. You can add one or more physical addresses for the contact.

12. You can select a specific ringtone for the contact that is used when they call you via FaceTime. You can also set a specific Text tone for Messages.

13. Swipe up to see more fields. You can even add custom fields and notes to a contact.

14. Tap the Done button to finish.

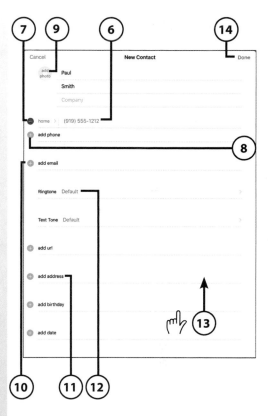

Siri: Call Me Ray

You can set a nickname field in a contact. When you do this, and the contact happens to be yours, Siri calls you by that name. You can also tell Siri: "Call me *name*," and it changes your nickname field even if you are not in the Contacts app at the moment.

You can also set relationships in your contacts by saying things like, "Debby is my wife."

Searching for a Contact

If you didn't have a lot of friends before, I'm sure you've gained quite a few since you got a new iPad. So how do you search through all those contacts to find the one you want?

1. Tap the Contacts app icon to launch the app.

2. Tap in the Search field. A keyboard appears at the bottom of the screen.

Contacts

Other Ways to Find Contacts

You can also drag (or flick to move quickly) through the contact list to find a name. In addition, the list of letters on the left side of the Contacts app enables you to jump right to that letter in your contacts list.

3. Start typing the name of the person you are looking for. As soon as you start typing, the app starts making a list of contacts that contain the letters you've typed. Keep typing until you narrow down the list of names and spot the one you are looking for.

4. Tap the name to bring up the contact.

5. Tap the Cancel button to dismiss the search.

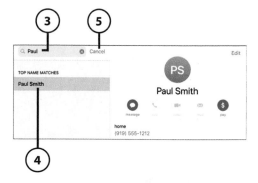

Siri: Show Me

You can also use Siri to find a contact. Try these phrases:

Show me John Smith.
Show me my contact.
Show me my wife.

Working with Contacts

After you have contacts in your iPad, you can do a few things from a contact in the Contacts app.

1. Tap and hold the name to copy it to the clipboard buffer.

2. Tap and hold the phone number to copy it to the clipboard buffer. You can tap and hold to copy with most pieces of information on this screen.

3. Tap the phone icon to place a FaceTime audio call.

4. Tap the FaceTime button to start a video chat with the user, providing they are also on an iOS device (or a Mac) and have set up FaceTime. You can start a FaceTime video call, or tap the phone-like button for an audio-only call.

5. Tap the email address to compose a new email in the Mail app. You can also tap the email icon.

6. Tap to the right of Notes to add more information without entering Edit mode.

7. Tap Share Contact to send the contact information via a text message or email, or by using AirDrop.

8. Start a text message conversation by tapping the message icon or the Send Message line. See "Conversing with Messages" in Chapter 8.

9. Tap Edit to enter Edit mode, which gives you the same basic functionality as entering a new contact.

10. Tap the Map to go to the Maps app and view the address location.

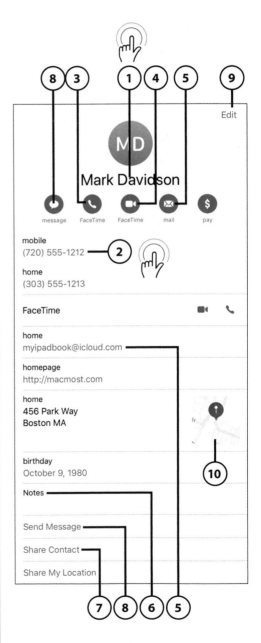

Using the Calendar App

Now that you have people in your Contacts app, you need to schedule some things to do with them.

Calendars, like contacts, are stored using Apple's iCloud service. Your calendars will sync over the Internet to your other iOS devices, and even your Mac, as long as you use the same iCloud account for each device.

Let's look at some things you can do with the Calendar app.

Creating a Calendar Event

1. Tap the Calendar app icon on the Home screen.

2. Tap the + button at the upper right.

3. Enter a Title for the event.

4. Enter a Location for the event, or skip this field.

5. Tap the Starts field to bring up a control for setting the starting time.

6. Tap the Ends field to bring up a control for setting the ending time for the event.

7. If the event covers the entire day, or a series of days, then turn on the All-day switch. The Starts and Ends fields change to dates only and don't include a specific time.

8. Tap Repeat to set an event to repeat every day, week, 2 weeks, month, or year.

Sunday		
27	①	
Calendar		

③ ④

Month	Year		Q +	②
Cancel	**New Event**	Add		
Title				
Location				
All-day		⬤		⑦
Starts	Feb 4, 2018	5:00 PM		⑤
Ends		6:00 PM		⑥
Repeat		Never >		⑧
Travel Time		None >		
Calendar	● myipadbook@gmail.com >			
Invitees		None >		
Alert		None >		

9. Tap Invitees to send an email invitation to another person for this event, if your calendar system allows this. If you and the other person are both using iCloud, they receive a notification of the event and have the option to accept or decline. If they accept, the event is added to their calendar. You are then able to look at your event's invitation list in this same location and see if they have accepted or declined.

10. Tap Alert to set the time for a notification alert to appear. This can be at the time of the event, or before the event, such as 5 minutes, 15 minutes, or even as much as a week before.

11. In addition, if you set Travel Time, your alert is adjusted so you have enough time to get to the event's location.

12. Tap Add to complete the event.

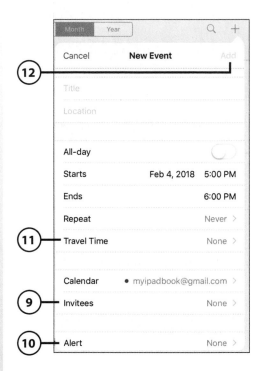

Siri: Creating Events

You can use Siri to create new events even when the Calendar app is not on your screen. Here are some examples:

Schedule a doctor appointment for 3 PM next Wednesday.
Set up a meeting with John tomorrow at noon.
Cancel my dentist appointment.

Deleting Events

To delete an event, scroll to the bottom of the event information while editing it to reveal a Delete Event button. This button also appears when you tap the event in any of the Calendar views. There is no real need to delete past events from your calendar—they take up almost no space and could be useful as a record of your past appointments.

Using Calendar Views

There are three main ways to view your calendar: Day, Week, and Month. Let's take a look at each.

Exploring Day View

The Day view is broken into two halves: The left side shows a timeline from morning until evening. Events are shown as blocks of color in this vertical timeline. The right side shows information for the event selected, if any.

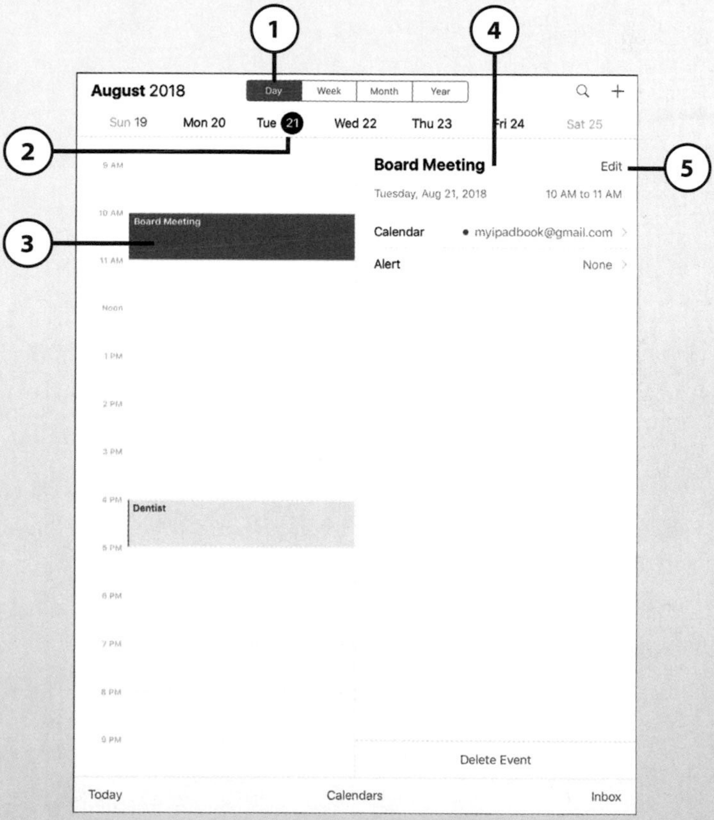

1. Tap Day to enter Day view mode.
2. You can tap any day shown at the top to jump to the list of events for that day. You can also drag left and right to see previous days and upcoming ones.
3. Tap any event shown to view information about that event.
4. The information appears on the right.
5. You can tap Edit to edit that event and change any aspect of it, or delete it.

6. You can drag up and down to view the entire day.

7. Tap Today to jump to the current day, in case you have moved to another day and want to return quickly.

8. Tap Calendars to select which calendars are shown. This is useful if you have set up multiple calendars in iCloud, or have subscribed to public calendars.

9. Tap Inbox to view any invitations you have received via email or messages. You can accept or reject them. Accepted invitations are added to your calendar.

10. Tap + to add a new event.

Year View

There is also a Year view, as you might have guessed because of the Year button at the top of the screen. This shows you 12 very small monthly calendars, with colored-in spaces on days where you have events. You can use this view to quickly navigate to an event in a different week or month. Or, you can use it to see when the days fall in the week.

Exploring Week View

To get a view of all the events for the week, switch to Week view. This gives you seven days across, but less space to preview each event. You can still select and edit events.

1. Tap Week to go to the Week view.

2. You can move to the previous week or the next by tapping and dragging in any blank part of the calendar. You can also drag vertically to see earlier in the morning or later in the evening.

3. Tap an event to view more information about it.

4. The information appears in a box to the left or right of the event.

5. You can tap Edit to edit the event right here. The familiar editing interface opens in an expanded box while you remain in the Week view.

6. Tap Today if you have navigated away from the current week and want to get back.

7. Tap + to add a new event while remaining in Week view.

Exploring Month View

To see the "big picture," you might want to use Month view. This gives you a grid of seven days across and six or more weeks vertically. While this view is similar to a monthly calendar, it doesn't necessarily have to show a single month. It can be used to show any group of six consecutive weeks.

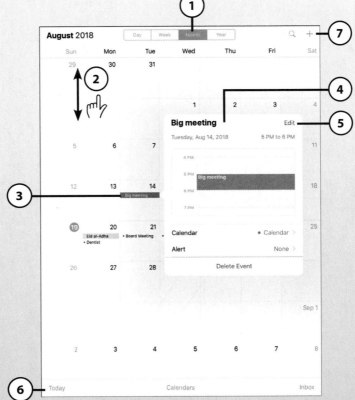

1. Tap Month to enter Month view.

2. While in Month view, you can tap and drag in blank areas to scroll up and down.

3. Tap an event to view more information.

4. The event information appears in a box.

5. Tap Edit to edit the information right here in Month view. The editing interface opens inside an enlarged box.

6. Tap Today to return to the current day if you have scrolled away from it.

7. Tap + to add a new event.

Siri: Checking Your Schedule

You can use Siri to see what events you have coming up, like this:

What do I have going on tomorrow?
What is on my calendar for this week?
When is my dentist appointment?

Creating a Calendar

You may have noticed in the previous tasks that you can select a calendar when you create an event. You can create multiple calendars to organize your events. For instance, you may want to have one for work and one for home.

1. From any calendar view, tap the Calendars button at the bottom center to display a list of your calendars.

2. You can scroll up and down this list and disable or enable calendars by tapping the check marks. A calendar without a check mark is hidden and won't appear in your views.

3. Tap the information icon to view and change information about a calendar, such as changing the color used as a background for events. You can also share calendars with other iCloud users.

4. Tap Add Calendar to create a new calendar.

5. Give the new calendar a name.

6. Set the color for the calendar.

7. Tap Done.

Deleting a Calendar

You can delete a calendar by following the steps 1–3 and then scrolling to the bottom of the information box. At the very bottom is a Delete Calendar button.

Default Calendar

Which calendar is used when you create a new event? You set the default calendar in the Settings app, under Mail, near the bottom of the list of preferences on the right.

>>>Go Further

SHARING CALENDARS

When you edit a calendar's information, you can also use the Add Person button that appears above the list of colors to share a calendar with a specific iCloud user. Below the colors list, you can choose to set the calendar to "public" and then share an Internet link that others can use to subscribe. For instance, you can create a schedule for your softball team and make it public, and then put a link to the calendar on the team's website. Anyone can subscribe to this calendar, but they can only view it. By default, others can edit it, but you can turn off Allow Editing by tapping the i button for the calendar, and then View & Edit next to the person's name with whom you are sharing it.

Using the Notes App

Another organization app that comes with your iPad is the Notes app. Although this one is much more free-form than the Contacts or Calendar app, it can be useful for keeping quick notes or to-do lists.

Creating a Note

1. Tap the Notes icon on your Home screen.

2. Notes opens up the note you were previously working on. To type, tap on the screen where you want the insertion point, and a keyboard appears.

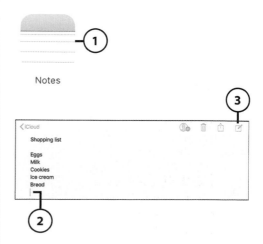

What's in a Name

The filename for a note is just the first line of the note, so get in the habit of putting the title of a note as the first line of text to make finding the note easier.

3. Start a new note by tapping the Compose button at the upper right.

4. View a list of all your notes, and jump to another note, by tapping the Back button.

5. Tap the name of the note you want to switch to.

6. Tap and type in the Search field to find text inside of notes. If you don't see the Search field, tap and drag down on the list of notes to reveal it just above the first note in the list.

7. Turn your iPad to horizontal orientation to have a permanent list of notes on the left. In this view, you don't need to tap Notes, as you did in step 4, to see the list.

8. Tap the Trash button at the top-right of the screen to delete the note you are viewing.

9. Tap the Share button at the top-right of the screen to share the note in a number of ways. For instance, you can start a new email message in the Mail app using the contents of the note, or print the note using AirPrint.

10. Share a note with someone else using iOS or Mac by tapping the Add People button. You then have the choice of inviting another iCloud user via Messages, Mail, Twitter, or Facebook.

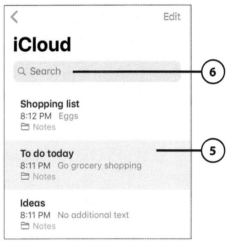

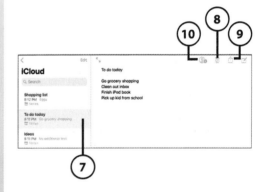

Notes in the Cloud

Notes are stored on Apple's iCloud server, just like calendar events and contacts. If you are using the same iCloud account on your Mac, for instance, you should see the notes appear almost instantly on your Mac, synced through iCloud. They also appear on your other iOS devices.

Notes Isn't a Word Processor

You can't actually use Notes for serious writing. There are only basic styles and no formatting choices. You can't even change the display font to make it larger. If you need to use your iPad for writing, consider Pages or a third-party word processing app. If you want to make some text bold, italic, or underlined, you can tap and hold a word, adjust the selection, and use the **B**/**U** button next to Cut, Copy, and Paste to apply a simple style to the selection.

Creating Checklists in Notes

You can already see that Notes is useful for creating lists. Apple has built in a list function to make it even easier to use in this way.

1. Start a new note, or continue typing in an existing one.

2. Tap the checklist button when you want to start a list. You can have text before and after the list; it doesn't have to be at the top of the note or the only thing in the note.

3. You see an empty circle appear on the line you are typing.

4. Type the first item in the list.

5. Tap Return on the on-screen keyboard, and you can continue entering more items, each with an empty circle to its left.

6. Tap the checklist button again when you want to resume typing normal non-list text.

7. You can tap any empty circle in the list to fill it with a check mark.

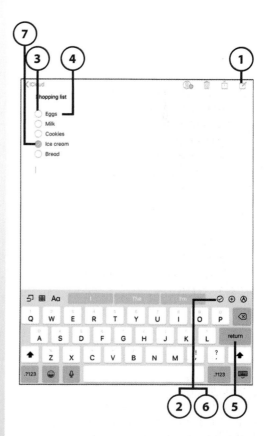

Notes Versus Reminders

Checklists in Notes are good for things like shopping lists, packing lists, party invitation lists, and so on. For to-do lists, use the Reminders app, which is covered later in this chapter.

Adding Photos and Sketches to Notes

You can also insert photos from your photo library into notes, take photos with the camera, or draw sketches with your finger to include in your notes.

1. Create a new note or use an existing one. Photos and sketches can co-exist with other text in any note.

2. Position the cursor where you want to insert the photo or sketch.

3. Tap the + button to choose a photo from your library, or take one with the camera. It is the same way you insert a photo into an email message or text message. You can choose a photo from your library or use the camera interface to take a picture.

4. Tap the sketch button to enter the sketching screen.

5. On this screen, you can draw anything you like using a few simple tools. Select the pen, marker, or pencil tool at the bottom.

6. Select a color. You can swipe from left to right across the colors to see two more sets of colors.

7. Tap and drag your finger to draw.

8. The eraser tool enables you to clear marks you have made.

9. You can use the undo and redo buttons to help draw.

10. Tap Done to return to the note.

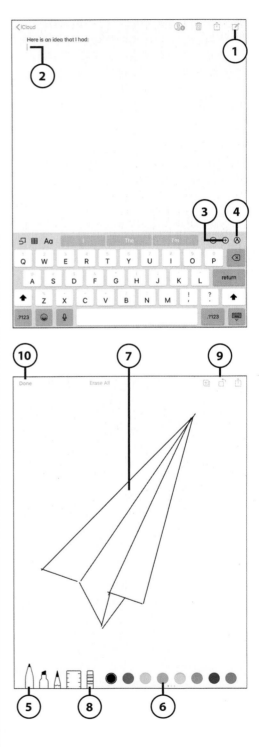

11. The sketch appears in your note. Tap it to return to the sketch screen to edit it. If you tap and hold the sketch instead, you see Cut, Copy, Delete, and Share options.

Multiple Sketches

You can add more than one sketch to a note. If you need to move a sketch to a different location in your note, or to a different note, tap and hold the sketch until you get the Options menu. Then use Cut to remove it and later use Paste to place it elsewhere.

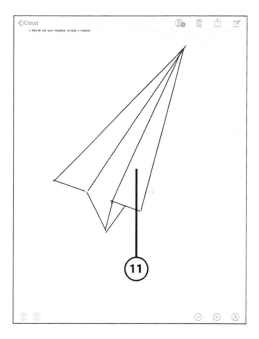

It's Not All Good

Don't See the Photo or Sketch Buttons?

The Photo and Sketch buttons are available only if your notes are being stored in a recent version of iCloud Notes. For instance, if you share your notes with a Mac using an older version of macOS, or an iPhone using an older version of iOS, then you can't create sketches in your notes because they are not compatible with the Notes app on those other devices.

Scanning Documents with Notes

With the Notes app, it is relatively easy to scan a paper document using your camera. Notes automatically focuses on the document and corrects the angle so the document appears flat even if it is slightly askew relative to the camera.

1. Get the document ready by placing it on a flat surface in front of your iPad. Launch the Notes app and start a new note.

2. Tap the + button to insert an image.

3. Tap Scan Documents to start the scan.

4. Position your iPad so you can see the entire document on the screen. A yellow area appears over the document if your iPad believes it can distinguish the edges of the document. Hold your iPad there for a second and the camera automatically takes and saves the image.

5. Alternatively, you can use the shutter button to snap the photo at any time.

6. If you would rather not use the automatic function, you can switch to Manual.

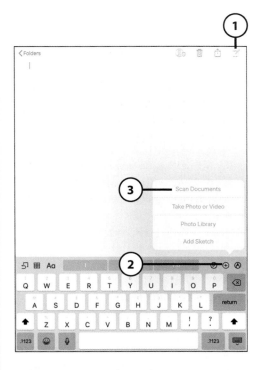

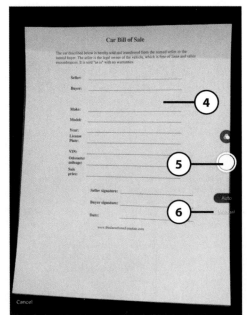

7. Use the Filter button to convert the image to grayscale or black and white if you prefer.

8. If this is a multi-page document, you can swap the paper out and the app automatically takes another shot, or you press the shutter button again.

9. Tap the Save button to save the scan(s) in your note.

10. The document appears in the note. Tap it to view it.

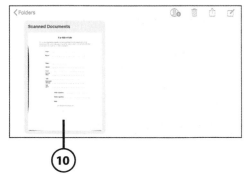

Signing and Sending Documents with Notes

If you need to sign a document, you could always sign it before scanning it in the previous task. With iOS 11, you also can sign a document after scanning it, and then send that document to someone using email or other methods.

1. After completing the previous task, you should be viewing the scan inside of the note.

2. Tap the Share button at the top right.

3. Tap the Markup button. If you don't see it right away, you might need to scroll the list of actions to the left to reveal it.

4. Tap the + button to add an element to the document.

5. Tap Signature to add a signature.

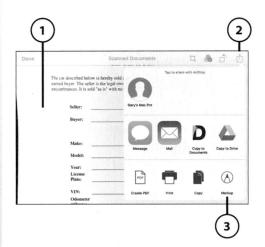

6. Use your finger, or the Apple Pencil if you have one, to write your signature.

7. Use the Clear button to clear it and try again. The signature you create here can be used over and over again, so it pays to take the time to get it right.

8. Tap Done to save the signature.

9. The signature appears on the document as a movable box. Drag and position it to the signature line.

10. Drag one of the corners to scale the signature so it fits in the space provided.

11. The next time you tap the + button, you have the option to use that same signature again, or add a new one.

12. Tap Done.

13. Tap the Share button.

14. Use the different methods of sharing to send the signed document via email, messages, and other methods.

Add Text and Shapes, Too

Notice that in step 5 there were also buttons for Text and some shapes, including circles and arrows. You could use these tools to fill out the other blank lines of the document or mark it up with the shapes. Filling out the document with computer-rendered text should make it easier to read than using handwriting. Also, you could use any of the pen tools at the bottom of the screen to draw on the document any way you want.

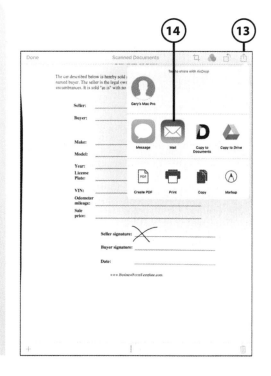

Using the Reminders App

Reminders is a to-do list application available on iPad, iPod touch, iPhone, and Macs. This app is for creating an ongoing list of tasks you need to accomplish or things you need to remember. These reminders can be similar to calendar events with times and alarms. Or, they can be simple items in a list with no time attached to them.

Setting a Reminder

1. Tap the Reminders icon on your Home screen.

2. Select the list you want to add a new reminder to.

3. Tap in a new line to create a new reminder.

4. Type the reminder and close the keyboard when done.

5. Tap the i button next to the reminder to bring up the Details dialog. If you don't see an i button, then tap any reminder item first.

6. Tap here to edit the reminder.

7. Slide the Remind Me on a Day switch to on to set a reminder alert.

8. Set a time for the alert to occur.

9. Add a note to the reminder if you want to include more details.

10. Tap outside of the Details box when you are finished editing the reminder.

Siri: Remind Me

You can create new reminders using Siri, like this:

Remind me to watch Doctor Who tonight at 8 PM.
Remind me to pick up milk when I leave work.
Remind me to check my stocks every day at 9 AM.

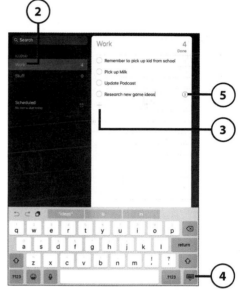

Reminders

11. Tap the button next to the reminder when you have completed the task. The item remains in the list temporarily.

12. Tap Add List to add a new reminders list.

13. Tap Show Completed to see completed reminders.

14. You can also search for reminders by typing the title or something from the content.

15. Tap Edit to remove reminders.

16. Tap the red – button next to a reminder to delete it.

17. Tap and drag the right side of the reminders to reorder them.

18. Tap Done when you are finished deleting and reordering the reminders.

19. You can also share a Reminders list with another iCloud user before leaving editing mode. Tap Sharing, and you can add one or more people from your contacts or manually add people with their Apple ID. Shared Reminders lists sync items to all people sharing them.

iCloud

Reminders sync by using the iCloud service from Apple. So, they are automatically backed up and should also appear on your Mac in the Reminders app, if you have OS X 10.8 Mountain Lion or newer. And if you use an iPhone, they should appear there as well.

Using the Clock App

The advantage of using an alarm rather than a reminder is that an often-recurring alarm, like your morning wake-up call or a reminder of when to pick up your child at school, won't clutter up your Reminders list or calendar.

Setting Clock Alarms

1. Tap the Clock app.

2. The main screen shows up to six clocks in any time zone you want.

3. Tap the + button to add a new clock.

4. Tap Edit to remove or rearrange the clocks.

5. Tap Alarm to view and edit alarms.

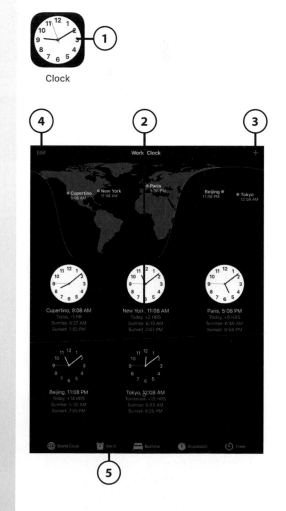

Clock

6. To add a new alarm, tap the + button.

7. Select a time for the alarm.

8. Select the days of the week for the alarm. Leaving it set to Never means you just want the alarm to be used once, as you might do if setting an alarm to wake you up early so you can catch a plane the next day. Otherwise, you can select from seven days of the week. So, you can set an alarm for Monday through Friday and leave out the weekend.

9. Tap Label to give the alarm a custom name.

10. Select a sound for the alarm. You can choose from preset sounds or your ringtone collection.

11. Leave the Snooze switch on if you want the ability to use snooze when the alarm goes off.

12. Tap Save to save all your settings and add the alarm.

13. The alarm shows up on the Alarm screen.

14. You can switch off the alarm, while leaving it in the calendar for future use.

15. Tap Edit on an alarm to edit or delete it.

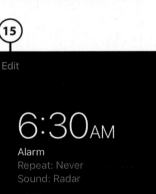

16. The alarm sounds and a message (in the middle of your screen) appears at the scheduled time. Even if your iPad is sleeping, it wakes up and displays a message on the Lock screen.

17. If you've enabled snooze, tap the Snooze button to silence the alarm and try again in 9 minutes.

18. Tap here to silence the alarm. If the iPad was awake when the alarm went off, you simply get a button to tap.

Wake Up!

When you set an alarm, it sounds even if you lower your volume to nothing, mute the sound with the side switch or Control Center, and switch into Do Not Disturb mode. This way, you can't accidentally turn off an alarm just because you wanted to avoid other distractions.

Siri: Create Alarms

You can use Siri to create and delete alarms and even set timers. Try these phrases:

Set an alarm for weekdays at 9 AM.
Create an alarm for tomorrow at 10 AM.
Cancel my 9 AM alarm.
Turn on my 9 AM alarm.
Turn off my 9 AM alarm.
Set a timer for 10 minutes.

The web is at your
fingertips with iPad's
Safari web browser

In this chapter, you learn about Safari, the browser built in to the iPad. You can use it to browse the web, bookmark web pages, fill in forms, and search the Internet.

→ Getting Started with Safari
→ Bookmarks, History, and Reading List
→ Working with Web Forms

Surfing the Web

The iPad is a beautiful web-surfing device. Its size is perfect for web pages, and your ability to touch the screen lets you interact with content in a way that even a computer typically cannot.

Getting Started with Safari

Undoubtedly, you know how to get to web pages on a computer using a web browser. You use Safari on your iPad in the same way, but the interface is a little different.

At the top of the Safari browser is a toolbar with just a few buttons. In the middle, the largest interface element is the address field. This is where you can type the address (URL) of any web page on the Internet, or enter a search query.

Tips for Typing a URL

A URL is a Universal Resource Locator. It can be a website name or a specific page in a website. Here are some helpful tips for entering URLs in Safari:

- For most websites, you don't need to type the www. at the beginning. For instance, you can type **www.apple.com** or **apple.com**, and both take you to Apple's home page. You never need to type http:// either, though occasionally you need to type https:// to specify that you want to go to a secure web page.

- Instead of typing .com. you can tap and hold the period button on the iPad keyboard. You can select .com, .edu, .org, .us, or .net.

Browsing to a URL and Searching

1. Tap the Safari icon on your iPad to launch the browser. Unless you have rearranged your icons, the icon is located at the bottom of the screen, along with your other most commonly used applications.

2. Tap in the field at the top of the screen. This opens the keyboard at the bottom of the screen. If you were already viewing a web page, the address of that page remains in the address field. Otherwise, it is blank.

Clear the Slate

To clear the field at any time, tap the X button located inside the field all the way to the right.

3. Start typing a search term or a URL such as apple.com or macmost.com.

Safari

4. As you type, suggestions based on previous pages you have visited and past web searches from other users appear. You might also see suggestions for apps you can install. To go directly to one of these pages, tap the page in the list. Skip to step 6.

Search This Page

Below the Google suggestions in the search suggestions drop-down menu is a list of recent searches and the occurrences of the phrase on the web page you are viewing. Use the latter to find the phrase on the page.

5. Otherwise, tap the Go button on the keyboard when you finish typing. If you typed or selected a URL, you will be taken to that web page.

6. Instead of typing a URL, you can type a search term and tap Go. This searches the web instead of going to a specific page. The term remains at the top and you get a page of search results.

7. Tap any result to jump to that page.

Siri: Search the Web

You can use Siri to search the web, even if you are not currently looking at the Safari screen. Sometimes Siri also answers general questions by suggesting a web search. The following are some example search phrases you can use:

Search for local plumbers.
Search Wikipedia for Paris.
Show me some websites about geology.
Google Denver news.
Search for iPad tutorials on MacMost.com.

Nothing Special, Please

Some websites present you with a special iPad version of the site. This is not as common as the special iPhone or iPod touch versions that many sites offer. If a website does not look the same on your iPad as it does on your computer, you might want to check for a link on the web page to view the standard web version, instead of a special iPad version. You can also tap in the address field in Safari, and then drag down on the list of Favorites that appears to reveal a Request Desktop Site option. This is especially useful if a site has lumped the iPad together with the iPhone and provided a needlessly simplified version.

>>>Go Further

SOME TIPS FOR SEARCHING THE WEB

Use these tips for more effective web searches:

- You can go deeper than just typing some words. For instance, you can put a + in front of a word to require it and a − in front to avoid that word in the results.

- You can use special search terms to look for things such as movie times, weather, flight tracking, and more. See https://support.google.com/websearch/answer/134479 for all sorts of things you can do with a Google search.

- Using iPad's Settings app, you can choose the search engine that Safari uses as its default. Tap the Settings icon and choose Safari on the left, and then look for the Search Engine setting. You can choose Bing, Yahoo!, or Duck Duck Go instead of Google, for instance.

- Using Google, you can search for much more than text on web pages. Look at the top of the search results, and you see links such as Images, Videos, Maps, News, and Shopping. Tap More and you can also search for things such as Blogs and Books.

- To explore the search results without moving away from the page listing the results, tap and hold over a link to see a button that enables you to open a link in a new tab, leaving the results open in the current tab.

- You can use many search settings with Bing or Google. These are not specific to the iPad but work on your computer as well when performing searches. Tap the Settings button (looks like a small gear) in the upper-right corner of the search results page to choose a language, filters, and other settings. Set up a Bing or Google account and log in to save these search preferences and use them between different devices.

Viewing Web Pages

Whether you typed in a URL or searched for a web page, after you have one open on your iPad screen, you can control what you view in several ways. You need to know these techniques to view the complete contents of a web page and navigate among web pages.

1. Navigate to any web page using either of the two techniques in the previous step-by-step instructions. When you arrive at the page, only the domain name shows at the top.

2. When you are viewing a page, you can touch and drag the page up and down with your finger. As you do so, notice the bar on the right side that gives you an indication of how much of the complete web page you are viewing at one time.

3. To zoom in on an area in the page, touch the screen with two fingers and move your fingers apart (unpinch). You can also move them closer together (pinch) to zoom back out. A double-tap restores the page to normal scaling. This works well on websites made for desktop computers, but mobile sites usually are set to fit the screen at optimal resolution.

4. You can also double-tap images and paragraphs of text to zoom in to those elements in the web page. A second double-tap zooms back out.

5. While zoomed in, you can touch and drag left and right to view different parts of the web page.

6. Tap a link to move to another web page from the current web page. Links are usually an underlined or colored piece of text; however, they can also be pictures or button-like images.

An iPad can shoot video, take photos, play music, and perform Internet functions such as web-browsing and emailing. Other functions – games, reference, GPS navigation, social networking, etc. – can be enabled by downloading and installing apps. As of March 2016, the App Store has more than one million apps for the iPad by Apple and third parties.

It's Not All Good

Where's the Link?

Unfortunately, it isn't always easy to figure out which words on a page are links. Years ago, these were all blue and underlined. But today, links can be any color and might not be underlined.

On the iPad, it is even more difficult to figure out which words are links. This is because many web pages highlight links when the cursor moves over the word. But with the touch interface of the iPad, there is no cursor.

Opening Multiple Web Pages with Tabs

Safari on the iPad enables you to open multiple web pages at the same time. You can view only one at a time, but you can hold your place on a page by opening a new tab to look at something on another page.

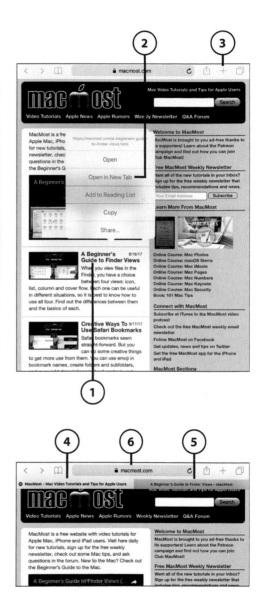

1. View a web page in Safari that has links to other pages, such as MacMost.com. Instead of tapping a link, tap and hold on a link until a contextual menu pops up above your finger.

2. Tap Open in New Tab.

3. Alternatively, you can tap the + button at the top of the screen to open a new tab that shows icons linking to the websites you have put in your Favorites.

4. You see two tabs at the top of the screen. The one on the right is in front of the one on the left and represents the visible page. You can tell which tab is the active one—it is in a lighter shade of gray than the others, and the Close Tab button (shown as an X) is visible.

5. You can switch tabs by tapping on the other tab; that tab now appears in front of the one on the right, and the screen area below shows that page.

6. When you enter a new web address, search, or use a book-mark, it changes the page of the current tab, but doesn't affect the other tab.

7. You can close the current tab by tapping the X button to the left of the tab's name.

8. Tap the Tabs button at the upper right to see all your tabs presented on one screen.

9. Tap any tab to jump to it.

10. The titles of tabs open on other devices using the same iCloud account are listed. Tap an item in the list to open its page on your iPad.

11. Tap Done to return to the tab you were viewing previously.

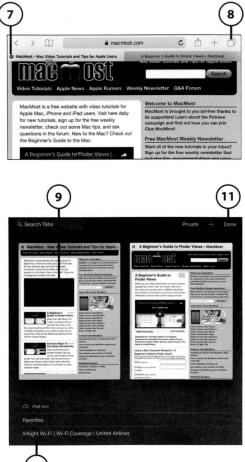

Private Browsing

When you use the tabs screen to select which tab to view, you also see a Private button at the top. Tap that and a new tab opens in private browsing mode. Web pages you view in this tab are not stored in your history. In addition, browser cookies are deleted after you close the tab. This does not hide your browsing behavior from your ISP or employer, but it could help you keep the surprise when buying a birthday present for someone who uses the same iPad.

Viewing Articles with Safari Reader

Web pages on the iPad can be vibrant and pretty. But sometimes the website tries to cram so much text and other junk onto a page that it can be painful to read. You can clear away all the clutter to reveal the text of a news article or blog post using the Reader feature.

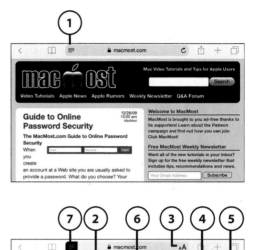

1. Look for the Reader button in the address field. If it is there, that means you can tap it to switch to Reader mode for this article.

2. In Reader mode, only the text and inline images of the article appear.

3. Tap the text appearance button to view options.

4. Tap the large or small "A" buttons to make the text size larger or smaller.

5. Tap the background color buttons to adjust the background.

6. Tap a font to change to that font.

7. Tap Reader again to return to the regular view of the page.

Bookmarks, History, and Reading List

You can always visit a web page by typing its address in the field at the top of Safari. But the app also has a way for you to get to your most frequently visited sites easily, find a page you recently visited, or save a page to read later.

Using Bookmarks and Favorites

Bookmarks allow you to save the web pages you visit most often and then access them with just a few taps. Favorites are bookmarks that appear at the top of the Safari browser for easier access.

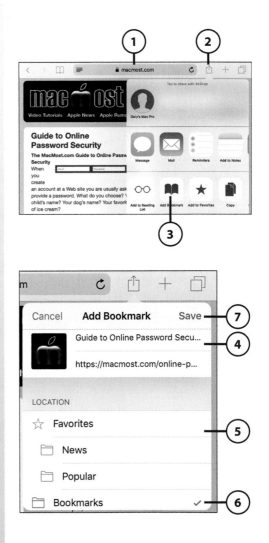

1. Use Safari to navigate to any web page.

2. Tap the Share button at the top of the screen.

3. Tap Add Bookmark.

4. Edit the title of the bookmark. The official title of the web page is prefilled, but you can use the keyboard to change it. You can tap the X to clear the text and start fresh.

5. You can choose to place the bookmark in Favorites, so it appears at the top of the Safari window where you can easily find it.

6. Or you can put it in another location, such as the main Bookmarks folder, where you can select it from the Bookmarks menu.

7. Tap Save to finish creating the bookmark.

8. To use a bookmark, first tap the Bookmarks button. This opens up a sidebar on the left. In vertical orientation, this sidebar closes when you choose a web page to view. In horizontal orientation, the sidebar stays until you tap the Bookmarks button again.

9. Find the bookmark in the list and tap it to go to that web page.

10. Alternatively, if you put the bookmark in Favorites or another folder, such as in step 6, you have to tap that folder name first to dig down to find the bookmark.

11. When you create a new tab, the bookmarks you put in your Favorites folder appear as icons for quick access to those pages. For more about tabs, see "Opening Multiple Web Pages with Tabs" earlier in this chapter.

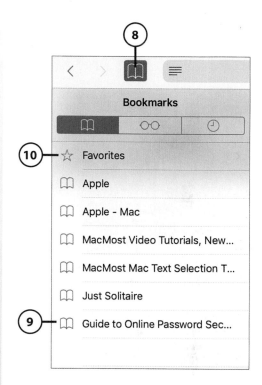

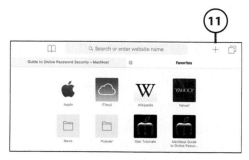

>>>Go Further

TIPS FOR BOOKMARKING WEBSITES

Use these tips to make the most of your bookmarked websites:

- The titles of web pages are often long and descriptive. It is a good idea to shorten the title to something you can easily recognize, especially if it is a web page that you plan to visit often.

- To create folders inside the Bookmarks folder, tap the Bookmarks button at the top of the Safari screen. Then choose the Bookmarks button at the top. At the bottom of that menu, tap Edit and then tap New Folder.

- You can create folders of bookmarks under Favorites. These appear as their own pop-up menu when you tap them, giving access to a subset of your bookmarks.

Using History

Safari keeps track of which web pages you have visited. You can use this history to find a page you went to earlier today, yesterday, or even several days back.

1. After using Safari to view several pages, tap the Bookmarks button at the top of the screen.

2. Tap the History button at the top of this menu to view your history.

3. Tap any item in the list to jump to that web page.

4. Previous pages you have visited are broken into groups by time, such as This Morning, Yesterday, and so on.

5. Tap the Clear button if you want to clear out your browsing history. For instance, are you about to hand your iPad to your spouse right after shopping for their birthday present?

6. You can also clear single items by swiping left across them and then tapping the Delete button that appears.

7. You can also search your history by keyword to find links you have visited in the past, without having to scroll down and carefully examine each item. To reveal the Search field, you might have to drag the list down slightly to reveal the field at the top.

Sync Your Bookmarks

If you are using iCloud, your bookmarks should sync between all your iOS and Mac devices. Safari on your computer gives you greater control over moving and deleting bookmarks. If you do your wholesale editing on your computer, those changes should be reflected in your iPad's bookmarks as well.

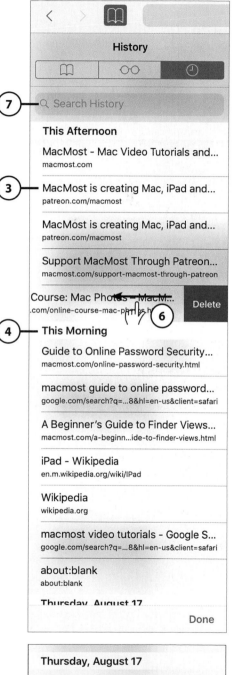

Creating Home Screen Bookmarks

If a web page is so important to you that you want even faster access to it than via a browser bookmark, you can save it as an icon on your iPad's Home screen.

1. Use Safari to navigate to any web page.

2. Tap the Share button at the top of the screen.

3. Tap Add to Home Screen. If you don't see this option, try dragging the bottom list to the left to reveal more options to the right.

Managing Home Screen Bookmarks

You can arrange and delete Home screen bookmarks in the same way you work with app icons. See "Arranging Apps on Your iPad" in Chapter 15 for details.

4. You can now edit the name of the page. Most web page titles are too long to display under an icon on the Home screen of the iPad, so edit the name down to as short a title as possible.

5. You can tap Cancel to leave this interface without sending the bookmark to the Home screen.

6. Tap Add to complete adding the icon to the Home screen.

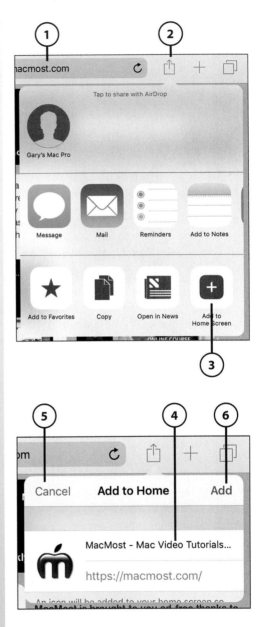

7. Press the Home button to return to your Home screen (not shown).

8. Look for the new icon on your Home screen that represents the bookmark you added. You might need to swipe through the pages of your Home screens to find it. Then, you can move it to any page or into a folder. The icon acts just like the app icons on your Home screen. See "Arranging Apps on Your iPad" in Chapter 15.

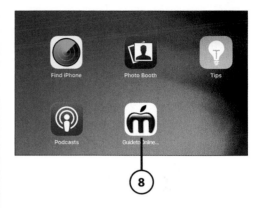

Website Icons

The icon for this type of bookmark can come from one of two sources. Web page owners can provide a special iPhone/iPad icon that would be used whenever someone tries to bookmark her page.

However, if no such icon is provided, your iPad takes a screen shot of the web page and shrinks it down to make an icon.

Building a Reading List

Your reading list is similar to bookmarks. You can add a page to your reading list to remember to return to that page later. When you do, it is removed from the Unread section of your reading list, but still appears in the All section.

1. Find an article you want to read later.

2. Tap the Share button.

3. Tap Add to Reading List. If this is the first time you are using the Reading List, you're asked whether you want to automatically save Reading List articles for offline viewing. If you choose not to use this feature, you won't be able to view the articles while offline.

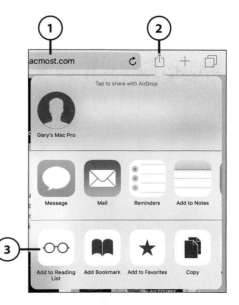

4. Tap the Bookmarks button to see your reading list.

Take it Offline

Pages you add to your reading list are downloaded to your iPad so that you can read them later, when you're not connected to the Internet.

5. Tap the Reading List button.

6. Tap any item to view the page. Even if you are not connected to the Internet, the page still shows because Safari stored the content when you added the page to the Reading List. You can also swipe left to Delete an item.

7. At the bottom you see either Show All or Show Unread. This lets you switch between the two lists. Show All shows everything in your Reading List. Show Unread does not show items you have already opened from the Reading List.

8. Tap Edit to be able to select and then delete items. You can also swipe right to left to reveal a Delete button on an individual item.

Reading List Syncing

The Reading List also syncs across your iOS devices and Macs using iCloud. So you can add it on your Mac and then see it appear in your Reading List on your iPad.

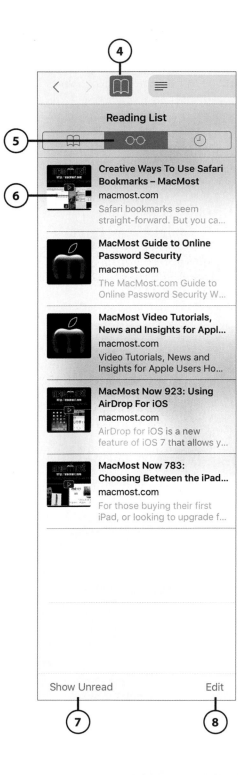

Working with Web Forms

The web isn't a one-way street. Often you need to interact with web pages, filling in forms or text fields. Doing this on the iPad is similar to doing it on a computer, but with a few key differences.

The keyboard shares screen space with the web page, so when you tap on a field, you bring up the keyboard at the bottom of the screen.

Also, pull-down menus behave differently than they do on a computer. On the iPad, you get a special menu showing you all the options.

>>>Go Further
SCANNING YOUR CREDIT CARD

When you encounter a web form that asks you to enter a credit card number, it can be a pain to have to enter all those digits. Instead, you can have your iPad read the number right from the card using your iPad's camera. Just tap in the credit card number field, and you see a Scan Credit Card button above the keyboard. Tap that and you are instructed to hold your card up to the camera. If the lighting is good and your number is clearly visible, the camera reads it and inserts the number into the field. If you don't see the Scan Credit card button, it could be because the web page isn't labeling its fields in a way that Safari can recognize. In that case, you need to enter the number manually.

Filling in Web Forms

1. Use Safari to navigate to a web page with a form. For demonstration purposes, try one of the pages at http://apple.com/feedback/.

2. Tap a field to type in it. The keyboard appears at the bottom of the screen.

3. Use the keyboard to type text into the field. The features of the keyboard depend on cues from the website. For instance, a site can set a text field to only accept numbers, in which case you see a numeric keyboard instead of a full keyboard.

4. Tap the Go button when you finish filling in all the required fields.

5. Select a check box or radio button by tapping it just as you would use your mouse to click it on your computer.

6. Tap a menu to select an item in a pull-down menu.

7. The special iPad pull-down menu reacts like any other iPad interface. You can tap an item to select it. You can touch and drag up and down to view more selections if the list is long.

8. A check mark appears next to the currently selected item. Tap that item or any other item to select it and dismiss the menu.

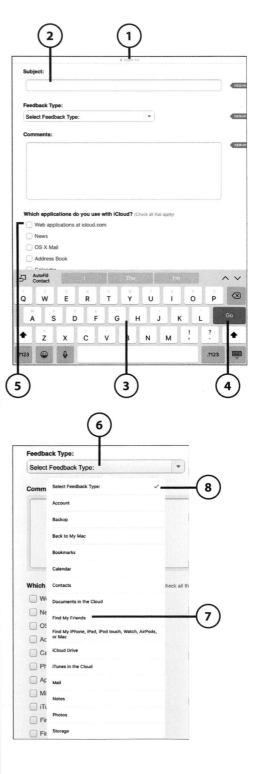

Special Menus

Some websites use special menus that they build from scratch, rather than the default HTML menus. When this is the case, you get a menu that looks exactly like the one you get when viewing the web page on a computer. If the web page is well coded, it should work fine on the iPad, though it might be slightly more difficult to make a selection.

>>>*Go Further*

TIPS FOR FILLING IN FORMS

Here are some additional tips for filling in forms with your iPad:

- You can use the AutoFill Contact button just above the keyboard to fill in your name, address, and other contact info instead of typing on the keyboard. To enable AutoFill, go into your iPad Settings and look for the Passwords & AutoFill preferences under Safari. Also make sure your own information is correct and complete in your card in the Contacts application. See "Saving Time with AutoFill," later in this chapter.

- To move between fields in a form, use the flat left and right arrow buttons just above the keyboard that move to the Previous or Next field. You can quickly fill in an entire form this way without having to tap on the web page to select the next item.

Saving Time with AutoFill

When you go to websites and fill out forms, it can be annoying to type basic information like your name and address, or your user ID and password. Furthermore, if you have to type your password every time you visit a site, or even on a daily or weekly basis, this encourages you to use simple, easy-to-guess passwords so you don't have to type long complex strings of characters.

The Keychain function built into Safari allows you to automatically fill in forms and login prompts. After you enter your information the first time, you never have to do it again for that website.

Setting Up AutoFill

To set up AutoFill in Safari, start by
going to the Settings app.

1. Tap Safari in the Settings app.

2. Tap AutoFill.

3. Slide the Use Contact Info switch
   on, if it's not. Now any time you
   go to a web page with a form that
   asks for basics like name, address,
   or telephone number, AutoFill
   uses your contact information
   in the Contacts app to fill those
   fields automatically.

4. Tap My Info to tell Safari which
   contact in the Contacts app
   is you.

5. Go to Passwords & Accounts in
   the Settings app.

6. Slide the Autofill Passwords
   switch on to have Safari remember user IDs and passwords when
   you log on to websites. As you see
   in the next section, Safari prompts
   you each time you enter a new
   User ID and Password so you
   can decide the passwords that
   are saved.

7. After you have visited some sites
   and saved some passwords, you
   can access the list of saved passwords by tapping Website & App
   Passwords.

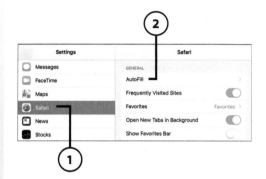

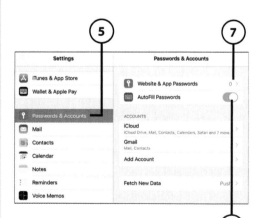

8. Tap any entry to view the ID, password, and the website it belongs to. This can come in handy if you need to view or copy and paste a password. For instance, you can grab your Amazon password to paste it into the Kindle app.

9. Tap + manually enter new passwords.

10. Turn on the Credit Cards switch to have Safari remember credit card information.

11. Tap Saved Credit Cards to see a list of your saved credit cards and to add new ones. When you add a credit card, include your name, the card number, the expiration date, and a short description. However, the security code for the card is not saved. Most websites ask you for this even after Safari has autofilled the information it has saved.

>>>Go Further
SAFETY AND SECURITY

If you add your passwords and credit card information for Safari to automatically fill in, isn't that incredibly insecure? Well, it is if you have not set a passcode for your iPad. The Settings app recommends you add a passcode when you turn these options on.

You set a passcode under Settings, General, Passcode Lock. Then, you should set the Require Passcode option to Immediately so as soon as you lock your iPad by closing the Smart Cover or pressing the Sleep button, the passcode is required to use it.

Even with the security enabled, using a simple passcode like 1234 or letting it sit around unlocked still presents a problem. You don't need to use AutoFill on every website. You could use it for unimportant sites like games and forums, and avoid using it for bank accounts and social media sites.

The advantage to using AutoFill for passwords is that you can use a long, random password for an account rather than a short, memorable one. It is more likely that your account will be broken into remotely when you use a short, common password than someone stealing your iPad and using it to gain access to that website. And even if they do, you can simply change your important passwords if your iPad is stolen.

Using AutoFill

After you have AutoFill set up, using it is relatively simple. You can use it with a form that asks for basic contact information, or for a login form. The process is the same.

1. Enter an ID or password at a website and tap the Sign In button, or press Return or Go on the virtual keyboard, to sign in.

2. If AutoFill is enabled, you might be prompted by Safari to save the password.

3. Tap Save Password to save the user ID and password.

4. Alternatively, tap Never for This Website to tell Safari that you don't want to save the password for this site, and not to ask again.

5. Tap Not Now to skip this step for now. This is useful if you have multiple logons for a site and don't want to save the one you are using at this moment.

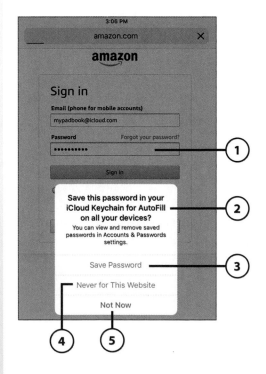

6. Log out and then return to the same website.

7. The ID and password are already filled in. The fields turn yellow to show that AutoFill has been used to fill them in.

8. Tap the button used by the site to complete the login.

9. If your ID and password don't appear at first, look for the Passwords button on top of the keyboard. This button also enables you to select from multiple sets of IDs and passwords if you have more than one account at the site.

Changing Passwords

So what happens if you change passwords for a site? Simply use the keyboard to erase and retype the password when logging into that site the next time. AutoFill will prompt you, asking if you want to save the new password, replacing the old one in its database.

It's Not All Good

AutoFill Not Working?

AutoFill works because forms use typical names for fields: ID, password, name, first name, last name, zip, and so on. If a website wants to get creative, or intentionally block AutoFill functions of browsers, then the site may obfuscate the names of fields to make it impossible for AutoFill to tell which field is which. Therefore, some websites might not work with AutoFill, whereas others do.

>>>Go Further
SAFARI EXTENSIONS

You can add new functionality to Safari with third-party extensions. For instance, you can use the popular 1Password app to insert passwords into login pages. You can use the Pinterest extension to pin web pages without leaving Safari.

To install an extension, first install the app from the App Store as you would any other app. (See Chapter 15 to learn how to find and install apps.) After you have installed an app that offers a Safari extension, tap the Share button at the top of Safari to start the process of activating it. This is the same button used to add a bookmark.

In the menu that appears, you see a list of ways to Share the page you are viewing, such as Message and Mail. You also have a list of more actions you can take with the page, such as Add Bookmark and Copy. Swipe either of these lists from right to left, and you see a More button as the rightmost item in the list. If the extension adds a way to share a web page, you find it by using the More button in the first list. Other extensions are behind the More button in the second list. Either way, switch the extension on to activate it.

After that, you'll find the extension along with the other items in either of these two lists as a button. For instance, with the Pinterest extension, you can tap the Share button, and then tap the Pinterest button to quickly add an image on the current page to one of your boards.

Send and
receive text
messages

Send and
receive email

In this chapter, you learn how to configure and use the Mail app to correspond using email and how to use the Messages app to send and receive messages.

→ Configuring Your iPad for Email
→ Reading Your Email
→ Composing a New Email
→ Deleting and Moving Emails
→ Searching Email
→ Customizing Your Email
→ Communicating with Messages
→ Expressing Yourself Through Messages

Communicating with Email and Messaging

Now that you have an iPad with a battery that seems to last forever, you have no excuse for not replying to emails. You need to be comfortable using the built-in Mail app that enables you to connect with your home or work email using standard protocols such as POP and IMAP. You can even connect with more proprietary systems such as AOL, Exchange, Gmail, and Yahoo! You can also send messages to your friends using Apple's iMessage system.

Configuring Your iPad for Email

It's easy to set up your email if you use one of the popular email services like Gmail, Yahoo!, AOL, or Microsoft. But if you use another kind of service, such as the email given to you by your local ISP or the company you work for, you need to enter more detailed information such as server addresses.

It is possible that your email account has already been set up for you. If you use Apple's iCloud as your email service, when you answered some questions while setting up your new iPad, you probably already gave your iPad your Apple ID and password and it set up your email automatically. You can use these steps to check to make sure that account is there, or add an additional account from another provider.

If you are using iCloud, Gmail, or any of the other services listed on the Add Account screen, all you really need to do is enter your email address and password. Your iPad sets up the account from those two pieces of information. But if you are using another type of email account, you need to enter several details about your account.

Set Up Your Email Account

1. Tap the Settings icon on your Home screen.

2. Find the Passwords & Accounts section.

3. If you are only using iCloud email, and you have set up your iCloud account on your iPad, you are all set. There is no need to set up email separately. If you want to check your iCloud email settings, you can tap here to view them.

4. Tap Add Account if you want to set up another kind of email account, such as one at Google, Yahoo!, your Internet service provider, or your employer.

Settings

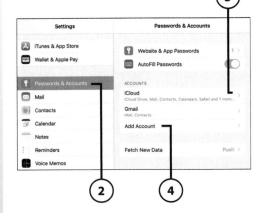

5. If you have an iCloud, Microsoft Exchange, Google, Yahoo! Mail, AOL, or Outlook.com account, tap the corresponding button. This example uses Google for a Gmail account.

Other

If your email account is from a cable or DSL Internet provider, or employers (depending on their system), you need to tap Other when setting up your account. Gather information such as your ID, password, email server address, and account type (such as POP or IMAP) before starting. Check with your provider's support department if you get stuck.

6. The next screen varies depending on the service you are using. Here you can see Google's authentication screen, so if you chose a different type of account, the screens for this step and the next few might look different.

7. Enter your email address. Make sure you enter it perfectly, as this is your ID for logging into this email service.

8. Tap Next to go to the next screen.

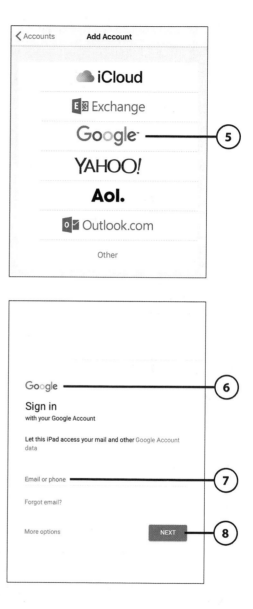

9. Enter your password for this email account.

10. Tap Next.

11. The next screen shows you what services the provider offers. For instance, Google's accounts not only provide email, but also contacts, calendars, and notes. You can leave all these turned on, or turn some off if you prefer not to use a service from that provider on your iPad.

12. Tap Save to continue.

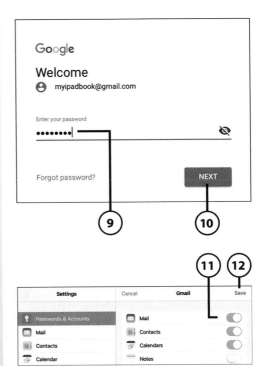

>>>Go Further
CHOOSING AN EMAIL PROVIDER WISELY

If you are using a cable or DSL provider, you might have an email address assigned to you by them. There are many good reasons to avoid using these email addresses and instead sign up for one such as Apple's iCloud or Google's Gmail service. The main reason is transportability. If you have a cable network email address now, you will lose it if you switch to another provider or you move out of your provider's territory. Another reason is that these ISP-provided email services tend to lack features like good junk mail filtering and the ability to send and receive email from multiple devices seamlessly.

Reading Your Email

You use the Mail app to read your email, which is much easier to navigate and type with your iPad turned horizontally. In horizontal mode, you can see the list of email messages to the left while you view the email message content to the right. In vertical mode, you view only one of these at a time.

Mail

1. Tap the Mail app icon on the Home screen.

< Mailboxes	Edit		🏳 🗀 🗑 ↩ ✎
Inbox		From: G Rosenzweig ›	
		To: Jane Jones ›	Hide GR
● **Johnny Zebra**	8:18 PM		
Hello			
Wanted to catch up. Let me know when		**Question about the new iPad**	
there is a good time to call. -- A		August 14, 2016 at 10:04 AM	
G Rosenzweig	8/14/16		
Question about the new iPad		Can I use the iPad as a laptop replacement? I only surf the web and write short text	
Can I use the iPad as a laptop		documents. I don't do any coding or video work? Thanks!	
replacement? I only surf the web and...			
		MM	
↓ 🖐			
Updated 2 minutes ago			
1 Unread			

2. On the left, you see a list of incoming mail. Tap an email in the list to view it.

3. On the right, you see the selected email.

4. If you want to check for new mail, drag the list of email messages down and release. It springs back up and asks the server to see if there are new email messages.

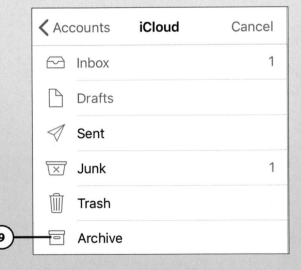

5. Tap the name or email address of the sender.

6. Tap Create New Contact to add the sender to your contacts.

7. Tap Add to Existing Contact to add the email address to a contact you already have in your Contacts app.

8. Tap the Folder button at the top of the email.

9. Tap a folder to move the current email to that folder.

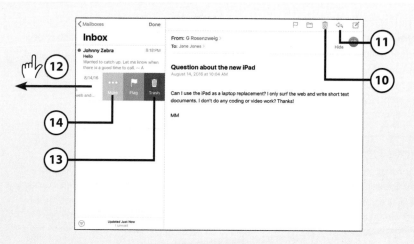

10. Tap the Trash button at the top of the email to send the email directly to the Trash folder.

11. Tap the Arrow button at the top of the email to reply to or forward the message.

12. If you tap and swipe right to left or left to right across the email in the left sidebar, you get more options. Be careful not to swipe too fast or instead of seeing options, you will quickly put the email in the trash.

13. Options include things like flagging or deleting the email.

14. Tap More to see a list of other options.

Customization

You can customize the Swipe options by going to the Settings app, selecting Mail on the left, and then Swipe Options. For instance, you can change the Swipe Right action from the default Mark as Read, to Archive.

15. In addition to actions like Reply and Forward, you can also select Notify Me, which gives you an alert when someone else replies to this email thread (any email with the same title).

Multiple Inboxes

If you have more than one email account, you can choose to look at each inbox individually or a single unified inbox that includes emails from all accounts. Just tap the Mailboxes button at the upper-left corner of the screen and choose All Inboxes. You can also choose to look at the inbox of a single account, or dig down into any folder of an account.

How Do You Create Folders?

For most email accounts—particularly IMAP, Gmail, and iCloud accounts—you can create folders using the Mail app. Use the back arrow at the upper-left corner of Mail to back out to the list of inboxes and accounts. Choose an account, then tap the Edit button to see a New Mailbox button at the bottom of the screen.

VIPs

You can make a contact a VIP by tapping Add to VIP when you select the sender's name in an incoming email. Then, their emails appear in your inbox as normal, but they also appear in the VIP inbox. So if you get a lot of email and want to occasionally focus only on a few very important people instead of everyone, choose your VIP inbox rather than your inbox.

If you are using VIPs with your iCloud email accounts, you'll see the same VIPs for your Mac and other iOS devices using that iCloud account.

Composing a New Email

Whether you compose a new email or reply to one you received, the process is similar. Let's take a look at composing one from scratch.

1. In the Mail app, tap the Compose button.
2. Enter an address in the To field.
3. Alternatively, tap the + button to bring up a list of contacts, and choose from there.
4. Tap in the Subject field and type a subject for the email.
5. Tap below the subject field in the body of the email, and type your email message.
6. Tap the Send button.

Siri: Sending Email

You can use Siri to send email by asking it to "send an email to" and the name of the recipient. It asks you for a subject and a body to the email, and then Siri displays the email. You can choose to send it or cancel. You can even do the whole thing through Siri by saying something like "Send an email to John Johnson with the subject hello and the body how are you doing."

Including Images

You can copy and paste inside a Mail message just like you can inside of any text entry area on your iPad. But you can also paste in images! Just copy an image from any source—Photos app, Safari, and so on, and then tap in the email body and select Paste. You can paste in more than one image as well.

Deleting and Moving Emails

While viewing an email message, you can tap the trash can icon and move it to the trash. You can also move a group of emails to a folder or the trash.

1. In the Mail app, go to any mailbox and any subfolder, such as your Inbox.

2. If you are viewing an email, you can delete it by tapping the trash can icon.

3. You can also start the process of deleting an email or several messages by tapping the Edit button.

4. Tap the circles next to each email to select them.

5. Selected emails are added to the middle of the screen in a neat stack.

6. Tap the Trash button to delete the selected emails.

7. Tap the Move button, and the left side of the screen changes to a list of folders. You can select one to move all the emails to that folder.

8. Tap the Cancel button to exit without deleting or moving any emails.

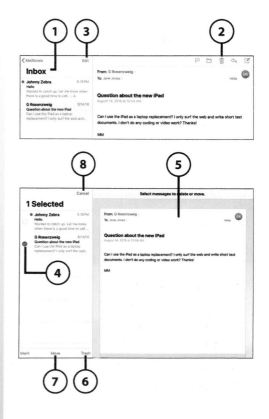

9. Alternatively, you can delete a single email by dragging just slightly right to left across the email in the list. This reveals Trash, Flag, and More buttons. If you drag all the way from the right to the left side of the screen, the Trash button enlarges and fills the space, and then the email is deleted with just this one gesture. Note that some email systems, like Gmail, favor archiving instead of deleting. In this case, you'll see a blue Archive button instead of a red Delete button.

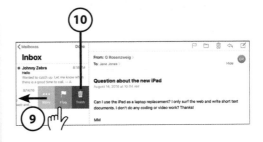

10. Tap the Trash button to delete the email. The More button allows you to reply, forward, flag, move, and perform various other actions on the email.

Oops—How Do I Undelete?

So you just tried to use step 9 to see what those buttons looked like, and you deleted the email by accident? You can always look in your Trash folder to select the email and move it back to the Inbox. But when you give your iPad a quick shake, you're prompted to undo the deletion.

Where's the Trash?

If you are just deleting the single email that you happen to be viewing, you can tap the trash can icon at the top. But sometimes that icon isn't there. Instead, you might see an icon that looks like a file box. This is an Archive button. Some email services, like Gmail, insist that you archive your email instead of deleting it. To facilitate this, they provide a nearly infinite amount of storage space, so you might as well use that Archive button.

What About Spam?

Your iPad has no built-in spam filter. Fortunately, most email servers filter out spam at the server level. Using a service such as iCloud or Gmail means that you get spam filtering on the server and junk mail automatically goes to the Junk folder, not your Inbox.

Searching Email

You can search your email using the Mail app.

1. The Search field is at the top of the email messages list in the left sidebar in the Mail app. It won't be visible at first. To see it, tap and drag down the messages in the left sidebar.

2. Tap in the Search field.

3. Type a search term.

4. You see people and emails in the results. Select an email to view it from the search results.

5. Tap Cancel to exit the search and return to the mailbox you were previously viewing.

Search What?

Searches work on From, To, and Subject fields and the body of the email message. Any messages you have in your inbox pop up right away, but any archived messages or ones stored in folders might or might not appear after a few seconds. The Mail app relies on your email server to return these results. Depending on what type of email server you have, it could take a while. Older results might not appear at all.

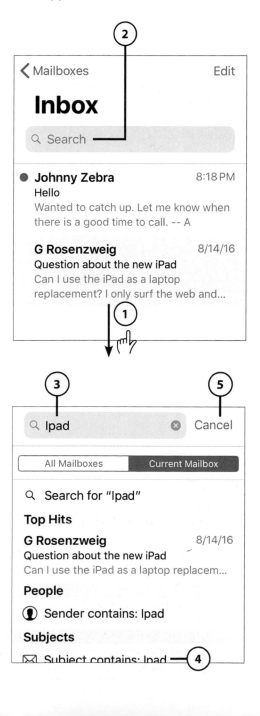

Customizing Your Email

You have more settings for email beyond the basic account setup. For instance, you can decide how you want to receive email, using either push delivery or fetch delivery (or manual). There are even more Email settings in the Settings app.

Configuring How You Receive Email

When you receive email, it is either fetched, pushed, or delivered manually when you choose. Fetch checks for email at regular intervals, whereas push receives emails soon after they have arrived at your email service. Depending on what your provider supports, you can choose between these settings.

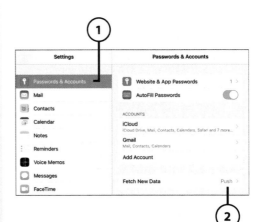

1. Go to the Settings app and find Passwords & Accounts.

2. Tap Fetch New Data.

3. Turn on Push to use push email reception, if you use email accounts that can send email via push.

4. Otherwise, select how often you want your iPad to go out to the server and fetch email.

5. Tap one of your email accounts to customize the settings for that particular account. Note that even some subscribed calendars have the ability to be set to push or fetch.

6. For each account, you can set your preferences to Fetch, Manual, or Push if available for that account. More options exist for some accounts, such as specifying which folders are pushed.

< Fetch New Data   iCloud

SELECT SCHEDULE

Push ✓ ──⑥

Fetch

Manual

If Push is not available, the Fetch schedule will be used.

PUSHED MAILBOXES

✉ Inbox ✓

📄 Drafts

✈ Sent ✓

🗑 Trash

🗄 Archive

🗙 Junk

📁 Notes

    📁 New Folder

    📁 To Do Items

📁 Project Alpha

Siri: Checking Email

You can ask Siri for a quick list of new email messages by saying, "Check my email." You get a list from within the Siri interface, and you can tap a message to read it in the Mail app. If you say, "Read me my email," Siri reads your new messages out loud to you.

No Thanks—I'll Do It Myself

The Manual setting is useful if you don't want to be disturbed throughout the day as you receive email. These accounts are checked only when you open the Mail app and look at the inbox for that account. Another reason to use Manual is to preserve battery so that your iPad won't use Wi-Fi or your mobile connection as often. You also might want to use Manual if you are concerned about bandwidth, like when you're traveling internationally and only want to check email when using Wi-Fi.

Creating a Signature

You can create a signature that appears below your email messages automatically. You do this in the Settings app.

1. In the Settings app, choose Mail.

2. Tap Signature, which is way down in the list on the right.

3. If you have more than one email account set up, you can choose to have one signature for all accounts or a different signature for each account.

4. Type a signature in one of the signature text fields. You don't need to do anything to save the signature. You can tap the Home button on your iPad to exit Settings if you like.

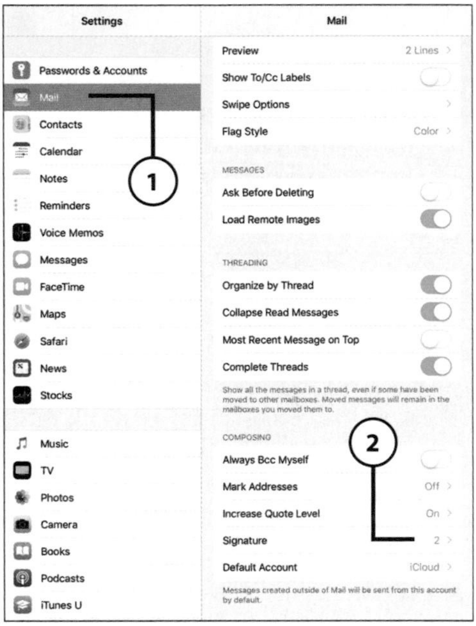

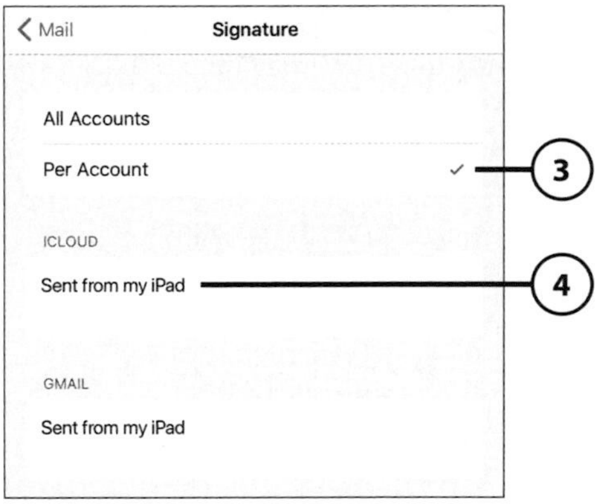

Case-By-Case Signatures

You can have only one signature for each email account. But the signature is placed in the editable area of the email composition field, so you can edit it like the rest of your message.

Settings	Mail
	Preview 2 Lines >
Passwords & Accounts	Show To/Cc Labels
Mail	Swipe Options >
Contacts	Flag Style Color >
Calendar	
Notes	**MESSAGES**
Reminders	Ask Before Deleting
Voice Memos	Load Remote Images
Messages	**THREADING**
FaceTime	Organize by Thread
Maps	Collapse Read Messages
Safari	Most Recent Message on Top
News	Complete Threads
Stocks	Show all the messages in a thread, even if some have been moved to other mailboxes. Moved messages will remain in the mailboxes you moved them to.
Music	**COMPOSING**
TV	Always Bcc Myself
Photos	Mark Addresses Off >
Camera	Increase Quote Level On >
Books	Signature 2 >
Podcasts	Default Account iCloud >
iTunes U	Messages created outside of Mail will be sent from this account by default.

① ②

< Mail	Signature

All Accounts

Per Account   ✓   **③**

ICLOUD

Sent from my iPad   **④**

GMAIL

Sent from my iPad

Styles and Images in Signatures

You can make some text in your signature bold, italic, or underlined by selecting the text and tapping on the selection. In addition to Cut, Copy, and Paste options, you also see a **B**/U option. Tap that button and you can style the selected text a bit. If you want to include an image in your signature, you can copy that image from another app and paste it in with the text. But try to refrain from pasting a photo or something large, as it might annoy your recipients to get a large image included with every email. A small company logo copied from your company's website might be more appropriate, although email etiquette points to keeping your signature simple and image-free.

More Email Settings

You can change even more email settings in the Settings app. Tap the Settings app on your Home screen, and then tap Mail to take a look at some of them.

1. If you don't want email messages to appear in search results on your iPad's Home screens, you can turn that off here.

2. Tap Notifications to change how and if onscreen alerts appear and sounds play when you get new email.

3. Tap Preview to choose how many lines of email message preview to show when stacking messages up in the list view.

4. Turn on Show To/Cc Labels to view "To" or "Cc" in each email listed so that you know if you were the primary recipient or someone who was just copied on an email to someone else.

5. When viewing email messages in your inbox, you can swipe left or right across the message in the list to take an action. You can set this up here. For instance, you can set a swipe to the right to mark an email as read, or you can set it to archive the message and remove it from the inbox.

6. Turn on Ask Before Deleting to require a confirmation when you tap the trash can icon in Mail.

7. Turn off Load Remote Images so that images referenced in an email but stored on a remote server are not shown in the email body.

Mail

ALLOW MAIL TO ACCESS

Siri & Search
Search & Siri Suggestions ⟩ — ①

Notifications
Badges, Sounds ⟩ — ②

MESSAGE LIST

Preview 2 Lines ⟩ — ③

Show To/Cc Labels ④

Swipe Options ⟩ — ⑤

Flag Style Color ⟩

MESSAGES

Ask Before Deleting — ⑥

Load Remote Images — ⑦

THREADING

Organize by Thread

Collapse Read Messages

Most Recent Message on Top

Complete Threads

Show all the messages in a thread, even if some have been moved to other mailboxes. Moved messages will remain in the mailboxes you moved them to.

COMPOSING

Always Bcc Myself

8. To group replies to an email under the original message, select Organize by Thread. This is handy when you subscribe to email discussion lists.

9. Turn on Always Bcc Myself if you want to get a copy of every email you send so that later you can move your copies of emails to your Sent folder on your computer. This might be a good idea if you are using an older email system. Modern email systems like iCloud and Gmail should save your sent emails to the server just like other messages.

10. Choose whether to indent the quoted text from the original email when replying to an email.

11. Tap Default Account to determine which account is used to send email by default if you have more than one account set up on your iPad.

12. In most apps from which you send emails, you can type an email and also change the account you use to send the email. To do this, tap the email address shown next to From and you get a list of all your accounts, including alternate email addresses for each account.

Mail	
Preview	2 Lines >
Show To/Cc Labels	
Swipe Options	>
Flag Style	Color >
MESSAGES	
Ask Before Deleting	
Load Remote Images	
THREADING	
Organize by Thread	
Collapse Read Messages	
Most Recent Message on Top	
Complete Threads	

Show all the messages in a thread, even if some have been moved to other mailboxes. Moved messages will remain in the mailboxes you moved them to.

COMPOSING	
Always Bcc Myself	
Mark Addresses	Off >
Increase Quote Level	On >
Signature	2 >
Default Account	iCloud >

Messages created outside of Mail will be sent from this account by default.

‹ Mail	**Default Account**	
iCloud		✓
Gmail		

Why Not Show Remote Images?

The main reason to not show remote images is bandwidth. If you get an email that has 15 images referenced in it, you need to download a lot of data, and it takes a while for that email to show up completely. However, remote images are often used as ways to indicate whether you have opened and looked at emails. So, turning this off might break some statistics and receipt functionality expected from the sender (including from spammers). Even if you have remote image turned off, you have the option to show them on a case-by-case basis as you view your email.

Communicating with Messages

Even though your iPad isn't a phone, you can send text messages. The catch is that you can message only other people who are also using Apple's iMessage system, which is anyone using iOS 5 or newer with an iPad, iPhone, or iPod touch, as long as they have signed up for the free service. Mac users can also send messages with the iMessage system.

Setting Up Messages

1. Tap the Settings app icon on your Home screen.

   You need to be signed into iCloud with your Apple ID to use Messages. If you didn't do that when you set up your iPad, or when you set up iCloud email, you need to go to the iCloud settings and sign in or create an iCloud account.

2. Tap the Messages settings.

3. Make sure iMessage is turned on.

4. If you turn this option on, when someone sends you a message they also get a notification when you have viewed the message.

5. Tap Send & Receive to control which email addresses can be used to find you, adding more and removing others. You can use any valid email address that you own for Messages, even if it is not the same as your Apple ID email address.

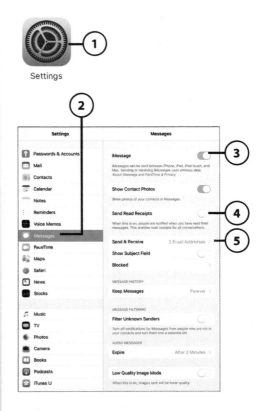

Settings

6. Apple's iMessage system can include a subject line along with the message, though most people don't use this.

7. Tap Blocked to add email addresses to block so individuals cannot send you messages.

8. Most people prefer to keep old messages around forever, to refer to them later. Text messages are small, so you don't have to worry about them using up any noticeable space on your iPad. But your iPad allows you to send audio and video messages as well, which do take up some space. You can choose to have those automatically disappear after you have listened to or viewed them.

9. You can opt to have messages received from senders not in your contacts list to be put in a separate list in the Messages app. You also won't receive notifications when someone not in your contacts list sends you a message.

10. Set how long to keep audio messages you receive. Typically, you want these to expire soon after you view them so that they don't fill up your iPad's storage space.

Blocking Messengers

There is an even easier way to block unwanted messengers when using the Messages app. You can tap the i button at the upper-right corner of the screen while viewing the conversation in Messages to get to the Details screen. Then tap the name, ID, or phone number at the top. This shows you more information about the sender. Scroll all the way down until you see the Block This Caller option. Use this and you'll never get another message from that account again. Better still, audio and FaceTime calls from them are blocked as well.

Conversing with Messages

After you have set up an account with Messages, you can quickly and easily send messages to others. The next time you launch Messages, you go directly to the main screen.

1. Tap the Messages app icon on your Home screen.

2. Tap the New Message button at the top of the screen.

3. In a new message, tap in the To field and enter the email address of the recipient. Note that they should already be signed up for iMessage or you will not be able to send them anything. Some iPhone users might use their phone number as their iMessage ID instead of, or in addition to, their email address. As long as the phone number is tied to an iMessage account, you can still converse with them using Messages on your iPad. You can add more than one recipient to start a conversation with a group.

4. If you want to send a picture or video, tap this button. You can choose a picture from your photo library, or take a picture with your iPad's camera.

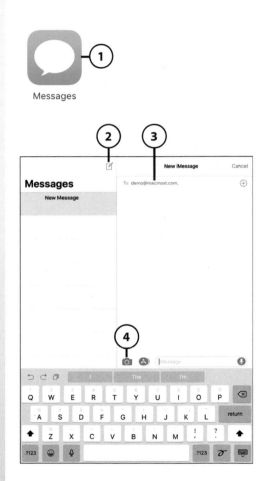

Messages

5. Tap the text field above the keyboard to type your message.

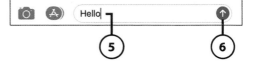

6. While you are typing your message, the button to the right side of the text field changes from a microphone to an up arrow. The microphone button can be used to record a voice message instead of typing a text message. When you start typing, the microphone button is replaced with the up arrow, which you can use to send your message when you're done typing.

Say It; Don't Text It

If you'd rather the person on the other end hear your voice, or you're just tired of typing, then use the microphone button in step 6 to record a short audio clip to send. The receiver will be able to play it back.

7. The conversation appears as a series of talk bubbles. Your bubbles are on the right.

8. When your friend responds, her comments are on the left side of the conversation panel.

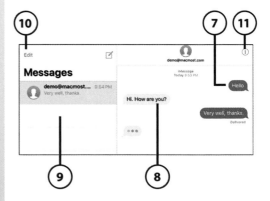

9. A list of conversations appears on the left side of the screen. You can have many going on at the same time, or use this list to look at old conversations.

10. Tap Edit to access buttons to delete old conversations.

11. Tap the info button to do various tasks, such as adding the person to your contacts or starting a FaceTime video chat. You can also send your current location to the people you are messaging, which saves you time if you want to tell someone to meet you at your current location.

12. A small bubble with three dots means that the other party is typing. You see this with other people using Apple's iMessage system, but if they are using a mobile phone with SMS or if their connection is poor, you might not see these indicators.

Siri: Sending Messages

You can use Siri to send messages. Simply tell Siri something like, "Send a text message to Gary," and Siri responds by asking you what you want to say in your message. Or, you can say something like, "Send a message to Gary. Tell him I'll meet him after the movie," and Siri creates the whole message for you. You can review the message before it is sent for truly hands-free operation. When you get a message, you can also ask Siri to "Read me that message," and you can listen to the message without ever glancing at your iPad's screen.

>>>Go Further
SMS ON YOUR iPAD

SMS, or Short Message Service, is the system of sending messages, sometimes called "texts," through your mobile carrier to other phone users. Unlike iMessage, SMS messages go through carriers like AT&T, Verizon, T-Mobile, and Sprint. So SMS is available on your iPhone, but not your iPad because your iPad isn't a phone and doesn't use these carriers for voice and messaging.

However, a feature called SMS Relay allows iPhone users to automatically forward SMS messages to their iPads and use their iPads to send SMS messages through the iPhone. This feature is available if both your iPhone and iPad use the same iCloud account, and they are both connected to the same Wi-Fi network. You receive an initial prompt asking if you want to enable SMS Relay. After you confirm, you're able to converse using SMS on your iPad as long as your iPhone is connected to the same Wi-Fi network.

This enables you to send messages from your iPad to friends who have non-Apple devices and use SMS.

Using Emojis in Text Messages

In addition to normal words, text messages also often include little pictures, called emojis. You're probably familiar with smiling face or heart emojis, but there are actually hundreds of different emoji symbols you can use.

1. Type a message in the Messages app.

2. Switch to the Emoji keyboard by tapping the keyboard switch button. If you have more than the default two keyboards (standard and emoji) active on your iPad, you might need to switch several times to get to the emoji keyboard.

3. Tap an emoji character.

4. The emoji is added to a message just like a normal letter would be.

5. Swipe left and right to reveal more emoji characters.

6. Tap a category button to jump to sections of the emoji character list. For instance, if you want to use the baseball emoji, chances are it is in the sports category.

7. Tap here to find your recently used emojis.

8. You can type spaces and delete without needing to switch back to the regular keyboard.

9. The Messages app highlights words that can be swapped for common emojis. For instance, you can tap the word pizza and it changes to the pizza emoji.

10. Tap to switch back to the regular keyboard.

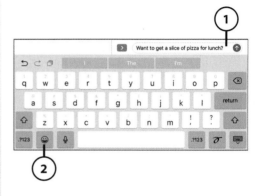

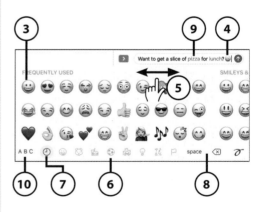

The Universal Language of Emojis

It is important to realize that emojis are part of a universal set of characters agreed upon by all device makers. So when you send a smiling face from your iPad, someone getting that message on an Android phone receives a smiling face. The actual drawing of the face might look slightly different, but it should always be similar enough to convey the same idea.

Emoji Skin Tones

Some emojis, like hand gestures and heads, come in a variety of skin tones. To see those, tap and hold an emoji character in the keyboard to see alternative versions in a pop-up. Tap the version you want to send.

Expressing Yourself Through Messages

When you send messages, there are many ways to express yourself beyond simply using words. You can send special quick replies, drawings, animated GIF images, and even full-screen animations. These special features work with others who are also using iOS 10 or later on their iPads or iPhones. They also work with Mac users who are using Mac OS Sierra. Other people usually see simplified or static images as a substitute.

Responding with Tapback Quick Replies

One of the many features of Messages is the ability to send quick responses to messages without typing anything. Apple calls this feature "tapback."

1. Tap and hold a message you have received.

2. A bubble appears above the message so you can tap one of several icons as a response: heart, thumbs up, thumbs down, ha ha, exclamation points, or a question mark.

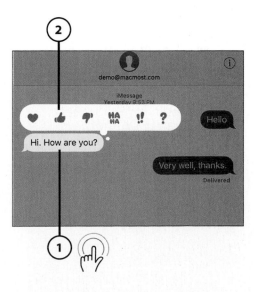

3. The icon response is added to the original message bubble.

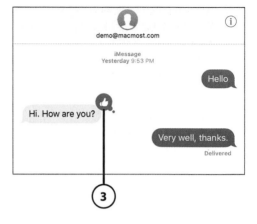

Sending Messages with Bubble Effects

Bubble effects change the way the bubble around the text looks. There are currently four effects.

1. Type a new message.

2. Tap and hold the up arrow button. Holding it for a second is important as a simple tap sends the message right now instead of showing you the bubble effects menu.

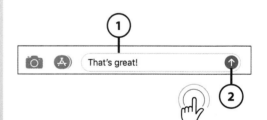

I Didn't Mean to Do That!

If you tap and hold the send arrow longer than you mean to, you can tap the X button to dismiss the Bubble effect menu and send the text as normal.

3. At the top of the screen you can switch between Bubble and Screen effects. Make sure you have Bubble selected. The next section covers Screen effects.

4. Tap one of the four bubble effects to see a preview of how this effect will look with the text you have selected.

5. The bubble animates according to the effect you selected.

6. If you like this effect and want to use it, tap the up arrow button. The message will be sent. Otherwise, tap the X to close the menu.

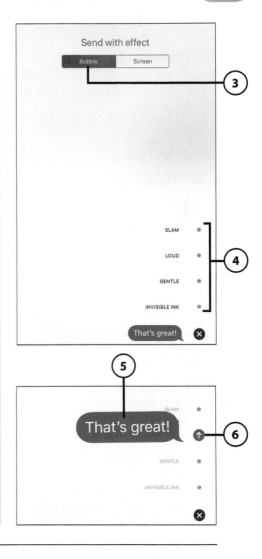

What Do the Effects Do?

It's hard to describe the animation of the four effects. It's best that you try them out for yourself the next time you get the chance. The general idea is to use Slam to provide maximum emphasis. Loud and Gentle can be used to relay emotion about the text. For instance, a "Sorry" said with the gentle effect gives the impression of a quiet apology.

The Invisible Ink effect is a little different. The text appears blurred until the receiver taps it. Then it becomes clear before becoming blurred again. This can be used to elicit a feeling of suspense—allowing the receiver to brace themselves before reading good or bad news. Or, it could simply give the receiver a chance to make sure no one is looking over their shoulder before they read the message.

Hide the Surprise

The Invisible Ink effect not only works with plain text message, but also with images. Just attach an image to the same message that you apply the Invisible Ink effect to, and the receiver has to tap the blurred image to reveal it.

Sending Messages with Animations

You can also send one of several full-screen animations with your messages.

1. Type a new message.

2. Tap and hold the up arrow button.

3. Tap Screen effects.

4. Right away the first screen effect, balloons, plays to show you what it looks like. The other four animations are falling confetti, a laser light coming from behind the message bubble, fireworks, and a flare arching across the screen.

5. Tap and drag right to the left to go to the next animation. Note that the five dots at the bottom indicate which animation you are currently viewing. You can drag left to right to go backward through the list.

6. Tap the up arrow button to send the message with the animation.

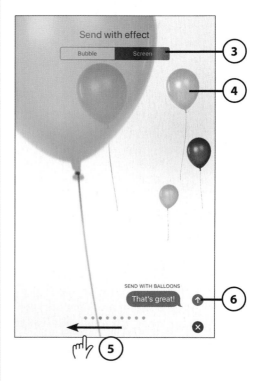

Sending Handwritten Notes

You can also send your own hand-writing, or even small sketches.

1. Start a message, but don't type anything.

2. Tap the sketch button on the virtual keyboard.

3. The keyboard changes to a simple sketchpad. Tap and drag your finger to draw.

4. Tap the Undo button to take back your last tap or stroke. You can use this multiple times to remove multiple errant strokes.

5. Tap here or swipe with two fingers to go to another page in this little sketchpad. This comes in handy if you want to try handwriting your message a few times and send only the best one.

6. Tap to resend your recent handwritten notes or sketches.

7. Tap to return to the regular keyboard.

8. When you are happy with your sketch or note, tap the Done button.

9. You can add text to appear alongside the sketch.

10. Tap the X to cancel the sketch.

11. Once you are happy with the sketch and any accompanying text, tap the up arrow to send it.

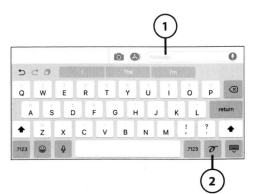

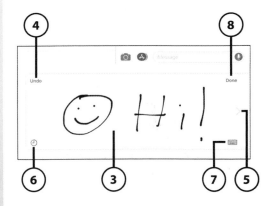

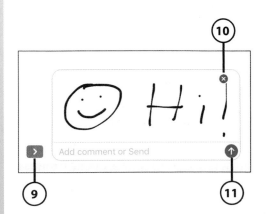

Sending Digital Touch Messages

Another way to express yourself with messages is to use special Digital Touch elements. These are animations, like heartbeats, kisses, fireballs, and even animated drawings over short video clips.

1. Tap the apps and special functions button before typing a message.

2. Tap the Digital Touch icon at the bottom. It looks like a heart with two fingers.

3. Tap here to select a color for your sketch.

4. Draw in this area by tapping and dragging.

5. Switch colors for each line if you like.

6. Tap the up arrow to send when you are done. What the receiver sees is the sketch re-created in real time with each stroke being drawn one-by-one just as you created it.

7. Alternatively, tap the X to cancel.

8. Tap the video button to use the camera on your iPhone to record video. Then you can draw over that video in real time to create a combination of video and a sketch.

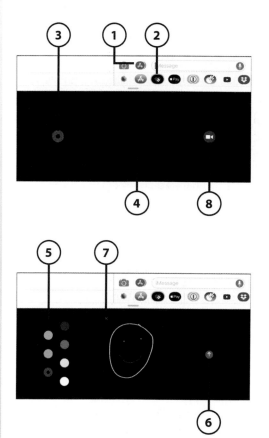

Other Digital Touch Options

In addition to drawing, you can tap and hold to create fireball animation, tap with one finger to send a ring animation, tap with two fingers to create a kiss animation, tap with two fingers and hold to create a heartbeat animation, and tap with two fingers and drag down for a broken heart animation.

You can also experiment to create other effects. For instance, tap with two fingers multiple times in different spots to send a parade of kisses. Use the video button in step 9 in combination with the fireball or ring animation. It takes some practice to create good effects, so send some of these digital touch messages back and forth with a friend and have some fun with it while practicing.

Keep or Let Expire?

When you receive a digital touch message, you see a small Keep button under it. If you tap that, the animated message remains in your conversation. If you don't tap it, the message disappears after a few seconds. This allows you to send and receive these fun messages without worrying about them cluttering up the text conversation.

Send Animated GIFs and Other Special Messages

You can also send animated GIFs and special images from Apple and third-party developers using messaging apps. These are apps you get in the App Store that allow you to send special items in the Messages app. You can read more about getting apps in Chapter 15.

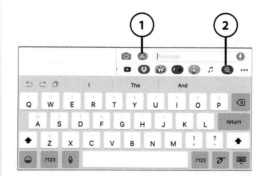

1. Tap the apps and special functions button before sending a message.

2. You should see this default example app already installed. Tap it to send a special image.

3. Some popular images and animated GIFs display. Tap one to send it.

4. You can search for images by topic. For instance, if you want to congratulate someone in a unique way, search for "congratulations" and see what animations come up.

5. Swipe left and right to see more. The left-most page of images are those you have recently sent.

6. Tap here to expand this interface to the full screen so you can see more images at once.

7. Tap here to return to the previous screen.

8. Tap to go directly to a screen in the App Store that shows featured messaging apps. You can then add more apps that can be available in step 2. (See Chapter 15 for more information about using the App Store.)

9. Tap the More (…) button to see what you have already installed and disable packages you no longer want.

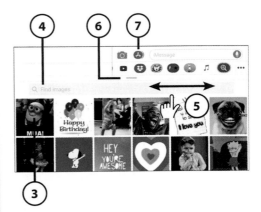

Browse your photos
on the iPad's
brilliant screen

Take pictures
with the iPad's
cameras

Take fun selfies
with Photo Booth

This chapter explains using the Camera and Photo Booth apps to take pictures. Then you learn how to view, edit, and share photos.

→ Working with Photos

→ Understanding Photo Sources

→ Working with Albums

→ Creating a Slideshow

→ For You and Memories

→ Marking Up Photos

→ Capturing the Screen

Taking and Editing Photos

In addition to replacing books, the iPad replaces physical photo albums. You can literally carry thousands of photos with you on your iPad. Plus, your iPad's screen is a beautiful way to display these photos. It can also replace your camera, as long as you don't mind the iPad's size compared to a smaller camera.

In addition to photos you take using your iPad, you can sync photos from your computer to your iPad, or use the iCloud Photo Library. Then you can use the Photos app to browse and view your photos.

Working with Photos

All iPads after the first generation include two cameras you can use to take a variety of photos that you can then edit and adjust as you need. One camera is located on the front, and one on the back. The primary app for taking pictures is the Camera app. Let's take a look at the things you can do with this app.

Taking Photos

Camera

1. Tap the Camera app icon on the Home screen. This brings up the Camera app, and you should immediately see the image from the camera.

Quickest Way to the Camera

If your iPad is locked and you want to take a picture quickly, no need to unlock it. Just swipe right to left on the Lock screen and you go right to the camera app interface. Take a picture and then tap the Home button to go back to the main Lock screen.

2. The camera app has six modes: Time-Lapse, Slo-Mo, Video, Photo, Square, and Pano. The first three are for video filming, and the other three take rectangular, square, and panoramic photographs. To switch between modes, you can tap and drag up and down in this area. Or, you could tap the word representing the mode you want, and the app switches to it. The option in yellow is the mode you are currently using. Switch to Photo mode if you are not in that mode already.

Mode Support

Not all iPad models support each mode. Pano requires at least an iPad with a Retina display (like the iPad Air). Slo-Mo requires an iPad Air 2 or newer model.

3. Tap to switch between front and rear cameras.

4. Tap anywhere on the image to specify that you want to use that portion of the image to determine the focus and exposure for the photo. A yellow box appears at that spot.

5. After you have tapped on the image, and if you are using the rear-facing camera, you can zoom in. To do that, tap and drag the dot up and down along this line.

6. Tap the HDR button to turn on High Dynamic Range Imaging. See the "High Dynamic What?" note for more information about this setting.

7. Tap the time delay button to set a timer for 3 or 10 seconds. This allows you to set your iPad down on a stand or lean it against something and get into the shot.

8. Tap the large shutter button at the right side of the screen to take the picture. Alternatively, press one of the volume buttons on the side of your iPad to take the picture. If you hold either button down, your iPad continues to take pictures in rapid succession.

9. Tap the thumbnail photo to go to the Camera Roll and see the pictures you have taken. You can edit and adjust the photo you have just taken, as described in the next task.

The Focus and Exposure Area

When you tap the screen as in step 4, the yellow box appears. This area is now used for both focus and exposure. After you tap the screen, you can tap and drag your finger up and down to make further exposure adjustments. The little sun icon next to the box moves up and down along the line as you do so.

If you hold your finger down for a few seconds, the box pulses and the text AE/AF Lock displays at the top of the screen. This means the focus and exposure are now locked and won't change as you move your iPad to point it at something different.

High Dynamic What?

High Dynamic Range Imaging is a process where multiple pictures are taken in quick succession, each using a different exposure. Then the multiple images are combined. For instance, if you are taking a picture of a person with a bright sky behind them, one picture will do better with the person, and the other with the sky. Combining the multiple images gives you a picture that shows them both better than a single shot would.

When you use HDR, be sure to hold your iPad steady so each shot captures the same image. They will be taken a fraction of a second apart, so HDR does not work well with moving objects or a moving camera.

It's Not All Good

You're Holding It Wrong

It is natural to hold your iPad vertically. You might use a majority of apps that way, so when it comes time to take photos or video, it is easy to forget and to continue to hold it vertically. This drives professional and amateur photographers crazy when they see a good photo ruined because a phone or iPad user forgot to turn the device before shooting the picture.

Although portrait photos have their uses, most pictures are best taken in horizontal orientation. Cameras are usually held horizontally, and when you view your photos on a computer screen or television, a horizontal photo fits nicely whereas a vertical photo needs to shrink to fit, with vertical space wasted on the left and right. Never shoot video in portrait orientation.

Editing and Adjusting Photos

You can start editing photos by tapping the photo icon, as in step 9 of the previous task. Or, you can enter the Photos app and edit photos from there. We look more at the Photos app later in this chapter.

1. If you don't see buttons at the top and bottom of the photo, tap the middle of the photo to bring up controls on the top and bottom of the screen.

2. Use the thumbnails at the bottom to select a specific picture to view your photos. Or just swipe left and right through the thumbnails to flip through all your photos. You can also swipe left and right on the photo itself to move through them one-by-one.

3. If you are editing a photo you just took using the Camera app, you can tap the Back icon on the left to exit viewing this one image and jump back to the camera interface. Otherwise, continue on to step 4.

4. Tap the Trash icon to delete the photo. Deleted photos are stored for 30 days in a special Recently Deleted photo album, where you can rescue them if the deletion was a mistake. You can also tap and hold in the middle of a photo and then select Hide to hide the photo from Years, Collections, and Moments views, though it is still shown in any album you have added it to.

5. Tap the Share icon to send the photo to someone else via message, email, AirDrop, or a variety of other methods depending on which apps you have installed. This is also where you can copy the image so you can paste it into an email or another app.

6. Tap the Favorites button to mark this photo as one of your best. You'll be able to find it quickly in the Favorites album in the Photos app.

7. Tap Edit to enter Editing mode and bring up controls on the side of the screen. The controls will appear on the side of the screen next to your Home button, either left or right depending on how you rotated your iPad.

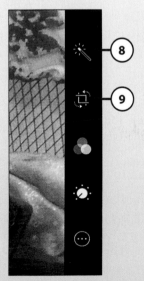

8. Tap Enhance to have the app examine the brightness and contrast in the photo and try to bring out the best image.

9. Tap the Crop button.

10. In this example, notice that the image automatically rotates slightly. The accelerometer in your iPad recorded the orientation of your iPad at the moment you took the photo, so it can now straighten the photo to be level. Tap and drag this angle dial up or down to rotate the photo manually.

11. Crop the photo by dragging any one of the four corners. Drag as many corners as you like to get the cropping just the way you want it.

12. Pinch in or out to zoom, or drag the photo to reposition it within the crop frame.

13. Tap Reset to set the rotation to 0 degrees and the cropping back to the full image size. Tap Reset again to rotate the photo automatically as it first appeared after step 9.

14. Tap this button to set the cropping rectangle to a specific size, such as 3:2 or square.

15. Tap the Rotate button to rotate the photo by 90-degree increments. This is useful when a photo is upside down or the wrong orientation.

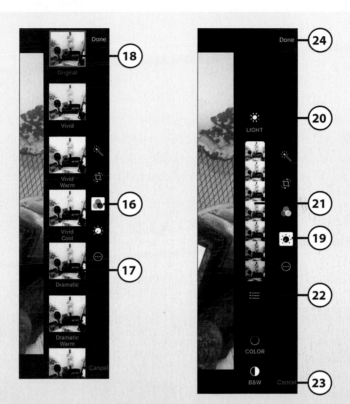

16. Tap the Filters button to apply a color filter to the photo.

17. Tap one of the filters in the list to preview the changes immediately.

18. Tap Original to remove the color filter.

19. Tap the Color Adjustments button.

20. Tap one of the three color adjustment types: Light, Color, or B&W.

21. Each type of adjustment has a filmstrip you can drag up and down to position the red line to indicate the level of adjustment you want. The main image on the screen shows you a preview of the result.

22. Use the List button to dig deeper into each adjustment and modify only one subsetting. For instance, you can adjust the contrast, brightness, or exposure.

23. Tap Cancel to leave the editor without saving the changes.

24. Tap Done to exit the editor and apply the changes to the photo.

>>>Go Further

EXTENDING PHOTO EDITING

You can add extensions to the Photos app that allow you to edit photos without leaving the app. When you install many third-party photo-editing apps, they add more functionality to photo editing. Look for a small button with three dots on the Photo app edit screen. You can see it just below step 19 in the screenshots. Tap that button, and then tap the More button to switch on an extension.

After it is switched on, tap the small three-dot button when editing a photo to select the extended functionality and apply interesting effects to your photo. Hundreds of third-party apps are available to give you all sorts of photo-editing fun.

Taking Panoramic Photos

If you have an iPad Pro, iPad Air, or an iPad mini with a retina display, the Pano option is available in the Camera app. This option allows you to take wide panoramic shots, covering a larger area than you could normally fit into a photo.

1. In the Camera app, slide the available capture types up until Pano is yellow.

2. Hold your camera in vertical orientation. Look at the rectangle in the middle of the screen. You will be filling this rectangle with images from the camera. Position it so the left side of the rectangle contains the portion of the scene you want to be on the left side of the finished panoramic photo.

3. Tap the camera shutter button, or the physical volume buttons, on your iPad to start taking the photo.

4. Slowly and steadily turn your body and your iPad from left to right to allow the camera to take in more of the image. As you move, the rectangle fills with the scene. Small parts of the top and bottom may remain empty if you tilt the iPad a little up or down. Try to keep these areas to a minimum, but a little of this is typically unavoidable.

5. You don't need to fill the entire rectangle. Most panoramic photos don't need to use the full horizontal area. Just get as much as you need to make a good photograph.

6. Tap the shutter button again to finish.

7. The result is just like a regular photo in your photo library, except that it is wider. You view it and edit it just like in the previous task.

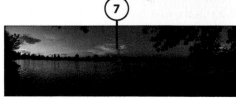

>>>Go Further
PANORAMIC TIPS

Use these tips when you're shooting a panoramic photo:

- Before you start taking the panorama, tap the arrow on the screen to reverse direction and take the photo from right to left.

- You don't need to restrict yourself to horizontal panoramas. You can hold your iPad in horizontal orientation and take a vertical one. This could be used to capture a skyscraper, or to get both the ground and a plane in the same shot.

- Panoramas don't have to be of scenery. For instance, you can capture a wide painting in an art museum even if there is not enough space to back up and get it in one shot. Or you can capture everyone sitting around a dining table in one shot.

- If there are moving objects in your panorama, such as soccer players running on a field, you might not get a clean shot. Sometimes a player who is moving fast might appear twice in the same panorama.

Using Photo Booth

In addition to the basic picture-taking functionality of the Camera app, you can also use the included Photo Booth app to take more creative shots using one of eight special filters.

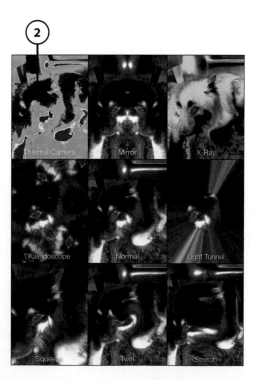

Photo Booth

1. Launch the Photo Booth app.

2. You see all the filters you can choose from. Tap one of the filters to select it. The screen changes to reflect the effect of that filter.

3. Tap the button at the bottom right to switch between the front and rear cameras.

4. Tap the button at the bottom left to return to the nine-filter preview.

5. Tap the shutter button at the bottom to take a picture.

6. Some filters also allow you to tap the live video image to adjust the filter. For instance, the Light Tunnel filter enables you to set the position of the center of the tunnel.

A Kind of Flash
When you take a picture with the camera on the front of the iPad, you get a kind of flash effect from the screen. It simply turns all white for a second. This helps in low-light situations.

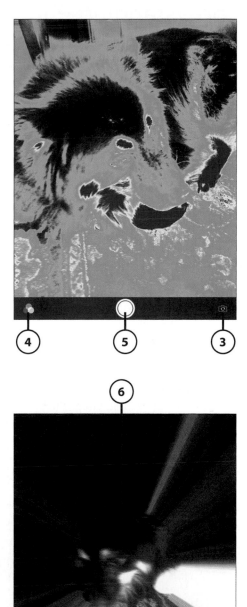

Understanding Photo Sources

Your iPad's Photos app can display photos from many different sources. You can then view them chronologically by Years, Collections, and Moments, which are covered in the next task. You can also organize them by albums that you create. Before we look at how to view your photos, it is important to understand where the photos come from. Here are all the possible sources:

- **Photos you take with your iPad's camera:** When you use the Camera app or the Photo Booth app to take a picture, it is added to your library with easy access through an album named Camera Roll.

- **Images from apps:** Many apps allow you to export images into your iPad's photo library. These photos are also available in the Photos app, and screen shots are included in this category. (Screen shots are covered later in this chapter.)

- **Synced from your computer:** iTunes on Mac and Windows computers can sync photos to your iPad. See "Syncing Photos" in Chapter 3, "Networking and Syncing." You can take pictures with a dedicated camera device, organize them on your computer, and then sync the ones you like to view on the iPad.

- **Transferred over a network:** You can use AirDrop on an iPod, iPhone, or Mac to send images to an iPad. You can also save some images you see on the web by tapping and holding over them, then selecting Save Image. You can save images attached to emails or messages. Sometimes third-party apps allow you to access images stored on other photo services and transfer these to your photo library as well.

- **iCloud Photo Library:** You can choose to store all your photos on Apple's cloud server and access them from all your iOS devices and Macs. When you use this option, you can no longer sync with iTunes on a computer because the two methods are mutually exclusive. You can turn this on in the Settings app, under Photos & Camera.

- **Photo Stream:** If you enable Photo Stream, every picture you take is automatically sent to iCloud's Photo Stream, where it also appears on your iPad, Mac, and even your Apple TV, if you have Photo Stream enabled on those devices. Think of this as a temporary email inbox for photos. Only the most recent 1,000 pictures from the last 30 days are stored in Photo Stream. You could take a picture on your iPhone and see it on your Mac and iPad, choosing to then move it to your main library if you want to keep it permanently. You can turn this on in the Settings app, under Photos & Camera.

- **iCloud Photo Sharing:** You can create iCloud photo albums and share them with others. Likewise, you can subscribe to someone else's shared album. Then you can view these shared album photos in the Photos app.

The big choice you need to make is whether to use iCloud Photo Library or sync photos using iTunes.

iCloud Photo Library is a great way to manage your photos as they will simply be available to you everywhere. But if you have a slow Internet connection at home, then you might want to stick with the old system of storing your photo library on your computer. (Although this might be a good excuse to call your service provider and get a faster connection.)

Browsing Your Photos

The Photos app on your iPad organizes your photos chronologically and breaks time into three levels: Years, Collections, and Moments. The photos taken on your iPad are combined with photos you synced from your computer or photos in your iCloud Photos Library. Let's take a tour of the Photos app to learn how to browse through your photos.

Photos

1. Launch the Photos app to view your photos.

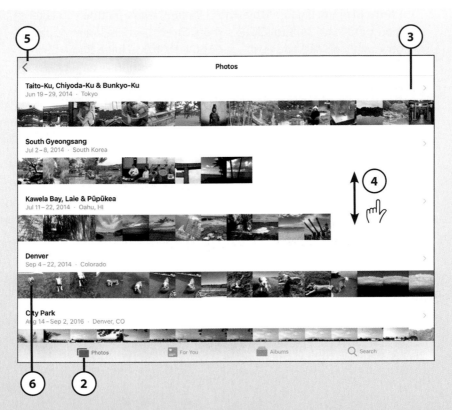

2. Tap Photos at the bottom to browse your photos.

3. You resume viewing your photos at the same level you were viewing them the last time you looked. The three levels are Years, Collections, and Moments. Which level you are at is indicated by the way the list of photos looks on the screen. In this case, the figure shows the middle level, Collections, which groups photos by sequential dates and nearby locations.

4. You can swipe vertically to scroll through your photos.

5. To move up a level, from Collections to Years or from Moments to Collections, tap the arrow in the upper-left corner. If you are viewing Collections, the label says Years to indicate that is the view you are moving back to.

6. Dig down to the next level by tapping one of the strips of photos. You can also tap and hold your finger over any photo until it pops out of the strip, and then release to jump right to viewing that photo.

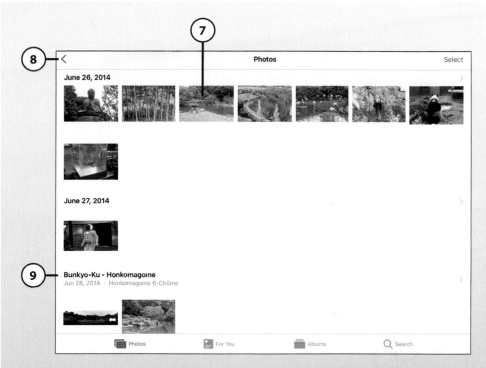

7. At the Moments level, you see the individual photos grouped with others that are the exact same location and date. Tap one to view it. (The next task covers viewing photos in more depth.) Note that Moments groupings are based both on time and location. So photos taken at a park in the afternoon and then at dinner later that day on the other side of town could be grouped into different Moments.

8. Tap the back arrow to go back up to the Collections level.

9. At the Moments or Collections level, tap any location name to go to a screen dedicated to that one moment.

10. The top of the screen shows a large title banner that fades through the pictures in the moment. Tap the Play button to start a full-screen slideshow. See "Viewing Photos as Memories" later in this chapter.

11. Below the banner are some of the pictures in the Moment. Tap one to view it.

12. Tap Show More to see all of the photos in a more uniform grid.

13. Swipe up to see more features on this screen.

14. The People section is a list of the people identified in the photos of this Moment. Tap one to view just those photos.

15.   The Related section includes other moments that are related to this one based on time or location.

16.   Tap the map to go into a map view of the moment.

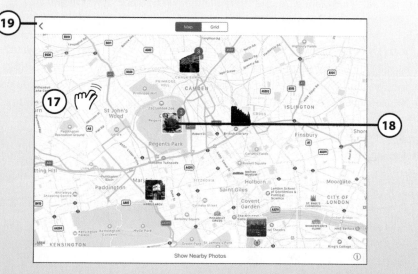

17.   The map resizes to contain all the photos in the Moments or Collections you are viewing. If the photos are all taken in the same city, you might get a city map. If they are taken across the world, you might see the whole planet. You can pinch to zoom, or tap and drag to move the map.

18.   Tap any single photo to view it, or tap a group of photos to see a screen that shows each one so you can scroll through them.

19.   Tap at the top left to return to Moments or Collections.

It's Not All Good

Where in the World Are You?

When you take pictures with a mobile phone like the iPhone, the location is automatically added to the photo. But most dedicated digital cameras, even expensive ones, do not have any GPS feature, so they don't know your location. iPads without a live Wi-Fi connection won't know, either. So your photo collection might have a lot of photos with no location information. These photos don't appear on maps and can't be accurately divided into Moments by location.

Searching Your Photos

Think back to a time before digital photos when you had to look in a physical photo album to find an old picture. You had to remember which album it was in and then flip through the pages to find it.

Until recently, finding a photo in your digital photo library wasn't much better. If you titled and tagged your photos, it was a bit easier. Using the People feature of Photos was a big plus, too. Now, though, the Photos app can actually identify objects in images. So you can search for something in a photo by typing the name of an object, and get results without ever having tagged or otherwise indicated that the object was in the photo.

1. In the Photos app, tap the Search button.

2. In addition to a Search field at the top of the screen, you see many suggestions for people, places, and categories. Tap any of these to search for that item.

3. Start typing a search term. You can use the names of people, locations, or a category. Hundreds of category terms are recognized. Examples include boat, bus, dog, tree, fence, house, water, hat… you get the idea. You might need to do a little trial and error to find a word that comes up with results.

4. As you type, some suggestions appear. The suggestions correspond to places, people, and categories found in your Photos library. You can tap any one to jump right to those search results. Notice the number of photos related to each suggestion is shown to the right. In this case, I typed *water* and that matched Waterloo, Water, Water Body, Waterfront, and Watercraft.

5. Alternatively, type the full term and tap Search to complete the search with the exact term you typed.

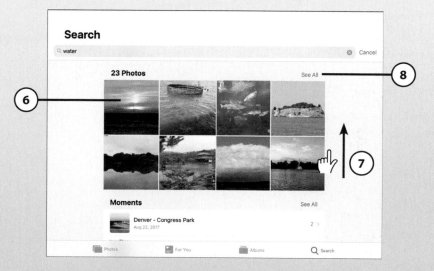

6. Tap any photo to view it.

7. Swipe up to see other matches, including entire Moments that match your search term.

8. Tap See All to see all photos that matched.

>>>*Go Further*

PHOTO SEARCH TIPS

Use these tips when you're searching your photos:

- This feature is very new and the entire concept of having computers recognize objects in photos is new, too. Don't expect perfect results, but do expect it to get better with each update to iOS.
- You can combine terms. Searching for *mountains water* returns photos that appear to have both mountains and water in them.
- You can also search for dates (*July 2015*), people (*Gary*), or places (*Colorado*). However, combining these in a single search gives mixed results.

Viewing Your Photos

Whether you are viewing a photo you tapped on at the Moments level, or you are viewing a photo in an album or from the Camera app, the interface is basically the same.

1. Tap in the middle of the photo to remove the buttons and text at the top and bottom of the screen so you can enjoy the photo. Tap again to bring the interface elements back.

2. Pinch out to zoom in on the photo. Once zoomed, you can tap and drag to see different areas of the photo.

3. When zoomed out to view the entire photo, you can swipe left or right to view the previous or next photo in the Moment or album.

4. Alternatively, you can tap or drag in the strip of photos at the bottom to move through the photos in the Moment or album.

5. Tap the Edit button to edit or adjust the photo. See "Editing and Adjusting Photos," earlier in this chapter.

6. Tap the Back icon to exit viewing this photo and return to the previous level, such as the album or Moment you were viewing. If you are viewing a photo from the cameras after taking a picture, this takes you back to the Camera app, plus there's an All Photos button to the right to open the Photos app.

7. Tap the Share button to share via AirDrop, email, social networks, and a variety of other methods. See the next section for more information about sharing.

>>>Go Further
ZOOM AND ROTATE

Here are a few tips on how to navigate your photos as you view them:

- Pinch or unpinch with two fingers to zoom out and in.
- Double-tap a photo to zoom back out to normal size.
- While a photo is at normal size, double-tap to zoom in on a spot of the photo.
- If you pinch in far enough, the picture closes, and you return to browsing mode.

Sharing Your Photos

You can share photos while viewing an individual photo, such as in step 7 of the previous task. You can also share from the Moments screen by tapping Share next to any photo.

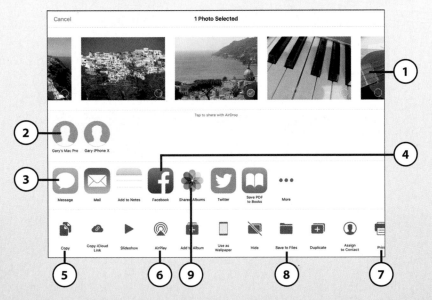

1. At the top of the Sharing screen, you see your selected photo—plus you can choose others in the same Moment or album to share. Tap any photo to include it. You see a check mark on photos that you have set to share.

2. You can share via AirDrop, sending the photo to another iOS or Mac user near you. See "Sharing with AirDrop" in Chapter 3.

3. You can send the photos using either the Messages or Mail apps.

4. You can also post directly to Facebook, Twitter, or Flickr, as long as you have configured these services in your Settings app.

5. You can copy a photo to use it in another app. You can also tap and hold in the middle of a photo while editing it, and select Copy.

6. You can use AirPlay to show the photo on an Apple TV connected to the same Wi-Fi network. See "AirPlay Mirroring with Apple TV" in Chapter 18, "iPad Accessories."

7. You can send the photo to a printer on your network. See "Printing from Your iPad" in Chapter 18.

8. You can export the photo to your iCloud Drive space, which puts it in your Files app and also into your iCloud Drive folder on your Mac. This is the iPad's equivalent to exporting the photo as a file. You can also select other locations accessible to your Files app, such as third-party cloud services.

9. You can use iCloud Photo Sharing to add the photo to an online shared album.

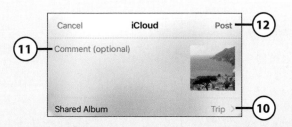

10. Set the online album where the photo should be placed. You're also given the chance to create a new album and to invite others, by email address, to see the album.

11. Add a comment that appears online with the photo.

12. Tap Post to send the photo to iCloud.

13. Tap Albums to see these online albums in the Photos app. You may need to swipe up to see the Shared Albums section. If you haven't shared an album before, the section won't be present yet.

14. You can create a new shared album from this screen by tapping the + button.

15. Or, to modify an existing shared album, tap to view it.

16. You see all the photos in that album. Tap a single photo to view it.

17. When looking at an individual photo, you can "like" the photo.

18. You can also add a comment. If you have been invited by someone else to share their album, then you can use steps 15–18 to view, like, and comment on their photos.

19. Tap the name of the album in the upper-left corner to go back to the previous screen.

20. Tap the blank space with the + sign to add more photos to the shared album. You can then browse your Photos list or other albums, or perform searches to find other photos to add.

21. While viewing a shared photo album that you have created, tap the People button to change the sharing options.

22. If you have invited others to share this album, you see their names here. You can also tap Invite People to add more people.

People   Slideshow   Select   (21)

Edit Shared Album

Invite People...   (22)

Subscribers Can Post

You and the people you invite can add photos and videos to this album.

Public Website   (23)

Share Link

Anyone can view this album at:

https://www.icloud.com/sharedalbum/#B0PGY8gBYnaM0R

Notifications

Show notifications when subscribers like, comment, or add photos or videos to this shared album.

Delete Shared Album

23. You can also turn on the Public Website option to let anyone view these photos. Then, tap the Share Link button to send people a link to the web page.

Results May Vary

You can share your photos in many ways, and it is likely that more ways will be added in the future. What you can use depends on what you have set up on your iPad. For instance, if you have Messaging and Twitter set up, you can use the Message and Tweet buttons to share using those services.

Working with Albums

Using the chronological Years/Collections/Moments views of the Photos app is a great way to find the photos you want to view. But, if you would rather organize your photos yourself, you can do so by creating albums.

You can make albums using the photo library software on your Mac, Photoshop Albums or Photoshop Elements on Windows, or file system folders on Mac and Windows. When you sync to your iPad with iTunes, you'll see these albums using the steps that follow. Or, if you are using iCloud Photo Library, you can create the albums on any device, and the albums also show up on all your other devices.

The important thing to realize about photo albums is that the photos aren't really *in* the album. Think of them as a list of references to photos, the same way a playlist in iTunes refers to songs stored in your music library.

A photo appears once in your photo library, and you can see it once in the Years/Collections/Moments views, but you can put a reference to that photo in multiple albums. For instance, you can have a photo appear in an album named "My Best Pictures" and also in an album named "Summer 2014." If you delete it from one or both, the photo is still in your library—it just doesn't happen to be in any album.

Viewing Albums

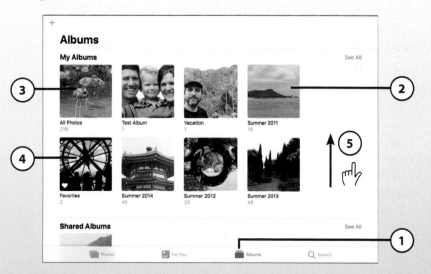

1. In the Photos app, tap Albums.
2. The Albums screen is a long list of albums—some are custom albums you have created, and some are preset albums that group together photos of the same type. The first section, My Albums, includes albums you have created.
3. All Photos is an album that simply shows every photo in your library.
4. Favorites is an album of every photo you have favorited by tapping the heart-shaped favorite button when viewing a photo.
5. You can swipe up to see more albums.

6. Tap People to see your photos grouped by the faces identified in the photos.

7. Tap Places to see your photos grouped by their locations. Naturally, only photos taken with a phone or other camera that tags photos with a location are in these groups.

8. You can also look at albums automatically compiled according to the type of photo. For instance, there may be albums for Videos, Selfies, Panoramas, and Screenshots. These kinds of albums appear in the list only if there is at least one photo of that type.

Getting Back to the Album

After you finish digging down into an album, you can go back to the list of albums by tapping the Back icon at the top left. But you also can pinch in all photos to group them in the middle of the screen and then release to move back to the albums list.

Creating Albums

You can create new albums on your iPad. If you are using iCloud Photo Library, these albums appear across all your devices. The process involves naming a new album and then selecting the photos to appear in the album.

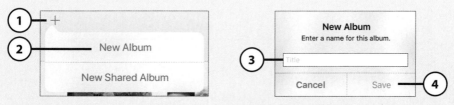

1. In the Photos app, tap Albums at the bottom to view your albums, and then tap the + button at the top left.

2. Select New Album.

3. Enter a name for the album.

4. Tap Save.

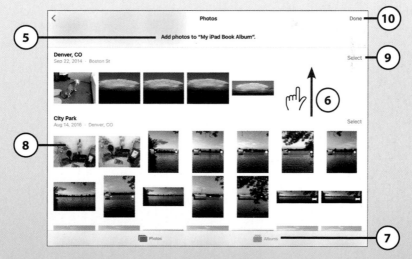

5. You see all your photos appear in the Moments view, just as they did in step 7 of the task "Browsing Your Photos," earlier in this chapter.

6. Tap and drag vertically to flip through your photos to locate the ones you want to include in this new album.

7. If you prefer Albums view, tap Albums to switch to that view.

8. Tap photos to add them to the album. Tap again to undo the selection.

9. Tap Select next to a Moment name to add that entire Moment to the album.

10. Tap Done when you have added all the photos you want to the album. You can always add more by viewing that album, tapping the Select button at the top, and then tapping the Add button at the top.

Creating a Slideshow

Another way to look at your photos is as a slideshow with music and transitions. You can quickly and easily create a slideshow with any group of photos in the Photos app that shows a Slideshow button at the top—for example, an album synced to, or that you created on, your iPad.

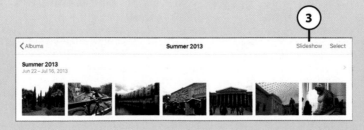

1. In the Photos app, tap Albums.

2. Tap an album to select it.

3. Tap the Slideshow button at the top of the album.

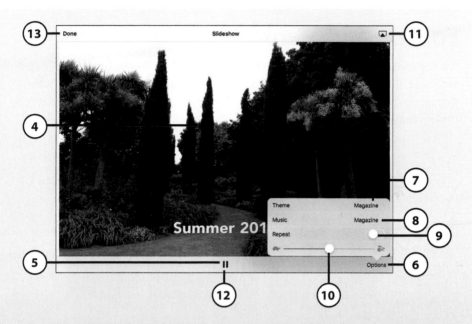

4. The slideshow immediately starts playing with default options. To customize it, first tap in the middle of the screen to bring up controls at the top and bottom.

5. Tap the Pause button to stop playback while you adjust the settings. The button changes to a Play button.

6. Tap Options at the bottom right.

7. Select from one of many themes for the slideshow.

8. Change the music to one of many presets, or use a song from iTunes.

9. Tap to set the slideshow to loop.

10. Use the slider to change the speed.

11. Slideshows can be played on your iPad's screen, or on any connected AirPlay video devices, such as an Apple TV connected to the same Wi-Fi network.

12. Tap the Play button that took the place of the Pause button to start the slideshow.

13. Tap Done to exit the slideshow.

Stopping a Slideshow

Tap anywhere on the screen to stop a slideshow. This takes you into the album. Start with the current photo. Then you can continue to browse that album normally swiping left or right and using the strip of thumbnails at the bottom.

For You and Memories

The For You section of the Photos app features automatically grouped collections called Memories, featured photos, and sharing suggestions. Memories is a Photos app feature that groups together photos taken at the same place and time. You can use these groups to play a different type of slideshow.

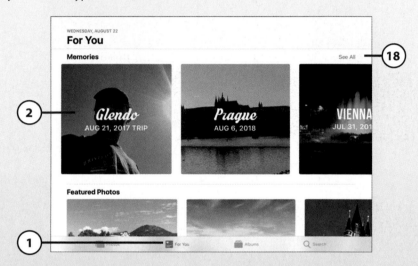

1. In the Photos app, tap the For You button to bring up the list of Memories, Featured Photos, and other items the Photos app is currently highlighting from your library. These items change daily. If none appear, you need to add more photos to your library for Memories to work.

2. Tap a memory to view it.

3. You can swipe up to see all the photos included in the memory, as well as people and places associated with the memory.

4. Tap the Play button on the large photo to start the Memories slideshow.

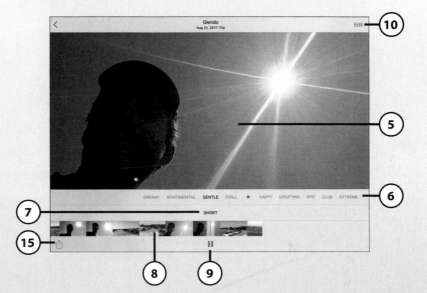

5. The slideshow starts playing. Tap in the center of the screen to bring up controls.

6. Slide this bar to change the mood of the slideshow by changing the music and transitions used.

7. Tap one of the length options to shorten or lengthen the slideshow. In this case there are only enough photos for the "short" option, but you may see "medium" and "long."

8. You can see the photos in the slideshow, and tap and drag them to move the slideshow forward or backward.

9. Tap the Play/Pause button to start or stop the slideshow.

10. Tap the Edit button to customize the Memories slideshow further.

Creating Memories from Moments

You can create a Memory from any Moment in the main Photos view. As you are viewing the Moment, scroll all the way to the bottom and tap the Add to Memories button.

11. Tap the items on the left to edit them: the title, music, duration, and even the list of photos and videos to include.

12. With Title selected on the left, you can edit the title and subtitle. If you select Music, you can choose the music, even using something from your Music library.

13. You can also edit the font used by the title.

14. Tap Done when you finish changing things and are ready to save the changes.

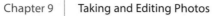

15. You can share the slideshow as a video.

16. Since Memories change on a regular basis, if you want to keep the Memory around for future use, tap the … button.

17. Tap Add to Favorite Memories.

18. You are now able to find this Memory by tapping See All on the For You screen. Then look for the Favorites button at the top right.

19. If you ever want to remove a memory, you can use the Delete Memory button.

It's Not All Good

Sharing Slideshows

Want to share a slideshow via a social network or YouTube? You can, but not by using the Photos app's Slideshow feature. Instead, use iMovie. See "Adding Photos to Your Video in iMovie" in Chapter 10, "Recording Video," to learn how to make a video that is a series of photos. See "Combining Clips in iMovie" in that same chapter to learn how to share a movie. You can also use one of many slideshow and photo-sharing apps from the App Store.

Marking Up Photos

In addition to editing photos to adjust color and light and to fix imperfections, you can also draw on photos with the Photos app Markup tool.

1. While viewing a photo, tap the Edit button.

2. Tap the … button.

3. Tap Markup.

4. To draw on the image, select one of the three drawing tools on the left. You can also select the fourth tool, an eraser, to erase drawing marks.

5. Select a color. You can choose one of the six colors shown, or tap the color wheel to choose from a larger palette.

6. Use your finger to draw.

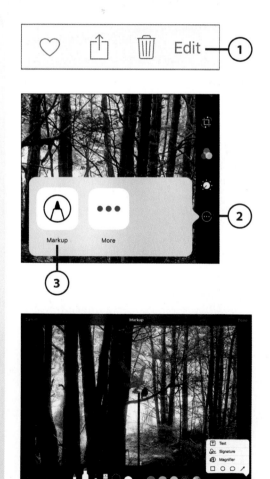

7. The Lasso tool lets you circle marks you have made on the image and then drag them around. It won't affect the photo itself, just the lines you have drawn.

8. Tap the + button to bring up more tools.

9. Tap to add a text field on the image and type some text. This is great for adding captions or watermarks.

10. Tap Signature to draw your signature on the screen, and then place it on the image. For example, you can take a photo of a document, and then you can sign it and send the signed version on to someone via email, messages, and so on.

11. Tap Magnifier to place a circle on the image, which you can move to magnify and draw attention to an area of the photo.

12. Tap any of the shape tools to draw that shape on the photo.

13. Tap Done to finish and leave the marks on the photo. Like with other editing tools, you can always Revert to Original to get rid of the marks and go back to the original photo.

Capturing the Screen

You can capture the entire iPad screen and send it to your Photos app. This feature is useful if you want to save what you see to an image for later.

1. Make sure the screen shows what you want to capture. Try the Home screen, as an example.

2. Press and hold the Wake/Sleep button and Home button at the same time. The screen flashes and you hear a camera shutter sound (unless you have the volume turned down).

3. An image of the screen capture appears at the bottom left for a few seconds. During this time, you can tap the image to go directly to editing it with the markup tools. Then tap the Done button at the top of the screen, which gives you the option to Save or Delete the screenshot.

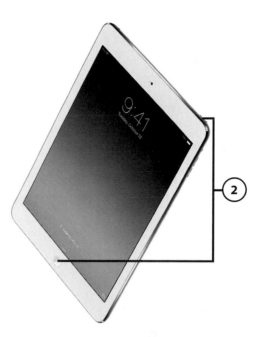

4. Go to the Photos app.

5. Tap Albums and then go to the All Photos album, or the Screenshots album listed under Media Types.

6. The last image in this album should be your new screen capture. Tap it to open it.

7. The screenshot displays just like any other photo. You can edit it or delete it with the buttons on the top right.

8. Tap the Share icon to email the photo or copy it to use in another application. Or you can leave the photo in your photo library for future use.

Photos

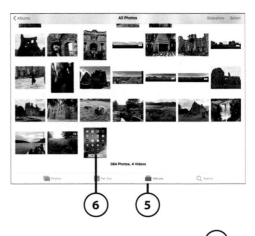

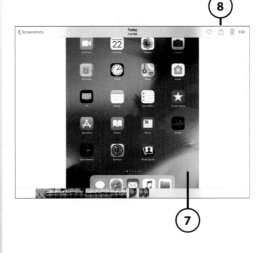

Make video calls
with FaceTime

Record video with your
iPad's cameras

Put together movies from
your video clips
and photos

In this chapter, you use the Camera, Photo Booth, and iMovie apps to shoot and edit video with your iPad. You also use the FaceTime app to make a video call.

→ Shooting Video
→ Trimming Video Clips
→ Editing in iMovie
→ Making Video Calls with FaceTime

Recording Video

You can record video using either of the two cameras on your iPad. The primary app for doing this is the Camera app.

In addition, you can edit video with the iMovie app. This app, which you can download from Apple in the App Store, lets you combine clips and add transitions, titles, and audio.

You can also use the cameras on your iPad to video chat with someone on another iPad, an iPhone, iPod touch, or a Mac using the FaceTime app.

Shooting Video

If you simply want to record something that is happening, you can do it with the Camera app.

Camera

1. Launch the Camera app. Also, turn your iPad sideways so you are shooting horizontal video, like you are used to seeing on TV and in movies. Your iPad can shoot in both vertical and horizontal orientations, but horizontal is better for playback on most screens.

2. Switch the camera mode to video by tapping this area and sliding the words "Time-Lapse, Slo-Mo, Video, Photo, Square, and Pano" so that "Video" is in yellow.

3. If needed, you can toggle between the rear and front cameras. Remember that the rear camera is much better quality than the front camera, so use the rear one whenever possible.

4. Optionally, tap in the image to set the best point for the exposure setting.

5. Tap the Record button to start recording. While you are recording, the red dot flashes and the length of the recording shows on the right side above the button. Tap the same button to stop recording.

6. Tap the image thumbnail to see your video when you are done.

7. You are now viewing an item in your photo library, the same place as you were in Chapter 9, "Taking and Editing Photos." But the interface looks different when you have a video instead of a still photo. Tap the Play button to watch the video.

8. Tap the Share button to email the video, send via a text message, or upload it directly to a service like YouTube, Facebook, or Vimeo. You can also stream it to an AirPlay device on your network, such as an Apple TV.

9. Tap the trash can to delete the video.

10. When you are done viewing your video, tap the Back button to return to the Camera app to shoot another video.

It's Not All Good

Emailing Compresses the Video

Video with the rear camera is shot at a resolution of 1920x1080. But when you email a video, it's usually compressed to a much smaller size. This is good because you won't be sending a massive video file, using your bandwidth and the bandwidth of the recipient. But don't use email to save your videos to your computer. Instead, use AirDrop or, if you use iCloud Photo Library, your video is stored there and appears on your Mac automatically.

>>>*Go Further*

TIME-LAPSE PHOTOGRAPHY AND SLO-MO VIDEO

A second video mode is Time-Lapse. Instead of filming video at a fast rate of 30 frames per second, your iPad can take video at a much slower rate, starting at around 1 frame per second. This allows you to capture slow-moving events like a sunset or a flower opening its petals.

To make a good time-lapse video, you need to find a way to keep your iPad completely stationary. Alternatively, you could take a moving time-lapse by having a passenger hold the iPad pointed out the front window of your car while driving.

With time-lapse, a 10-minute period of time unfolds in 30 seconds. If you want more control over the exact rate of the time-lapse, search for "time lapse" in the App Store—you'll find all sorts of third-party time-lapse photography apps that allow you to control the frame rate and much more.

Slo-Mo is the opposite of time-lapse and is only available on more recent iPad models. It takes video at a high frame rate, and then shows the start and end of the video at normal speed, whereas the middle of the video is in slow motion. You can adjust the portion of the video that is shown in slow motion using a slider control that appears just above the trimming control, which is discussed in the next section.

Trimming Video Clips

While viewing a video in your photo library, you can also trim it to cut some unneeded footage from the start and end of the video.

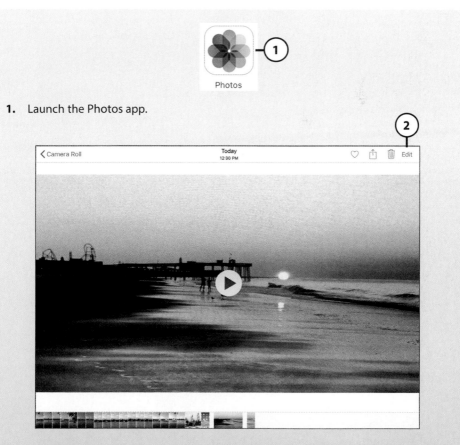

1. Launch the Photos app.

2. Find a video you want to trim and view it. Then tap the Edit button at the upper right. Notice that in the previous task, after initially taking the video with the Camera app, you also get that same button so you can go right from shooting video to trimming it.

3. You see a timeline of sorts at the bottom of the screen.

4. Drag the left side of the timeline to the right to trim from the start of the video.

5. Drag the right side of the timeline to the left to trim from the end of the video.

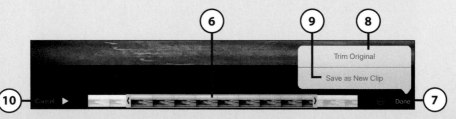

6. The section you have selected is outlined in yellow. Areas to the left and right of this area will be removed.

7. Tap the Done button.

8. Tap Trim Original to replace the video with the trimmed version.

9. Tap Save as New Clip to keep the original, and also save your trimmed version as a separate clip.

10. You can tap Cancel to quit without trimming if you want.

Editing in iMovie

The trimming functionality of the Camera and Photos apps gives you the basic ability to edit a video clip, but you can go a lot further if you download the iMovie app from Apple. Although it's not a full-featured editor like you might have on your computer, you can combine clips, add titles and transitions, and produce a short video from your clips.

iMovie Editing Without Leaving the Photos App

You can add extensions to the Photos app that allow you to edit videos without leaving the app. Extensions come with apps like iMovie when you install them. After you have iMovie, you get a small button with three dots on the Photos app video edit screen. Tap that button, and then tap the More button to switch on the extension.

After it is switched on, you can tap the small, three-dot button when editing a video to enter a special iMovie editing screen. This screen enables you to trim, apply filters, add music, and add titles. So, if you just want to do something quick to a single video clip, using the extension is the way to go.

iMovie

1. Launch the iMovie app. Turn your iPad to look at the screen horizontally. iMovie is a little easier to use in that orientation.

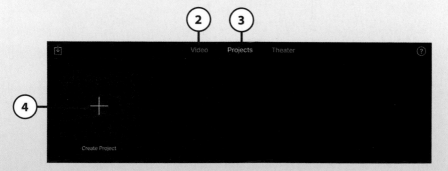

2. Tap Video to view your video clips.

3. Projects allow you to combine clips into longer movies with transitions and titles. Tap Projects to see a list of your projects.

4. Tap the + Create Project button to create a new project.

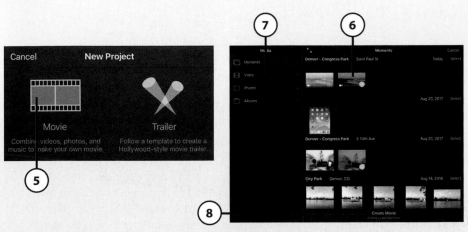

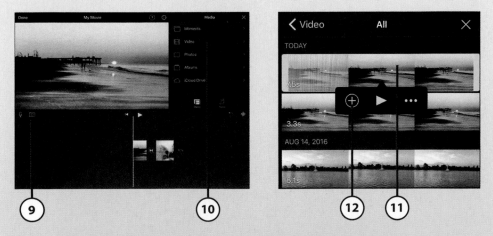

5. Tap Movie.

6. Tap items (both videos and photos) to add them to your movie project.

7. You can switch between all Moments in your Photos library, just Video, just Photos, or viewing by Album. Use whichever view you prefer for finding media for your project.

8. Tap Create Movie when you are done. In this example, I'm not adding any media at this stage. You can add media after you have started the project.

9. Tap the Camera button to record a new video clip right here and now.

10. Tap either Moments, Video, Photos, or Albums to start looking for items to use in your project. Tap iCloud Drive to take media files directly from your iCloud Drive storage space.

11. Dig down into your library and find the video you want to add. Tap it.

12. Tap the + button to add the video to your movie project.

13. Continue to add more clips. Each one will be appended to the end of the project.

14. The line indicates the current position of the video.

15. The preview area shows you the image at the current position.

16. Drag the project timeline left and right to scroll through it.

17. Pinch in and out to shrink or enlarge the timeline.

18. Tap Play to play the video in the preview area. If the line is at the end of the video, it jumps back to the start of the video first.

19. Tap and hold a clip until it "pops" off the timeline; then you can drag it to a different part of the project timeline.

20. Tap the Done button when you are done editing. There is no need to "save" your project—the current state of the project is always saved.

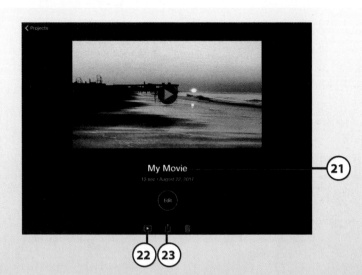

21.   Tap the name of the project to edit the name.

22.   Tap the Play button to view the finished project.

23.   Tap the Share button to save the video to your photo library, send it via email or Messages, or upload it to YouTube, Vimeo, Facebook, and a variety of other video services.

Best Way to Share with Friends?

While it might seem to be a good idea to simply email a video to your friends, remember that video files are usually very large. Even if you have the bandwidth to upload them, your friends need the bandwidth to download them. Some might use services that have restrictions on how large email attachments can be.

So, the video-sharing options in iMovie are better for all concerned. You can upload to your Facebook or YouTube account and even set the video to "private" or "unlisted." Then just let a few friends know about it with the link in an email instead of a huge file attachment.

Editing Transitions

Between each clip in your iMovie project is a transition. You can choose between a direct cut (no transition), a cross-dissolve transition, or a special theme transition. But first, you must select a theme.

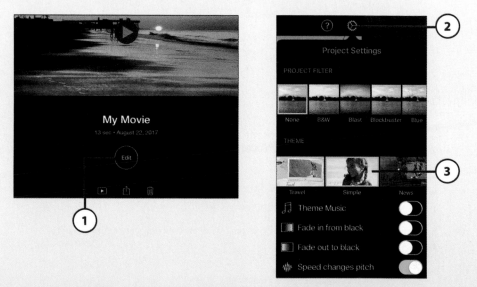

1. Tap the Edit button to open up the project you created in the previous task.

2. Tap the Settings button to select a theme.

3. Swipe through the themes and choose one.

4. Tap one of the transition icons that appear between each clip. This should bring up the Transition Settings menu along the bottom of the screen.

5. Tap None (the first one) if you want no transition at all and just want one clip to cut right into the other.

6. Tap the star icon to use the special theme transition. These vary depending on which theme you choose.

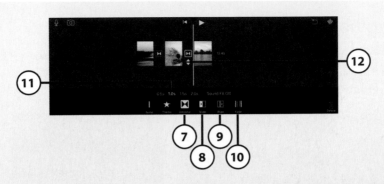

7. Tap Dissolve if you want one clip to fade into the other. This is the most common transition for most purposes.

8. Tap Slide for a transition that moves the next clip over the current one. When you tap this transition, you see some other icons appear above it. Pick one for the direction of the slide.

9. Tap Wipe for a transition that wipes and replaces one clip with the other, starting at one edge. You can pick the direction here as well.

10. Tap Fade for a transition that fades out and then fades in the next clip. You can choose to fade to black or white.

11. Tap a duration for the transition.

12. Tap the triangles below the transition button to expand into a precision editor.

13. Move the transition area to select how you want the two clips to overlap during the transition. To make it easier to move the yellow bars, you might want to pinch out to zoom in for a closer look at the area.

14. Tap the triangles to leave the precision edit mode.

Adding Photos to Your Video

You can also add photos from your Camera Roll or any album on your iPad. You can just use a series of photos in a video, or mix photos and video clips.

1. Continuing with the previous example, scroll the timeline all the way to the left.

2. Tap Photos in the Media area to find a photo to insert.

3. Tap the photo you want to insert in your project.

4. The photo appears in the timeline at the current position. Tap it to select it.

5. Tap and drag the yellow bars to change the duration of the photo in the timeline. It starts with a default of 5 seconds. But, for example, you could increase it to 10 seconds.

6. The photo will be animated, starting at one zoom and pan location and ending at another. This is called the Ken Burns effect. Tap the Start button that appears in the preview area. Then adjust the photo by pinching, zooming, and dragging to get it just as you like. For instance, pinch in so the photo fits into the frame. This is the start position of the animation.

7. Tap the End button to set the end position for the picture. For instance, unpinch to zoom in on a specific area.

8. Tap the Ken Burns Enabled/Disabled button to turn off this animation effect and have the photo appear as a static image instead.

9. Tap outside the photo in the timeline when you finish adjusting both the start and end positions.

10. Slide the timeline back and forth to preview how the movement in the picture will work.

You can continue to add pictures just as you would add video clips. Add as many as you like. You can even create a slideshow of just photos without ever shooting a single second of video footage.

>>>Go Further
GETTING CREATIVE WITH PICTURES

You can even create a video slideshow without any photos. For example, you could use one of the drawing programs mentioned in Chapter 16, "Must-Have Apps," such as Autodesk SketchBook, Brushes Redux, ArtStudio, or Adobe Illustrator Draw, to create images with text and drawings on them. Create a series to illustrate an idea or story. Then bring them together as a series of pictures in an iMovie project. Add music and a voiceover to make something very interesting.

Adding Video Titles

You can also add titles that overlay clips or photos in iMovie. Like the transitions, the style of the titles depends on the theme you are using.

1. Tap a clip to select it.
2. Tap Titles to select a title style.

3. Tap a title style. As you do so, a preview appears in the preview area.

4. Tap one of the text field areas in the preview to bring up the keyboard and enter text.

>>>Go Further
MUSIC AND VOICEOVERS

You can also do a lot with the audio in iMovie. You can add any song from your iPad's iTunes collection to the video as the background track. There are also a number of theme music tracks included that you can use.

You can also add from a collection of sound effects the same way. However, sound effects can appear at any point in your movie, whereas music covers the entire span of the video.

You can also have four audio tracks: the audio attached to the video, background music, sound effects, and a voiceover.

To learn how to use all the additional features of iMovie, look for the Help button at the bottom-left corner of the projects screen. This brings up complete documentation for the app.

Making Video Calls with FaceTime

Another major use of the video cameras is FaceTime. This is Apple's video-calling service. You can make video calls between any devices that have FaceTime, including recent iPhones, iPod touches, iPads, and Macs. As the number of people with FaceTime increases, this app becomes more and more useful.

All that's required to make a FaceTime call is a free account. You can use your existing Apple ID or create a new one. You can also assign alternative email addresses to be used as FaceTime "phone numbers" that people can use to contact you via FaceTime.

Wi-Fi Preferred

You still need to be connected to the Internet with a Wi-Fi connection. Some mobile carriers do support FaceTime calls with their iPad data plans. If you have an iPad data plan with a wireless carrier, contact your provider for details.

Setting Up FaceTime

Settings

1. Launch the Settings app.

2. Tap FaceTime on the left.

3. Turn on FaceTime if it isn't already on.

4. An Apple ID is needed for FaceTime even if you don't plan to use that same email address with FaceTime calls. If you haven't used FaceTime before, you will be prompted to enter your Apple ID and password.

5. This list contains email addresses others can use to reach you via a FaceTime call. By default, your Apple ID email address will be here. But you can add another one and even remove your Apple ID email address if you never want to use that for FaceTime.

6. The Caller ID represents your default email address used to place FaceTime calls. It is what others see when you call them. You see this if you have two or more email addresses assigned to your Apple ID account.

7. If you also have an iPhone and it is set to the same Apple ID, you can turn on Calls from iPhone. When your iPhone rings with a FaceTime video or voice call, your iPad also rings, and you are able to take the call on either the iPad or the iPhone.

Multiple Email Addresses

By using different email addresses for different iOS devices, you can more easily specify which device you are calling. For instance, if you and your spouse both have iPhones, and you share an iPad, you can give the iPad a different email address (maybe a free email account). That way you can specify which device you want to call.

Placing Video Calls with FaceTime

After you have your account set up in FaceTime, you can place and receive calls.

1. Launch the FaceTime app.

2. The left side of the screen shows a list of people previously called. You can tap one of them to call them again.

3. Alternatively, tap the + button to call someone else.

4. Tap the + button to call someone in your contacts.

5. Alternatively, type the email address or iPhone phone number of someone to call them.

6. You can also type a name and you will get a list of suggestions from your contacts that matches. You can tap one of those suggestions to make a call.

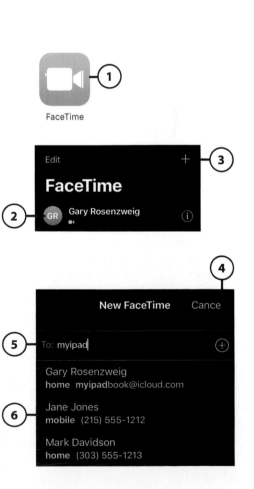

7. After you finish typing an ID or select a name, choose whether you're making an audio or video FaceTime call. Choose Audio if you only want to speak to the other party.

8. Choose Video to use FaceTime to start a video chat.

9. Wait while the call is placed. You hear ringing. You can tap the X button to cancel the call before you connect.

10. After the other party has answered the call, you can see both his image filling the whole screen and your image in a corner. You can drag your image to any of the four corners.

11. Tap the screen to bring up the controls while you're talking.

12. Tap the Mute button to mute your microphone.

13. Tap the X button to end the call.

14. Tap the … button to bring up more options.

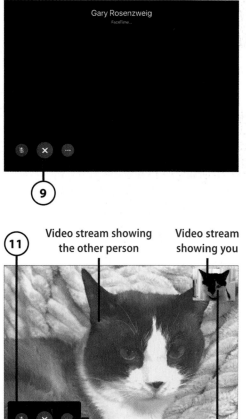

Video stream showing the other person

Video stream showing you

15. The Flip button switches between the iPad's two cameras. This way you can show the view in front of you instead of your face to the other person.

16. You can switch to sending messages in the Messages app. The FaceTime video conversation still continues in a smaller window while you send messages. This allows you to send text, pictures, files, and other message content while using FaceTime.

17. You can mute the other person.

18. You can turn off your camera for a moment of privacy.

19. You can also see some information about your current conversation.

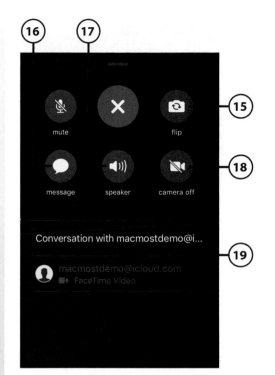

Two-Way Street

To place a FaceTime call, the recipient also needs to have FaceTime set up, of course. If you try to place a call and they do not have FaceTime, you get a message telling you so. It might be that they have simply not given you the correct email address to use for them for FaceTime calls.

Receiving Video Calls with FaceTime

After you have a FaceTime account, you can receive calls as well. Make sure you have set up FaceTime by following the steps in the "Setting Up FaceTime" task earlier in this chapter. Then it is a matter of just waiting to receive a call from a friend.

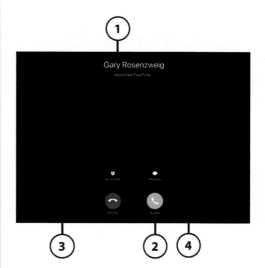

1. If you aren't currently using your iPad, it rings using the ringtone you choose in Settings, Sounds. When you pick up your iPad, you see something similar to the Lock screen, but with a live feed from your camera (so you can see if you look good enough to video chat) and the caller's name at the top.

2. Tap the Accept button to wake up your iPad and go immediately into the call. If you are using your iPad at the time the call comes in, FaceTime launches and you get a screen with two buttons. The screen still shows your camera's image and the name of the caller.

3. You also have the option to dismiss the call. You can do this by simply pressing the Wake/ Sleep button at the top of your iPad. Or, you can tap the Remind Me button, which dismisses the call and sets a reminder for one hour later so you can call the person back.

4. You can also tap the Message button to dismiss the call and send a polite text message to the caller.

5. Choose a message from the list.

6. Alternatively, tap Custom to type a message.

7. After the conversation starts, tap the screen to bring up controls.

8. Tap this button to mute your microphone.

9. Tap End to end the call.

10. Tap ... to access more functions, as described in the previous task.

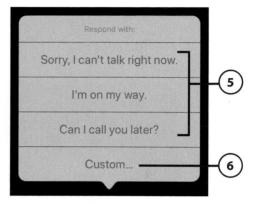

Ring Ring

Remember that you can set your ringtone in the Settings app under Sounds. You can even set the volume for rings to be unaffected by the volume controls on the side of your iPad. That way you don't miss a call because you left the volume turned down.

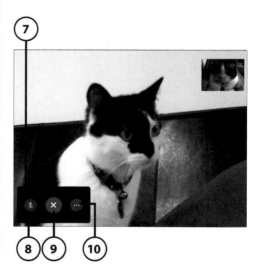

>>>Go Further

SO WHAT IF IT DOESN'T WORK?

FaceTime is set up to be simple. It just works. Except when it doesn't. There are no network settings to fiddle with. So the problem usually lies in the Wi-Fi router at either end of the call. If someone has security on their modem or Wi-Fi router, then it could be interfering with the call. See this document at Apple's site for some FaceTime troubleshooting tips:

https://support.apple.com/en-us/HT204168.

Create and edit word
processing documents
with Pages

In this chapter, you begin to get work done on the iPad by using Pages to create and format documents.

→ Creating a New Document
→ Styling and Formatting Text
→ Creating Lists
→ Inserting Images
→ Document Setup
→ Sharing and Printing Documents

Writing with Pages

The iPad is great as a personal media device, with your music, pictures, and videos. But it can also be used to get some work done. If you write for work or leisure, you'll want to download the Pages app from the App Store. Pages is a basic word processor, which you can use to write anything from short essays to long novels. You can also use images and formatting tools to build simple reports and newsletters.

Word Processing Alternatives

Microsoft Word: Although many apps will display Word documents, and a few allow you to edit Word documents, it is worth getting the official Microsoft Word app if you are already an Office 365 user. However, if you don't subscribe to Microsoft's Office 365 cloud service, then you won't be able to really use the app.

Google Docs: Google also has a suite of office tools that are usually accessed in a web browser. But they have an iPad app that lets you access and work on your documents directly.

iA Writer: This is a word processor designed for simplicity. The idea is to let you focus on writing, not styles and formatting.

Creating a New Document

Let's start off simple. The most basic use of Pages is to create a new document and enter some text.

1. Tap the Pages app icon on the Home screen.

Pages

2. If this is the first time you have run Pages, you go through a series of screens welcoming you to Pages and asking if you want to set up iCloud as the storage space for Pages documents. This is the best way to use Pages, Numbers, Keynote, and other apps. All of your documents will sync with all of your iOS and Mac devices, so you will have one collection of documents available everywhere. If you have worked in Pages before, you can skip to step 5.

3. The next screen asks if you want to create a new document right away. Instead, tap Use iCloud to go to the documents screen that lists all your iCloud documents. If this is your first time using Pages with iCloud, then it shows that you have no documents.

Welcome to Pages

The most beautiful word processor ever designed for a mobile device.

The Search for Perfect Color

Continue

iCloud for Pages

iCloud keeps your documents up to date on all your devices. And you can edit them at iCloud.com from a Mac or PC browser.

Later   Use iCloud

4. Tap My Documents.

5. Tap Create Document.

6. You are then faced with the template choices display. You can scroll vertically to see more. Tap the Blank template to go into the main editing view.

7. Type some sample text in the document just to get the feel for entering text.

8. Return to your documents list by tapping Documents.

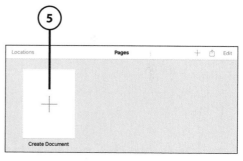

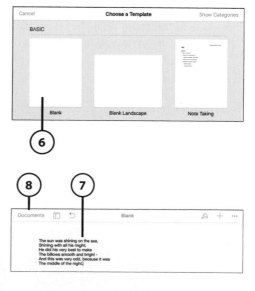

9. You can now see the new document. Tap the name of the document, Blank, to assign a proper name to it.

10. Tap the document to open it later to continue working with it.

11. Tap Edit to move into Edit mode where you can delete or duplicate any selected document.

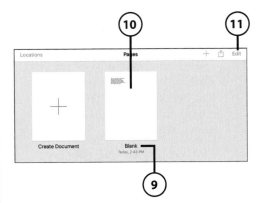

A Real Keyboard

If you plan on using Pages on your iPad often, you might want to invest in a physical keyboard for your iPad. You can use the Apple Wireless keyboard or almost any Bluetooth keyboard. Apple also has a version of the iPad dock that includes a keyboard. See Chapter 18, "iPad Accessories," for details.

Styling and Formatting Text

One of the most basic things you'll need to do in a word processor is to change the style and format of text. This example shows how to use the built-in paragraph styles of Pages, how to set the font and style of text, and how to set text alignment.

1. Create a new document and type some text. In this example, the first line is the title of a poem, the second is the author's name, and the rest is the body of the poem.

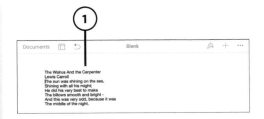

2. Tap in the first line of text to place the blinking cursor there. It doesn't matter where in the line of text the cursor appears—you are about to set the paragraph style, which applies to an entire line of text.

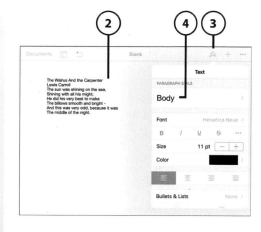

3. Tap the paintbrush button. This brings up controls to adjust the appearance of text.

4. The Body style is indicated under Paragraph Style. Tap it to choose a new style.

5. Tap Title to assign this style to the line of text.

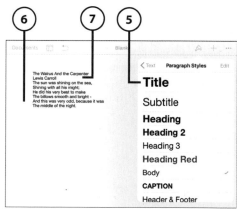

6. Tap outside the controls to dismiss them.

7. Place the cursor in the second line of text and repeat steps 3–5, but this time apply the Subtitle style to the second line.

8. To style the remaining text, you need to select it. Double-tap any word in the text so the word is highlighted in blue and has selection markers on the side. Then drag the selection markers so the entire set of lines is selected.

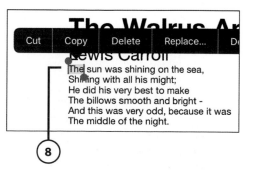

9. The highlighted area should now encompass all the lines.

10. Tap the paintbrush button.

11. Tap the + button next to the size of the font several times to increase the size of the font.

12. Tap the color chip next to the word Color.

13. Since the text is currently black, you see black, white, and gray text colors. The current color has a check mark.

14. Tap Color to view a color palette.

15. Select a color.

16. Tap Text to return to the previous set of controls.

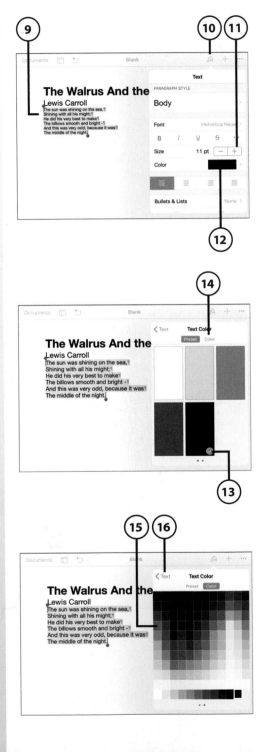

17. Tap the font name.

18. Select a different font for this text. You can drag the list up and down to see all of the available fonts.

19. Tap outside the controls to dismiss them.

20. Select all the text, including the title and author lines. You're going to center all this text.

21. You could use the alignment buttons in the style tools, but instead use the handy buttons that appear right above the keyboard at the bottom of the screen. Tap the Alignment button there.

22. A menu of alignment settings appears. Tap Center to center all the text.

Notice that there are two ways to access most style and alignment settings in Pages. The first way is to tap the paintbrush button at the top of the screen and then go to the Styles section of those controls. The second is to use the toolbar that appears above the keyboard.

You can also access the basic text styles of bold, italic, and underline using either method.

Undo Mistakes

At the top of the Pages screen, there is an Undo button. Use that to undo the last action you took—whether it is typing some text or changing styles. You can use Undo multiple times to go back several steps.

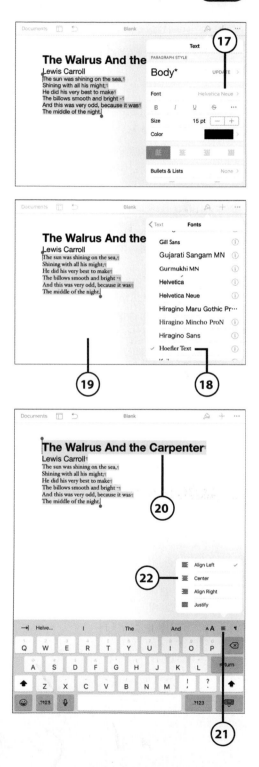

>>>Go Further

NO CUSTOM PARAGRAPH STYLES

It would be nice to define your own Title, Subtitle, and Body styles. Pages for iOS doesn't have any way to do this. You are stuck with the predefined paragraph styles, and you need to set your own font, size, and format if you don't like these.

One way around that works if you are a Mac user and use Pages on your Mac. There, you can alter and create new paragraph styles. Then when you save the document in iCloud and open it in Pages for iOS, you see those paragraph styles.

You can also select text in Pages for iOS, tap the Style option in the context controls that appear above the selection, and select Copy Style. Then you can repeat the process with another selection and select Paste Style. This is a quick way to take specific styles and formatting from one piece of text and apply it to others.

Creating Lists

You can easily create lists in Pages, just like in a normal word processor.

1. Create a new document in Pages using the Blank template.

2. Type a word that could be the first item in a list. Don't tap Return on the keyboard.

3. Tap the paintbrush button on the toolbar.

4. Tap Bullets & Lists.

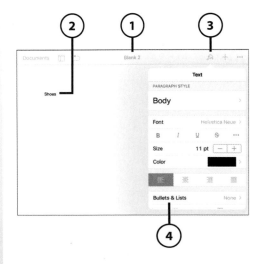

5. Tap the Bullet option to turn the text you just typed into the first item in a bulleted list.

6. Tap outside the controls to dismiss them.

7. Use the on-screen keyboard to tap Return and type several more lines. Tapping Return always creates a new line in the list. Tapping Return a second time ends the list formatting.

8. Select the entire list.

9. Tap the paintbrush button.

10. Tap Bullets & Lists.

11. Tap Numbered to change the list to a numbered list.

12. Tap outside the controls to dismiss them.

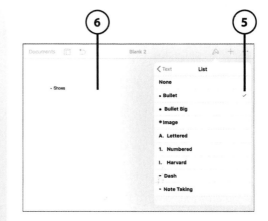

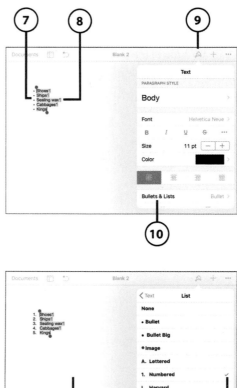

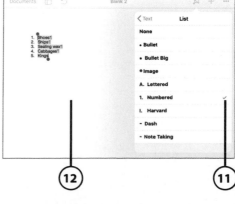

13. Tap one line of the list to place the cursor in it.

14. Tap the paintbrush icon again.

15. Tap the Move Right button that is right under the Bullets & Lists item to indent the line and create a sublist. You can create sublists as you type or by selecting lines and using the arrow buttons to format after you type.

16. Alternatively, you can use these buttons in the toolbar above the keyboard to indent items in the list without bringing up the paint-brush controls. Tap here to bring up a menu that lets you Indent, Outdent, or add another Tab character.

Inserting Images

You can place images into your Pages documents. You can even wrap text around the images.

1. Start with a document that already has some text in it. Tap to place the cursor where you want to insert the image.

2. Tap the + button.

3. Select the Pictures icon to insert a picture, and give Pages permission to access your media (if this is the first time you've inserted a picture).

4. You see a list of sources. Tap Photo or Video to browse your Photos app library for an image. Find the image in that album and tap it. Then tap outside the controls to dismiss them. You could also use other sources, such as Insert from, which enables you to find an image saved among your iCloud Drive files.

5. Tap the image to select it.

6. You can delete the image with the context menu that appears.

7. Drag any of the blue dots around the edges of the image to resize it.

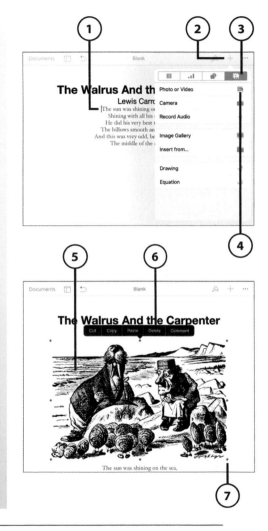

But I Don't Want To Use a Photo

You can insert any image that lives in your photo library. But, it doesn't have to be a photograph you took. You can import images and clipart from the web, email messages, and other apps. For instance, in Safari if you tap and hold an image, you get the option to Save Image. This puts it in your photo library, and you can now insert it into a Pages document. You can also use AirDrop to send images from other iOS devices or Macs.

8. Double-tap the image to scale and mask it.

9. Use the slider to resize the image. Notice that as you enlarge the image, the parts outside the visible area are dimmed. This gives you an idea of which parts of the image will be visible after you are done scaling.

10. You can drag and position the image so a different area is visible.

11. Tap Done when you are finished.

12. With the image selected, tap the paintbrush button.

13. Tap Style.

14. Choose a frame style.

15. Use Border, Style, Scale, and Shadow to further customize the frame.

16. Tap Arrange.

17. Change the text wrapping setting to Around to make sure the text wraps around the image.

18. Tap outside the controls to dismiss them.

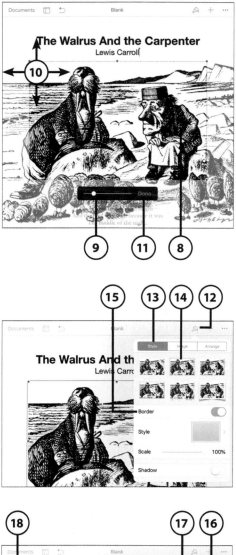

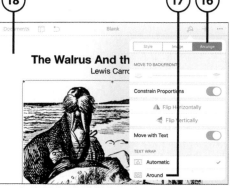

19. Wrapping text around images works well with multiple columns of text. So, make the text layout two columns so the text wraps around the image. Select all the text except the title and author line.

20. Tap the paintbrush button.

21. Scroll up to get to the Columns setting.

22. Increase the number of columns to two.

23. Notice that the text now wraps around the image on both sides. Also notice that you only converted the paragraphs of the poem to two columns; the title and author lines are still a single column.

Rearranging Images

After you place an image in your document, you can drag it around and resize it as much as you want. Pages automatically snaps the edges of the image to the margins and center lines of the page as you drag it around.

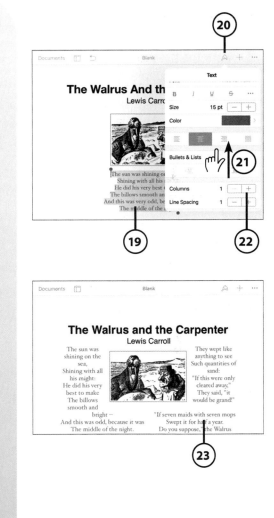

>>>Go Further

SHAPES, TABLES, AND CHARTS

In addition to inserting images, you can also add three other types of graphic elements: shapes, tables, and charts. With Shapes, you can choose from a variety of types, such as rectangles, circles, arrows, and stars. Each shape can have a different border and fill color. You can also put content inside of shapes, such as text or images.

Tables are like little spreadsheets inside your documents. You can fill cells with information or numbers, and even perform basic calculations with formulas. You can also represent numbers as charts, selecting from line, bar, or pie charts of many different types and styles.

Create a sample document and try adding each of these elements by tapping the + button. Play around with all the different styles by selecting the element and tapping the paintbrush just as you did with images.

Document Setup

You can change a variety of your document's properties in Pages.

1. Open a document or create a new one.

2. Tap the ... button.

3. Choose Document Setup.

4. Drag the arrows at the four edges of the page to adjust the width and height of the page.

5. Tap to change the paper size from Letter to A4, or use a custom size. You can also switch between portrait and landscape orientation.

6. Tap the + button to add content that will appear in the background of every page in the document. For instance, you could add a rectangle shape, fill it with a texture, and stretch it to fill the entire page to add a textured background. Or, you could use an image as the background.

7. Tap in the header or footer to add text to the top or bottom of every page in the document. There are three sections to the header and footer that you can add text to: left, middle, and right.

8. You can add any text to these boxes. For instance, you can put the name of your document or your name in one of these sections.

9. You can also choose to add a page number that automatically increments for each additional page.

10. Tap one of the page number options to add that element.

11. Tap Done when you are finished.

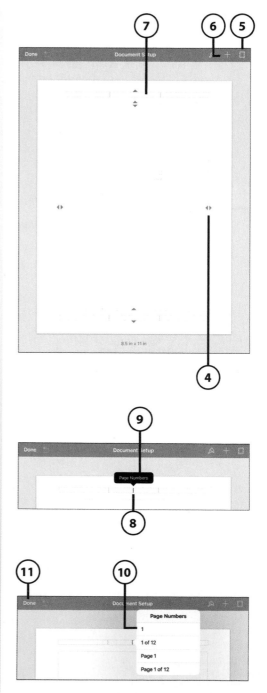

Sharing and Printing Documents

Thanks to iCloud, sharing documents with Pages, Numbers, and Keynote among your own devices is very easy. Any document you create on any device is available to the other devices. But you can also share your document with another person by emailing it, printing it, or sending it to a network server.

1. Tap the … button.

2. You can invite someone else to view or collaborate using iCloud. You can send invitations via email, messages, and other methods. You can also upload the document to iCloud and create a link that can be used by anyone to view the document.

3. Tap the Export button.

4. You can export your Pages document to third-party apps that can accept PDF or ePub formats.

5. Tap the Share button.

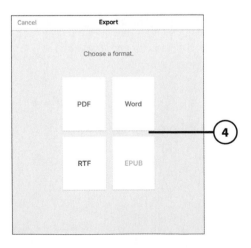

6. You can send the document to another device using AirDrop.

7. Tap Mail or Message to send the document as an attachment using those methods.

8. To print the document, tap here.

9. Tap to select a printer. The name of the printer will appear here and should be selected by default the next time you print. AirPrint is used to print wirelessly from your iPad. See "Printing from Your iPad" in Chapter 18 to set up AirPrint.

10. You can select a range of pages to print.

11. You can also select the number of copies.

12. Tap Print to send the document to the printer.

Pages Does Word

You can put more than just Pages documents into the iTunes list to import. Pages can also take Microsoft Word .doc and even .docx files.

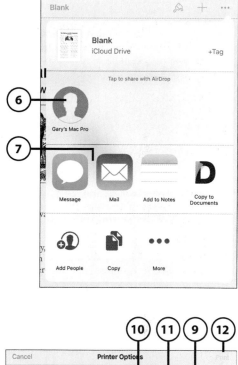

Create and enter data into spreadsheets

With Numbers, you can create data spreadsheets, perform calculations, and create forms and charts.

→ Creating a New Spreadsheet
→ Calculating Totals and Averages
→ Styling Tables and Cells
→ Creating Forms
→ Using Multiple Tables
→ Creating Charts

Spreadsheets with Numbers

Numbers is a versatile program that enables you to create the most boring table of numbers ever (feel free to try for the world record on that one) or an elegant chart that illustrates a point like no paragraph of text ever could.

Creating a New Spreadsheet

The way you manage documents in Numbers is exactly the same as you do in Pages, so if you need a refresher, refer to Chapter 11, "Writing with Pages." Let's jump right in to creating a simple spreadsheet.

1. Tap the Numbers icon on your Home screen to start.

Numbers

2. Tap + and then tap Create Spreadsheet to see all the template choices.

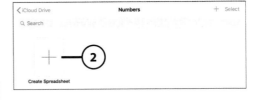

3. Tap Blank to choose the most basic template.

Numbers Terminology

A grid of numbers is called a *table*. A page of tables, often just a single table taking up the whole page, is a *sheet*. You can have multiple sheets in a document, all represented by tabs. The first tab in this case represents "Sheet 1." Tap the + to add a new sheet.

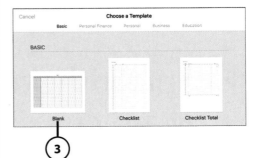

4. Double-tap in one of the cells to select the sheet. An outline appears around the cell.

5. Tap the keyboard button to bring up the keyboard so you can type data into the cell.

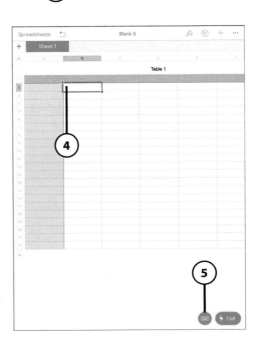

6. The keyboard in Numbers has many different modes. What you see when you first open the keyboard is text mode, where you can enter text and labels into cells. To get to the numeric entry keyboard to enter a value, tap here to switch to number mode.

The Action Menu

Notice that when you have selected a cell or other item in Numbers, you see an Action Menu button at the lower right. It has the name of the selected item, such as Cell, and a lightning bolt symbol. If the keyboard is open, the button appears at the top-right corner of the keyboard.

Tap this button to see some common actions for the selected item. For instance, for a cell you might see buttons to insert the current date, start a formula, copy, paste, or clear.

7. Use the keypad to type a number.

8. Tap the upper Next button, the one with the arrow pointing right.

9. The cursor moves to the column in the next cell. Type a number here, too.

10. Tap the Next button again and enter a third number.

11. Tap the space just above the first number you entered.

12. Tap the letters ABC above the keyboard to switch back to alphanumeric text input. The ABC changes to a 123.

13. Type a label for this first column.

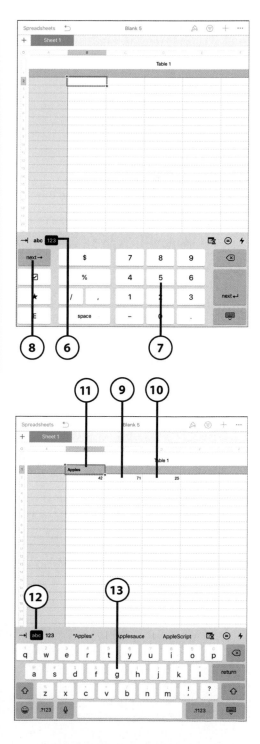

14. Tap in each of the other two column heads to enter titles for them as well.

15. Tap to the left of the first number you entered. Type a row title.

16. Now enter a few more rows of data.

17. Tap the button at the bottom-right corner of the keyboard (looks like a mini keyboard with a down arrow below it) or tap outside of the table to dismiss the keyboard.

18. Tap any cell in the table to select the table.

19. Tap and drag the circle with two lines in it to the right of the bar above the table. Drag it to the left to remove the unneeded columns. To do this, you might need to drag the whole screen to bring the right side of the table into view.

20. Tap and drag the same circle at the bottom of the vertical bar to the left of the table. Drag it up to remove most of the extra rows, leaving two at the bottom for future use.

21. Double-tap the title of the table and give it a name.

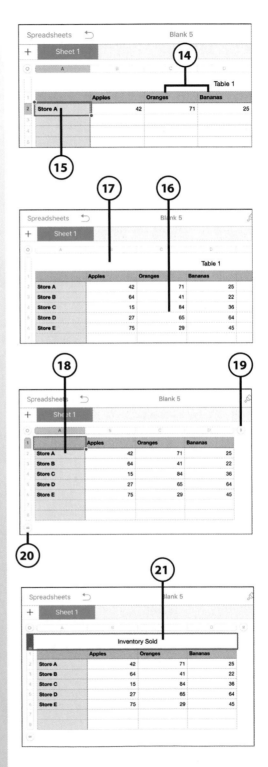

Calculating Totals and Averages

One of the most basic formula types is a sum. In the previous example, for instance, you might want to total each column. You might also want to find the average of the numbers in the columns.

With tables, you typically put these kinds of calculations in footer rows. So, your table has header rows with the title of each column and footer rows with things like sums and averages.

1. Start with the result of the previous example. Select any cell in the table. Then tap the paintbrush to bring up the controls.

2. Tap Headers & Footer.

3. Increase the number of Footer Rows to 2. This turns the last two rows in the table into footer rows.

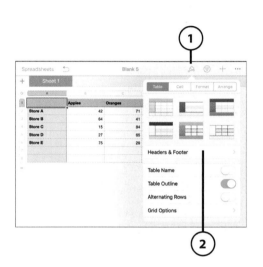

The Advantage of Footer Rows

You can put a formula to perform calculations in any cell of a table. So why bother with footer rows? They give you two nice features. First, you can now ask for the sum or average of an entire column, and Numbers knows to not include values in header and footer rows. Second, if you are entering values in the last cell of the last row above a footer row, and you tap the New key on the keyboard, Numbers inserts a new row and automatically moves the footer rows down.

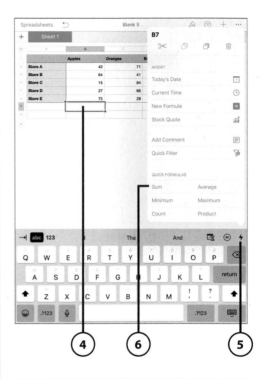

4. Double-tap in the cell just below the bottom number in the first column.

5. Tap the Action Menu button to bring up common actions.

6. Tap the Sum button to place a SUM formula in the cell. Numbers knows that if you are entering a SUM formula into a footer cell, you want to get the sum of all the cells in that column, excluding the header and footer cells.

7. The formula for the cell appears in the text field. Because you are using a footer row, Numbers automatically assumes you want the sum of this column, so it puts the name of the column into the formula. Otherwise, you would have to tap the column letter at the top of the column, manually enter B, or select a range of cells such as B2:B6 for the formula.

8. The result of the formula instantly appears in the spreadsheet.

9. Tap here to dismiss the keyboard.

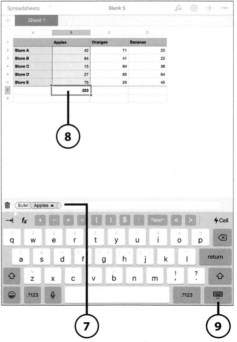

10. Repeat steps 4 through 6 for the other columns in the table.

11. Double-tap the last cell in the first column.

12. Tap the = button to go to the formula entry keyboard to manually enter the formula this time, instead of using the Action Menu button as shown in step 5. This gives you access to many more functions, and the ability to use basic operators like addition, multiplication, and so on.

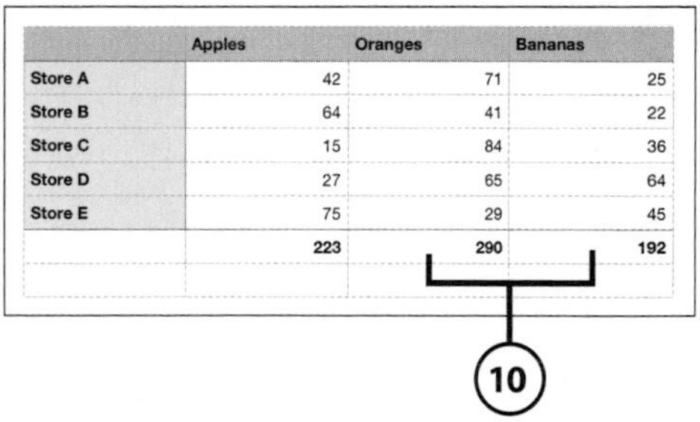

	Apples	Oranges	Bananas
Store A	42	71	25
Store B	64	41	22
Store C	15	84	36
Store D	27	65	64
Store E	75	29	45
	223	290	192

10

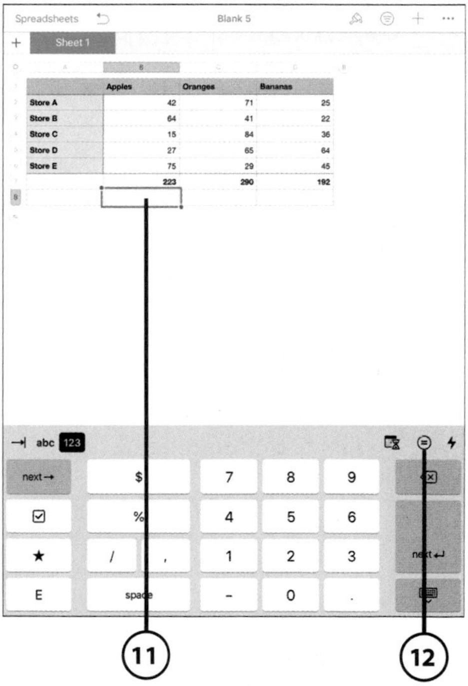

11   **12**

13. Tap the functions button.

14. Tap Statistical to dig down into those functions. If you don't see it, make sure Categories is selected, not Recent.

15. Tap AVERAGE in the list that appears.

16. Immediately after tapping AVERAGE, tap the column heading B, to indicate that you want the average of column B.

17. Tap Return to dismiss the keyboard and complete the formula.

18. Do the same for the next two columns. Or, you can select the first cell, copy it, then paste it into the second and third. When you do, select Paste Formula so the formula, and not the value, is pasted. The references to the columns shift automatically so each averages the appropriate column.

19. You can also enter labels for these two footer rows.

	Apples	Oranges	Bananas
Store A	42	71	25
Store B	64	41	22
Store C	15	84	36
Store D	27	65	64
Store E	75	29	45
Total	223	290	192
Average	44.6	58	38.4

Automatic Updates

If you are not familiar with spreadsheets, the best thing about them is that formulas like this automatically update. So if you change the number of Apples in Store C in the table, the sum in the last row automatically changes to show the new total.

Styling Tables and Cells

When working with tables, you can assign many different style options. It is easy to set the style for an entire table, but you can also make design choices for a single cell or group of cells.

1. Start with a table like the one we have been working with in the previous tasks. Select any cell in it.

2. Tap the paintbrush button.

3. Select Table.

4. Select a style. You see it reflected in the table immediately.

5. You can switch off the table name so it is no longer visible.

6. You can switch off the thin outline that surrounds the entire table.

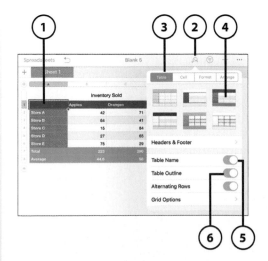

7. Rows in the table normally alternate between light and dark background shades to make it easier to read. You can turn this off as well.

8. Grid Options lets you decide where lines appear between cells.

9. Swipe up for more controls. You can change the font and size used by the table.

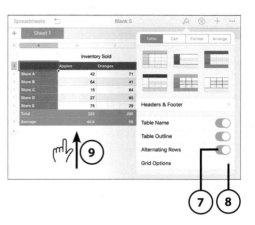

10. Select a single cell or group of cells. In this case, select a cell to highlight to point out something in the table.

11. Tap the paintbrush button.

12. Tap Cell.

13. Tap any of the style buttons at the top to apply a style, such as bold.

14. Change the size of the text.

15. Tap to bring up a control to change the color of the text.

16. Tap Cell Fill to change the background color of the cell.

17. Tap Format.

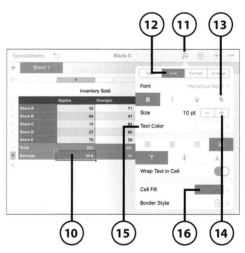

18. This menu allows you to set a format for the cell. For instance, you could choose Currency, and a currency symbol, such as $, would be placed before the number. There are a wide variety of different formats to choose from.

Creating Forms

Forms are an alternative way to enter data in a spreadsheet. A form contains many pages, each page representing a row in a table. As an example, let's create a sign-up table where people attending a meeting can enter their names, phone numbers, and email addresses.

1. In Numbers, create a new spreadsheet.

2. Enter titles for three columns, such as Name, Phone, and Email.

3. Shrink the table by grabbing the handle at the bottom left. You should end up with only the header row, the header column, and blank cells in the first row.

4. Tap the paintbrush button. Then go to Table, Headers & Footer, and change the number of header columns to 0.

5. Tap and enter a title for the table.

6. Tap the + button.

7. Tap New Form. This option only appears when you already have a table with labels in the header columns.

8. Select a table in one of the other sheets in this document. In this case, there is only one option, the Sign In Sheet table.

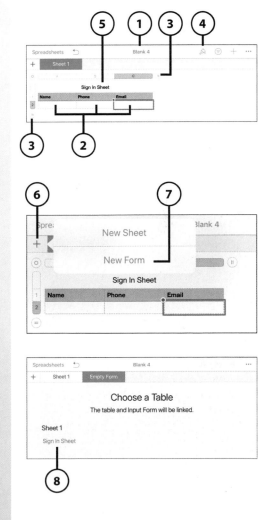

9. You are now in form entry mode. You can enter data in the three fields in the form.

10. Tap + to enter another row of data. Enter a few sample rows.

11. When you are done with some examples, tap the Sheet's tab to go to the spreadsheet.

12. The data in the form is also in the spreadsheet table. The table and the form are linked, so changes to one are reflected in the other.

13. You can return to the form at any time by tapping its tab.

14. In the form, you can use the arrow buttons to move through the rows of data.

15. You can tap and drag this array of dots to flip quickly through large sets of data.

16. You can use the trash button to delete a row.

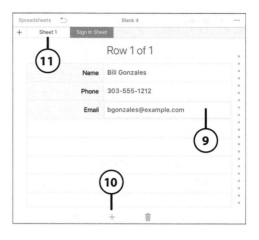

Using Multiple Tables

The primary way Numbers differs from spreadsheet programs such as Excel is that Numbers emphasizes page design. A Numbers sheet is not meant to contain just one grid of numbers. In Numbers, you can use multiple tables. By using multiple tables, you can track data more efficiently. Let's look at an example.

1. Continuing with the example from earlier in this chapter, keep the current table and move it down to make space for another. Tap the + button at the top right to add a second table.

Selecting a Table

It can be difficult to select an entire table without selecting a cell. Tap in a cell to select it. Then tap the circle that appears in the upper-left corner of the table to change your selection to the entire table.

2. Using what you have learned in this chapter so far, create a small second table with prices as shown.

3. Expand the original table by adding one more column.

4. Name this column Revenue. Notice that when you expand the table, the total and average formulas in the footer columns are automatically added. The average now gives an error because it is attempting to find the average of an empty column.

5. Double-tap the first empty cell in the new column to bring up the keyboard.

6. Tap the keyboard button, then the = button at the top of the keyboard to start entering a formula.

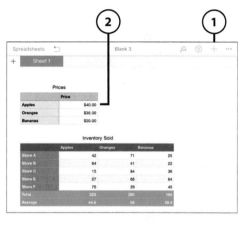

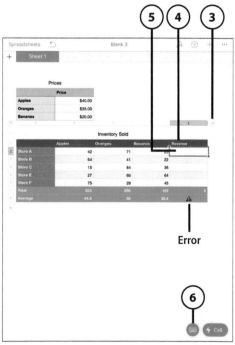

Error

7. You want to multiply the number of items in each cell by the price that matches it. Tap the cell that represents Apples from Store A, tap the X symbol on the keyboard, and then tap the cell that represents the price of Apples in the upper table. Tap + in the keyboard and do the same for Oranges and Bananas.

8. The plan is to copy and paste this formula into all rows. When you do that, the references in the formula change to match the relative position of the cell it is being pasted into. You want that for the Inventory numbers, but you don't want that for the prices. You want those to stay fixed. So tap the little up arrow next to the Price Apples item in the formula to bring up a menu.

9. Switch on all Preserve options for this item. This ensures that as you paste the formula elsewhere, it always points to the price of apples in the upper table.

10. Do the same for Price Oranges and Price Bananas.

11. The formula should now look like this. Notice the $ symbol is used to indicate that a reference is absolute and not relative to the position of the formula. Tap the green check mark to finish the formula.

12. Tap to select this cell.

13. Tap Copy from the context menu.

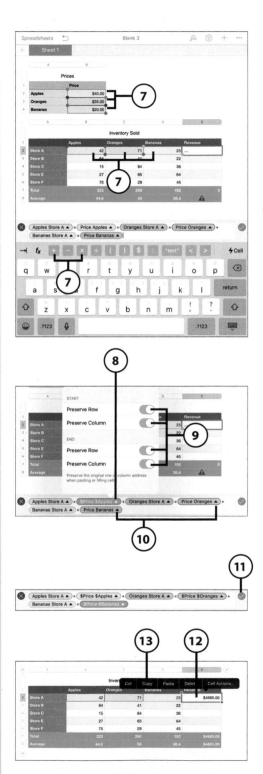

14. Tap the next cell, and then expand the selection to include all the empty cells in that column.

15. Tap Paste in the context menu.

16. Tap Paste Formulas.

17. The values for all the rows are calculated.

18. Note that the total and averages are calculated as well.

19. If you change one of the prices in the upper table, all the values for revenue change instantly to reflect it.

Enhance the Sheet

Another thing you can do is add more titles, text, and images to the sheet—even shapes and arrows. These not only make the sheet look nice, but can also act as documentation as a reminder of what you need to do each month—or instruct someone else what to do to update the sheet.

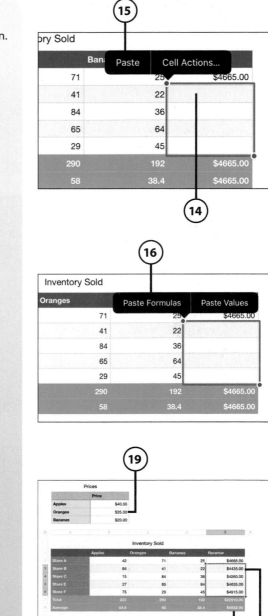

Creating Charts

Representing numbers visually is one of the primary functions of a modern spreadsheet program. With Numbers, you can create bar, line, and pie charts and many variations of each.

1. Start with a table similar to the one you have been working with in this chapter. Select the whole table. Numbers uses the header column and header row, along with the numbers in the body of the table, to build the chart.

2. Tap the + button.

3. Select charts.

4. You can select 2D, 3D, or Interactive charts. For this example, stick with a simple 2D chart. But take the time to explore the others as well.

5. You can swipe horizontally to see different chart styles. There are several pages of them.

6. Tap a chart to insert it into your sheet.

7. A chart is created using the data from your table. In this case, each store is represented along the horizontal axis, with a bar for each product. The vertical axis shows you the number sold.

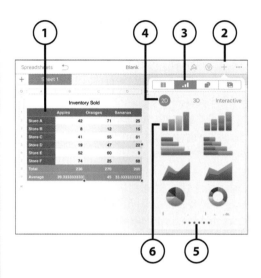

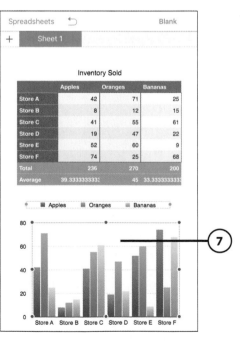

8. With the chart selected, tap the paintbrush button.

9. Tap Chart.

10. You can select a different style for the chart.

11. You can turn various elements on or off.

12. You can also customize the text in the chart.

13. Swipe up for more options, such as the ability to change the chart type.

14. Tap X Axis or Y Axis.

15. You can turn off various portions of the chart related to the selected axis.

16. So what happens if you choose a different type of chart? Numbers tries its best to match the data to the chart. If you choose a pie chart, only one row of data is used. You can see when the chart is selected that the table above it uses colors to show which cell matches which slice of the pie.

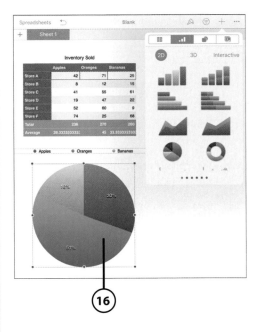

Create and display business and educational presentations

In this chapter, you use Keynote to build and display presentations.

→ Building a Simple Presentation
→ Building Your Own Slide
→ Adding Transitions
→ Organizing Slides
→ Playing Your Presentation

Presentations with Keynote

You can't have a suite of business apps without having a presentation tool, and Keynote is that tool on the iPad. The basics of using Keynote are the same as for Pages and Numbers. So let's get right to making presentations.

Building a Simple Presentation

Keynote works best in horizontal screen orientation because presentations are usually given on horizontal screens. So after you launch Keynote, turn your iPad on its side. The way you manage documents in Keynote is exactly the same as you do in Pages and Numbers, including the ability to use iCloud to store your documents. If you need a refresher, refer to Chapter 11, "Writing with Pages."

1. Tap the Keynote icon on the Home screen. If this is the first time you are using Keynote, you get a series of introduction screens. Continue until you are viewing an empty list of your presentations.

2. Tap the Create Presentation button to create a new presentation.

3. Choose either a standard or widescreen format. If you plan on presenting using a modern TV screen, you might want to use widescreen to get the best fit.

4. Choose a theme. We use Gradient for the task.

5. Double-tap the first line of text that reads Double-Tap to Edit.

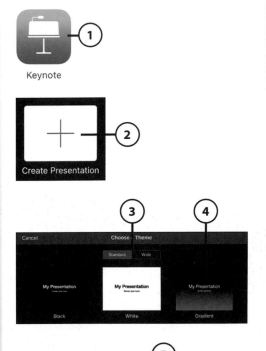

6. Type a title using the on-screen keyboard.

7. Double-tap the subtitle area and type a subtitle.

8. Tap the + button at the top of the screen.

9. Tap the media tab. You are asked to allow permission to access your media, if this is the first time you've used it.

10. Choose a photo. You might need to tap Photo or Video first, and then dig down into your Photos library albums.

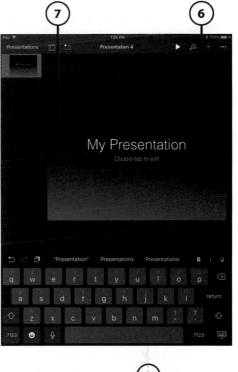

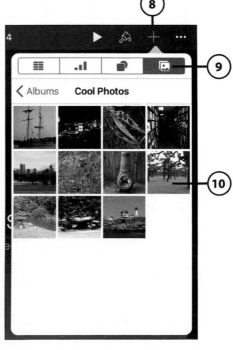

11. Tap the photo and use the blue dots at the corners and on the sides to resize the photo. Tap and drag in the middle of the photo to position it.

12. Tap the + button at the bottom-left corner to bring up a list of slides.

13. Tap any of the slide templates to add a slide. You now have two slides in your presentation.

>>>Go Further
STARTING NEW PRESENTATIONS

Keynote presentations are made up of slides. The slides in the current presentation are shown at the left of the screen. The selected slide takes up most of the screen. The slides are built from one of many slide templates, which you can modify as needed.

Be aware that there is no way to switch themes or to access the design of another theme after you start a new presentation. If you're used to working with Keynote on a Mac, you might be disappointed by this.

You can copy and paste entire slides between presentation documents, though. So if you want a document that mixes themes, you can achieve it by copying and pasting.

Building Your Own Slide

You can remove items and add your own to any template. You can practice adding your own elements to a slide by using the blank template.

1. Start a new document or continue from the previous example. Tap + to add a new slide.

2. Scroll down in this list and choose the blank slide to the lower right.

3. Tap the + button at the top to add an element.

4. Tap the media button.

5. Select an album, and then select a photo from that album.

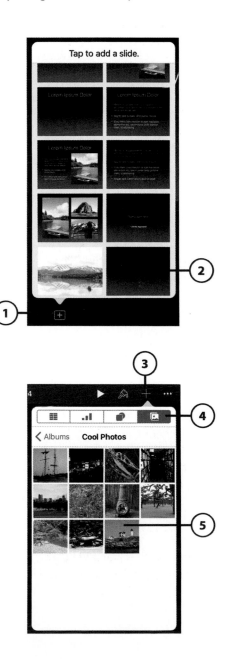

6. With the photo selected, grab one of the blue dots and shrink the image.

7. With the image selected, tap the paintbrush button and then tap Style.

8. Tap the bottom right of the six basic image styles or tap Style Options to customize the look of the photo even more.

Select All

To select all objects, tap a space with no objects. After a short delay, tap there again, and then you can choose Select All.

9. Add two more images using steps 3 through 8.

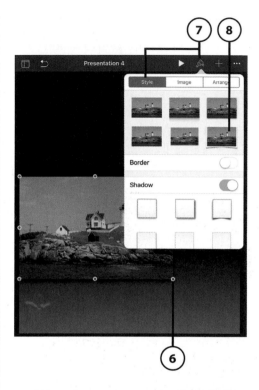

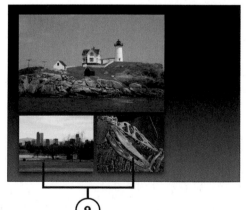

10. To select multiple items, use two fingers. Tap the first image with one finger and hold it. Use a second figure to tap the other two images to add them to the selection. Then drag all three images into a better position.

11. Tap the + button to add another element.

Tables and Charts Anyone?

You can also add tables and charts, even basic shapes, in the same way you would do it in Pages. There are a lot of similarities between using Pages and using Keynote.

12. Tap the shapes and text button.

13. Tap the first element, a plain text box.

14. Tap outside the menu to dismiss it.

15. Tap the text box to select it.

16. Drag it to a new position and expand it.

17. Double-tap in the text box to enter some text.

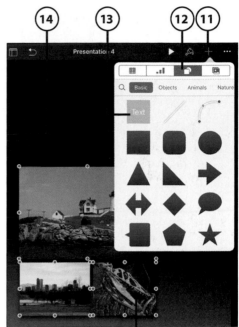

18. Close the keyboard and select the text box. With the text box selected, tap the paintbrush button.

19. Tap Text, and then change the font style and size.

20. Make the text bold by tapping B.

21. Tap outside the menu to dismiss it.

22. Your text is now bold. You now have a custom slide with three pictures and some text.

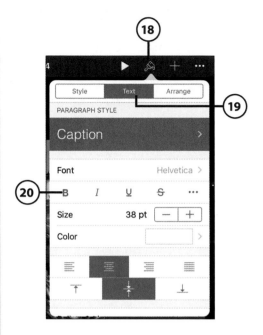

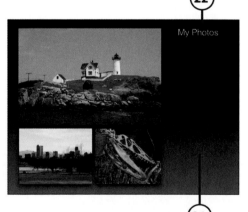

Adding Transitions

Just like other presentation programs, Keynote on iPad has a number of transition options. To practice working with transitions, start with a sample presentation, such as the one you have been working on, or create a new document with some sample slides.

1. Select the first slide on the left and then tap it again.

2. Tap the Transition button that appears.

3. Scroll through the transitions and pick one. Try Cube. The slide animates to show you the transition.

4. Tap Options.

5. Select any options associated with the transition. For example, the Cube transition has a duration setting.

6. Use the Play button to preview the transition.

7. Tap outside the control to dismiss it.

8. You're in a mode where you can continue to add transitions to slides. Tap an existing transition to edit it.

9. Tap another slide to add a transition.

10. Tap Done in the upper-right corner of the screen to exit.

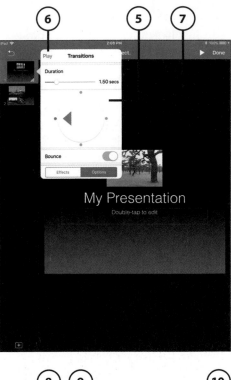

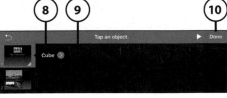

Magic Move

Another type of transition is the Magic Move. This is where objects on one slide are the same as the objects on the next, but they are in different positions. The transition between the slides moves these objects from the first position to the second.

1. Select a slide with several objects on it, such as three images. Tap it.

2. Tap Transition.

3. Choose Magic Move.

Unique Effects with Magic Move

The great thing about the Magic Move transition is that you can create some unique effects. For instance, in the example, you could bunch all the photos into a tiny space on the first slide and then spread them out in the second slide. The transition would make it seem like the photos are bursting out and falling into place.

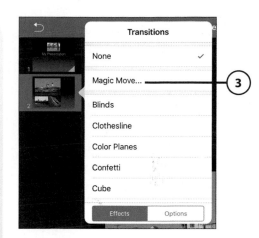

4. Tap Yes to duplicate the current slide so that you have two identical slides from which to create the Magic Move transition.

5. Slides 2 and 3 are identical, and slide 3 is the current slide. Move the objects around to reposition them or resize them. The stars indicate which elements are taking part in the Magic Move. In this example, the images will be swapping places. The Magic Move transition causes them all to flow from one position and size to the other.

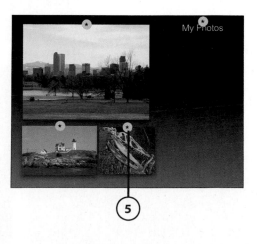

6. Tap the second frame.

7. Tap the arrow next to Magic Move and then tap play to preview the transition from slide 2 to slide 3. You need to tap the screen to proceed from the second slide to the third one and see the transition.

8. Tap Done in the upper-right corner of the screen.

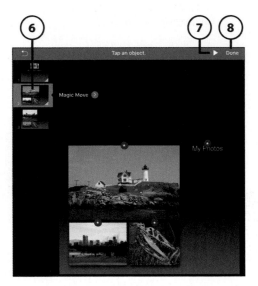

Object Transitions

In addition to the entire screen transforming from one slide to the next, you can also define how you want individual elements on the slide to appear.

1. Start off with a slide that includes a title and a bullet list. Tap the slide's title text.

2. Tap Animate.

3. Tap the build in button.

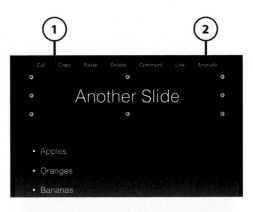

4. Tap Blast to see a preview of the animation.

5. Tap the bullet list.

6. Tap build in.

7. Scroll down to Move In and tap it.

8. Tap Delivery. You can also explore the Options and Order parts of the menu, but for this task you leave those settings alone.

Don't Build the First Object

A common mistake is to set every object to build, as you have in this example. Because the first object, the title, builds in, it means that nothing appears on the slide at first. You start off blank. Then the title appears and then the bullet items. Sometimes, though, you should start a slide with the title already on it.

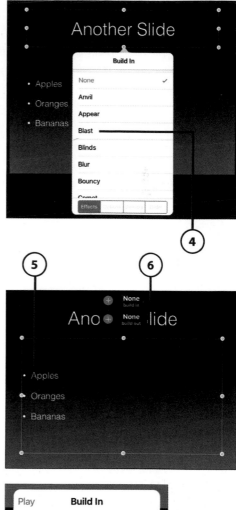

9. Tap By Bullet and then tap Done in the upper-right corner of the screen. The effect works by first showing you a blank screen, and then when you tap the screen, the title appears with the Blast transition. Each of your next three taps makes a bullet appear.

Play	**Build In**
All at Once	
By Bullet	✓
By Bullet Group	
By Highlighted Bullet	

| Effects | Options | Delivery | Order |

2 – 4

Organizing Slides

As you create presentations on your iPad, you might discover you need to re-order your slides, but that's no problem with Keynote. To practice, use a presentation that has several slides.

1. Create a presentation that includes several slides.

2. Tap and hold the third slide. It grows slightly larger and begins to follow your finger so that you can drag it down into another position.

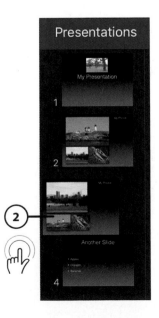

Grouping Slides

There are two options when you drag a slide and place it back in the list. The first is to place it flush left, where it inserts normally. If you move the slide slightly to the right, though, you are grouping the slide with the one above it. Groups are a great way to put slides that belong together as a single element. That way, you can move them as one unit if you need to. To move them as a group, you close the group by tapping the triangle next to the parent slide. Then move the parent slide around, and all children come with it.

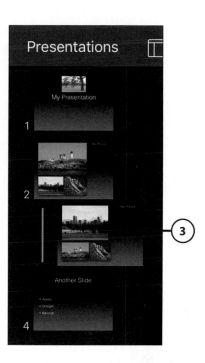

3. Drag slide 3 to the right so it inserts in a group owned by slide 2.

4. Tap the triangle on the left of slide 2 to close the group.

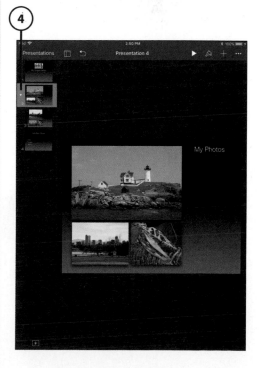

5. Tap slide 1 with your finger and continue to hold.

6. Use your other hand to tap slide 2 and then release your finger. You can now move this group of two slides as one unit.

7. Tap once to select a slide. Then tap a second time after a short delay to bring up a menu.

8. Use Cut, Copy, and Paste as you would while editing text. You can duplicate slides using Copy.

9. Tap Delete to remove a slide.

10. Tap Skip Slide to mark a slide as one to skip during the presentation. This comes in handy when you want to remove a slide from a presentation temporarily, perhaps while presenting to a specific audience.

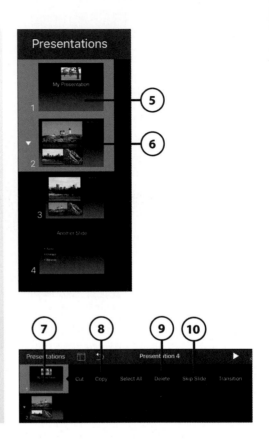

Playing Your Presentation

After you create your presentation, or if you want to preview what you've done, you can play your presentation.

1. With a presentation open in Keynote, tap the Play button.

2. The presentation fills the screen. Tap the center or right side of the screen to advance to the next slide. You can also tap and drag from left to right.

3. To go back to the previous slide, drag right to left.

4. Tap the left edge of the screen to bring up a list of slides.

5. Tap one of the items in the list to go directly to that slide.

6. Tap outside of the list of slides to dismiss the list.

7. Pinch in at the center of the screen to end the presentation and return to editing mode.

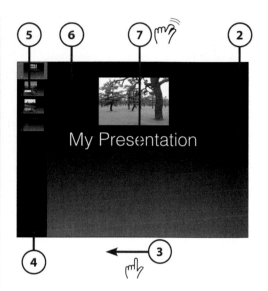

>>>Go Further
WHICH VIDEO ADAPTER?

One way to get Keynote's presentation out to an external screen is to use an adapter. There are two main choices: the VGA adapter or the HDMI adapter. Get the VGA adapter if you plan to present over a traditional meeting room projector. However, newer televisions and maybe some advanced projectors would use an HDMI connection. You can also convert VGA to fit other video connections. For instance, if you need to connect to a TV using a component or s-video, you should find some VGA adapters that work. See if you can find one that has been verified to work with an iPad before buying.

8. Tap and hold in the middle of the slide to bring up special pointer controls.

9. A row of tools appears at the bottom. Select a color.

10. Use your finger to draw on the slide.

11. Tap to undo your drawing.

12. You can use the laser pointer dot instead of drawing.

13. Use the arrow buttons to navigate between slides.

14. Tap Done to return to normal presentation mode.

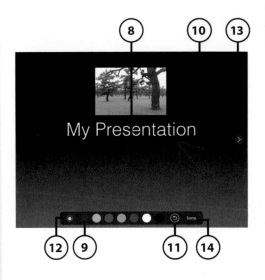

>>>Go Further

PRESENTING ON AN EXTERNAL DISPLAY

Presenting on your iPad with people looking over your shoulder probably isn't your goal. You want to present on a large monitor or a projector, which you can do with a Lightning to VGA Adapter (see Chapter 18, "iPad Accessories," for more information).

You can also use the AirPlay ability of an Apple TV (2nd generation or newer) to send your presentation wirelessly to a TV. See "Using AirPlay to Play Music and Video on Other Devices" in Chapter 4 to set up AirPlay mirroring. When you tap the Play button to play your presentation, mirroring goes into a special mode, with the actual presentation on the TV and your presenter layout on your iPad's screen, so you can control the slides.

Presenting with an external display works slightly differently than without one. Your iPad's screen shows the time and some buttons at the top. You can bring up the list of slides on the left, but it only appears on your iPad's screen, not the external display.

Search for locations and
get directions with Maps

In this chapter, you learn to use the Maps app to find locations and get directions.

→ Finding a Location
→ Searching for Places and Things
→ Getting Directions
→ Getting a Better View with Maps Settings
→ Getting Traffic Reports

14

Navigating with Maps

The Maps app is a great way to plan a trip—whether you're going across the country or to the grocery store. You can search for locations on the map, view satellite images, see optimized driving routes, and even get information and reviews of local businesses.

Searching with Maps

You can search for a specific address. You can also use a general area or the name of a place or person, and Maps does the best it can to locate it. For example, you can try three-letter airport codes, landmark names, street intersections, and building names. The search keeps in mind your current maps view, so if you search for a general area first, such as Denver, CO, and then for a building name, it attempts to find the building in Denver before looking elsewhere in the world.

Finding a Location

The simplest thing you can do with Maps is find a location.

1. Tap the Maps app on your Home screen.

2. Type an address or the name of a place in the Search field.

3. As you type, you get a list of suggestions. You can tap one of these if you notice it matches your search closely enough.

4. Otherwise, finish typing the address or name and tap the Search button on the on-screen keyboard.

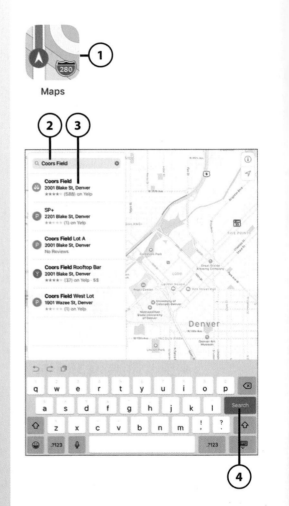

Maps

5. The map shifts to that location and zooms in.

6. Tap the location name to get more information.

7. You see information about the location, such as the telephone number and website. You can tap these to call the location or visit the web page.

8. Tap Directions to get directions to the address.

9. Drag up to reveal more information below.

10. You can see a few reviews from Yelp, or tap here for the Yelp app. You are directed to its listing in the App Store if you don't have it installed.

11. Tap Create New Contact or Add to Existing Contact to add the name, address, phone number, and other information to your Contacts app.

12. Tap Report an Issue to help Apple improve its maps database. If the location happens to be a business you are associated with, and you want to correct some missing or inaccurate information, this is the place to start.

13. Tap the X button to close this information overlay and see more of the map.

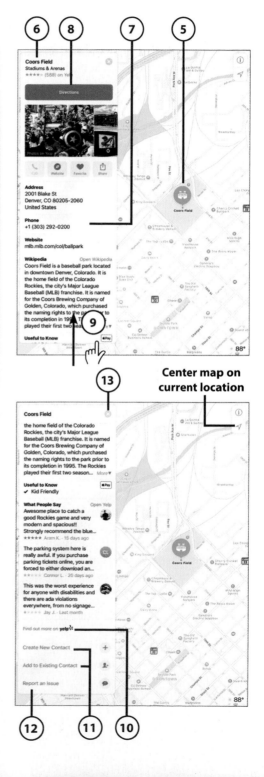

Center map on current location

Where Am I?

Want to quickly center the map on your current location? Tap the GPS button (it looks like a blue arrow) at the top-right corner of the screen. Even if your iPad doesn't have a GPS receiver, it takes a good guess as to your current location based on the local Wi-Fi networks it can see.

Searching for Places and Things

You can also use Maps to search for something that has more than one location. For instance, you could search for restaurants, grocery stores, bars, coffee shops, or even the location of Apple Stores.

1. Start in Maps. You should see the last area you were viewing. If it is not your current location, search for that location or tap the GPS button to go there.

2. Tap the Search field and enter the name of a store. Don't always restrict yourself to specific names such as "Apple store." You can type in general terms such as "coffee" or "restaurant" to get a broader selection of results.

3. Pins appear on the map for all locations matching the search term in the general area. The locations also appear in a list, with the closest one at the top. Note that the blue dot represents your current location.

4. Tap the name for more information about that location.

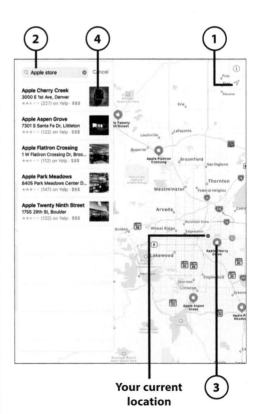

Your current location

Sometimes Maps Gets It Wrong

The maps database is huge, which means it also contains errors. Sometimes an address is wrong or the information is out of date, so you find yourself in front of a shoe shop instead of your favorite restaurant.

Siri: Finding Map Locations

You can ask Siri to find locations even when you're not already in the Maps app. A small map displays in the Siri interface, and you can tap it to open the Maps app, centered on that location. Try commands like:

Where is Coors Field?

Show me Broadway and First Avenue on the map.

Map 6th and Colorado Boulevard.

Getting Directions

Say you want to do more than just look at a location on a map—you actually want to go there. Apple Maps can help you with that by giving you turn-by-turn directions you can follow while you drive. Your iPad can even speak them out loud. However, if your iPad is Wi-Fi only, you most likely won't have a connection while driving. In that case, you can still bring up a list of directions on your iPad before you leave home.

1. After searching for and finding a location, tap the Directions button.

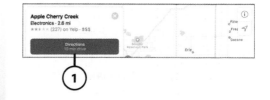

2. At the top of the screen you see a To and a From. Usually the From field is labeled Current Location. You can tap it to search and start your trip from another location.

3. You can edit the From and To fields to change your route start and end points.

4. You can swap these two fields if your directions have you going in the wrong direction.

5. Tap Route to accept the changes and return to the previous screen.

6. Tap Driving Options to change the type of route.

7. Tap to choose to avoid tolls or highways on your route.

8. Tap Done to return to the previous screen.

9. Tap Walk or Transit to switch from driving directions to walking or public transit directions. Apple Maps offers public transit directions only for some cities.

10. Different routes may be shown on the map, and in the list on the left. Tap in the map or on the list to pick one.

11. Tap a Go button to start the turn-by-turn directions. This is only useful if you have a mobile connection to the Internet while you are using your iPad to navigate.

12. Alternatively, tap the Details button to see a list of each step in the journey.

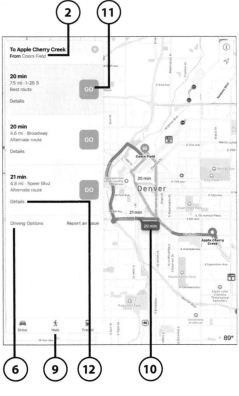

13. Tap the Share button under the list to print the directions, or send them to your iPhone or someone else's iPhone via AirDrop.

Spoken Turn-By-Turn Directions

For those who have a wireless mobile connection on their iPad, directions become much more useful. You can use your mobile connection as you drive and the Maps app will follow along, updating the steps in your route as you make progress. You even get spoken directions as you approach each turn, so you don't need to take your eyes off the road.

Siri: Getting Directions

The easiest way to get the Maps app to show you directions is to ask Siri. With or without the Maps app open, try phrases like:

How do I get to Denver International Airport?

Take me to the nearest coffee shop.

Plot a course to Colfax Avenue and Colorado Boulevard.

Take me home.

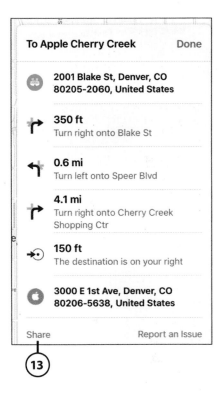

To Apple Cherry Creek	Done

2001 Blake St, Denver, CO
80205-2060, United States

350 ft
Turn right onto Blake St

0.6 mi
Turn left onto Speer Blvd

4.1 mi
Turn right onto Cherry Creek Shopping Ctr

150 ft
The destination is on your right

3000 E 1st Ave, Denver, CO
80206-5638, United States

Share   Report an Issue

⑬

Getting a Better View with Maps Settings

The default mode of Maps shows clean colorful lines, but you can also switch to satellite views, 3D models, and even a 3D photographic view.

Using Satellite View

Satellite view is like the standard map view in that you can search for places and get directions. But you can also get a better sense of what is at a location.

1. In Maps, tap the i button at the top right.

2. Tap Satellite to see a satellite view of your location.

3. Tap the X button to return to the map.

4. Unpinch in the center of the map to zoom in.

5. The closer view helps show you what the streets actually look like.

6. Tap the i button again and then tap Map at the top to return to the regular map view.

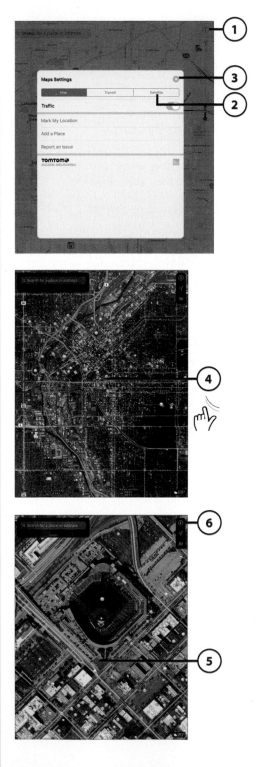

Using 3D View

Another way to view a map is with a 3D view. This allows you to see the height and shape of buildings to get a better understanding of the area.

1. Start by looking in Maps using the standard view. Pinch in to be fairly close to the street.

2. Drag up with two fingers to change the viewing angle of the map and initiate 3D view. If the map simply moves instead of switching to 3D, then it probably means you haven't zoomed in close enough. It could also mean that 3D views aren't available in this area.

3. The flat top-down view is replaced by a perspective view. Pinch to zoom in closer.

4. Larger buildings in downtown areas are now 3D objects. Use two fingers to rotate the image, and you can see the buildings from all angles.

5. Tap the info button and switch to satellite view.

6. The 3D models are replaced with textured models of buildings and terrain. You can still zoom and rotate in 3D satellite view, even getting so close to the ground that you can virtually move between buildings.

7. Use two fingers and swipe up to tilt the 3D effect for a more horizontal view.

8. Tap to turn off 3D mode and return to standard top-down flat mode.

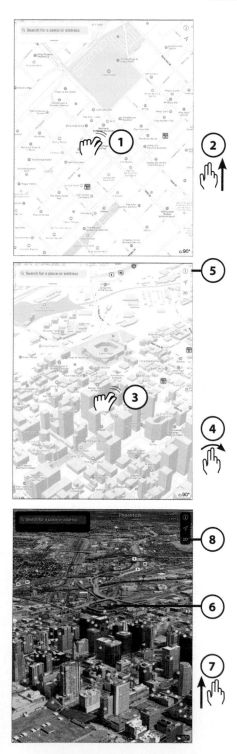

Not in My Town

Although 3D view is great for those of us who live in big cities, it isn't available for every location. For there to be 3D models and textures, an Apple-hired airplane has to take pictures of your city. They have gotten a lot of the world's major cities, but not everywhere yet.

Getting Traffic Reports

The Maps app includes a way for you to see up-to-date traffic flow and information.

1. Bring up a map view that shows some highways and major boulevards.

2. Tap the i button.

3. Make sure Traffic is turned on.

4. Tap the X button to close the Maps Settings overlay.

5. The map shows red or yellow lines where traffic is slow.

6. You can also see the locations of accidents or construction sites that are affecting traffic. Tap for details. Other symbols you see represent road closures, police activity, or other things that might affect traffic. You can tap them to see more information.

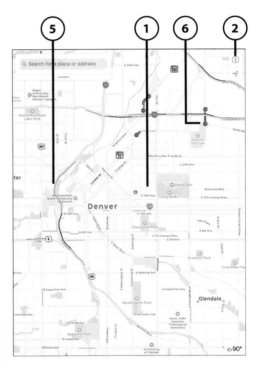

Siri: Traffic Reports

You can quickly bring up the map with traffic reports turned on by asking Siri:

What's the traffic like?

What's the traffic like in San Francisco?

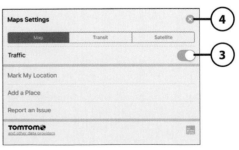

>>>Go Further

GET MORE WITH GOOGLE MAPS

There are many other map apps in the App Store, but Google Maps stands out as almost a must-have for anyone who uses maps. It has similar functionality to the built-in Apple Maps app, but uses different map data and information about locations. It comes in handy to have two map apps in case one doesn't list or have enough details about a location.

Google Maps has also been around for a lot longer than Apple Maps, so it has some features you can't find in the latter, such as biking trails. It also has something called Street View, where you can view 360-degree pictures taken right on the streets.

See Chapter 15, "The World of Apps," to learn how to use the App Store to find and install new apps like Google Maps.

Control apps with
Siri Shortcuts

Search the App Store
for thousands of useful,
educational, and
entertaining apps

Learn to work
with multiple apps
at the same time

In this chapter, you learn how to go beyond the basic functionality of your iPad by adding more apps using the App Store. You also learn how to multitask using more than one app at the same time to complete a task.

15

→ Purchasing an App

→ Organizing Apps on Your iPad

→ Working with Apps

→ Dragging and Dropping Between Apps

→ Getting Help with Apps

→ Monitoring and Managing Your Apps

→ Watching Your iPad Usage with Screen Time

→ Controlling Apps with Siri Shortcuts

The World of Apps

Apps that come with your iPad and Apple's office apps, Pages, Numbers, and Keynote, are just the tip of the iceberg. The App Store contains hundreds of thousands of apps from third-party developers, with more added each day.

You use the App Store app to shop for and purchase new apps—although many are free. You can also rearrange the app icons on your Home screen pages to organize them.

Purchasing an App

Adding a new app to your iPad requires that you visit the App Store. You do that, not surprisingly, with the App Store app on your Home screen.

1. Tap the App Store icon on your Home screen.

2. The bottom of the screen has buttons that take you to screens with today's featured apps and featured game apps. Tap the third option, which shows you non-game, featured apps.

3. Swipe left to view more featured apps in any of the horizontal lists. You can do the same for the sections in the lower part of the screen, which often change to feature different types of apps.

4. Swipe up to scroll down and see more featured app categories.

App Store

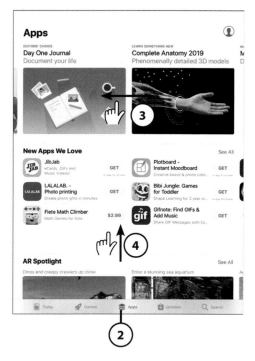

5. Continue to swipe up until you see Top Paid and Top Free lists, as well as Top Categories.

6. Tap See All for any of the lists to see more apps.

7. Tap any category to go to the page of featured apps in that category.

8. Tap Search to search for an app by keyword.

9. Type a search term to look for apps by name or keyword.

10. Tap a suggestion to complete the phrase and perform the search.

11. Alternatively, tap the Search key at any time to start the search.

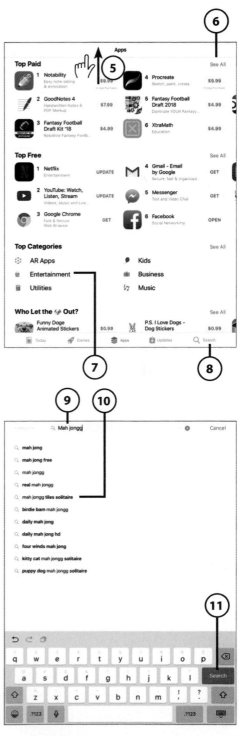

12. Tap Filters to narrow the search.

13. Tap to filter between iPad apps and iPhone apps. Apps that are optimized to work well with both screen sizes appear in both categories.

14. Select whether you want to see apps that are free or both free and paid.

15. Select a category to narrow the search results.

16. Choose how you want the results to be ordered: relevance, popularity, ratings, or release date.

17. Select an age group if you would like to only see apps suitable for children.

18. Results are displayed. You can tap any one to jump to the page for that app. You can also tap the Get button (which instead is labeled with a price if the app is not free) to get the app.

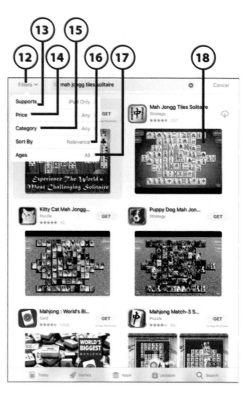

Redeem Codes

If you go to the bottom of the Today, Games, or Apps pages in the App Store app, you see a button marked Redeem. Use this to enter any redemption code you get for a free app. You may get a code because someone sends you an app as a gift. Developers also send out a handful of these codes when they release a new app or app version.

Automatically Download New Apps

If you go to the Settings app, look for the iTunes & App Store category. There you can turn on automatic downloads for apps, as well as for music and books. After you turn this on, purchasing an app on your Mac or PC in iTunes, or on another iOS device with the same Apple ID, automatically sends this app to your iPad as well.

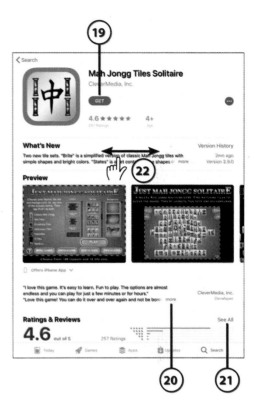

19. If an app is free, this button is labeled Get. If it's a paid app then you see the price in your local currency. Tap the button, and it changes to a Buy button. Tap it again. If the app is already on your iPad, the button is labeled Open, and you can launch the app by tapping the button

Purchased Apps

If you have purchased the app in the past, but don't currently have it on your iPad, you will see a cloud/download button that lets you download the app again. You do not pay again for an app you have already purchased.

20. Tap the More button to see the full description of the app.

21. Tap See All in the Rating & Reviews section to look at reviews for the app.

22. Scroll left and right to flip through the screenshots for the app.

23. Tap the … button to send a link to the app to friends via email, Messages, and so on. You can also pay for and send a non-free app to a friend as a gift, or add a non-free app to your wish list to remember it for future consideration.

24. Verify the app name, icon, rating, and other information on the confirmation screen. Tap the Install button to install the app, or tap Cancel if you've changed your mind.

25. When you purchase an app, it starts installing, and you can watch the progress from the app's information page in the App Store app or from the location of the app's icon on your Home screen.

Redownloading an App You Already Purchased

Once you buy an app, you own it forever—at least as long as you keep using the same Apple ID. At the top of the App Store app in Today view, you see a button with the outline of a person. Tap that to see your account information. Tap Purchased to see a list of all apps you have bought, even if you have removed them from this iPad, or maybe never even downloaded them in the first place. Perhaps you previously bought an app on your iPhone or iPod touch. You can quickly jump to any of these apps and download them to your iPad without paying for them a second time.

>>>*Go Further*

FREE, PAID, AND FREEMIUM

Some apps in the App Store are free, and others you need to pay for before downloading and installing. But some apps are free for the basic version, and then you need to make in-app purchases to use advanced functions or buy more content. These are called "freemium" apps.

It is up to the developer of the app to design the method of making purchases. Most apps show you a preview of the function or content and then include a purchase or buy button. Before any app can charge your iTunes account for an in-app purchase, you see a standard Confirm Your In-App Purchase prompt.

Photo apps might use in-app purchases to charge you for additional filters or effects. Drawing apps might charge for new brushes or tools. Some free apps have advertising and allow you to make an in-app purchase to be able to use the app ad-free.

Often games have a variety of items you can purchase to alter gameplay. But instead of a long list of in-app purchases, they simply charge you for in-game currency such as tokens, gems, or gold. Then you can use these to purchase items inside the game.

There's no risk in trying free apps that offer in-app purchases. If you find that the purchases in the app are not worth it for you, simply do not purchase anything. If the app isn't useful, you can delete it without spending a penny.

Finding Good Apps

Finding good apps might be the biggest problem that iPad users have. With more than one million apps in the App Store, it can be hard to find what you want, so here are some tips.

1. When viewing an app, always tap the More button in the description and read the description carefully. Make sure the app is what you are looking for before downloading it. The title of the app itself is not going to be enough to determine this.

2. You might want to check out the version history. Established apps have a long list of versions and improvements showing that the developer is actively updating and maintaining the app.

3. Ratings can be deceiving, especially if there are only a few of them. Three stars doesn't mean much when there are only 5 ratings. It could be that two people gave the app a poor rating simply because it wasn't what they were looking for.

4. If an app has few ratings, tap the developer's name to view other apps by that developer so you can get an idea of the quality of the app.

5. Swipe up to see more information.

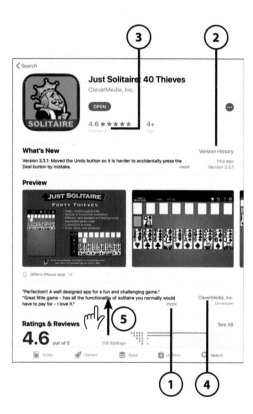

6. Don't pay too much attention to a single review. Since anyone can say anything in a review, it is hard to judge from just one. Instead, look for reviews that seem to present thoughtful information about the app and help you judge whether it is the right app for you.

7. You can often check out the developer's website. Their site can give you an idea of the quality of the app and the level of support they provide.

8. Good developers also provide a link here for support requests.

9. Swipe up to see more information.

10. In the list of more apps by the same developer, keep an eye out for free or demo versions of the same app. Sometimes a developer provides a limited-feature, free version of a paid app. You can use the free version to try out the app to test the quality.

11. At the bottom of the page is a list of similar apps. If you think the app on the page may not be the right one for you, then you can start looking for something else here.

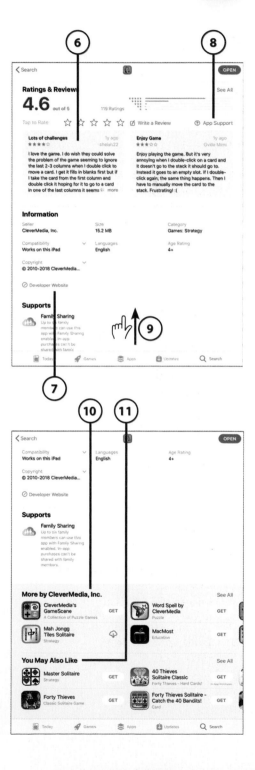

>>>Go Further

USING RESOURCES OUTSIDE THE APP STORE

Many good resources for finding apps aren't part of the App Store. Following are a few suggestions:

- Search using Google. For example, if you want another spreadsheet app, search *iPad App Spreadsheet*.

- After you find an app that you want, try another Google search using the name of the app followed by the word *review*.

- Find sites that feature and review apps. Many are out there, but be aware that some sites are paid by developers to review an app, so the review might not be the most objective.

- The author provides a list of recommended apps at **http://macmost.com/ featurediphoneapps**.

Organizing Apps on Your iPad

It doesn't take long to have several pages of apps. Fortunately, you can rearrange your app icons in two ways. The first is to do it on the iPad Home screen and allow apps to appear on multiple pages of the screen as each page fills up. In addition to spreading your apps across multiple pages, you can also group them in folders so that several apps take up only one icon position on a screen.

Arranging Apps on the Home Screen

1. Tap and hold an icon until all the icons start to jiggle.

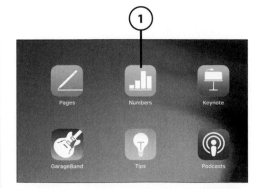

2. The icon you are holding is a little larger than the others. Drag it and drop it in a new location.

3. To carry the icon to a different page of apps, drag it to the side of the screen.

4. Delete an app from your iPad by tapping the X at the upper left of the icon. Note that the X does not appear over all apps, as some of the default apps that come with your iPad cannot be removed, such as Contacts, Settings, and App Store.

5. When finished, press the Home button (not shown).

Move Multiple Apps

If you want to move more than one app to another screen, you can do that by tapping and holding an app until the icons jiggle and have the little X next to them for deleting. Then start to move that one app. After moving it a bit, you can tap on other apps on the screen with another finger. This adds these apps to a stack of apps you are moving. You can then move them to another screen by dragging to the edge of the screen to flip the page.

>>>Go Further

OFFLOAD APPS TO SAVE SPACE

Once you have purchased an app, you can always download it from the App Store again. You can delete an app to save space on your iPad and then download it again when you need it. Just know that deleting the app also removes data, settings, and preferences for it.

If you are running out of storage space on your iPad, you can "offload" apps. This removes the large app, but saves your data for that app. Go to Settings, General, iPad Storage, and then look through the list of apps. Tap any app to see how much space it uses. You can then tap the Offload App button to offload it but keep its data around.

In Settings, General, iPad Storage is also an Offload Unused Apps setting that automatically offloads an app if you haven't used it in a while and you need the space.

When an app is offloaded, its icon is still on the Home screen, but it's dimmed. When you tap the icon to open the app, the app is first redownloaded, and then it opens.

Moving Apps to and From the Dock

Although you might have two, three, or even dozens of Home screen pages filled with apps, you have only one Dock. The Dock is the row of apps at the bottom of the Home screen. It remains the same no matter which Home screen page you're viewing. You can add and remove apps from the Dock.

1. Tap and hold an app icon on the Home screen, just for a second, before it "pops" out a bit and you can drag it around.

2. Drag the icon to the Dock at the bottom of the screen. Place it on the left side of the Dock in the position where you want it to stay. The left side is defined by a thin vertical line (in the figure, it's to the left of the Settings app icon).

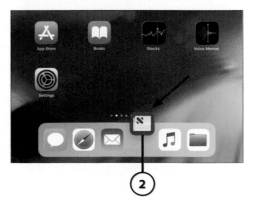

3. You can use the same technique to move icons around in the Dock. Icons you add to the Dock must stay on the left side.

4. To remove an icon from the Dock, press and hold an icon, but drag up and out of the Dock and place the icon on the main part of the Home screen.

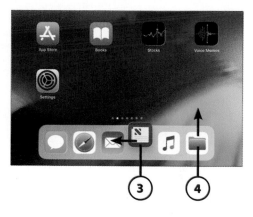

The Right Side of the Dock

The left side of the Dock contains apps that you place there. You have total control over what is on the left side. On the right side are other recently accessed apps and sometimes predictions of which app you might want to use next. You can remove the right side of the Dock completely by going to Settings, General, Multitasking & Dock, and turning off Show Suggested and Recent Apps.

Using the Dock While in Apps

Not only is the Dock available on all pages of the Home screen, but it is also available while you are using an app.

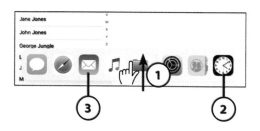

1. While in an app, tap below the bottom of the screen and move your finger slowly up to about 2 inches above the bottom. Don't go any further or you'll launch the App Switcher.

2. The Dock appears. You can tap and drag it back down to the bottom of the screen to get rid of it.

3. Tap an app to launch it.

Show Recent Apps

In addition to apps you specifically place in the Dock, you also see some apps on the right side of the Dock. These are apps you have recently used or your iPad thinks might come in handy right now according to the time of day or the app you are currently using. Whether these suggestions appear depends on the setting in the Settings app under General, Multitasking & Dock, Show Suggested and Recent Apps. Toggle that on or off as you prefer.

Creating App Folders

Grouping apps in a folder enables you to de-clutter your Home screen if you find you have too many apps competing for space on the screen.

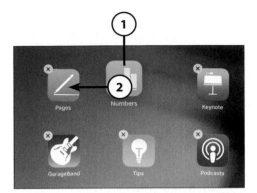

1. Identify several apps that you want to group. Tap and hold one of those apps until the icons start to jiggle.

2. Continue to hold your finger down, and drag the icon over another icon you want to have in the group.

3. An app folder appears and enlarges to fill the center of the screen.

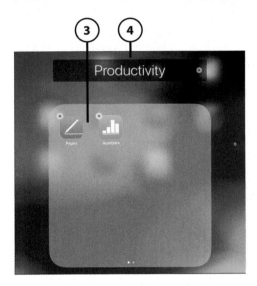

4. Change the name of the app folder by tapping the default name and editing it with the virtual keyboard.

5. Press the Home button once (not shown) to dismiss the name editor, and again to return to your Home screen.

6. The app folder is on your Home screen. You can drag other apps to this folder using steps 1 and 2.

Working with Folders

After you have created an app folder, you can access the apps in it by first tapping on the folder and then tapping the app you want to launch. Tapping and holding any app in the folder gives you the opportunity to rename the folder, rearrange the icons in the folder, or drag an app out of the folder.

>>>*Go Further*

WORKING WITH APP FOLDERS

Here are a few more things you can do inside app folders:

- To remove an app from a folder and put it back into a position on the Home screen, tap and hold the icon until it jiggles. Then drag it out to the surrounding area outside of the folder.

- Inside app folders, you can have more than one page if you have more than nine apps stored in it. You can swipe left and right to move between pages while the folder is open.

- While apps in the app folder are jiggling, you can move them around inside the folder and off to the left or right to move them between pages inside the folder.

- You can move app folders around your Home screen and between Home screen pages just as you can with an app icon.

Working with Apps

You can have many apps running at once on your iPad. In fact, after you launch an app, it remains running by default even if you switch back to the Home screen and run another app. You can even view a second app at the same time you're running another one, or set up video to run picture-in-picture with another app.

The iPad has some powerful features that enable you to view and use more than one app at a time. Some of these were introduced with iOS 10 and iOS 11 but have been improved in iOS 12.

Viewing Currently Running Apps

Apps running in the background use little or no resources. You can think of them as paused apps. You can switch back to them at any time, and most apps resume right where you left off.

1. Tap below the bottom of the screen and move your finger up. Keep moving up, and you'll see the current app shrink and the App Switcher screen appear under it. You can also get here by double-pressing the Home button.

2. The App Switcher shows all your currently running apps in a grid, the Dock at the bottom, and the Control Center at the right. The app you currently are using appears to the top right, and the previous app that you used is below that. Other apps move off to the left, and you can tap and drag left to right to scroll through them.

3. Tap any app to jump to it.

4. Drag any app up off the top of the screen to force it to quit. It is rarely necessary to force-quit an app unless it is misbehaving or frozen.

5. Get back to the current app by tapping it, or by pressing the Home button once.

Moving from App to App with a Gesture

If you have several apps running, you can quickly move between them by using four-finger gestures. Just swipe left or right with four fingers at the same time to move from app to app without needing to go back to the Home screen, or use the list of recent apps.

>>>*Go Further*

RESTARTING APPS

There is a method for restarting an app that works when the app is the one currently onscreen.

Press and hold the Wake/Sleep button on the top of your iPad for about three seconds. You see the Slide to Power Off control appear.

Don't use the Slide to Power Off control or press the Cancel button. Instead, hold the Home button down for several seconds. This quits the app and restarts the app. In some cases, the app quits, but you have to relaunch it.

Using More Than One App at a Time

You can use more than one app at the same time on your iPad. In fact, there are many ways to do this. Let's take a look at some of the ways you can manipulate apps on the screen to use more than one.

1. Start with an app on the screen. This example shows Safari on the screen in the horizontal orientation.

2. Tap just below the screen. Drag up an inch or two to reveal the Dock. Don't drag any further or you'll go to the App Switcher.

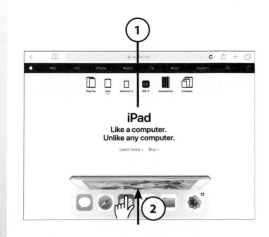

3. Tap another app. Hold for a second so it "pops" and you can drag it up and to the right.

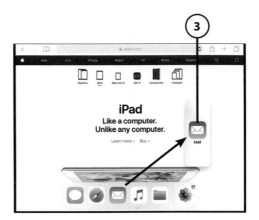

4. Move the icon to the right side of the screen, and it should push Safari to the left, making room for the new app to the right. Release your finger.

5. The new app takes up about a third of the screen to the right. You could also have moved to the left to have the new app take up the left third.

6. The previous app still remains on the screen, using the left two-thirds. Both apps are active and usable.

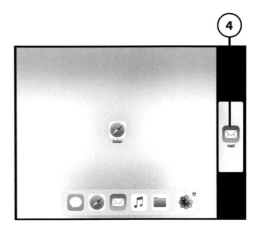

7. A line divides the apps. You can tap and drag the middle portion of that line to the left or right. You can drag it to the left to give each app one half of the screen, or the left app the left third and the right app the right two-thirds. You can also drag all the way left or right to hide one app and let the other use the full screen.

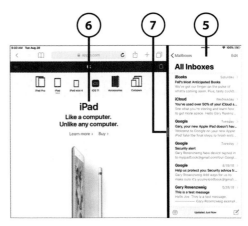

8. Tap and hold the small line, or handle, at the top of the app, and then drag it down slightly to give the main app the entire screen. The secondary app window floats above the primary app. (You could have done this in step 4 by simply not dragging the new app so far to the right.)

9. Drag this handle to the left side of the screen to move the window there.

10. Drag the top handle all the way to the right, off the screen, to make the window disappear.

11. Drag starting from off the right side of the screen to bring the window back.

   There are many more ways to interact with these windows. For instance, if you drag the handle down slightly you see you have the chance to make the window a static one-third of the screen again, pushing the other app to the other two-thirds.

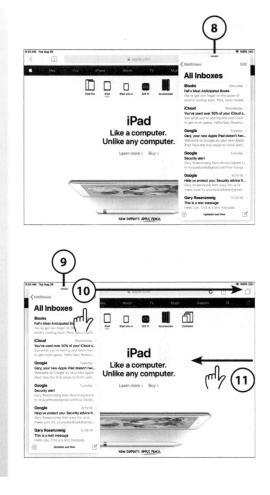

It's Not All Good

Not All Apps Support Multitasking

It is up to third-party app developers to support and allow multitasking. Some apps might not allow it because it is difficult for the app to be shown in a one-third or one-half screen window. You can count on most standard Apple-created iPad apps to work with multitasking. In some cases, a third-party app might work as the full-screen app with another app on top of it in a window, but not the other way around.

Viewing Video with Picture-in-Picture

Another method for multitasking is specific to video. While you are watching video in some apps, like Safari, you can keep the video playing on the screen while you move to another app. This example uses a video on a web page.

1. Start on a web page that has an embedded video. Sometimes you need to start the video to see the controls.

2. Look for this Picture-in-Picture button and tap it. If you don't see it, it means that the video isn't being presented in a format that is compatible with picture-in-picture on your iPad.

3. The video is replaced with a "This video is playing in picture in picture" message.

4. The video moves to a corner of the screen.

5. You can tap and drag the whole video to move it to another corner of the screen.

6. Tap this button to restore the video to its normal place in the web page or app you are using. If you don't see these buttons, tap once in the center of the video to reveal them.

7. Tap the Pause button to pause playback. It changes to a Play button so you can use it to resume playback.

8. Tap the X button to close the video.

9. Press the Home button to go to the Home screen, or use any method to go to any other app (not shown).

10. The picture-in-picture window remains over the Home screen or new app so you can continue to watch while you do other tasks.

11. You can also pinch open to enlarge the picture-in-picture window.

Using iPhone/iPod touch Apps

Most apps in Apple's App Store are built for both the iPhone (and iPod touch) and iPad. Both devices run iOS, but the iPhone has a much smaller screen than the iPad. If a developer has created an app specifically for the iPhone's screen, and not the iPad, you can use a special feature of the iPad to enlarge the app to make it fill most of your display.

1. To enlarge the app, tap the expand button.

2. If the app looks blurry when it's enlarged, tap the shrink button to return to normal size.

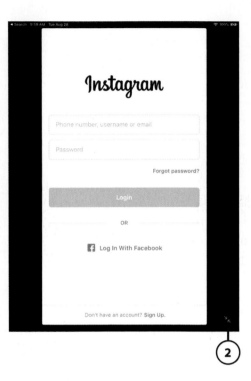

Dragging and Dropping Between Apps

You can drag and drop items between apps. This works in a similar way to using a desktop computer. There's no definitive list of what types of objects can be dragged and dropped and which apps support them, but you'll find it works in many cases, especially with the built-in apps from Apple.

Inserting Photos into an Email Message

This first example shows you how to add an image to an email message. Start with the Mail app open and a new email on the screen.

1. The Mail app is open with a message in the process of being written.

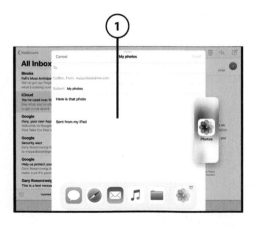

2. Drag up from the bottom of the screen just enough to bring up the Dock. For the example, I added the Photos app to the Dock in advance, so I can use it in multitasking.

3. Tap the Photos app and wait a second for it to "pop" so you can drag it. Then drag it up and to the right.

4. Release it about here, so it appears as a window, allowing the Mail app to remain full screen under it.

5. Inside the window with the Photos app, navigate to the album with the photo you want.

6. Tap and drag the photo to the message. A green + symbol appears to let you know that the image will be inserted. Do not release your hold on the photo.

7. While you are dragging the photo with one finger, you can use another finger to tap a second image and add it to the drag. You can include as many as you want. The number appears next to the green + symbol.

8. After you finish, you can drag the Photos app out of the way by grabbing the top handle and moving it to the right. It then will be offscreen, but can easily be brought back later by dragging from offscreen right to left.

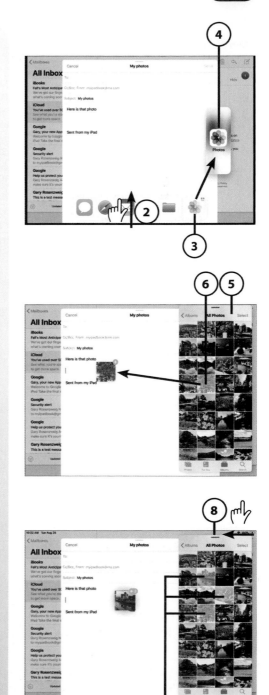

Dragging Text from a Web Page to Notes

Here is another example. In this case, say you want to do some research online, so you are in Safari. Now you see some text you want to put into a note in the Notes app.

1. Safari is being used to view a page.

2. Drag up from the bottom of the screen just enough to bring up the Dock.

3. Drag the Notes app from the Dock to the upper right. (For this example, the Notes app is on the right side of the Dock because it was recently used.) Bring the app all the way to the right so it takes the right one-third of the screen, and Safari maintains the left two-thirds.

4. The Notes app is now on the right. It is open to a note.

5. Select some text from the web page in Safari.

6. Tap and drag the selection from Safari to Notes. The green + indicator shows that this text will be inserted into the note.

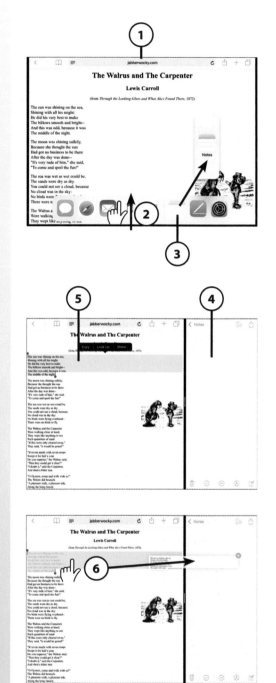

7. Release and the text is now copied to the note.

Note that you could have done the opposite here, with the same result. You could have had the Notes app taking up the left two-thirds of the screen, or even the full screen, and Safari on the right or as a floating window. The drag action would work just as well.

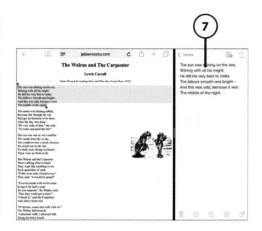

It's Not All Good

Not All Apps Support Drag and Drop

For drag and drop to work, both apps need to support it. For instance, the current version of Keynote doesn't support it, so dragging an image from Safari to a Keynote slide doesn't work. Fortunately, you can still copy and paste with both apps on the screen, so that solution is an alternative in some of these cases.

Exporting Photos to Files

Let's take a look at one more example. This example demonstrates dragging from the Photos app to the Files app. On a Mac or PC, this would be the equivalent to exporting photos as files.

1. The Photos app is running and open to some photos.

2. Drag up from the bottom of the screen to bring up the Dock.

3. Tap the Files app in the Dock and hold until it "pops;" then drag it up and to the right to use it as a window.

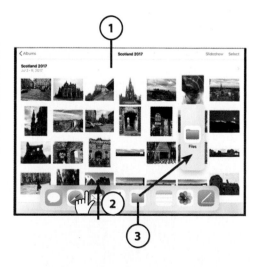

4. The Files app is now a movable window on the right side.

5. Tap and drag the first photo, but do not drop it into the Files app yet. Keep holding it.

6. While holding the first photo, tap two other photos with another finger. This adds them to the stack of photos you are dragging.

7. Drag the photos into the Files app and release.

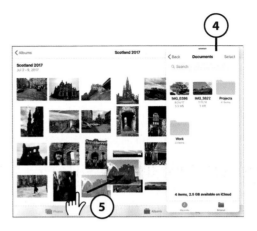

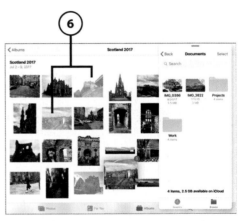

8. The three photos are exported from Photos and now also exist as files in the Files app.

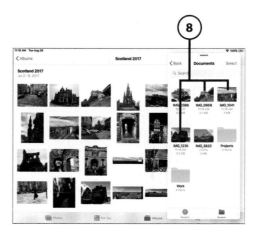

Getting Help with Apps

Apps are developed rapidly by both large and small companies. Because of Apple's restrictions on app distribution, apps are difficult to test, which means it is common to find bugs, have problems, or simply need to ask a question.

1. Check in the app to see if you can contact the developer. For example, in the Word Tiles game app, there is an About/Feedback button that takes you to a page of frequently asked questions and contact information.

2. If you don't find a way to contact support in the app, launch the App Store app and search for the app there. Then scroll down the page to the description.

3. Look for the App Support button, which would take you right to a page at the developer's website with support information.

4. Alternatively, you might find a link to the developer website, which would also have support information or a way to contact the developer.

5. If you need support, don't leave a review asking for support. Although developers can respond to a review on this page, it is difficult to communicate this way and get actual help with a problem. The developer has no way to contact you directly through a review.

>>>Go Further
SHARING APPS

When you buy an app, it can be put on any iPad (or iPhone/iPod touch if it works there, too) registered to your iTunes account. So if you have an iPad and an iPhone, you can buy the app on one and put it on the other at no extra charge. You can use the Family Sharing feature of iOS to also share that app purchase with other members of your family. See "Sharing Purchases with Your Family" in Chapter 4, "Playing Music and Video," to learn more about Family Sharing.

Monitoring and Managing Your Apps

Most users don't need to do anything extra to keep apps running smoothly. However, you do have a variety of tools that let you see how much storage space and battery power your apps are using, and whether they are accessing your location and other information.

Viewing App Storage Information

To see how much storage space each app is using on your iPad, go to the Settings app.

1. Tap the Settings app icon.

2. Tap General.

3. Tap iPad Storage.

Settings

4. At the top of the iPad Storage screen is a graph showing what types of data take up space on your iPad.

5. You can offload apps to save space. See "Offload Apps to Save Space" earlier in this chapter.

6. The list of apps at the bottom of this screen doesn't appear instantly; it takes a few seconds to generate. All your apps are listed, sorted by storage space with the app that takes up the most space listed first. Tap an app for more details.

7. Apps can show different information on this screen. In this case, the breakdown of storage between the app itself and the data stored by the app is shown.

8. Tap to offload the app, which keeps the data around but deletes the app. On the Home screen, the app's icon is dimmed, and you can tap it to re-download the app and resume using it.

9. Tap to delete both the app and its data.

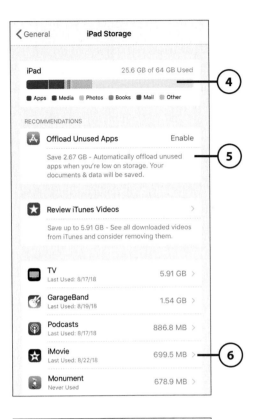

< General   iPad Storage

iPad   25.6 GB of 64 GB Used

● Apps ● Media ◌ Photos ● Books ● Mail ◌ Other

RECEMMENDATIONS

🅰 Offload Unused Apps   Enable

Save 2.67 GB - Automatically offload unused apps when you're low on storage. Your documents & data will be saved.

★ Review iTunes Videos   >

Save up to 5.91 GB - See all downloaded videos from iTunes and consider removing them.

▢ TV   5.91 GB >
  Last Used: 8/17/18

🎸 GarageBand   1.54 GB >
  Last Used: 8/19/18

🎙 Podcasts   886.8 MB >
  Last Used: 8/17/18

☆ iMovie   699.5 MB >
  Last Used: 8/22/18

▨ Monument   678.9 MB >
  Never Used

< Back   iMovie

★ iMovie
  Apple

App Size   688.2 MB

Documents & Data   11.3 MB

Offload App

This will free up storage used by the app, but keep its documents and data. Reinstalling the app will place back your data if the app is still available in the App Store.

Delete App

This will delete the app and all related data from this iPad. This action can't be undone.

10. In other cases, you see information specific to the app. For instance, with the Music app, you see the total space used by all songs. You also see a list of all artists.

11. You can tap to dig down into an artist's albums, or swipe to the left to reveal a Delete button to remove all songs by the artist. Other apps might let you delete documents, videos, images, or whatever types of data the app uses.

Viewing Battery Usage

If you notice your iPad's battery life isn't as long as you think it should be, it could be because an app is using more than its share. You can check the battery usage for each app in the Settings app.

1. From the Settings app, tap Battery.

2. You see a lot of data about your battery level over the last 24 hours or 10 days, and your activity over that time, too.

Days Vary

The number of days you see in Last X Hours or Last X Days can vary based on your usage.

3. Tap here to switch between the 24-hours or 10-days view.

4. The list gives you an idea of which app might be an energy hog. Keep in mind that it is relative. In this example, this game app had just recently consumed the most battery power simply because I'd used it the most.

5. Tap to toggle between power usage and the amount of screen time and background time to help you determine if an app is using too much power relative to the amount of use you have for it.

Viewing Location Usage

Another thing apps use is information; of particular use is your location. This helps mapping and information apps to give you relevant results, for instance. You can see which apps use your location and how often they access it in the Settings app.

1. In the Settings app, go to the Privacy settings.

2. Tap Location Services.

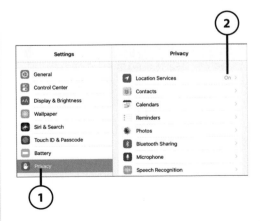

Location by Wi-Fi

Remember that your iPad can get your location even if you do not have a mobile wireless data plan. It looks at which Wi-Fi hotspots are near, and figures out your location from a database that knows where these hotspots are located.

3. Here you see a list of apps that access your location. Some apps access your location only while they are the app you are currently using. Other apps access that information even while they are running in the background. Keep in mind that this is about permissions, not usage. Just because an app has been given permission to access your location in the background doesn't mean it is always doing so.

4. The little compass needle icons are color-coded to let you know how often your location is used by the apps. For instance, three apps show a gray icon, which means that they have used your location in the last 24 hours, but not recently.

5. You can tap any item to revoke location access, or in some cases change it from Always to While Using the App.

What Is a Geofence?

The Location Services screen in the Settings app shows a hollow purple arrow next to an app that is using a geofence. This simply means the app checks to see whether you are in a certain area. For instance, a shopping app may check to see if you are in the store. The MLB At the Ballpark app uses this to see if you are in the stadium and customizes the information based on that fact.

❮ Privacy   **Location Services**

Location Services

Location Services uses Bluetooth and crowd-sourced Wi-Fi hotspot locations to determine your approximate location. About Location Services & Privacy...

Share My Location   >

"Gary Rosenzweig's iPad" is being used for location sharing.

	App Store	◀ While Using >
	Apple Store	While Using >
	Apple Support	While Using >
	Calendar	While Using >
	Camera	While Using >
	Find Friends	While Using >
	Home	While Using >
	Maps	◀ Never >
	News	While Using >
	Photos	While Using >
	Safari Websites	While Using >
	Siri & Dictation	While Using >
	Weather	◀ Always >
	System Services	◀ >

◁ A hollow arrow indicates that an item may receive your location under certain conditions.

◀ A purple arrow indicates that an item has recently used your location.

Viewing Information Sharing Permissions

Some apps communicate with each other. For instance, Keynote might have access to your photo library, or Skype might have access to your Contacts database. You are usually asked for permission when this first happens. For instance, the first time you insert an image into a Keynote presentation, a dialog pops up asking for you to grant permission for Keynote to access your photos.

You can view these connections between apps in the Settings app. You can also revoke these permissions.

1. In the Settings app, tap Privacy.

2. You see a list of apps that share information. Tap one of them.

3. In this case, two apps have asked for permission to access the camera.

4. You can switch off access to any app. Keep in mind that this could have consequences and the app might no longer be able to get the information it needs to operate.

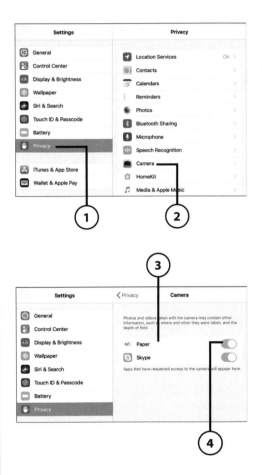

Modifying Notifications Settings

When you start using an app, it might ask you if it is okay for it to send you notifications. The notifications are little alert boxes in the middle of your screen, or messages at the top of your screen, that appear when something happens that the app wants you to know about. Apps need your permission to show you these notifications, which is why they ask. You can change your decision later by using the Settings app.

1. Open the Settings app and tap Notifications.

2. Tap an app to view its specific notifications settings.

3. Tap on a notification type to switch it on or off. For instance, switching off Banners means that neither temporary nor persistent banners will appear.

4. Tap here to select the banner type: temporary or persistent. The latter remains on the screen until you dismiss it, whereas the former appears only for a few seconds.

5. Turning on Badges means that the app's icon shows a number over the Home screen icon when there is a message.

6. Many apps let you set the specific sound used. Tap Sounds to specify the sound the app uses.

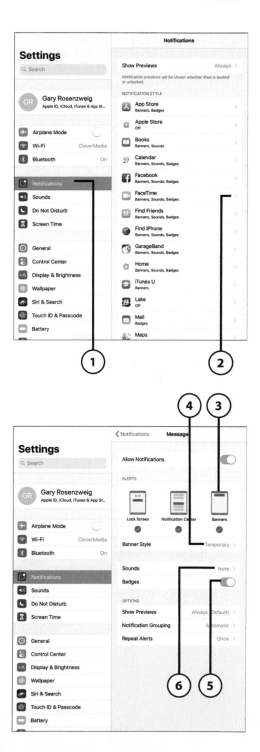

7. Turn off Show Previews if you prefer that the small preview of the message does not appear with the alert.

8. Notification Grouping is a new feature of iOS 12 that groups together notifications on the Lock screen and Notification Center so you see a single item even if this app has multiple notifications. You can tap it to reveal all the individual notifications.

9. Tap Repeat Alerts to configure whether the alert repeats after a few minutes, and how many times. It is useful to have an alert repeat in case you missed it the first time.

10. If you want to completely disable an app's ability to send you notifications, switch off Allow Notifications.

Apps Vary

Each app has its own set of settings, so take a few minutes to go through them all and see what options are offered. As you add new apps to your iPad, any that use the Notifications Center are added to this list; so it is a good idea to occasionally review your settings.

Watching Your iPad Usage with Screen Time New!

A new iOS 12 feature is Screen Time in the Settings app. This feature shows you how much time you spend on your iPad and in each app. You can also submit yourself to voluntary restrictions to try to limit your time on your iPad and in each app. You can even block content completely.

Checking How You Spend Your Time

1. In the Settings app, tap Screen Time.

2. A general graph shows how you spend the time on your iPad. It's broken into categories like Productivity, Games, and so on.

3. Tap here to dig down into usage by time of day and individual app.

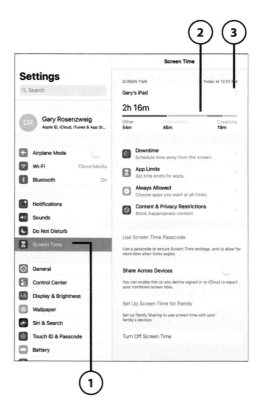

4. You can see your total iPad time for today, plus a break-down for each hour.

5. You can also see how much time each app was used. If you tap an app name, you can see an hourly break-down and even add a voluntary limit on that app. We look at limits in the next section.

6. Websites are also listed.

7. Only the top apps and sites are shown. But you can tap Show More to see a longer list.

8. Swipe up to see more.

< Screen Time

| Today | Last 7 Days |

Gary's iPad

SCREEN TIME   Today at 12:46 PM

2h 34m

12 AM   6 AM   12 PM   6 PM

Other   Productivity   Creativity
58m   46m   19m

MOST USED   SHOW CATEGORIES

Safari
47m

Settings
37m

Notes
19m

Photos
19m

Instagram
18m

App Store
16m

macmost.com
16m

Show More

PICKUPS

0 per hour

9. You can see how many times you physically picked up your iPad.

10. You can also see the number of notifications you have received. Tap these to adjust the notifications settings for any app so you can cut down on notifications you don't really need.

Screen Time Widget

You can also see how much time you have been spending on your iPad on the Today View, which you reveal by swiping left to right on the first Home screen. The widgets there include a Screen Time item. You can learn about using these widgets in Today View in Chapter 1, "Getting Started." If you don't see a Screen Time widget, you can add it by using the Edit button at the bottom of the widgets.

Shared Screen Time

If you turn on the Share Across Devices option in Screen Time, it will combine all the statistics for your iOS devices. So, if you have an iPhone and an iPad, it totals the usage amounts. These devices would be linked through your Apple ID, so any iOS device using your Apple ID is counted.

‹ Screen Time	Today	
Safari	47m	›
Settings	37m	›
Notes	19m	›
Photos	19m	›
Instagram	18m	›
App Store	16m	›
macmost.com	16m	›

Show More

PICKUPS

0 per hour

12 AM　　6 AM　　12 PM　　6 PM

Total Pickups	5
Most Pickups	2 between 11 AM – 12 PM

NOTIFICATIONS

1°

Around 0 per hour

12 AM　　6 AM　　12 PM　　6 PM

Limiting Your iPad Time

Now that you know how much time you spend on your iPad, you might decide to limit yourself and cut down on that screen time. You can do this with the App Limits tool.

1. Go into the Screen Time section of the Settings app.

2. Tap App Limits.

3. Tap Add Limit.

4. Choose from a category of app, such as Games.

5. Tap Add.

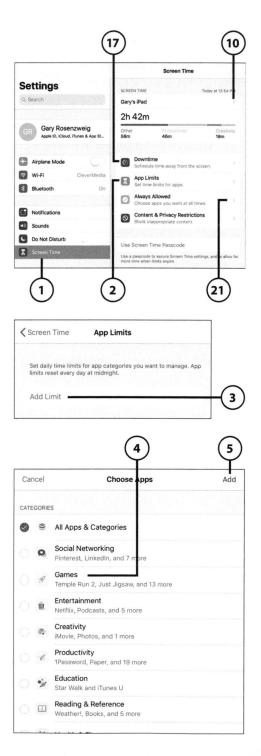

6. Set an amount of time.

7. Tap the back button when you are done.

8. The limit is listed. You can tap it to edit or delete the limit.

9. These limits apply to an entire category of app. If you want to set a limit on a specific app, you can do that, too. Tap the back button.

10. Tap the name of your iPad to bring back the Screen Time list of apps.

11. Tap an app.

< App Limits   **Games**

Time   Set

58
59
0 hours   0 min
1   1
2   2

App limits apply to all devices that are using iCloud for screen time. A notification will appear five minutes before the limit expires.

APPS & CATEGORIES

Games
Temple Run 2, Just Jigsaw, and 13 more

Edit Apps

Delete Limit

< Screen Time   **App Limits**

Set daily time limits for app categories you want to manage. App limits reset every day at midnight.

Games   2 hr >

Add Limit

MOST USED   SHOW CATEGORIES

Settings
51m >

Safari
47m >

Notes
19m >

Photos
19m >

Instagram
18m >

App Store
16m >

macmost.com
16m >

Show More

12. Tap Add Limit.

13. Set a time.

14. You can also set this limit to apply only for certain days of the week.

15. Tap Add.

16. Tap the back button and then tap the next back button to return to the main screen for Screen Time.

17. You can also set a time limit for the entire iPad. Tap Downtime.

16

⟨ Today   **Safari**

SCREEN TIME   Today at 1:01 PM

47m

12 AM   6 AM   12 PM   6 PM

Daily Average   6m

INFO

Safari

Age Rating   No Rating

Developer   Apple Inc.

LIMITS

Add Limit

12

13   **14** **15**

Cancel   **Safari**   Add

Time   1 hr

                         58
                         59
        0
              1 hour   0 min
               2   1
               3   2

Customize Days   >

App limits apply to all devices that are using iCloud for screen time. A notification will appear five minutes before the limit expires.

APPS & CATEGORIES

Safari

    Edit Apps

18. Turn on Downtime.

19. You can set a start and end time. Between these two times, you will be allowed to use only selected apps that you have designated.

20. Tap the back button.

21. You can tap Always Allowed to choose apps that will be allowed even during "downtime."

22. Tap the green button next to an app to move it to the top list so it will be allowed at all times.

23. Tap the red button next to an app to remove it from the list of apps always allowed.

Set It, Lock It

If you are setting up these time limits for another person, such as a child, you also might want to set a passcode for Screen Time so that this person cannot change the limits. You can do that with the Use Screen Time Passcode button on the main Screen Time screen. We previously looked at this and the content restrictions settings of Screen Time in Chapter 2, "Customizing Your iPad."

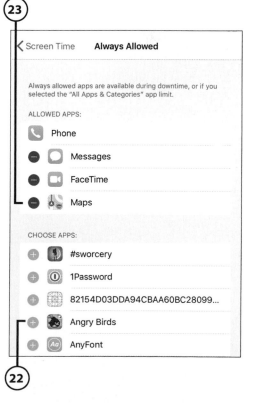

Controlling Apps with Siri Shortcuts New!

While Siri has been around for a while now, iOS 12 brings some new and powerful functionality. You can now define your own Siri voice commands that perform tasks in one or more apps. These are called Siri Shortcuts.

There are some ready-to-use Siri Shortcuts. You can also create your own by writing simple programs using drag-and-drop in a special Shortcuts app.

Using Pre-Built and Suggested Siri Shortcuts

You can find some pre-built shortcuts, plus shortcuts that are automatically generated based on your most frequent behavior. To start using these, you need to enable them, and assign a voice command to them.

1. Go to the Settings app and tap Siri & Search.

2. Look for the Suggested Shortcuts section. What you see will be different from the figure because the choices are based on your most common behaviors. For this example, I'm using the See Stories from Today item with a News app icon. There is also an expanded list of suggestions if you tap All Shortcuts.

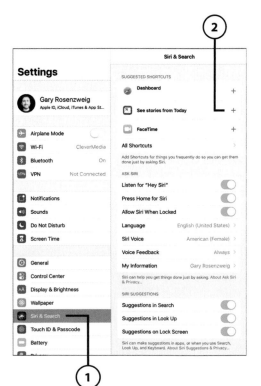

3. The next screen shows you the Siri Shortcut again, with the app icon for the app it controls, plus the name of the app.

4. Tap the large red Record button to record your voice command that will trigger this Shortcut.

5. As you speak, the waveform reacts, and the words appear in the middle of the screen. Use a command that is easy to remember, but not too long. In this case I used, "Show me today's news."

6. Tap the red Stop button when you are done with the command.

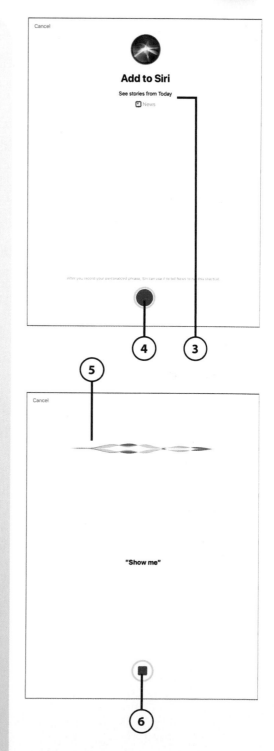

7. The next screen shows you the completed command.

8. You can tap Re-Record Phrase if you change your mind or if your iPad didn't hear you correctly.

9. Tap Done to exit.

10. You see a list of all your Shortcuts.

11. Tap Edit to edit, delete, or re-record your Shortcuts.

12. Press the back button to return to the main screen for Siri & Search.

13. You can get back to your list of Shortcuts at the top of the Siri & Search settings screen now that you have created a Shortcut.

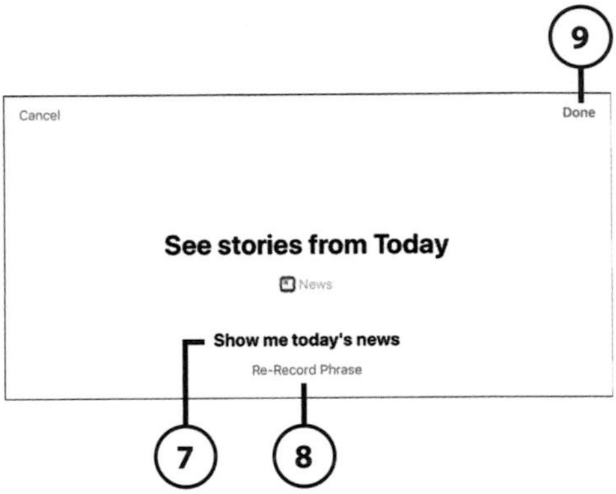

(9)

Cancel   Done

See stories from Today

News

Show me today's news

Re-Record Phrase

(7)   **(8)**

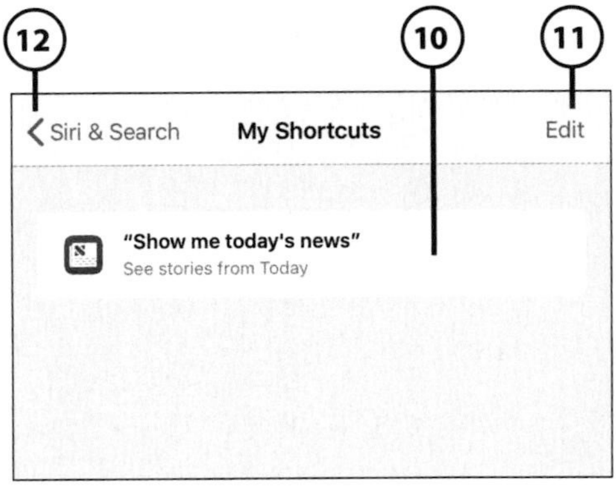

(12)   **(10)**   **(11)**

< Siri & Search   **My Shortcuts**   Edit

"Show me today's news"
See stories from Today

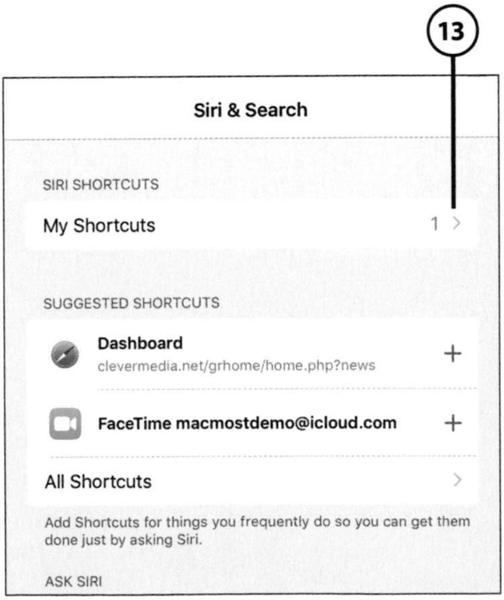

(13)

Siri & Search

SIRI SHORTCUTS

My Shortcuts   1 >

SUGGESTED SHORTCUTS

Dashboard   +
clevermedia.net/grhome/home.php?news

FaceTime macmostdemo@icloud.com   +

All Shortcuts   >

Add Shortcuts for things you frequently do so you can get them
done just by asking Siri.

ASK SIRI

Creating Your Own Siri Shortcuts

To make your own Shortcuts, you need the Shortcuts app. If you don't already have this on your iPad, look for it in the App Store. It is a free app from Apple.

Shortcuts allows you to use building blocks to create a Siri Shortcut that commands one or more apps to perform tasks. You can design countless variations. To explain the basics, I'm building a Shortcut that takes a photo and sends it as a message to a specific person.

1. Launch the Shortcuts app.

2. There are two views: the Library view and the Gallery view. The Gallery contains some prebuilt Shortcuts that you can use or alter. We'll start with the Library view that shows you your current Shortcuts, including some to start off with.

3. Tap the Create Shortcut button. You can also use the + button at the top right.

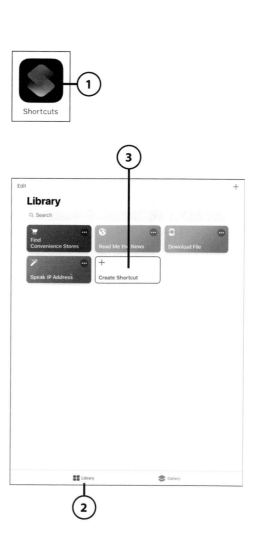

4. You build a Shortcut using a series of "actions." On the left side you see a list of some of the most commonly used actions. To see a list of all actions, organized by category, tap the Search field at the top.

5. You can continue typing to search for a specific action, or you can tap a category in the list. After completing these steps, you will want to return here and take your time to explore all the different actions in each category to see what is possible with Shortcuts. Tap Photos & Video.

6. Now you see a list on the left of all the photo- and video-related actions. The action we want is right near the top, called Take Photo. Tap that. You could also tap the "i" button next to each one for a description of the action.

7. The new action appears in your Shortcut to the right.

8. In this case, a message states that you need to give Shortcuts access to the camera. Tap Allow Access and then tap OK when asked to give access.

9. Actions often have options. For instance, with the Take Photo action, you can choose the front or back camera, the number of photos that will be taken, and whether you see a preview of the photo when it's done.

10. Tap the back button to go back to the long list of actions to add another action to the Shortcut.

11. Swipe up until you see Messages in the list.

12. Tap Messages.

13. Tap Send Message to add that action to the list on the right.

14. Tap Allow Access to give it access to your Contacts.

15. The new action is now part of your Shortcut.

16. Turn off Show When Run because you don't need to see that step; you just want it to perform automatically.

17. Add the recipient. You can use the name or email address from your Contacts app.

18. Tap here and type a short message to include.

19. To finish the Shortcut, tap the Settings button.

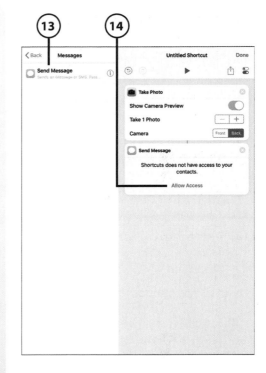

20. Tap here and type a name for this Shortcut.

21. Tap here to select a color and icon for the Shortcut.

22. Tap to add an icon for the Shortcut to the Home screen.

23. Tap Add to Siri if you want to add this Shortcut as a Siri command, and then go through steps 4 through 9 of the previous task.

24. Tap Done.

25. The Shortcut is added to your Library. You can run it by tapping the button.

26. Tap the … button to edit the Shortcut. To delete it, tap and hold the button; the Shortcuts jiggle so you can select them and delete them with the Trash icon.

(23) **(21)** **(20)** **(24)**

Settings   Done

Name   Send Daily Picture >

Icon   >

Add to Siri

Run this shortcut with your voice by adding it to Siri.

Show in Widget

Show in Share Sheet

Add to Home Screen

Share Shortcut

Import Questions   >

(22)

(25)

Edit   +

Library

Q Search

Find
Convenience Stores   Read Me th News   Download File

Speak IP Address   Send Daily Picture   +
                                               Create Shortcut

(26)

Want To Do Some Coding?

The actions in the Shortcuts app aren't just commands for other apps to perform. There is also a category of actions named Scripting. The actions here include things like Repeat, If, Choose From Menu, List, Calculate, Set Variable, and Get Variable.

If you've done any programming, you'll realize that these actions give you a lot of power. You can create shortcuts that use variables and even arrays. They can branch with If statements and repeat with loops.

Although the drag-and-drop interface makes it difficult to create long, complex programs, you can certainly do some interesting things. Shortcuts is like Automator on the Mac in that it lets you build programs, or "scripts," that will make common and repetitive tasks easier for you.

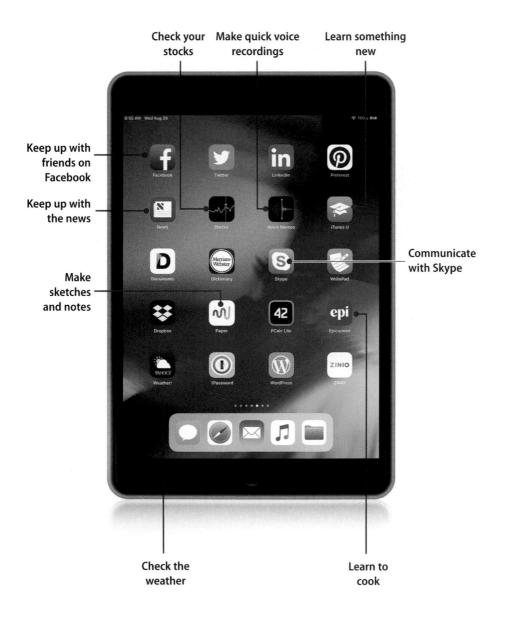

Check your stocks

Make quick voice recordings

Learn something new

Keep up with friends on Facebook

Keep up with the news

Make sketches and notes

Communicate with Skype

Check the weather

Learn to cook

In this chapter, you take a look at various apps that you should add to your iPad to make it even more useful.

→ Connecting with Friends on Facebook
→ Reading the News
→ Checking Your Stocks
→ Recording Voice Memos
→ Adding a Dictionary
→ Making Phone Calls with Skype
→ Handwriting Notes with WritePad
→ Sketching Ideas with Paper
→ Adding a Calculator with PCalc Lite
→ Finding Recipes with Epicurious
→ Checking the Weather
→ Learning New Things with iTunes U
→ Other Useful Apps

16

Must-Have Apps

Ask almost anyone what the best feature of the iPad is and you'll get the same answer: all the apps! The App Store is not only a source of more than one million useful, interesting, and fun apps, but it grows each day as third-party developers and Apple add more. Here's a look at how to use some of the most popular apps for the iPad to perform various useful tasks.

Connecting with Friends on Facebook

Many people now spend more time on Facebook than the rest of the Internet combined. If you are one of those people, the official Facebook app is probably the first third-party app you should put on your iPad.

With the Facebook app, you can browse your wall, post status updates, send messages, post photos, and do most things that you can do on the Facebook website, but the environment is designed for iPad users.

1. Search the App Store for the Facebook app. Tap Get to download and install it. After the app has downloaded, the button changes to Open. Tap it to launch the app.

2. When you first run the Facebook app, you need to sign on with your email address and password.

3. If you don't have a Facebook account yet, you can sign up within the app.

4. Scroll up and down to view your News Feed.

5. Like posts just as you would on the Facebook website.

6. Tap Comment to add a comment to a post.

7. View and handle friend requests.

8. Tap to find out whether you have any direct messages. However, you cannot use the Facebook app to view or respond to Facebook messages. Frustrating, right? Facebook insists that you use their Messenger app for that. Search the App Store for "Facebook Messenger," which you can install for free.

9. See your list of Facebook notifications.

10. Tap the More button to access different parts of Facebook.

11. Tap your name to examine your own timeline and edit your profile.

12. Tap Most Recent to see recent items in your Facebook feed instead of just what Facebook deems important.

13. See a list of your friends and view their information and their timelines.

14. Post to Facebook by tapping the empty post field. You can also use the Photo button to jump right to your photo library to choose a photo to post. If you don't see this empty post here, drag the screen downward until you are at the very top of your News Feed and it will appear.

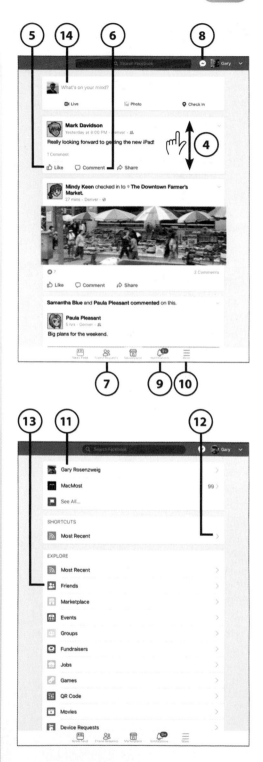

15. Type the text of your update.

16. Add friends who are with you to the update.

17. Add a photo from your photo library, or take a new photo using your iPad's cameras.

18. Tap to include your location in the post.

19. Tap to start streaming live video using your iPad's cameras.

20. Post the update to Facebook.

Cancel	**Create Post** — (20)
Gary Rosenzweig	
👥 Friends ▾	
What's on your mind? — (15)	
🖼 Photo/Video — (17)	
👤 Tag People — (16)	
😊 Feeling/Activity/Sticker	
📍 Check In — (18)	
🏷 Sell Something	
📹 Live Video — (19)	

It All Looks Different

If there is one consistent thing about Facebook, it is change. Facebook loves to change how its website and apps look. So if the Facebook app looks different than what you see here, it could simply be that Facebook has, once again, decided to redesign the interface.

Post from Outside

You don't need to use the Facebook app to post pictures. You can do it right from the Photos app and other image-handling apps. You need to have the Facebook app installed and you need to have signed in, but other apps allow you to post directly to Facebook without needing to switch to the Facebook app. You can do things like post pictures from the Photos app, post links from Safari, and ask Siri to "update my Facebook status."

>>>*Go Further*

MORE SOCIAL MEDIA APPS

Facebook is undoubtedly the primary social media platform for most people. Other platforms do exist, and they also have apps you might want to try. If you use any of these services, the app is worth adding to your iPad.

 Twitter: Twitter is a hugely popular app for sharing short messages with others and following the tweets of friends and public figures.

 LinkedIn: For many business professionals and job-seekers, LinkedIn is even more important than Facebook.

 Pinterest: A fun way to visually share your interests with others.

 Google+: Google's social network is similar to Facebook, but part of the Google ecosystem.

 Instagram: A very popular way to share photos and videos with friends. Unfortunately, this app is still optimized for iPhone screens, though you can use it on your iPad as well.

 Snapchat: Snapchat is very popular, especially with teens. Unfortunately, the Snapchat app is iPhone-only. You can get the app for your iPad, but it is simply the iPhone app enlarged to fit the iPad screen. It's maybe not a great way to post snaps, but it is useful for following others.

Reading the News

With the News app that comes with your iPad (with a new design for iOS 12), you can read news stories from hundreds of newspapers, magazines, blogs, and other sources. The articles are presented in a nice design that makes it easy to browse through stories and bookmark some for later reading. Better still, you can pick which news sources you see and which interests you have, so you are essentially getting a newspaper customized for you.

1. Launch the News app. It is a default app that comes with your iPad. If this is the first time you are running News, you might see a series of welcome screens.

2. The Today screen is usually where you start when you go to the News app. If you have previously been reading an article, however, you are returned to that page. The Today screen shows you Top Stories, Trending Stories, and stories tailored for you based on what you have previously read and liked.

3. Swipe up to see the different sections of the Today screen.

4. Tap any story to jump into it and read more.

5. Tap to open a menu. Alternatively, tap and drag from the left edge of the screen to the right. If you are holding your iPad in horizontal orientation, then this menu is always present.

6. The top of the menu shows you the date and current temperature in your area.

7. Tap Today to jump back to the Today screen.

8. Tap Spotlight to view the current spotlight article, usually a feature or in-depth analysis of some topic.

9. Tap a specific publication or topic that you follow to jump to it. This list starts with some default sources and topics, but you can edit it to suit your taste.

10. A list of suggestions gives you the chance to customize the news you see. Tap the Like or Dislike icons to like or dislike a topic. Swipe up to see more topics. At the bottom of the menu is a Discover Channels & Topics button you can use to delve deeper into which publications and topics you want to see more articles from.

11. Tap Edit to remove publications and topics from your Following list.

12. Type in the Search field to find specific publications and topics. If you don't see the Search field, tap and drag down on the menu to reveal it. Thousands of newspapers, magazines, TV stations, and other news sources publish to Apple News.

13. In this example, I'm searching for local news.

14. If you see a channel or topic you want to add, tap the heart icon next to it.

15. Tap a topic to get news articles from a variety of sources instead of just one publication.

16. Alternatively, you can type a topic in the Search field to find current articles on the subject.

17. Tap an article on any page, as you did in step 4, to expand the article to full screen.

18. If the left side menu is in the way of the article, tap anywhere on the right side of the screen to dismiss it.

19. Tap this button to adjust the font size in most articles.

20. Tap the Like button to see more articles like this. You can also tap the Dislike button to tell the News app you aren't interested in articles like this.

21. Tap the Share button to share the article via Messages, Mail, and other methods.

22. Tap to save an article to read later.

23. Bring up the left sidebar menu again. Scroll to the bottom.

24. Tap Saved Stories to see your saved news articles.

25. Tap History to look back at stories you have recently viewed.

9:57 AM   Wed Aug 29

APPLE NEWS
AUGUST 29   62°

Technology

Science

Travel

Business

Fashion

Entertainment

Health

Food   (23)

Sports

Saved Stories ————————(24)

History ————————————(25)

PERSONALIZE YOUR NEWS
Follow your favorite channels and topics to improve your reading experience.

Discover Channels & Topics

Manage Notifications   >

>>>*Go Further*
LOCAL NEWS AND MORE

Using search in step 12 enables you to quickly find sources that don't show up easily when browsing. For instance, you can search for the name of your city, state, or country to see if any local news sources appear. Sometimes there are topics that pertain to your location, such as a sports team.

>>>*Go Further*
MORE NEWS READING APPS

For reading news, you have two types of apps: ones like News that aggregate news from many sources and apps from a single news source.

 USA Today: This daily newspaper features concise news stories and other articles in an easy-to-browse format.

 Flipboard: This third-party app is very similar to Apple's News app, but it has been around a lot longer.

 Feedly: This news reader lets you subscribe to any syndicated (RSS) content.

Zinio: Although some magazines have their own apps, many others can be found inside the app called Zinio. It is kind of a clearinghouse for hundreds of magazines that publish with a standard format. Browse sample articles for free, and then look for magazines you can purchase either as a single issue or as a subscription. You can even get European and Asian magazines that are hard to find in the U.S. A similar app is Texture, recently acquired by Apple.

Checking Your Stocks New!

The Stocks app has been around since the beginning of iOS, but only on the iPhone. iOS 12 adds this useful app to the iPad, and does a complete overhaul of the old app to add news and other features.

1. Look for the Stocks app on your Home screen and launch it. If this is your first time using Stocks, you might see a welcome screen.

2. On the left side, you see some stock quotes and indexes.

3. On the right side you see news, starting with the top business news. You can tap any story to read it.

4. Swipe down to see news sections based on each of the items on the left side.

5. Tap a stock or index to dig down into the numbers.

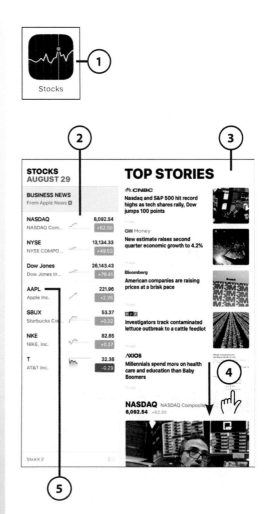

6. You see a detailed chart and information like the day's low, high, volume, and so on.

7. You also see news stories related to this index or company.

8. Tap the time durations to change the chart. For instance, you can tap 3M to see a three-month chart.

9. Tap the Manage button.

10. Tap a red button next to any item to remove it from your watch list.

11. Tap the + button to search for a stock or index by name or symbol and add it to your watch list.

12. Tap Done after you have customized your watch list to suit your interests.

Tracking Non-Stocks

Finding stocks to track is easy because you just search for the company name or symbol. But other things like the S&P 500 index or the price of gold are tricky to find. Keep in mind that the data comes from Yahoo Finance, so you just need to use the same symbols you would use at Yahoo's site. For instance, a quick web search reveals that ^GSPC shows you the S&P 500 index, and XAUUSD=X is a symbol for the price of gold.

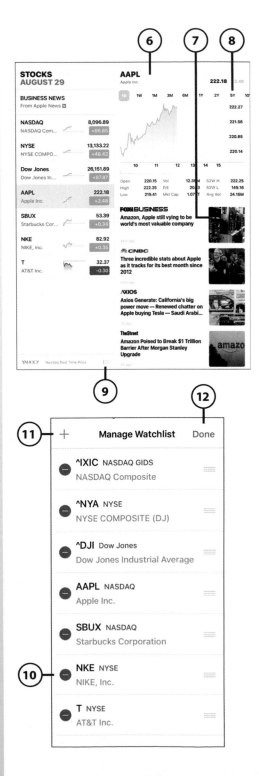

Recording Voice Memos New!

Another app that has been around on the iPhone for a long time but is making its debut on the iPad is the Voice Memos app. This simple app uses the iPad microphone to record audio. You can use this as an alternative to typing notes.

1. Launch the Voice Memos app. If this is your first time using Voice Memos, you see a welcome screen.

2. To record a voice memo, tap the red Record button.

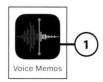

3. As you talk, a waveform indicates it is recording.

4. You can tap the Pause button at any time to pause the recording. It changes to a Resume button you can tap again to continue recording.

5. You can keep track of the length of the recording as you talk.

6. Tap Done when you are finished recording.

7. The recording is named based on your location. You can change that by tapping the name and editing the text.

8. Tap the Play button to play back the recording.

9. Use the Skip Back and Skip Ahead buttons to move through the recording quickly.

10. You can also drag the playback line to jump around in the recording.

11. Alternatively, swipe back and forth to move around in the recording.

12. Tap Trash to delete the memo.

13. Tap the Share button to export the recording as a file to the Files app or to another app that accepts audio recordings as input.

14. You can also go back into the recording and replace the entire thing, a section, or resume recording at the end.

15. All your voice memos are listed on the left. You can jump to any one or use the Edit button to select and delete them.

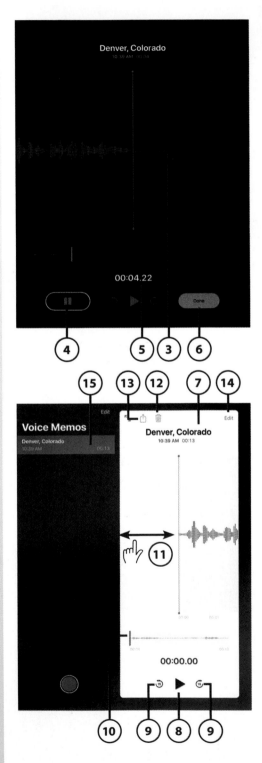

You Can Even Trim

Although Voice Memos seems like a simple app, it has the capability to do complex editing, like trimming the recordings. When you tap the Edit button to edit a recording, you see a trim button at the top left. You can move the start and end of the recording and delete that section or trim the recording to include only that section.

Adding a Dictionary

It would be a crime to have to carry a dictionary with you in addition to your iPad. Of course, the solution is to get a dictionary app for your iPad. The Merriam-Webster Dictionary HD app is a free download from the App Store. There is also a premium version that removes the ads and includes illustrations and other features for a few dollars.

1. Find the Merriam-Webster Dictionary HD app in the App Store. Tap Get to download and install it.

Use Any Online Dictionary

Of course, if you prefer another dictionary that doesn't have an iPad app, you can always just bookmark its site in Safari. You can also create a Home screen bookmark as explained in Chapter 6, "Organizing Your Life."

2. Tap in the Search box and enter a word to look up.

3. Tap the Microphone button to speak the word and look it up. This is handy if you don't know how to spell the word.

4. The word and definition appear.

5. Tap the speaker icon to have the word spoken so you can hear its pronunciation.

6. The app can also be used as a thesaurus. A list of synonyms appears at the bottom. Tap any one to jump to that word. In fact, you can tap any red word in the definition to jump to that word for further clarification.

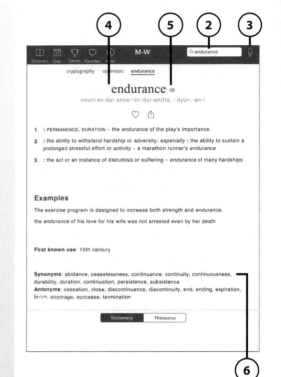

>>>Go Further

MORE DICTIONARY APPS

 Oxford English Dictionary: An alternative to the Merriam-Webster dictionary is, of course, the Oxford. The app is comparable, with a similar set of features.

 Urban Dictionary: Sometimes a standard dictionary isn't enough. If you want definitions for slang words and text message abbreviations, this app can help. Note that this dictionary also includes lots of modern profanity.

 Wikipedia: If you want an encyclopedia instead, you can use Wikipedia's official app for access to entries in their huge user-created database.

Don't forget about using a Google search as another alternative to a dictionary. Google can often take the oddest misspelling and come up with the correct word. Then, the search results include definitions, as well as Wikipedia entries and links to articles about the subject that might help even more.

Siri: Define It For Me

You can ask Siri to define a word, too. Naturally, that works best in situations where you know how to pronounce the word.

Define existential.

What is the definition of existential?

Making Phone Calls with Skype

Your iPad works quite well as a phone when you use a VoIP (voice over IP) app. Skype is probably the most well known. Of course, you can use FaceTime to make both video and audio calls, but that only works if the other person is part of the Apple ecosystem using an iOS or Mac device. If they are on an Android, Windows, or Linux device, Skype is a good alternative.

1. Search for Skype in the App Store. Make sure you look for the iPad app, not the iPhone/iPod touch app of the same name. Tap Get to download and install it, and then tap the Open button to launch the app.

2. Tap Skype Name, Email, or Mobile to sign in using your Skype account. You can also sign in with a Microsoft account. Complete the sign-in process by entering your ID and password. Alternatively, if you do not have a Skype account, enter your email address to start the process to create one.

Get a Skype Account

You need a Skype account to use the Skype app. You can get a free one at https://www.skype.com/. If you find the service useful, you might want to upgrade to a paid account, which lets you call landlines and other phones. The free account lets you call only other Skype users.

3. On the main Skype screen, you can view recent calls, your contacts list, and your Skype info. Tap Calls.

4. Tap the Dialpad button.

5. Use the on-screen keypad to enter a phone number. You need a country code, too, which means using a 1 for U.S. calls. It should be there by default.

6. Tap the Call button.

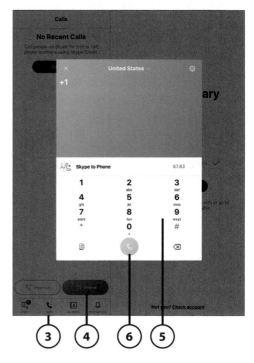

7. While placing a call, you see the status, including the phone number and the elapsed time.

8. Additional buttons are available across the bottom for things like mute, keypad (for touch-tone menus), add callers, and hang up.

9. Tap the End Call button to hang up.

How Do You Hold Your iPad to Talk?

The microphone is at the top of your iPad. The speaker is at the bottom on the back. The best way to hold it during a call might be to just put the iPad in front of you and ignore the locations of both. Or, you can get a set of iPhone EarPods, which include the speakers and the microphone.

How About Skype Video?

You can also make video calls with Skype using your iPad's cameras. But you must be connecting to another Skype user who also has a video camera connected to their computer, or perhaps they are using an iPad as well.

Handwriting Notes with WritePad

You'd think with a touchscreen that the iPad could recognize your handwriting instead of making you type on an on-screen keyboard. The WritePad app enables you to take notes by typing or by using the touchscreen to write with your finger.

1. Search for WritePad in the App Store. Tap the price (currently it's $4.99) to download and install it, and then tap the Open button to launch the app.

2. The first time you use WritePad, you are guided through some setup screens.

3. After setup, you are taken right to an empty document. Instead of typing to add text, draw the text with your finger. Note that the cursor is at the upper left, but you don't need to write there. Write anywhere on the screen.

4. The text appears at the cursor.

5. Tap the Documents button to see all of your WritePad notes.

6. Tap on a note document to open it.

7. Tap the + button to add a new note.

>>>Go Further

MORE ALTERNATIVES TO TYPING

MyScript Nebo: This app keeps your notes in handwritten form, but lets you convert them to text later. It works well when you need to combine text and drawings, and it works especially well if you have an Apple Pencil.

Dragon

Dragon Anywhere: iOS does a good job understanding speech and converting it to text using the built-in speech recognition (see "Dictating Text" in Chapter 1, "Getting Started"). But to take things to the next level, you can use this app from the leader in dictation software. It responds to dictation commands and spelling out words for a completely hands-free solution.

Sketching Ideas with Paper

Perhaps you don't want your handwriting converted to text, but instead want to sketch out ideas or doodle on your iPad. Probably the most popular app for that is the simple Paper by FiftyThree.

1. Search the App Store for Paper by FiftyThree. Tap Get to download and install it, and then tap the Open button to launch the app.

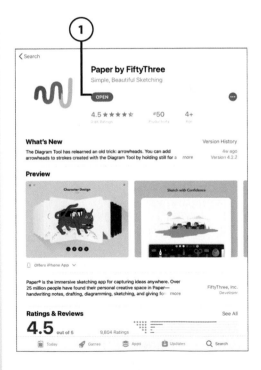

2. When you first run Paper, you go through a series of introductory messages. After that, you see a screen with some sample journal books. You can create your own journal by tapping the + button.

3. If this is an existing journal, you see the pages displayed; you can swipe to flip between the pages. You can also tap a page to edit it.

4. Tap the + button to create a new page.

5. Anything you sketched previously appears on the current page.

6. Tap in the middle or pinch out to zoom in on a page so you can sketch. Pinching in far enough returns to the previous screen showing all the pages of the grid.

7. Tap a pen tool to draw.

8. Tap and drag your finger to draw lines.

9. Tap a color to change colors.

10. Tap the eraser tool and drag your finger on the page to erase.

11. Tap the X or pinch in to zoom back out to view the whole grid of pages.

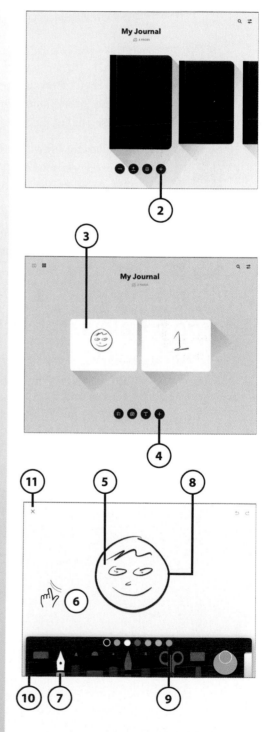

>>>Go Further
MORE SKETCHING APPS

 Autodesk SketchBook: Unlike Paper by FiftyThree, SketchBook is specifically for illustration. Professional artists have used it to create some amazing pieces.

 Adobe Illustrator Draw: This sketching app uses vector-based tools, so it can be a good starting point for artists who need to take their sketches into other Adobe software later. It also has some interesting color tools.

 Brushes Redux and **ArtStudio:** Two other excellent drawing tools with layers, and lots of brush and color options.

Adding a Calculator with PCalc Lite

Your iPad is a powerful computer, capable of processing data and performing calculations. So, how do you calculate a simple restaurant tip? There's no calculator built in to your iPad, but you can easily add one with a third-party app. Let's look at using the free PCalc Lite app. If you search for "calculator" in the App Store, you can find dozens of other different free and paid calculator apps.

1. Find the PCalc Lite app in the App Store and tap Get; then tap the Open button to launch the app.

2. You can enter numbers just like with a real calculator. For instance, enter 68.52, the cost of dinner for two at a nice restaurant. No wine, but desserts.

3. Tap X to multiply by the next number.

4. Tap 20 to indicate 20 percent. Good service with a smile. And then tap % to indicate that 20 is a percent (0.20).

5. The answer appears in the display. By all means, round up to $14. The waiter refilled your water three times without being asked.

6. Tap AC (all clear) to begin your next calculation.

7. In many ways, an app calculator is better than the real thing. For instance, there is an Undo button.

8. Tap the Settings button.

9. You can choose to customize the look of the calculator by changing the theme and the look of the digits. Some calculator apps feature tons of options.

10. If you are a scientist, mathematician, or engineer, you might want to use the calculator in Reverse Polish Notation mode; tap the RPN switch to turn it on. If you don't know what Reverse Polish Notation is, then you don't want to use Reverse Polish Notation mode.

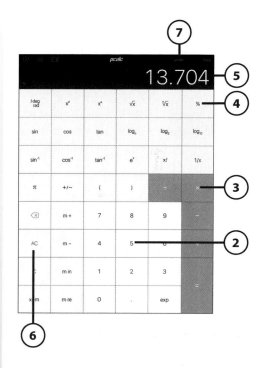

>>>*Go Further*

MORE CALCULATOR APPS

 MyScript Calculator: This app allows you to actually write your numbers as you would on a sheet of paper. You can use operations and mathematical symbols and it calculates what you are asking and gives you an answer. It can even find the value of variables in short algebraic equations.

 The Calculator: This alternative to PCalc includes both standard and scientific calculator modes.

 Calculator HD: This other alternative lets you see your results history in a list.

Siri: Calculations

You can ask Siri to do math for you as well.

What is 6 times 7?

What is 20% of $73.80?

What is the square root of 99?

Finding Recipes with Epicurious

One application for early personal computers was to store and recall recipes. With the Internet, we can also share those recipes. And now with the iPad, there is finally a way to easily have these recipes with you in the kitchen while cooking. The Epicurious app is a favorite for such tasks.

1. Search for Epicurious in the App Store. Tap Get to download and install it, and then tap the Open button to launch the app.

2. Tap here to create an account that lets you store your favorites.

3. Tap Search to look for a specific recipe.

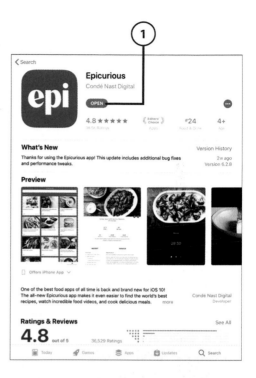

4. Tap to browse using categories. For instance, you can list recipes by their main ingredient or dietary considerations.

5. Search for a specific dish.

6. When you dig down to a recipe page, you see a picture and other information.

7. Read a summary of the dish and preparation time estimates.

8. Review the ingredients list.

9. Review the preparation instructions.

10. Return to the main screen.

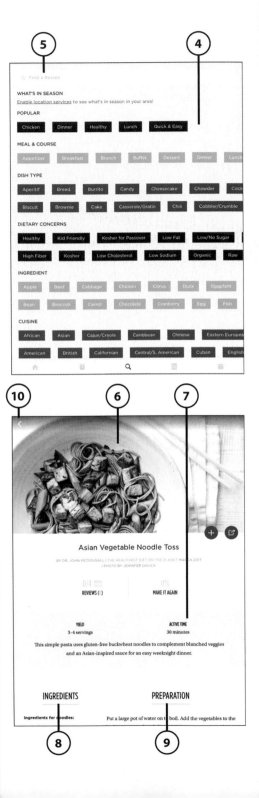

>>>Go Further

MORE COOKING APPS

Food Network In the Kitchen: This app gives you more than just recipes. You get videos featuring the TV network's stars showing you how to make the dishes.

Yummly: An alternative recipe database to Epicurious.

Allrecipes Dinner Spinner: Another alternative—this one includes videos as well.

Checking the Weather

The iPhone comes with a Weather app preinstalled, but the iPad does not. However, you can find many good weather apps in the App Store. Download any one of those to add this important information to your iPad. As an example, let's look at the Yahoo Weather app.

1. Search the App Store for Yahoo Weather. Tap Get to download and install it, and then tap Open to launch the app.

2. If this is the first time you have used the app, you might be asked if you want to enable daily weather notifications. You are also asked if you want to allow the app to use your location, which allows it to focus on your local weather without requiring you to enter your location. After that, the first screen you see shows you the current conditions for your location.

3. Tap and slide up to reveal more weather information.

4. You can view the hourly forecast for the rest of the day.

5. You also see a 10-day forecast.

6. Swipe up again to reveal more information.

7. You can find more detailed information about the current conditions.

8. You can see basic information like sunrise, sunset, and moon phase.

9. At the bottom, you can see the current radar map. To the right of the map, you can use buttons to switch between satellite, heat, wind, and radar maps.

10. Tap the + button to add another location. When you have more than one location, you can swipe left and right to switch between locations to check the weather in different places.

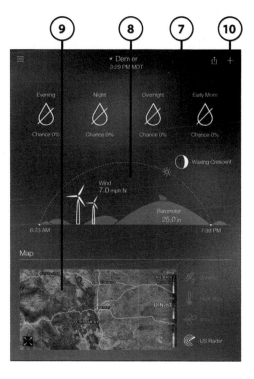

>>>Go Further

MORE WEATHER APPS

 The Weather Channel: This is a comprehensive weather app from the cable network.

 Weather Underground: This app from one of the most well-respected weather sites predicts the weather based on numerous sources and user reporting.

 WeatherBug: Another good alternative weather app.

 Living Earth: View a 3D globe showing conditions and forecasts.

Learning New Things with iTunes U

You have an entire school in your iPad—many universities, in fact. Apple's iTunes U app is your gateway to free educational content provided by many of the world's top colleges.

1. Search the App Store for the iTunes U app. Tap Get to download and install it, and then tap Open to launch the app.

2. If you start with a blank library of courses, tap the button at the bottom to enter the Featured courses screen.

3. Tap the More button for a complete list of categories.

4. Tap in the Search field to search the catalog for a course.

5. Tap a course to view more information.

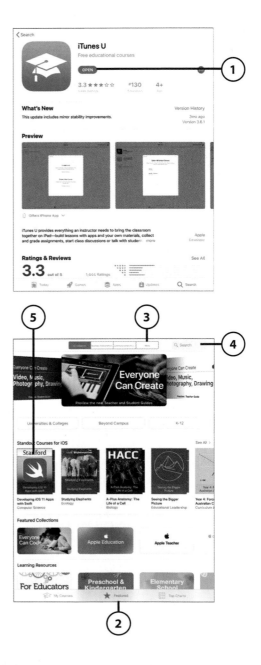

Don't Stop with iTunes U

If you search the App Store, you can find apps that teach you just about anything. Want to learn to play guitar? How to bowl? How to repair your car? There are all sorts of apps for these. And when you can't find an app, you can use the YouTube app to search for tutorial videos.

6. Read the description of the course.

7. Swipe up the page to move down and see all the course materials. Icons to the right of the names indicate what type of material: audio, document, video, and so on.

8. Tap to download an individual item.

9. Tap to subscribe to the whole course, which will put it in your library and take you to your library screen.

10. Tap My Courses to go to the My Courses screen.

11. Tap a course in your library.

12. Tap Materials to see a chronological list of the course materials.

13. Tap an item to view or listen to it.

14. You can download an item to listen/read/view it later.

Is It Really Free?

Yes, for the most part. Many major universities provide these courses for free. However, just like with a real course, you sometimes need to purchase extra materials to follow along. For instance, there may be a book, app, or other item listed. Sometimes you can purchase the item right on your iPad, such as a book in the Apple Books Store.

>>>Go Further

MORE EDUCATIONAL APPS

Craftsy: You can purchase video courses for things like crochet, knitting, quilting, baking, weaving, and other crafts. You browse their catalog and buy the course with an in-app purchase. Then you follow along with video tutorials. You can also take notes and ask questions of your instructor.

TED: This app gives you access to thousands of educational and inspirational videos from TED conferences around the world.

Other Useful Apps

So many useful apps are in the App Store that it is impossible to cover them all in a book. Here are some quick mentions of others you can check out. Some are free; others you have to pay for.

 1Password: Mac users already know about the popular 1Password for Mac, which gives you a place to securely store passwords and other important information and conveniently access them through Safari.

 MindNode: If you use mind-mapping software to organize your ideas and plan projects, then you'll be happy to know there is a pretty advanced tool that lets you do this on the iPad.

 WordPress: This app lets you write, edit, and maintain your blog posts. It works for the WordPress.com blogging service and for WordPress blogs set up on independent sites. **Blogsy** is an app that also lets you work with your WordPress blog, as well as many other popular blogging platforms.

 Day One Journal: For those who like to keep journals, your iPad can replace physical paper with apps like Day One Journal. You can include photos and keep it completely private with a password. **Momento** is another journaling app to check out. And **Heyday** is one with a focus on keeping travel journals.

 StarWalk 2: This is a must-have app for anyone even vaguely interested in astronomy. Even if you aren't, the beautiful, up-to-the-minute renderings of the night sky on your iPad will impress your friends. You can see what the sky looks like right now, right where you are, and use it as a guide to identifying what you see.

 WolframAlpha: Want to compare two stocks, see the molecular structure of sulfuric acid, or calculate the amount of sodium in your breakfast? Would you believe that one app does all three and has hundreds of other interesting answers to all sorts of questions? It is also the answer engine behind a lot of what the iPhone's Siri feature does, so you get a little bit of Siri on your iPad.

B **Bloomberg:** The iPhone comes with a weather app, a calculator app, and a stocks app. The first two have good alternatives mentioned earlier in this chapter. For the last one, you also have good options. The Bloomberg app lets you track your stocks and keep up with financial news. **Yahoo Finance** is a decent alternative, as well. If you use an online broker, search for their app—most of them produce one.

 VNC Viewer: You can use your iPad to share your computer's screen. With VNC viewer, or any similar tool such as **iTeleport** or **Mocha VNC Lite**, you connect to a Mac using OS X's screen sharing or a PC using a VNC server. Then you not only can see what is on your computer's screen, but you can tap and type to control it.

Compose music

Stream movies and television

Play games

In this chapter, you look at apps that exist for entertainment purposes such as viewing movies, reading comics, listening to music, or playing games.

→ Composing Music with GarageBand

→ Watching Videos with YouTube

→ Watching Movies and TV Shows with Netflix

→ iPad Games and Entertainment

Games and Entertainment

You can view a lot of information and get a lot of work done on the iPad, but it is still a great device for entertainment. The majority of entertainment apps out there are games, but there are also some general entertainment apps that you can take a look at.

Composing Music with GarageBand

It is hard to sum up GarageBand in just a few pages. This brother to the Mac GarageBand application is a very big app. It could almost deserve a book all to itself. Let's look at how to create a simple song.

1. Download and install GarageBand from the App Store. If you already have it, launch it from the Home screen. See "Purchasing an App" in Chapter 15, "The World of Apps," for instructions on how to find and download apps.

2. There are many ways to create and add musical tracks to songs in GarageBand. One way is to use Live Loops, a grid system of looping sound segments. But this example uses the virtual keyboard. You need to make sure you are using the Tracks option to see the virtual instruments.

3. Now you can choose an instrument to start. Select the keyboard.

4. Tap the keys to play notes. The force at which you hit the keys and the spot on the key determines the exact sound it produces.

5. Tap the Instrument button and swipe left or right to change from Grand Piano to one of dozens of other instruments.

6. Tap the Record button to record what you are playing. A metronome counts down, so wait one measure before starting. Try just a few notes, a handful of measures.

7. Tap the Stop button, which appears instead of the Rewind button in this location, when you are done recording.

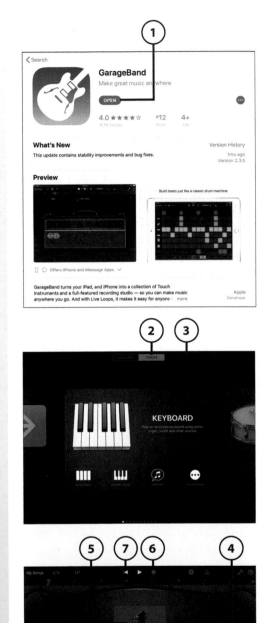

8. Tap the Undo button if you didn't get the notes quite right. Then try again.

9. After you have recorded a bit of music, the View button appears. You can use that to switch to the Tracks view. It then changes to a Keyboard button to switch back to the Keyboard view.

10. In Tracks view, you see the bit of music you recorded. Tap it once to select it. Tap again to bring up a menu that includes Cut, Copy, Delete, Loop, Split, and Edit. Tap Loop.

11. The music you recorded is set to loop for the entire section of the song. Tap the Play button to test it.

12. Tap the Loop button to view premade loops that you can add to your song.

13. Tap Apple Loops if it isn't already selected.

14. Use the Search field to look for loops, or tap the Instrument, Genre, or Descriptors buttons below the Search field to narrow your list of loops.

15. Select a loop to test it. You can even have your loop playing at the same time by tapping the Play button at the top and then tapping a loop from the Apple Loops menu to see how they sound together.

16. Drag a loop from the list to the area right under the loop you created.

17. Now you have your original loop and a drum loop. Tap Play to hear them together.

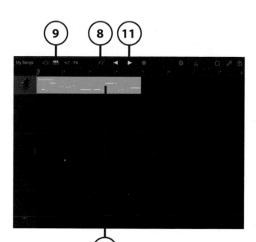

You can continue to add loops. Add a bass line and maybe some guitar. You can also double-tap on the left side of each track where you see the image of the instrument, to return to the instrument view and switch instruments or record more notes.

Besides the piano, you can also play guitar, bass, or drums. And each instrument has several variations. Plus, there are smart instruments, such as the smart guitar, that only allow you to play notes and chords that fit well together.

See http://macmost.com/ipadguide/ for more tutorials on using GarageBand for iPad.

Watching Videos with YouTube

Although you can watch YouTube videos by browsing YouTube.com with Safari, the official YouTube app from Google gives you a dedicated video player for the millions of user-created videos on the service.

1. Search the App Store for the YouTube app for iPad. Tap Get to download and install it, and then tap Open to launch the app.

2. If you have a Google (Gmail) account, log in to access your playlists and comment on videos. To simply search and view videos, you do not need an account, you can just use the app as a guest.

3. You see a list of videos recommended by YouTube. Tap the Trending button to see what others are watching.

4. Swipe up to move down the page and see more YouTube topics.

5. Use the Search tool to search for any video on YouTube.

6. Tap a video to view it. You might want to rotate the iPad to horizontal orientation because videos are horizontal.

7. As the video plays, tap the middle of the video at any time to bring up playback controls.

8. Use the Pause/Play button to pause and resume the video.

9. You can tap and drag the circle left and right to move back and forth in the video.

10. Tap the expand button to expand the video to full screen.

11. Tap to add a video to Playlist, Favorites, or the Watch Later list (not shown). You need to be signed in to your YouTube account to see this button. You can also share it with friends using email, messages, or social networks.

12. Tap the back button to return to the list, or search results you were looking at before choosing this particular video. The current video you are watching continues to play and shrinks to a box at the bottom right.

13. You can tap any related video to just go right to it.

14. If you are signed in, you can comment or give a thumbs up or down to the video.

15. Tap Subscribe if you are signed in to add the channel to your subscription list and receive notifications when new videos are added.

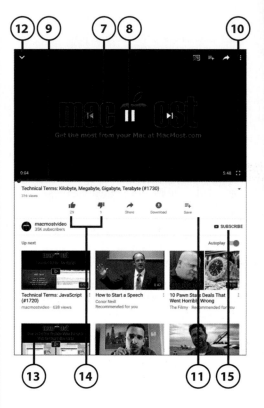

>>>Go Further
WHAT ELSE CAN I DO?

Want to contribute? Another app from Google called YouTube Capture lets you record video with your iPad's camera and upload it to YouTube. You can also share your videos from the Photos app or iMovie to YouTube with the Share buttons in those apps. Get ready for your 15 minutes of fame!

Watching Movies and TV Shows with Netflix

One of the most essential apps for the iPad is the Netflix app. Netflix subscribers can use it to watch movies right on their iPads.

1. Search the App Store for the Netflix app. Tap Get to download and install it, and then tap Open to launch the app.

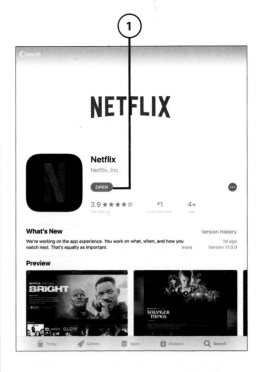

2. If you don't have an account, you can sign up for a trial account right on your iPad.

3. If you have an account, you can sign in. After the first time, you should be automatically signed in.

4. On the main Netflix screen is a list of movies and TV shows.

5. You can also use the Search function to find movies and TV shows.

6. If you are in the middle of watching videos, whether on your iPad or another device where you use Netflix, you have the ability to jump right in and continue watching.

7. When you choose a new video, whether from the front screen or through a search, you are first taken to an information screen. Read the information to find out more about the video.

8. In this example, the item is a TV series; you can scroll down to see a list of episodes. Tap the Play button in the center of a picture to watch it.

9. The video should start after a few seconds. It plays in horizontal orientation, so you need to turn your iPad on its side. There are Play and Pause controls at the bottom of the screen.

10. After the video starts playing, the controls disappear. To bring up the controls again, tap in the center of the screen. You can double-tap in the center of the screen to enlarge the video, or just turn your iPad sideways for a better view.

11. Use the large slider at the bottom to jump around in the video.

12. Tap the back button to return to the previous screen.

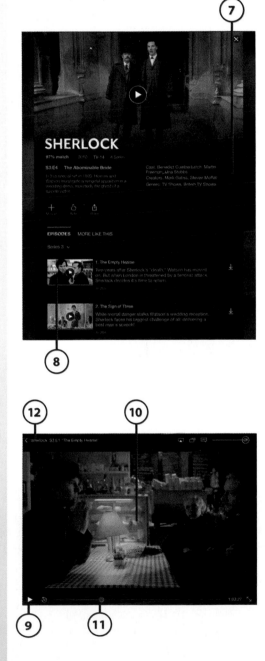

Connection Required

Although watching movies in the Netflix app is unlimited, you can't download and store the movie for later viewing. You need to be online to watch. iTunes rentals, on the other hand, can be stored and watched while offline, like on an airplane flight.

>>>*Go Further*
MORE STREAMING VIDEO

Netflix is not the only main choice for streaming video. Another app called Amazon Prime Video gives you access to similar content with lots of movies and TV shows. Instead of subscribing to Netflix, you can subscribe to Amazon's service through your Amazon account.

Hulu, another service that streams TV shows and movies, also has an iPad app called Hulu. It works with the same Hulu account that you might already be using to view shows on the Hulu website.

In addition, many TV networks provide their own apps that let you watch videos provided you get that channel through your local cable network or satellite provider. For instance, the HBO Go app lets you watch HBO shows on your iPad after you have proven that you get HBO at home. The separate HBO Now app lets you pay for access to HBO's programming if you don't get HBO at home.

iPad Games and Entertainment

Even if you purchased your iPad to stay connected, get work done, or watch videos, you might want to check out the rich and wonderful world of games.

With the touchscreen and accelerometer control, the iPhone and iPod touch turned out to be fertile ground for game developers. Add to that the large screen and fast processor of the iPad, and you have a powerful and unique gaming device.

Let's take a look at some of the best games for the iPad.

Monument Valley and Monument Valley 2

Games look beautiful on the retina display of the iPad. Monument Valley and its sequel are exploration games with fantastic design but simple gameplay. You guide a character through challenging puzzle levels that play with geometry and reality. These games have won many awards for a reason. Start with the original. It has stood the test of time over the last few years to remain one of the iPad's top games.

Minecraft: Pocket Edition

You have probably heard of Minecraft before, even if you haven't tried it. For some people, the iPad is simply a "Minecraft-playing machine" and hardly anything else. In this game, you explore a world and also reshape it. Build whatever you like. You can also see what others have built and even build together with others online.

Other world-exploring and building games include **Terraria** and **The Blockheads**.

Prune

You'll find many of the best games have almost no instructions. Part of the fun is figuring them out. In Prune, you are given a hint that you start with a fast-growing tree and prune some branches to encourage it to grow in other directions. As you experiment, you figure out there are things you want to grow toward and things you want to avoid. It turns out to be a very serene and almost meditative experience.

Superbrothers: Sword & Sworcery EP

There are hundreds of adventure games for the iPad where you move from screen to screen exploring lands and solving puzzles. Superbrothers is part retro-adventure and part of the next generation at the same time. Plus, it has an emphasis on music with an award-winning soundtrack that ties into the gameplay.

Also look for other popular adventure games like **Monkey Island 2 Special Edition, Machinarium, The Bard's Tale,** and **Broken Sword: Director's Cut.**

Kingdom Rush

A major genre of touch device gaming is tower defense. In these games, you build defensive structures to stand up against a never-ending onslaught of enemy troops. The most popular in this group right now is Kingdom Rush.

The enemies come down the road and head for your kingdom. You place towers of various sorts on the road to stop them. You are fighting orcs, goblins, trolls, wizards, and demons with your archers, sorcerers, and cannons. Also check out **Field Runners** and **GeoDefense**.

Where's My Water

Some of the best iPad games have premises that are a little bizarre. For instance, Disney's Where's My Water game has you digging in the dirt to let water flow down to some pipes so an alligator can take a bath. Yes, that's the game.

But what makes this crazy game so good is the realism—at least how realistically the water flows as you swipe through the environment. Each level presents a more difficult challenge. You can buy in-app purchases of new packs of levels that tell stories.

Cut the Rope

Another strange premise is needing to cut ropes to swing candy into a monster's mouth. This time the physics puzzle is about the way the ropes react as you cut them. Not only do you need to break the ropes in the right places, but you need to be quick so you do it at the right time.

Cut the Rope has a free version with ads and a paid version without. Each level presents new challenges, such as puffs of air and spiders that crawl on the ropes.

Harbor Master HD

One of the new game genres that appeared on the iPhone was the draw-to-direct type of game. It first appeared with a game called Flight Control, which is also available on the iPad.

Harbor Master HD takes the genre a little further. The idea is you direct ships into docks by drawing with your finger. Simply draw a line from the ship to the dock and the ship follows the path.

The game gets harder as you go along, with more and more ships unloading cargo and then sailing away. You have to make sure the ships find a dock and that they never collide.

Angry Birds HD

Many people purchase games to play on an iPad. But some people buy an iPad to play a game. When that is the case, the game responsible is usually Angry Birds HD.

In this game, you shoot birds at a structure using a slingshot. Your goal is to destroy the pigs living in the building. Sounds a bit strange, but behind the premise is a good physics simulation that presents challenges with every level. And it has also spawned some sequels, like **Angry Birds Seasons HD, Angry Birds Rio, Angry Birds Space HD,** and **Angry Birds Star Wars HD**.

Plants vs. Zombies HD

Zombies are attacking your house, and you need to defend it. So, what do you use? Strange mutant fighting plants, of course.

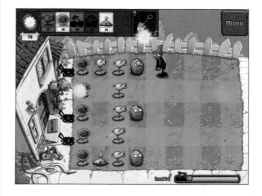

It sounds weird, and it is. But as a fun strategy game, it works. It plays like a tower-defense style game but with fun elements that you find in those $20 PC game downloads. Plus, if you like it, there is a sequel: **Plants vs. Zombies 2.**

Scrabble for iPad

There are thousands of word games for the iPad, and one of the best is one of the original word board games—Scrabble. Not only can you play against a tough computer opponent, a friend on Facebook, or your local network, but you can also play against a friend in the same room, using your iPhones.

You both download the Tile Rack app for the iPhone and then use the iPad as the main game board; your tiles appear only on your iPhones. Another popular word game to check out is **Words With Friends**. The author also has several other popular games, including **Word Tiles by CleverMedia**, **Word Spell by CleverMedia**, and **Word Swipe 2 by CleverMedia**.

Temple Run 2

The original Temple Run spawned an entire genre of iOS apps called "endless runners." The character you control in the game runs forward at full speed. All you do is control whether the character jumps, slides, turns left, or turns right.

It sounds pretty simple, and when you start you only last for a few seconds. This leads to wanting to try it again and again to improve your score. Before you know it, you'll be making impossibly long runs. There are some other variations you can search for, such as **Temple Run: Brave** and **Temple Run: Oz**. An excellent game in the same basic genre is **Pitfall!**

The Room, The Room Two, The Room Three

Here's a series of mystery puzzle games with beautiful graphics. You manipulate objects in a room using natural gestures to solve puzzles. As you progress, a story unfolds.

You need to explore the small 3D game environment in order to notice tiny clues and interpret messages. They are slow-paced games for those who like to think instead of furiously tap and swipe. Anyone who is a fan of old-style games like Myst will like these games.

Gold Strike

I'll go ahead and mention some of my own games here. Gold Strike was first a web-based game, then a PC game, and then an iPhone game. Once you try it, you'll see that it was really an iPad game all along, just waiting for the iPad to come along.

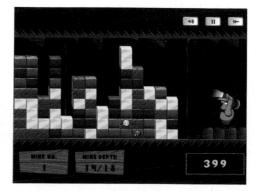

You tap groups of blocks to remove them before the mine fills up. Gold blocks give you points, and the larger the group, the more points you get. The iPad version also includes some game variations for extended play.

Just Mah Jongg Solitaire

Tile-matching games have been around for a while, but they seem to have been made for the iPad. The combination of touch and a large, bright screen make it perfect for these games.

Just Mah Jongg Solitaire includes different tile sets and layouts. You can play the standard Mah Jongg matching game, or use a set like Halloween or Egyptian Nile tiles for variety. One key feature of the game is that it creates solvable arrangements. Although ultimately solving a layout is up to you and the choices you make while playing, every game you play has at least one solution.

You can check out all of the author's iPad games at http://clevermedia. com/ipadgames/.

Extend your iPad with printers, cases, connectors, and keyboards

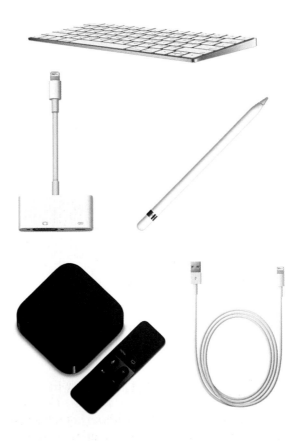

This chapter looks at some optional accessories like printers, video adapters, keyboards, headphones, and cases. It also covers the Home app, which allows you to control electronics around your home.

→ Printing from Your iPad
→ AirPlay Mirroring with Apple TV
→ Video Output Adapters
→ Using Wireless Keyboards
→ Importing Photos with an SD Card and USB Adapters
→ Charging Your iPad with Power Accessories
→ Listening with EarPods
→ Protecting Your iPad
→ Apple Pencil
→ Controlling Your Home with Your iPad

iPad Accessories

Many accessories available for your iPad perform a variety of tasks, protect it, or just make it look pretty.

You might already have some things that work with your iPad— printers and wireless keyboards, for instance. Let's look at a variety of accessories to see how to use them.

Printing from Your iPad

You can print from your iPad without connecting any cables. Apple calls this function AirPrint. You can print a web page or document directly from your iPad over your wireless network.

The one catch? It works only with printers that support AirPrint. Fortunately, the list is pretty large and includes printers by many companies. You can find an updated list of AirPrint printers at https://support.apple.com/HT201311.

Printing from the Notes App

Assuming you have one of these printers and have set it up on your local network, here's how you print, using the Notes app as an example.

1. In the Notes app, with the note you want to print open, tap the Share button.

2. Tap Print. If you don't see Print in this list, you might need to drag the list to the left to reveal more buttons to the right.

3. At the bottom of the overlay that appears is a preview of what you are about to print.

4. Listed next to Printer you will see the name of the last printer you used, as long as the iPad is still connected through the network to this printer. But if you have never printed before, or the printers available have changed, tap Select Printer.

5. If the printer is on and has been configured to your network, it should appear in the list. Tap it to select it.

6. The printer name is showing. Tap its name again to select a different printer.

7. If there are any options to select, you see them listed. If there is more than one, you might simply see an Options button—if you tap that, it expands to show all the options. In this case, the printer can be switched between color and black and white.

8. Tap the –/+ buttons to set the number of copies to print, or leave it at 1 Copy.

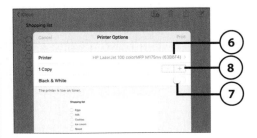

9. Tap Print to send the note to the printer.

    At this point, your iPad launches a special Print Center app. You might not notice it unless you quickly double-press the Home button to bring up the list of apps. You then see this Print Center app running as the left-most app in the list. If your document is small and your printer is fast, it might print so quickly that you will never catch the Print Center app running.

10. That's all you need to do. But if you want to monitor the progress of your printout, double-press the Home button to bring up the list of apps currently running on your iPad. You should see a Print Center app. If you are just printing one page and your network and printer are fast, it could appear and disappear before you even get a chance to see or select it.

11. You can see the status of the printing process and other information.

12. Tap Cancel Printing to stop printing.

Cancel   **Printer Options**   **Print**

Printer   HP LaserJet 100 colorMFP M175nw (63B6F4) >

1 Copy   − +

Black & White

The printer is low on toner.

Print Summary

Document   Shopping list

Printer   HP LaserJet 100 colorMFP M175nw (63B6F4)

Copies   1

Options   Single-sided, Letter

Started   Today at 10:44 AM

Status   Printing 1 of 1...

Cancel Printing

Different for Other Apps

How you initiate printing differs from app to app. Using Pages, for example, you go to the Tools button at the top of the screen and select Share and Print. You see Print as one of the options. But for most apps, you initiate printing by looking for a Print option in the Share button that looks like a box with an arrow pointing up.

Printing When You Can't Print

Not all apps include the ability to print. But that doesn't mean you can't print what you see on the screen. Just capture the screen by pressing the Sleep/Wake button and Home button simultaneously (see "Capturing the Screen" in Chapter 9, "Taking and Editing Photos"). Then, go to the Photos app and look for the new image. You can print that image using the Share button in the Photos app.

What If Your Printer Doesn't Have AirPrint?

Although not all Wi-Fi printers support AirPrint, there is a way to cheat. Some enterprising third-party developers have come up with software for desktop computers that sets up a printer connected to the computer as an AirPrint printer. You aren't really printing directly to a printer—you are going through the computer. Still, it might be a good option for some. Search on the Web for Printopia (Mac), handyPrint (Mac), or Presto (PC).

AirPlay Mirroring with Apple TV

The Apple TV might be the best iPad accessory of them all. It enables you to display the screen of the iPad on a high-definition television. And it does this wirelessly, using the local Wi-Fi network and something called AirPlay Mirroring.

Setting Up AirPlay

You need to make sure several things are in place before you can use Air-Play Mirroring.

1. Make sure that both your iPad and Apple TV are connected to the same local network.

2. Make sure both your iPad and Apple TV are up to date. Using older or mismatched versions of software on the devices could prevent AirPlay from working.

3. Turn on AirPlay on your Apple TV. To do this, go into Settings, AirPlay, and turn it on (not shown).

4. On your iPad, swipe down from the top-right corner of the screen up to bring up the Control Center. See "Using Control Center" in Chapter 1, "Getting Started."

5. Tap the Screen Mirroring control. Note that it might not appear if you do not have at least one AirPlay device, such as an Apple TV, connected to your network and enabled.

6. Select which Apple TV you want to mirror the iPad's screen.

7. When you want to stop mirroring, repeat steps 4 and 5, but select Stop Mirroring. This button only appears if you are currently mirroring.

The Benefits of Apple TV

The Apple TV is a worthwhile device to have just for the ability to use AirPlay to show your iPad on a TV screen. However, you also get many other great features such as iTunes movie rentals, YouTube, Netflix, and many other video and gaming apps, depending on your specific Apple TV model.

The Mirror Crack'd

Some apps won't mirror to Apple TV at all. Certain video streaming apps have purposely restricted mirroring due to licensing issues and other reasons. So you might not be able to mirror when using apps from certain cable networks. But usually there are Apple TV apps for some of those networks, so you have to get those shows directly on your Apple TV anyway.

>>>Go Further
MORE ABOUT AIRPLAY

Mirroring your iPad's screen through an Apple TV is just one of many functions of AirPlay. You can also find AirPlay buttons in other apps, such as the Music app and other third-party audio apps. You can send just the audio stream from these apps to Apple TV to play music through your TV or home theater system.

You can also get audio-only AirPlay devices, such as Apple's own Airport Express base station and many small speaker systems and home theater attachments. These devices appear when you try to use AirPlay from an audio app.

You can also use the Bluetooth ability of your iPad to send audio from some apps to wireless speakers. Check out https://www.apple.com/shop/accessories/all-accessories/headphones-speakers for Apple's list of audio devices for iPad. Select the connection type on the left and choose Bluetooth to see only Bluetooth devices. Or, go to your favorite shopping site and search for Bluetooth or Airplay.

Video Output Adapters

In addition to using an Apple TV to wirelessly mirror your iPad's screen to a TV or projector, you can also use one of two cables to directly connect your iPad to a screen.

There are two models. One is for VGA connections, such as you might find on many boardroom and classroom projectors. The other is an HDMI connector, which works for most HD televisions produced in the last few years. However, you will find televisions with VGA connectors and projectors with HDMI connectors. Check your device before purchasing one of the two adapters. If you have both types of connections, get the adapter for the more modern and versatile HDMI connection.

Both adapters have a Lightning connector on the one end that plugs into the bottom of your iPad. The other end has either the HDMI or VGA connector, plus a port to connect a Lightning cable. This is for connecting your iPad's power adapter so your iPad is receiving power at the same time it is sending the video signal to the TV or projector.

Apple's Lightning Digital AV Adapter   **Apple's Lightning to VGA Adapter**

You don't need to use this Lightning port—you can run your iPad on its battery while it's connected to the screen. However, connecting your iPad to AC power prevents your battery from draining and your iPad from running out of power while you are presenting. Wouldn't want to have to stop your presentation just before the slide where you ask the board members for money, would you?

1. Connect the adapter to the dock port on your iPad.

2. Connect the other end of the adapter to a standard HDMI or VGA cable. You cannot hook the adapters directly to a TV or projector because they have female connectors. A male-to-male connector bridges the gap between the adapter and the TV or projector, just like it would if you were connecting to a laptop computer.

3. Connect the other end of the cable to a monitor or projector that accepts either HDMI or VGA.

4. If you are using the VGA adapter and also want audio, then use an audio mini jack to connect the headphone port of the iPad to the line in the projector. The exact type of cable you need depends on what audio input the projector takes.

5. At this point, the video on the projector or monitor should mirror that of the iPad. Some apps might show different things on the iPad's screen and the external display. For example, Keynote shows the presentation on the external display, whereas you have the presentation plus controls on the iPad's screen.

TV Compatibility

The video coming from the iPad is compatible with both 720p and 1080p HD televisions and video devices. It also includes audio over the HDMI cable. Many televisions support only 1080i, not 1080p. In that case, the video might be shown in 720p instead.

Using Wireless Keyboards

If you have a lot of typing to do and are sitting at a desk anyway, you can use Apple's wireless Magic Keyboard with your iPad. This is the same wireless keyboard that you would use with a Mac. You can also use just about any other Bluetooth-compatible wireless keyboard.

Apple Magic Keyboard

Choosing the Right Wireless Keyboard

If you have an older Apple wireless keyboard, it might not work with your iPad. The Apple Store warns that only "newer" keyboards can successfully connect to the iPad. Reports from people with older wireless keyboards indicate that this is true. However, you don't need to stick with Apple's wireless keyboard. Most Bluetooth keyboards work fine with the iPad. Search your favorite online store for all kinds of compact wireless Bluetooth keyboards. Check reviews to see if anyone has mentioned trying the model with an iPad. If you are having trouble connecting to a keyboard or any Bluetooth wireless device, Apple has some troubleshooting tips at https://support.apple.com/HT201205.

1. To connect to the Apple Magic Keyboard, first make sure it is charged. Older Apple keyboards use AA batteries, but the latest Magic Keyboard needs to be plugged in occasionally to charge.

2. Tap the Settings app on your iPad and tap Bluetooth.

3. Make sure Bluetooth is turned on.

4. Turn on your Apple Wireless Keyboard by pressing the button on its right side (not shown). You should see a small green light turn on at the upper-right corner or back edge of the keyboard.

5. After a second or two, the keyboard should appear on your iPad screen. Tap it.

6. Look for a four-digit number in the message displayed. Type that on your wireless keyboard. Then press the Return key.

7. After the connection is established, you should see Connected next to the name of your keyboard.

8. After you connect, the iPad automatically uses the physical keyboard by default, rather than bringing up the on-screen keyboard (not shown). To use the on-screen keyboard again, you can either disconnect or power off your Apple Wireless Keyboard, or you can press the Eject button at the upper-right corner of the keyboard to switch to the on-screen keyboard at any time.

9. If you want to disconnect the keyboard so it is no longer paired with your iPad, tap the i button, and then tap Forget this Device.

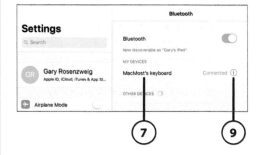

The iPad Pro Smart Keyboard

If you have an iPad Pro, in addition to being able to use a wireless keyboard, you can also purchase Apple's Smart Keyboard. There is a different model for each size of iPad Pro. This keyboard isn't wireless. It attaches to the side of the iPad and acts like both a stand and a screen cover as well.

The keyboard isn't permanently attached to your iPad. It is held in place by magnets and gets power through that surface, so there is no need for batteries or charging. There are also third-party keyboards that use the same connection.

>>>*Go Further*

SPECIAL KEYS

When you use a wireless keyboard or the Smart Keyboard with your iPad, there is more to using a keyboard with your iPad than just typing letters. There are also special controls.

When you hold down the Command key on the keyboard a list of keyboard shortcuts pops up on the screen. The list changes depending on context, so it shows different shortcuts if you are in Notes than if you are on the Home screen.

In addition to these shortcuts, some of the following keys may perform special functions. It all depends on whether your keyboard has these keys. For instance, the Magic Keyboard has F1 through F12 keys, but the Smart Keyboard does not.

- **Brightness (F1 and F2):** Changes the brightness of the iPad screen.
- **Volume (F10, F11, and F12):** Mutes, lowers, and raises the volume.
- **Eject (to the right of F12):** Brings up or dismisses the on-screen keyboard.
- **Arrows:** Navigates editable text.
- **Arrows+Shift:** Selects editable text.
- **Command:** Can be used with X, C, and V for Cut, Copy, and Paste inside editable text.
- **Command+Z:** In many writing apps, you can use this to undo, just like when typing on a desktop computer.
- **Audio Playback Keys (F7, F8, and F9):** Goes to previous track, play/pause, and next track.
- **Command+Space:** Starts a search, just as if you were on the Home screen and swiped down from the middle of the screen.

Importing Photos with an SD Card and USB Adapters

The Lightning to SD Card Camera Reader lets you take an SD card and connect it to your iPad. That means you can take pictures with your standalone camera or video recorder, pull out the SD card, and then connect that card to your iPad to add the photos or video to your Photos library. If you are using iCloud Photo Library and are connected to the Internet, then the photos would be added to your library and available on other devices as well.

You can also buy a Lightning to USB adapter from Apple that lets you connect some cameras directly to your iPad. Either way, the Photos app launches and allows you to import the photos it finds.

Here is how to import photos directly from your camera or SD card.

1. Connect the SD card reader to your iPad's dock port with the SD card in it (not shown). Or, connect your camera using the USB connector. If you are connecting a camera, you will most likely need to switch the camera on and into the same mode you use to transfer pictures to a computer.

2. After a slight delay, the Photos app should launch and images on the camera or card should appear on your iPad's screen. You might need to tap the Import button at the bottom of the screen to see the photos.

3. Tap Import All to import all the photos on the card.

4. Tap the Trash button if you want to delete the images without ever importing them into your iPad.

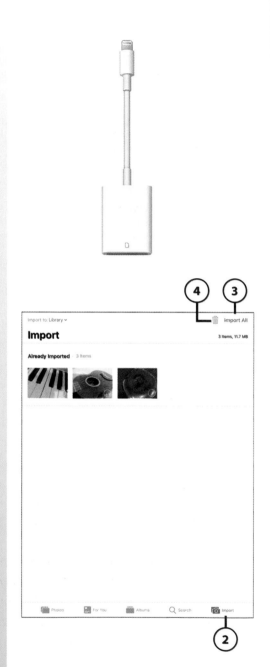

5. If you don't want to import or delete all of the images, tap one or more images to select them instead.

6. Tap Import All.

7. Tap Import Selected to bring in only the selected photos.

8. After importing the photos, you are given the chance to delete them from the camera or card. Tap Delete to remove them.

9. Tap Keep to leave the images on the camera or card.

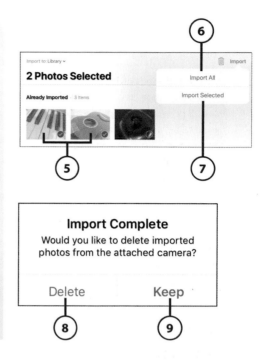

Charging Your iPad with Power Accessories

A power user of any gadget usually acquires additional power chargers and cables. For instance, you might want to charge your iPad at home and at work, or even while traveling. Here are some suggestions for accessories that will keep your iPad charged. All of these are available in Apple Stores, the Apple online store, other online retailers, and many computer and electronics stores.

If you travel between two locations, such as home and work, or home and school, then carrying your one-and-only power adapter with you might be a problem. It is too easy to forget to bring it along.

You can buy a second charger and dock cable from Apple that is the equivalent of the one that came with your iPad. Alternatively, the iPad Dock from Apple enables you to stand the iPad up vertically while it's either plugged in to a power outlet or docked with your computer. You can also use the iPad in this position and even pipe the audio into external speakers through the dock.

Here is a list of items you might want to consider:

- **Apple Lightning to USB cable**: An extra dock cable to plug your iPad into a Mac or PC for syncing and slow charging. Many cars and some public places like airports now have USB outlets that you can use with this cable or the one that came with your iPad. It is always good to have a spare cable, as losing your only one means you can't charge your iPad.

Apple iPad 12W USB power adapter

- **Apple iPad 12W USB power adapter:** Charges the iPad at full speed, faster than a standard USB port. This doesn't come with a cable, so if the plan is to have a complete set of power adapters and cables in two locations, make sure you pick up the aforementioned USB cable, too.

- **Car Charger:** You can find car USB phone chargers very cheap at superstores and online, and then use your own Lightning cable to connect your iPad. Make sure that the device outputs at least 10 watts of power, or it will charge your iPad slowly or not at all. Apple doesn't have an official car charger, but it sells several third-party brands in the Apple Store.

Belkin Car Charger

- **External Battery**: If your needs are extreme, and the 10+ hour normal battery life of your iPad isn't enough, you can shop for an external battery pack. You charge them up before you leave home, and then you plug your iPad into them with your Lightning cable—the iPad thinks it is getting power from a wall charger. Apple sells some in its store that can add a few more hours, or even as much as a full charge, to your iPad.

Not All Power Is the Same

Your iPad requires extra power to charge properly. With the power supply that came with your iPad, a 10- or 12-watt model, it should charge fully after about 4 hours. But with a smaller 5-watt iPhone power supply, or while hooked up to a standard 6-watt USB port on a computer, it takes twice that amount of time. Some low-power USB ports on computers won't charge the iPad at all.

Listening with EarPods

Although you can use any standard earphones with your iPad, the official Apple EarPods headphones come with a controller on the cord that gives you additional functionality.

You don't get a set of EarPods when you buy an iPad, but you do get a set when you buy a new iPhone or iPod, so you may already have these. You can also purchase them separately from Apple in Apple Stores and online.

In addition to the controls, the EarPods have a microphone that usually gives you better quality recording than using the one on the body of the iPad, which is typically farther from your mouth. It is a good idea to use the EarPods mic when making FaceTime or Skype calls, or recording using audio apps.

Here's what you can do with the controller on the EarPods while you have music playing with the Music app. These also work in many third-party music apps and even audiobook players. You don't need to have the audio app on the screen, or even your iPad unlocked to use these. The audio just needs to be playing.

1. Press the + button to raise the volume.

2. Press the − button to lower the volume.

3. Press the center button once quickly to pause the music. Press again to resume.

4. Press the center button twice quickly to skip to the next song. If you hold the second press, the current song fast-forwards until you release.

5. Press the center button three times quickly to go to the previous song. If you hold the third press, the current song rewinds until you release.

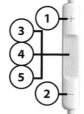

EarPod Alternatives

The EarPods are not only inexpensive, but regarded as pretty high quality. However, if you do prefer other headphones, note that they usually do not come with controls on the cord. Sometimes you will find only the volume controls, and other times you will find all three buttons—but the center button only serves to pause music and won't perform other actions.

Another option is Apple's latest earphones, the AirPods. These are completely wireless. The AirPods are priced much higher than EarPods and are usually associated with the iPhone, not the iPad. But they are compatible with the iPad mini 2 through 4, iPad Air 1 and 2, and all iPad Pro models. Pairing these wireless earphones with your iPad is easy; simply hold the EarPods inside the case near your iPad, and you should be prompted on your iPad to set them up.

>>>*Go Further*

MORE FUN WITH EARPODS

Here are a few other uses for your EarPods:

FaceTime: If you get an incoming FaceTime call while the EarPods are connected, you can press the center button to answer the call. To decline the call, hold the button down for a few seconds.

Siri: You can also use the center button to activate Siri. Just press and hold the center button for a few seconds until Siri appears. The microphone on the EarPods comes in handy so you can talk to Siri through it as well.

Camera: What? There's a camera in your EarPods headphones? No. But you can use the + button on the cord to trigger taking a photo with the Camera app. It works just like the onscreen camera button. You can also use the volume up button on the side of the iPad. This allows you to take a photo while not physically holding your iPad.

Protecting Your iPad

Most iPad users buy something to protect their iPad. Protection ranges from large impact- and weather-resistant cases to thin screen coverings. Some users even buy multiple cases to use in different situations.

iPad Smart Cover

A cover is just a cover, right? But Apple didn't make "just a cover" for the iPad. They made a "smart cover." By using magnets, this cover sticks to the front of the iPad without hiding the rest of the iPad's design. And it is highly functional, acting as a stand as well. It does not, however, work with the original iPad.

The Smart Cover also performs two other functions. First, your iPad can detect when it is closed or opened. You can turn this option on or off by going to the Settings app, under General settings, and looking for the Lock/Unlock option.

Another function your Smart Cover performs is to clean the screen. The material on the inside of the cover gently wipes the screen each time you open and close the cover. Your screen might still need a good wipe-down with a soft cloth every once in a while, but the Smart Cover does keep it a little neater.

The iPad Smart Cover

Apple makes Smart Covers for all models of iPad. Naturally, you have to make sure you purchase the one that fits your model. They also make a leather sleeve for most models that protects your iPad while you are carrying it around.

Third-Party Protective Covers and Cases

Instead of the Smart Cover, or in addition to it, you might want to get a protective cover for your iPad. The problem here is not finding one, but choosing from the hundreds of models already available.

Some covers cover only the back and sides of the iPad, leaving the screen open. Often these covers work in conjunction with an Apple Smart Cover, allowing you to use both at the same time.

The advantage of a cover over a case is that the cover stays on the iPad while you use it. So if you drop your iPad while trying to use it, the cover provides some protection.

A case or sleeve, on the other hand, is something you would put your iPad inside of in order to protect it when you're not using the iPad. Then you would take the iPad out to use it.

Some cases fit loosely enough to allow you to also put a cover on the iPad, giving double the protection. There are also many products that are between a cover and a case, offering the protection of a case, but allowing you to still use the iPad without taking it out—at least to a certain extent. Some manufacturers use the terms "cover" and "case" interchangeably.

When looking for a case, there are many things to consider. Don't look only in a local Apple Store—it stocks only a few cases. Look online to discover a wide variety. Pick one that fits your needs and style.

Size Matters

Remember that each version of the iPad is physically different. They are slightly different dimensions and thicknesses. The port on the bottom and the locations of the buttons are different as well, which means some cases may not have a properly sized or aligned opening. Check the product carefully to make sure you are getting one that fits your device.

A Keyboard and a Cover

Some covers and cases combine protection with a keyboard. They allow you to unfold the cover so the iPad, and a keyboard built into the case, resembles a small laptop computer. If you like using an external keyboard, and want to carry the keyboard around with your iPad, this might be the best setup.

Apple Pencil

The Apple Pencil is a stylus that works with the some of the latest iPad models. It allows artists to use the iPad as a canvas. You can draw using Apple's tools, such as the drawing tools in Notes or Pages. You can also draw using third-party apps like Paper by FiftyThree, mentioned in Chapter 16, "Must-Have Apps."

The Pencil senses where the tip of the pencil hits the iPad's touchscreen. It also knows the amount of force you are applying and the angle you are holding the Pencil.

Although it is easy to see why an artist may want to use an Apple Pencil, it can also be useful for non-artists. For instance, you can use it with Microsoft Office apps to mark up a document with notes and symbols.

In the Notes app, you can simply start using your Pencil at any time while working in a note. The app recognizes that you want to draw and allows you to add sketches to your note.

The Apple Pencil

Controlling Your Home with Your iPad

The Home app allows you to control electronics and appliances in your house. Unfortunately, it won't just magically control any device. You need to have devices that are compatible with Apple's remote control standard, called HomeKit. For instance, you can get a thermostat that is compatible with HomeKit and use that to control the temperature of your house from your iPad.

There are also light bulbs that can be controlled, either to be turned on or off, or to even change color. The simplest type of device is a plug that turns on and off some electric device, such as a lamp.

Controlling an Appliance with the Home App

As an example, here is how to add a simple switch that controls power to a lamp.

1. Launch the Home app.

2. When you first start the Home app, you see a default location— My Home. You can tap the location button to rename it.

3. Because accessories are made by different companies, you might need to refer to the instructions that came with the accessory to get started. But for many devices, simply connecting it to power is enough.

4. On your iPad, tap Add Accessory.

5. There are many ways to connect a device. Devices often come with a serial number either on the device or on a piece of paper that came with the device. The Home app starts by letting you scan the code from the device using the iPad's camera.

6. If you don't see a code, or your iPad doesn't recognize it, tap here to add the device in other ways.

7. If the device is working, you might see it appear here. You can tap it to enter the code manually.

8. Even if you don't see the device, you can still tap here to enter the code and see if that works.

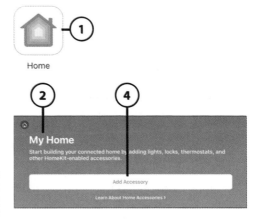

Home

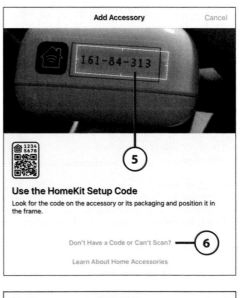

9. Enter the code from the device.

10. The Home app takes care of many of the details for you, like telling the device all it needs to know to connect to your Wi-Fi network. Tap Allow to grant permission for the accessory to use your Wi-Fi network.

11. From here, you can change the name of the device. Chances are the default name does not fit the use in your house. For instance, a better name for this device may be "Living Room Side Table Lamp."

12. Tap Done.

13. The device appears on your main screen in the Home app. Because this is an on/off switch, you can simply tap the button to turn it on or off. More complex devices might take you to screens with a variety of controls.

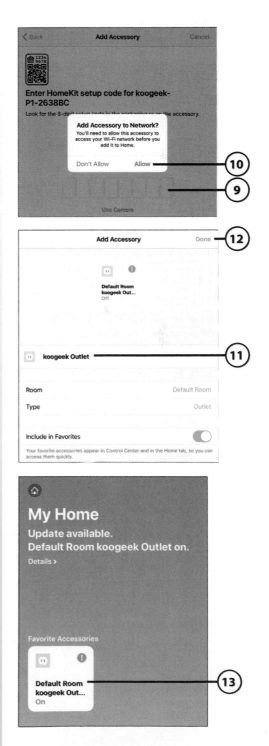

Automating Appliances

To automate electronics with Apple's HomeKit technology, you need to have a device designated as the control hub. Previously, an Apple TV was the only option, but starting with iOS 10 you can designate an iPad as the control hub. After you do that, you can automate tasks, such as having a light turn on or off at certain times.

1. Start by going to the Settings app. Tap Home on the left.

2. Turn on Use This iPad as a Home Hub.

3. In the Automation app, tap the Automation button at the bottom of the screen.

4. Tap Create New Automation.

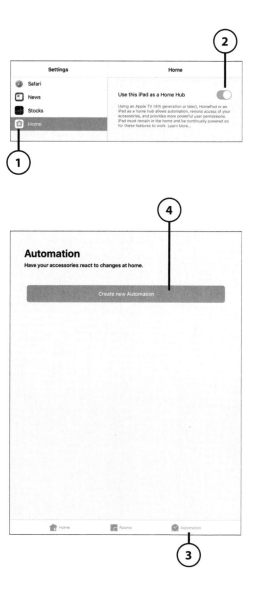

5. Tap A Time of Day Occurs to have an action occur at a specific time.

6. Set the time that will trigger this event. You can also choose Sunrise or Sunset, which adjusts according to your location and the time of year. You can also remove days from this schedule by tapping the circles at the bottom.

7. Tap Next.

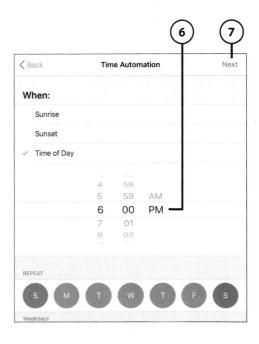

8. Choose the device that will be affected.

9. Tap Done.

10. The automation event has been set. You can see it in the list, and tap it to adjust or delete it.

11. To add another automation, tap the + button.

Honey, I'm Home!

You can also choose People Arrive in step 5 to have the action take place when you leave or arrive home, or leave or arrive at any location. Of course, you would have to add an iPhone that is always with you to your HomeKit automation system so that the system knows where you are. Your iPad stays home and acts as the hub for this system, but it knows you are located where your iPhone is located. You can have the lights come on in your house as you arrive!

9

‹ Back   6:00 PM, Weekdays   Done

When:

🕐 6:00 PM, Weekdays

Accessories:
Press and hold to adjust accessories.

DEFAULT ROOM

Default Room
koogeek Ou...
Turn On

Test This Automation

Turn Off   Never

Accessories turned on by this automation will not be turned off.

8

10 **11**

9:17 AM Thu Aug 30   🛜 100%

➕

Automation
Have your accessories react to changes at home.

🕐 6:00 PM, Weekdays
koogeek Outlet

🏠 Home   ▪️ Rooms   ✅ Automation

Set the Scene

You can also create "scenes" in the Home app. A scene may include multiple commands, like turning some lights on or off, setting others to a dim amount, and turning on some music. Then you can just tap on that scene and all of those commands are given.

Siri: Talk to My House

After you have things set up in the Home app with your iPad or Apple TV as the hub, you don't even need to go into the Home app to do many tasks. For instance, if you have defined Office Lamp as a device, you can simply tell Siri to "Turn off the office lamp."

If you have more complex devices, you use commands like:

Set the temperature to 72 degrees.

Dim the lights to 50 percent.

Set my bedtime scene.

Keep your
apps up
to date

Find your
iPad if it
is lost

Get tips about
how to use
your iPad

Keep your
iPad's
operating
system
up to date

Get help
online

As you continue to use your iPad, you might have questions about how to do things and face problems you can't solve. There are many ways to seek advice and help. You should also take steps to secure your iPad against theft.

→ Getting Help on Your iPad

→ Getting Help from Apple

→ Keeping Your iPad Up-To-Date

→ Securing Your iPad

Maintaining Your iPad and Solving Problems

Apple provides excellent support for their products. You can visit one of the Apple Stores for direct hands-on help. Apple also has a place on their website where you can seek out information and communicate with other iPad users. Additionally, there are often ways to get help from inside some apps and by using the iOS Tips app included on your iPad.

Getting Help on Your iPad

The Tips app offers general advice on using your iPad. Some apps include extensive help information inside the app.

Using the Tips App

The Tips app offers bits of useful advice about using your iPad. It does this by presenting a single tip on a screen, along with a graphic or animation.

1. Tap the Tips app icon on your Home screen.

2. Tap a section, such as Genius Picks or Essentials or What's New to get to the tips.

3. Each screen has a single tip.

4. Swipe to the left to go to the next tip.

5. Tap Collections to see more tips that are organized into small collections.

6. Tap the Share button to share the tips by sending a link to the tip via Messages or email. Each link goes to the corresponding tip at Apple's **https://tips.apple.com** website.

Updates

Apple should be updating the Tips app with new tips on a regular basis. So check back every so often to see what is there and learn something new. You might also get notifications from Apple when new items appear in the Tips app.

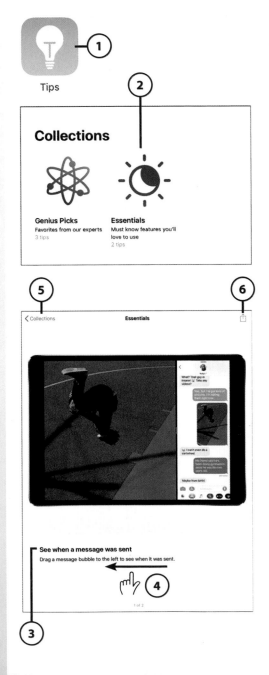

Getting Help Inside Apps

Many apps have how-to and help information inside them. Where to find it and how to use it depends on how the app developer designed the app. Pay careful attention to the buttons and navigation toolbars inside of apps to look for this information.

For instance, let's take a look at Pages. It has extensive documentation.

1. Tap the Pages icon to open it. Then, open an existing document or start a new one. See Chapter 11, "Writing with Pages," to learn how to start a new document.

2. Tap the … button at the top right.

3. Swipe up to get to the last items in the list.

4. Tap Pages Help.

Pages

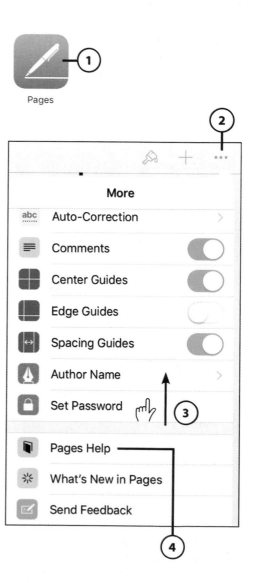

5. You see some general help information. Tap the Contents button to see a list of help topics instead.

6. Tap a subject to see a list of subtopics. Tap a subtopic to read more.

7. Read about the particular subtopic.

8. Tap a reveal arrow to open more text.

9. Tap the List button to return to the table of contents.

10. Use Search to look for information in the documentation.

11. Tap Done to close the documentation window.

External Documentation

Many app developers put documentation on their websites. Be sure to look for links to this inside the app, but also use the App Store to find the name of the developer and search for his or her website. Sometimes the App Store listing includes a direct link to the website. Some developers don't include documentation, but they have instructional videos or support forums that might help.

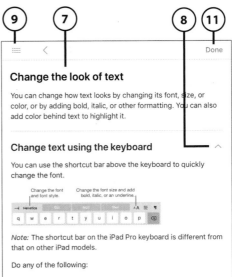

Getting Help from Apple

Apple offers various support options. You can ask a question online, or take your iPad to the Genius Bar in any Apple Store. Your iPad comes with a warranty, which you can extend for up to two years.

One of the most straightforward and easy ways to get help from Apple is to use the Genius Bar. This is an area inside every retail Apple Store. If you have an Apple Store at a nearby mall, then you have a Genius Bar there, too.

Although you can walk into the store and ask for an appointment, you usually have to wait a while, or come back later. It is easier to make an appointment online at Apple's site and then show up at the appointed time.

Appointments at the Genius Bar are free. You don't need to be covered by a warranty or even have bought your iPad at that store. All you need is to have a question about an Apple product. If you have a question about your iPad, whether if it's about how to do something or if you think it is broken, you should bring your iPad with you.

Using the Apple Support App

You can get help from Apple by using the special Apple Support app. Search for it in the App Store and download it. Here's how you would use it to get help with an iPad problem.

1. Download and launch the Apple Support app in the App Store.

2. If this is your first time running the app, you're asked to sign in to your Apple ID. You see a welcome screen. Tap Get Started.

3. If you are logged into your Apple ID in the Settings app, and you have registered your Apple devices, then you should see them listed here.

4. You can swipe up to see other help topics, such as iCloud, Apple Pay, Billing & Subscriptions, and so on.

5. Tap your iPad to continue.

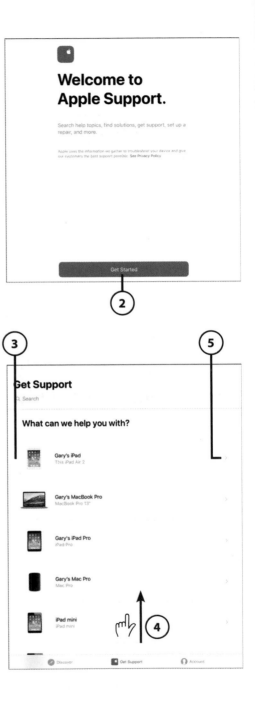

6. Choose a topic that best represents your issue.

7. Alternatively, type in the Search field to search by keyword.

8. Scroll carefully through the list of problems to find your issue.

9. Tap your problem if you see it.

7

6

‹ Get Support   iPad Air 2 Support

Q Search

Popular Topics

Repairs & Physical Damage   ›

Battery & Charging   ›

System Performance   ›

More Topics

Apple ID & iCloud   ›

Apps & Features   ›

Update, Backup & Restore   ›

Subscriptions & Purchases   ›

Discover   Get Support   Account

8

‹ iPad Air 2 Support   **Repairs & Physical Damage**

Recommended Articles

If your iPhone, iPad, or iPod touch won't turn on or is frozen

If your device has a frozen screen, doesn't respond when you touch it, or becomes stuck when you turn it on, learn what to do

What best describes your issue?

Buttons not working   ›

Headphone, cable or USB adapter replacement   ›

Accidental damage   ›

Device frozen or unresponsive device   ›

Not starting up as expected   ›

Display not working as expected   ›

Discover   Get Support   Account

9

10. You can choose to get phone support from Apple—either immediately or scheduled for a specific time.

11. You can also choose to chat online.

12. If you feel you need to bring your iPad in to the Apple Store for direct help, tap See All to see more options, and then tap Bring in for Repair to start scheduling a Genius Bar appointment.

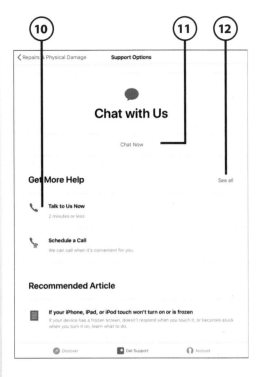

Using the Apple Support Website

Have you spotted the problem with using the Apple Support app to get help with your iPad? If your iPad isn't working, then how are you supposed to be able to run the app?

If you have a serious problem, you might need to use a computer or other device to reach out to Apple. In that case, you can simply go to the Apple website. The process is similar and can work with almost any device you use to visit the Web.

1. Go to **support.apple.com**.

2. Tap Support at the top of the page.

3. Look for iPad in the list of topics. You might need to scroll down to find it.

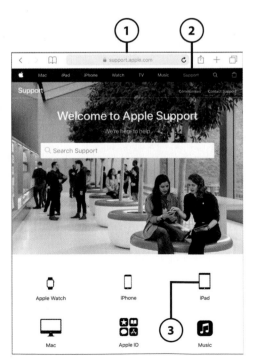

4. Scroll through the page to see if any options or articles help you with your issue.

5. As an example, say your iPad has a cracked screen. The Repair Options link is the most likely path to help.

6. There is plenty of good information on this page about repairs, including a price list.

7. Whether you decide to bring your iPad in to the store or mail it to Apple, the next step is to tap Contact Apple Support.

8. You go to a website that is similar to the Apple Support app in the last task. Tap Repairs & Physical Damage and continue to answer questions on the next screens.

9. Eventually, you get to a screen where you can start to schedule an appointment. Tap Bring in for Repair.

10. Alternatively, you can arrange to send your iPad back to Apple for repairs.

11. If you are unsure what to do, you can always use the phone or chat options to talk to someone from Apple.

Don't Know What To Do?

If your iPad has stopped working or isn't functioning properly and you think it might need to be replaced, the Genius Bar should be your first stop. If they determine it needs to be replaced or repaired, they can start that process for you. Although the initial appointment at the Genius Bar is free, repairs might cost you, depending on whether you are still covered by Apple's warranty. See "Extending Your Apple Warranty," later in this chapter.

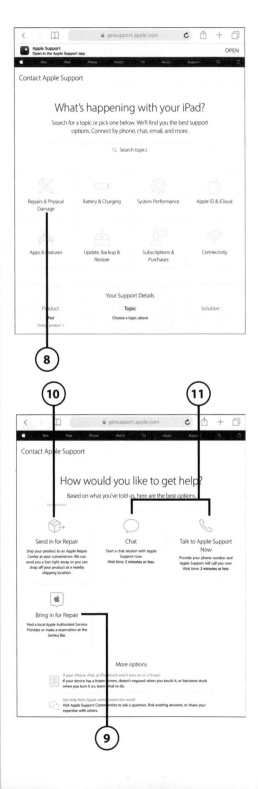

Asking a Question Online

What if your question isn't critical or urgent? You can always tap into the huge community of iPad users by asking a question on Apple's discussion forums.

1. Using the web browser on your iPad, or any computing device, go to **https:// discussions.apple.com**.

2. Tap iPad.

3. You can tap a discussion to read the question and replies.

4. Swipe up to move down the page and see more. If you scroll down far enough, there is a Search field, and you can search for a discussion.

5. Tap Start a Discussion to ask a question, but be sure that you have searched exhaustively first. It is much better to find that your question is already there than to ask it again and wait for a reply from a member of the community.

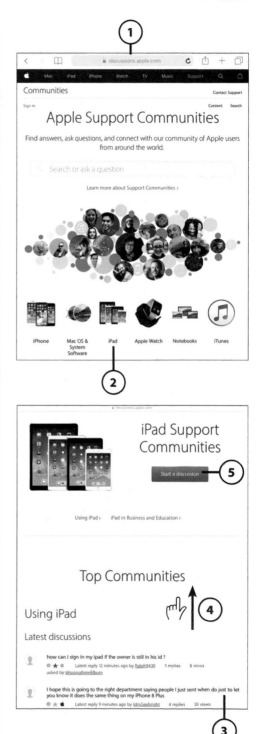

6. Type a title for your question that is short but accurately summarizes your problem. A title of "iPad Problem" is much too vague. A better title would be something like "iPad Screen Too Dark."

7. Describe the problem with as much detail as you can. Be sure to include your exact model of iPad, your version of iOS, details about the problem, and things you have tried so far. Then check back later to see if you have any replies.

It's Not All Good

No One from Apple Is Here

The Apple discussion boards are all about users helping users. There are no Apple support personnel answering questions there. It is just other users like yourself, though some might have more experience than you and be able to help.

Another mistake people often make in the discussion boards is to make product suggestions or give feedback that's intended for Apple. There's no guarantee that Apple will see it in the discussion boards. However, there is a place where you can leave suggestions. Go to https://www.apple.com/feedback/ipad.html and fill out the form there. You most likely will not get a response, but someone from Apple will see your feedback; and if others also feel the same way, you just might see a new feature in an upcoming version of iOS or the next iPad.

>>>Go Further

EXTENDING YOUR APPLE WARRANTY

Apple calls their warranty AppleCare. When you buy a new iPad from Apple or an authorized retailer, you get one year of AppleCare, plus 90 days of phone support. You can see the details at https://www.apple.com/support/products/ipad.html.

You can extend your warranty by buying AppleCare+. This gives you two years of AppleCare and two years of phone support. Prices might change, but in 2018 in the U.S., AppleCare+ costs $69 for the iPad and $99 for the iPad Pro. You don't need to buy AppleCare at the same time as your iPad. Currently, you can purchase it any time up to 60 days later.

Typically, you might think that a warranty covers defects, but not accidents. If your iPad stops working through no fault of your own, Apple will replace it. But, what about if you drop it? Then you are out of luck, right?

Actually, AppleCare+ comes with some amount of accident coverage. If you break your iPad, you can get it repaired or replaced for a small fee—currently just $49. Prices and conditions can change, so be sure to check the latest details before you buy AppleCare+. Look at https://support.apple.com/ipad/repair/screen-damage for the latest prices with and without AppleCare+.

Keeping Your iPad Up to Date

One of the most important things you need to do to keep your iPad running smoothly is to make sure it gets all the latest software updates.

Updating iOS

Apple comes out with regular free updates to iOS. Some are minor updates that fix problems and make your iPad more secure. Others include new features.

1. Tap the Settings icon on your Home screen to open it.

Settings

2. Tap General.

3. Tap Software Update.

4. In this space, you should see a message telling you that your version of iOS is up to date. Otherwise, you might see a Download and Install button and some instructions that allow you to perform an update.

   Your iPad should alert you when an update is available. But it is a good idea to periodically check the Settings app to make sure you didn't miss an update.

Updating Apps

You should keep your apps updated as well. Just as with iOS, minor updates will fix problems, and major updates often introduce new features.

1. Tap the App Store icon on your Home screen to open it. Note that if you see a number in a red circle, it indicates that you have some apps that need updating. But even if that red circle is not there, you might want to check anyway—it would force the App Store app to see if there are any updates.

App Store

2. Along the bottom of the screen, look for and tap the Updates button.

3. Look for available updates, which are listed under the Pending heading. If you don't see it, that means all of your apps are up to date.

4. Tap an Update button to immediately update a single app. If you have a lot of updates but are short on time, you might want to update the apps you know you use right now, and then save the others for a more convenient time.

5. Alternatively, tap Update All to update all of the apps.

6. You can also read information about the updates. Each update entry includes information from the developer about what is new. Sometimes you need to tap the More button to read the full text.

Automatic Updates

In the Settings app, in iTunes & App Store, there is a setting for app "Updates" under the Automatic Downloads heading. If you have that turned on, then apps should automatically update without requiring that you go through these steps. But you can still use this process to check to see what has been updated and what notes are included with the update.

Securing Your iPad

Not only is your iPad valuable, but the information you have on it is valuable as well. If your iPad is lost or stolen, you want to make sure no one gets your information, and that you have a chance of getting your iPad back.

Basic Security Measures

There are four main actions you need to take to secure your iPad and your information.

- **Set a passcode:** This is covered in "Password Protecting Your iPad" in Chapter 2, "Customizing Your iPad."

- **Secure your Apple ID and iCloud account with a strong password:** A strong password means you should not use a word that appears in the dictionary, a name, or a date in any format. Even a combination of those will make it easier for a malicious hacker to break into your iCloud account. Choose a password with random letters and digits, even mixing the case of the letters.

- **Make sure Find My iPad is turned on, and you know how to use it:** This is covered in the next section.

- **Back up your iPad often:** See "Back It Up!" in Chapter 3, "Networking and Syncing." You can back up your iPad to a computer using iTunes. You can also turn on iCloud backups by opening the Settings app, tapping iCloud, and then tapping Backup. There's no reason you can't do both. These options help you restore your documents and settings to a new iPad if the need arises. Of course, using iCloud to store your data, such as with Pages, Numbers, and Keynote, also means that all your documents would be in your iCloud account and accessible to your other devices.

Best Security: Apple Two-Factor Verification

In addition to setting a strong password for your Apple ID, you want to use Apple's two-factor verification system to make it even harder for someone to access your data. See https://support.apple.com/HT204915 to get started.

Using Find My iPad

So what happens if your iPad is missing? Your main tool in dealing with that is the Find My iPad feature built into iOS. It does more than its name suggests: Not only can you locate your missing iPad but you can also remotely wipe all your personal information from it.

Setting Up Find My iPad

Find My iPad should be on by default when you set up your new iPad and sign in with your Apple ID. Use the Settings app to check whether Find My iPad is on.

Settings

1. Launch Settings.

2. Select your Apple ID.

3. Select iCloud on the right.

4. Make sure Find My iPad is turned on. If it isn't, tap it to switch it on. You'll go to a simple screen with an on/off switch to turn it on.

    That is all it takes to add a huge security feature to your iPad. Now let's learn what to do if your iPad is missing.

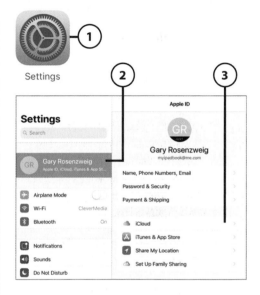

Locating a Lost iPad

Now your iPad is missing, and it is time to take action. You can log on to iCloud on any computer, another iPad, or pretty much any device with a browser. In fact, you can use a special Find My iPhone app you can download from the App Store. It also works for iPads and even Macs. If you have an iPhone, or a second iPad, it is worth having this app on both devices so you can use it in case the other goes missing.

For this example, I've used a computer to log in to iCloud.com.

1. Go to https://icloud.com in a web browser. Alternatively, you can use the Find My iPhone app on your iPhone, if you have one, or on another iPad.

2. Sign in with your Apple ID and password.

3. Tap Find iPhone.

4. This is where you keep your fingers crossed. If your iPad has been turned off, wiped by an evil genius, or destroyed in some way, then you might not be able to locate it. But give it a few minutes to try.

5. Whew! None of those things happened. There's your iPad on a map. You can zoom in and figure out where the iPad is before going any further. Perhaps you simply left it at a friend's house, in your car, or it fell behind the sofa. Best to be sure.

6. Tap the green dot to see some information in a bubble. You see the name of your iPad and the last time a signal from it was received.

7. If you have more than one device registered with Find My iPhone/iPad/Mac, use the pull-down menu to focus on only one.

8. Once you are focused on one device, you see information about it in an overlay.

9. Tap to have your iPad play a sound. Even if the volume has been turned down and muted, a sound plays at full volume. Use this if you see that your iPad is somewhere nearby, and you have simply misplaced it.

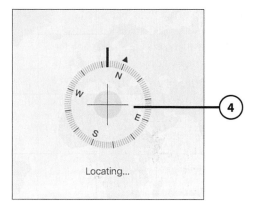

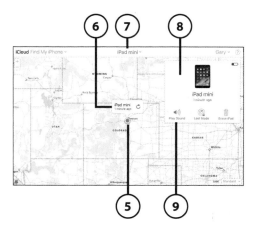

10. Tap to put your iPad into Lost Mode, which locks it. Because you have already set a passcode for your iPad, this should be redundant. But you can also use this to display a message on your iPad's screen, which can be useful if you have simply forgotten your iPad in a friendly location, and you want to see if someone has found it and is willing to help you by contacting you.

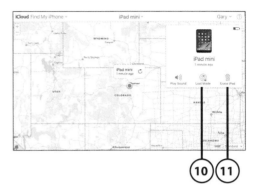

11. Tap Erase iPad, which is the nuclear option. It wipes the memory of your iPad, clearing all your personal information. The downside is that you can no longer track your iPad using Find My iPad. So use this option when you have completely given up finding it and simply want to secure your information.

>>>Go Further

YOUR SECRET WEAPON: ACTIVATION LOCK

When you turn on Find My iPad, you are also turning on Activation Lock. This is an iOS feature that prevents anyone else from erasing your iPad and reactivating it with a new Apple ID. You also can't turn off Find My iPad, and thus can't turn off Activation Lock, without your Apple ID and password.

This basically makes your iPad useless to anyone who steals it. They can't unlock it because you have a passcode. They can't wipe it because they don't know your Apple ID and password.

Activation Lock continues to work even after you have used the Erase iPad option of Find My iPad. Your iPad is still useless to anyone else without your Apple ID and password. So you get the last laugh, sorta.

It's Not All Good

So Why Would Anyone Steal an iPad?

With Activation Lock, a thief can't use your iPad. So why steal it? There are still reasons why someone would swipe an iPad. First, some people don't turn on Find My iPad or set a passcode. So some thieves might find it worthwhile to steal an iPad, hoping they took an unsecured one. And even if the iPad is locked, there might still be a way to make a buck from it by selling it for parts.

It's Not All Good

I Found It...Now What?

Say that your iPad was stolen and you've located it. It is probably not a good idea to confront a potential criminal on your own. Call the police. Be sure to tell them that you are able to track the iPad and know exactly where it is. Stories of people doing this are all over the Web. Sometimes the police are very helpful, and sometimes a small theft isn't enough to take their attention from larger matters. Most stories seem to end with the police happy to help in a straightforward case of recovering stolen property.

Index

Symbols

2D charts, creating, 318-320
2-factor verification, 508
3D charts, creating, 318-320
3D view (Maps), 351-352

A

accessories
    AirPrint printers, 467, 470
    Apple Pencil, 485
    Apple TV, 470-471
    docks, 479-480
    EarPods, 481-482
    power, 479-480
    protective covers/cases,
        483-484
    SD cards, 477-479
    USB adapters, 477-479
    video output adapters,
        472-474
    wireless keyboard,
        474-477
accident coverage, 505
accounts
    Amazon Instant
        Video, 456
    Apple ID, 508
    Apple Music, 101-102
    email accounts,
        192-193, 206
    Hulu Plus, 456
    iCloud, 508
    Skype, 426
    two-factor
        verification, 508
    YouTube, 452

Actions, Siri Shortcut, 402,
    406-407
Activation Lock, 512
adapters
    power, 480
    USB, 477-479
    video output, 472-474
Add Account option (Mail
    Settings), 192
Add a Fingerprint
    command, 48
Add Bookmark command
    (Safari), 174
Add Calendar command
    (Calendars), 147
Add List option
    (Reminders), 160
Add Songs button (Music), 93
Add to Existing Contact
    command (Mail), 196
Add to Home Screen option
    (Safari), 178
Add to Reading List option
    (Safari), 179
Adobe Illustrator, 432
AE/AF Lock (Camera), 225
AirDrop
    alerts, 81
    enabling, 80
    sharing files with
        Contacts, 81
        photos, 234, 244
        video, 263
Airplane mode, 34
AirPlay, 340
    mirroring with, 470-471
    playing music/video
        with, 115
    speaker systems, 472
    viewing photos with, 244
Airport Extreme base
    station, 64
AirPrint, 301, 467, 470
Alarm button (Clock), 161
alarms, 161-163
albums, photo, 246-247
    creating, 249
    deleting photos from, 247
    iCloud Photo Library, 249
    iCloud Photo Sharing,
        245-246
    viewing, 247

alerts
    AirDrop, 81
    Do Not Disturb feature,
        52-53
    settings, 43-43, 389-390
alignment options
    (Pages), 291
Allow Notifications
    setting, 390
All Recipes Video
    Cookbook, 437
Always Bcc Myself option
    (Mail), 206
Amazon Instant Video, 456
Angry Birds HD, 461
Animate button
    (Keynote), 334
animations in text messages,
    216, 219-220
answer apps, Wolfram
    Alpha, 443
Apple Airport Extreme base
    station, 64
AppleCare, 505
AppleCare+, 505
Apple EarPods, 481-482
Apple ID
    changing password for, 68
    compared to email
        address, 68
    creating, 67
    security, 508
    signing in with, 67-68
Apple iPad 12W USB power
    adapters, 480
Apple iPad Smart Cover, 7
Apple Lightning to USB
    cables, 480
Apple Magic Keyboard,
    474-477
Apple Maps. See Maps app
Apple Music, 76, 79, 97, 100
    cancelling, 102
    discovering new music,
        105-106
    playing music with,
        102-104
    radio stations, 106
    subscriptions to, 101-102
Apple Pencil, 485
Apple Store Genius Bar,
    497, 502

Apple support
    AppleCare, 505
    AppleCare+, 505
    Apple Support app,
        497-500
    Apple Support website,
        500-502
    discussion forums,
        503-504
    Genius Bar, 497, 502
    warranties, 505
Apple TV, 340
    AirPlay Mirroring and,
        470-471
    benefits of, 471
    viewing photos with, 244
Apple Watch, 219
appliances, controlling
    Home, 486, 491
    HomeKit, 486-490
App Limits tool, 394-397
apps. *See also* specific
    app names
    accessing Dock from, 367
    battery usage, 385-386
    deleting, 365, 384
    developer information
        for, 496
    documentation for,
        495-496
    downloading, 359-360
    dragging and dropping
        between, 376-381
    finding, 362-364
    free, 361
    fremium, 361
    games, 361
    help, 381-382
    images from, 234
    in-app purchases, 361
    information-sharing
        permissions, 388
    location services, 386-387
    notification settings,
        389-390
    offloading, 366, 384
    organizing, 364-369
    paid, 361
    purchasing, 356-360
    quitting, 6
    ratings, 359-362
    recommended, 364
    redownloading, 360

removing from
    folders, 369
restarting, 371
reviews, 359-362
sharing, 360-382
storage information,
    383-385
switching between, 371
syncing with iCloud,
    66-71
troubleshooting, 381-382,
    495-496
updating, 506-507
using simultaneously,
    372-373
viewing
    *currently running
    apps, 370*
    *Picture-in-Picture
    feature, 374-375*
App Store
    developer
        information, 496
    downloading apps from,
        359-360
    finding apps in, 362-363
    free apps, 361
    fremium apps, 361
    games, 361
    paid apps, 361
    purchasing apps from,
        356-360
    ratings and reviews,
        359, 362
    redeeming codes in, 358
    searching, 357
App Switcher, 370
Archiving email, 200
arranging apps
    on Dock, 366-367
    on Home screen, 364-365
    with folders, 368-369
articles, viewing with Safari
    Reader, 173
arts and crafts apps, 442
ArtStudio, 432
Ask Before Deleting option
    (Mail), 205
asking questions
    in Apple discussion
        forums, 503-504
    of Siri, 31-32

Ask to Join Networks
    option, 60
astronomy apps, 443
attachments, email, 199,
    205, 301
audio. *See* sound
Auto-Capitalization, 50
Auto-Correction, 50
Autodesk Sketchbook, 432
AutoFill, 183-188
    filling out web forms with,
        186-187
    security, 185-186
    setting up, 184-186
    troubleshooting, 188
automation
    app updates, 507
    appliances/electronics,
        488-490
    automatic downloads,
        57-58, 359
Auto-Night Theme switch
    (Books), 124
Averaging columns, 307-311

B

Back Up Now button, 74
backups, 508
    iCloud Backup, 70, 74
    syncing with, 74
badges, 389
bandwidth, 207
banners, 389
batteries
    charging, 479, 480
    external batteries, 480
    usage, viewing, 385-386
Battery option (Settings),
    385-386
Bcc label (email), 206
Beats 1 radio station (Apple
    Music), 106
blocking senders, 208
blogging apps, 443
Bloomberg, 444
Bluetooth devices, 474-477
Bookmarks, creating in
    Books, 127
Bookmarks button
    (Books), 127

bookmarks
  Books, 127
  Safari, 174-176
    creating, 174-176
    Home screen
      bookmarks, 178
    syncing, 177
books
  buying, 119-121
  Collections, 128
  customization, 123
  finding, 122
  in iCloud, 130
  organizing, 127-130
  PDFs in, 120
  reading
    in Books, 122-127
    in Kindle app, 130-131
    with Google Play
      Books, 132
    with Nook app, 132
    with iTunes, 79
brightness, 56-57, 123
browser. See Safari
Brushes Redux, 432
bubble effects in text
  messages, 214-216
bulleted lists, creating, 293
buying items
  apps, 356-360
  books, 119-121
  in-app purchases, 361
  iTunes, 95-97, 114
  with Touch ID, 49

C

cables
  Apple Lightning to
    USB, 480
  HDMI, 472-474
  VGA, 472-473
calculator apps
  Calculator, 434
  Calculator H, 434
  MyScript Calculator, 434
  PCalc Lite, 432-433
  Siri, 434
Calendar, 15
  calendars
    creating, 147-149
    default, 148
    deleting, 148
    sharing, 149

events, deleting, 142
syncing
  with iCloud, 66-71
  with iTunes, 79
text, 57
views, 143-147
Calendars setting (iCloud), 69
Calendar widget, 15
calls
  FaceTime, 279-283
  holding iPad during, 427
  Skype, 425-427
  video, 277-281
    receiving, 282-283
    setting up, 277-278
    troubleshooting, 283
    Wi-Fi connections, 277
Camera, 223
  AE/AF Lock, 225
  Camera Roll, 225
  exposure, 225
  focus, 225
  HDR, 225
  modes of, 224
  photos
    editing, 227
    orientation of, 226
    panoramic, 230-231
    taking, 224-225, 234
  switching between
    front/rear cameras, 225
  time delay, 225
  video, 262-264
Cancel button (Mail), 199
capitalizing text, 21, 50
car chargers, 480
cases/covers, 483-484
Cc labels (email), 205
cell styles, 311-312
cellular data, 58, 65-66
Cellular Data option
  (Settings), 65-66
charging iPad, 479-480
charts
  adding to
    presentations, 329
  creating, 318-320
  inserting into
    documents, 298
checklists, creating in
  Notes, 151
clips, editing. See iMovie
Clock, 161-163

Collections
  Books app, 128
  Photos, 236-239
color
  adjustments to
    photos, 229
  applying to text, 290
  Books themes, 124
columns, 307-311
comments
  photos, 245
  YouTube, 452
Compose button
  Mail, 198
  Notes, 149
composing
  email, 198-199
  music with GarageBand,
    447-450
configuring iPad. See setting
  up iPad
connecting
  to iCloud, 67-70
  to Wi-Fi, 63-64
Contacts
  adding, 135-138
  composing email to, 140
  copying, 140
  creating, 196
  editing, 140
  in iCloud, 135
  nicknames, 138
  searching for, 138-139
  sharing, 81, 140
  syncing
    with iCloud, 66-71
    with iTunes, 79
  VIP, 198
Contacts setting (iCloud), 69
Control Center, 33-36
  Airplane mode, 34
  closing, 36
  Do Not Disturb mode, 36
  orientation lock, 35
conversations (text
  messages), 209-210
cooking apps
  All Recipes Video
    Cookbook, 437
  Epicurious, 434
  Food Network In the
    Kitchen, 437
  Yummly, 437

Copy command, 29
copying
    contacts, 140
    text, 29
correcting text, 50
covers/cases, 483-484
Craftsy, 442
Create a New Apple ID
    option, 67
Create Document command
    (Pages), 287
Create New Contact
    command (Mail), 196
Create Shortcut button, 401
Create Spreadsheet
    command (Numbers), 304
credit cards, scanning, 181
cropping photos, 227-228
cross dissolve transitions
    (video), 272
customization. See setting
    up iPad
Cut the Rope, 460

D

Data Roaming option
    (Settings), 66
Day One, 443
Day view (Calendar), 143-144
Default Account option
    (Mail), 206
default calendar, 148
Define button (Books), 125
Delete button (Keynote), 338
deleting
    apps, 365, 384
    calendars, 148
    clock alarms, 162
    email, 197-200, 205
    events, 142
    photos, 227, 247
    reminders, 160
    slides, 338
    songs from playlists, 91
    text messages, 208, 219
    video, 263
Delivery button
    (Keynote), 335
developer support, 381-382
dictation, 27-28, 430

dictionaries
    Google as, 425
    Merriam-Webster
        Dictionary HD, 423-424
    Siri as, 425
    Urban Dictionary, 424
    Wikipedia Mobile, 424
digital touch messages, 219
directions. See driving
    directions
Discover Channels & Topics
    button (News), 415
discussion forums (Apple),
    503-504
Display settings, 56-57
displays, external, 340-341
doc/docx files, importing into
    Pages, 301
Dock, 23, 366-367, 479-480
Docs (Google), 285
documentation, app, 495-496
documents. See Pages
    documents
Done button
    Contacts, 137
    Keynote, 340
    Pages, 296
    Reminders, 160
Do Not Disturb settings, 36,
    52-53
downloading
    apps, 359-360
    automatic downloads,
        57-58
    GarageBand, 448
    Netflix, 453
dragging/dropping
    between apps
    app support for, 379
    photos
        exporting, 379-381
        inserting into email,
            376-377
    web page text, dragging
        to Notes, 378-379
Dragon Dictation, 430
drawing apps, 361
    Adobe Illustrator, 432
    ArtStudio, 432
    Autodesk
        Sketchbook, 432
    Brushes Redux, 432

Paper by FiftyThree,
    430-431
driving directions
    Google Maps, 353
    Maps, 347-349
    sharing, 349
    Siri, 349
    traffic reports, 352
Dropbox files, 86-87
DVDs, importing, 112
Dvorak keyboard, 50
Dynamic wallpaper, 41

E

EarPods, 481-482
Edit button (Clock), 161
editing
    clock alarms, 162
    contacts, 140
    photos, 226-236, 243
    text, 28-29
    video, 265-269
        music, 276
        photos, 273-274
        titles, 275
        voiceovers, 276
        transitions, 271-272
educational apps
    Craftsy, 442
    iTunes U, 440-442
    TED, 442
    YouTube tutorial
        videos, 441
email. See Mail
emojis, 212-213
Ends field (Calendar), 141
Enhance button (Photos), 227
enhancing photos, 227
Entire Music Library option
    (iTunes), 75
Epicurious, 434
Erase Data feature, 46
Erase iPad option, 512
events, deleting, 142
exposure (photos), 225
extended Apple
    warranty, 505
extensions, Safari, 188
external batteries, 480
external displays, 340-341

F

Face ID, 49
Facebook, 410-412
    posting photos to, 244
    posting video to, 263, 270
FaceTime
    calls, 279-283
    configuring, 277-278
    EarPods, 482
    troubleshooting, 283
    Wi-Fi connections, 277
fade transitions (video), 272
Family Sharing, 98-100, 382
Favorites
    Photos, 227
    Safari, 174-176
Featured podcasts, 109
feedback for Apple,
    submitting, 504
Feedly, 418
fetch delivery (email), 202
Fetch New Data setting
    (Mail), 202
files
    Dropbox, 86-87
    exporting photos to,
        379-381
    Files app, 83-87, 379-381
    Google Drive, 86-87
    iCloud Drive, 83-85
    moving between
        machines, 83
    PDFs, adding to Books
        library, 120
    sharing
        with AirDrop, 80, 81
        from iCloud Drive, 85
    storing
        on iCloud Drive, 83-85
        on other cloud services,
            86-87
Files app, 83-87, 379-381
filling in web forms
    AutoFill, 183-188
        security, 185-186
        setting up, 184-186
        troubleshooting, 188
    manually, 182-183
filtering photos, 229, 232-233
Filters option (App
    Store), 358

finance apps
    Bloomberg, 444
    Yahoo Finance, 444
Find My iPad, 70, 508-512
fingerprints, Touch ID, 48-49
flash (photos), 233
Flickr, 244
Flipboard, 418
files, 83
focus (photos), 225
folders
    creating, 198, 368
    naming, 368
    organizing apps in,
        368-369
    removing apps from, 369
Font button (Kindle), 131
fonts
    Books, 124
    Pages, 291-292
Food Network in the
    Kitchen, 437
footer rows (Numbers), 308
For You, Photos, 252
forgotten passcodes, 47
Format option
    (Numbers), 312
formatting
    cells, 312
    text in Pages, 288-292
forms, creating, 313
forums, Apple discussion,
    503-504
forwarding email, 197
free apps, 361
fremium apps, 361
functions
    AVERAGE, 307-311
    SUM, 307-311

G

Gallery view (Siri
    Shortcuts), 401
games, 361
    Angry Birds HD, 461
    Cut the Rope, 460
    Gold Strike, 463
    Harbor Master HD, 460
    Just Mah Jongg
        Solitaire, 464

    Kingdom Rush, 459
    Monument Valley, 457
    Plants vs. Zombies
        HD, 461
    Scrabble for iPad, 462
    Superbrothers: Sword &
        Sworcery EP, 458
    Temple Run 2, 462
    The Room, 463
    Where4s My Water, 459
GarageBand, 447-450
General Settings, 61
    Keyboard, 49-52
    Language & Region, 28
    Reset, 60
    Restrictions, 54
    Spotlight Search, 60
generations of iPads, 3-5
Genius Bar, 497, 502
geofence, 387
gestures
    pinching, 42
    shaking, 9
    swiping, 197, 205
    switching between apps
        with, 371
Get Sample button
    (Books), 121
GIF in text messages, 219-220
Gmail
    account setup, 192-194
    archiving, 200
    spam filters, 200
    YouTube and, 451
Gold Strike, 463
Google
    dictionary function, 425
    Google+, 413
    Google Docs, 285
    Google Drive, 86-87
    Google Maps, 353
    Google Play Books, 132
    searching for apps
        with, 364
    YouTube and, 451-453
GPS button (Maps), 346
Grid Options (Numbers), 312
grouping
    apps in folders, 368-369
    slides, 337
    text messages, 208

H

Handbrake app, 112
Handoff, 81-82
handwriting notes, 217
  MyScript Memo, 430
  WritePad, 427-428
Harbor Master HD, 460
HBO Go, 456
HBO Now, 456
HDMI adapters, 339
HDMI cables, 472-474
HDR (High Dynamic Range
  Imaging), 225
Headers tools (Numbers), 307
headphones, 481-482
help
  app developer support,
    381-382
  Apple support
    AppleCare, 505
    AppleCare+, 505
    Apple Support app, 497,
      500
    Apple Support website,
      500-502
    discussion forums,
      503-504
    Genius Bar, 497, 502
  AutoFill, 188
  external app
    documentation, 496
  internal app
    documentation, 495-496
  Tips app, 494
Heyday, 443
Hey Siri feature, 33
Highlight button (Books), 125
highlighting books, 125-126
History (Safari), 176-177
Home button, 5-6
  No Home button, new
    iPad Pro, 5-6
home controls
  (appliances/electronics)
  Home, 486, 491
  HomeKit, 486-490
Home screen, 12
  bookmarks, 178
  organizing apps on,
    364-365
  wallpaper, 42

home videos, 112
hotspots, 65
Hulu Plus, 456

I

iA Writer, 285
iBooks. See books
iCloud
  backups, 70, 74
  connecting to, 67-70
  contacts, 135
  email, 192-194
  iCloud.com website, 71
  iCloud Drive, 71,
    83-87, 244
  notes, 150
  Photo Library, 234-235,
    249, 263
  Photo Sharing, 235,
    244-246
  Photo Stream, 235
  purchased books in, 130
  reminders, 160
  security, 508
  signing in, 67
  syncing with, 66-71
  text messages, 207
images. See also photos
  in documents, 295-298
  in email, 199, 204-207
  moving, 42
  in slides, 327-330
  in text messages, 212-213
  wallpaper, 40-42
  zooming in/out, 42
iMessage, 207
iMovie
  editing video in, 267-269
    music, 276
    photos, 273-274
    titles, 275
    voiceovers, 276
    transitions, 271-272
  Ken Burns effect, 274
  sharing video with, 270
importing
  DVD, 112
  photos, 477-479
in-app purchases, 361
inboxes, email, 198

information-sharing
  permissions, 388
Instagram, 413
installing Safari
  extensions, 188
Interactive charts, creating,
  318-320
interface elements, 19-20.
  See also keyboards; Siri
International data
  roaming, 66
Internet connections
  cellular, 65-66
  Wi-Fi, 63-66
investments apps, 444
Invisible Ink effect, 215-216
invitations to photo
  albums, 246
iOS updates, 5, 505-506
iPad Pro
  Apple Pencil, 485
  Home button removed
    from new model, 5-6
  Smart Keyboard, 7,
    476-477
iPad Storage (Settings),
  383-385
iPassword, 443
iPhone apps, 375-376
iPod touch apps, 375-376
iTeleport, 444
iTunes, 455. See also Apple
  Music
  copy protection, 114
  Family Sharing, 98-100
  iTunes Match, 76
  iTunes U, 440-442
  Multi-Passes, 115
  purchasing from, 95-97
  season passes, 115
  syncing, 72-73, 97
    Apple Music, 79
    books, 79
    Calendar, 79
    Contacts, 79
    movies, 79
    music, 75-76, 79
    photos, 77-80
    podcasts, 79
    TV shows, 79
  time-delayed rentals, 115
  video, 114-115

J

Joining Wi-Fi networks, 63-64
Join option, 64
journaling apps, 443
Just Mah Jongg Solitaire, 464

K

Ken Burns effect (iMovie), 274
keyboard (on-screen), 20,
   288. *See also* dictation
   on-screen
      capitalizing text, 21, 50
      copying/pasting
         text, 29
      correcting text, 50
      customizing, 49-52
      Dvorak layout, 50
      editing text, 28-29
      Keyboard Clicks
         setting, 44
      Mail app and, 25
      modes of, 20-22
      predictive text, 26, 50
      QWERTY keyboard, 50
      Safari web browser
         and, 25
      shortcuts, 24-25, 51
      special controls,
         476-477
      splitting, 22-23, 51
      as trackpad, 30
      undocking, 22-23
   protective covers/cases
      for, 484
   third-party, 52
   wireless, 474-477
Keyboards button, 50
Keychain setting (iCloud), 70
Keynote presentations, 323
   building, 323-326
   playing, 338-340
   presenting on external
      display, 340-341
   slides
      building, 327-330
      charts, 329
      deleting, 338
      grouping, 337
      images, 327-330
      organizing, 336-338

   selecting, 338
   shapes, 329
   skipping, 338
   tables, 329
transitions, 331-336
Kingdom Rush, 459

L

Label option (Clock), 162
Language & Region
   settings, 28
libraries
   Books, 120
   iCloud Photo Library,
      234-235, 249, 263
   iTunes video libraries,
      114-115
Library button (Books), 123
Library view (Siri
   Shortcuts), 401
Lightning to SD Card Camera
   Reader, 477-479
limiting screen time, 394-397
LinkedIn, 413
List button (Photos), 229
listening
   with EarPods, 481-482
   to music, 90-92,
      102-104, 115
   to podcasts, 108
lists, creating, 292-294
Living Earth app, 439
Load Remote Images option
   (Mail), 205
local news, finding, 418
locations. *See also* directions
   location information in
      photos, 239
   location usage, viewing,
      386-387
Location Services (Settings),
   386-387
locking
   Lock Sounds setting, 44
   missing iPads, 512
   orientation, 35
Lock screen, 10, 11, 42
loops (GarageBand), 449
lost iPads
   erasing, 512
   finding, 510-512
   locking, 512

Lost Mode, 512
Loud and Gentle effect, 215
Love button (Music), 92

M

magazines, Zinio, 418
Magic Move transition,
   332-334
Mail app, 191
   accounts
      changing, 206
      setting up, 192-193
   addresses, 68, 278-279
   email
      archiving, 200
      Bcc label, 206
      checking for, 195
      composing, 198-199
      creating contacts
         from, 196
      deleting, 197-200, 205
      forwarding, 197
      moving, 199
      photos in, 199, 205,
         376-377
      previewing, 205
      reading, 195, 203
      receiving, 202
      recovering deleted, 200
      remote images in,
         205-207
      replying to, 197, 206
      searching, 201
      sending, 198-199
      signatures, 204
      To/Cc labels, 205
      undeleting, 200
   fetch delivery, 202
   folders, 198
   keyboard shortcuts, 25
   Manual setting, 203
   multiple inboxes, 198
   providers, 194
      Gmail, 451
      iCloud, 192-194
   push delivery, 202
   settings, 202-205
   spam filters, 200
   syncing, 66-71
   swipe options, 197, 205
   Trash, 197-200
   VIP, 198

maintenance
 backups, 508
 updates
  apps, 506-507
  iOS, 505-506
Manage Storage setting
 (iCloud), 69
Manually Manage Music and
 Videos option, 74-76
Manual setting (Mail), 203
Maps app, 343
 3D view, 351-352
 directions with, 347-349
 errors, 347
 GPS button, 346
 locations in, 344-346
 Satellite view, 350
 Siri and, 347-349
 traffic reports, 352
media, 114-115
Memories slideshow, 253
memos, voice, 421-423
menus, 19
Merge command, 23
Merriam-Webster Dictionary
 HD, 423-424
messages. *See* Mail app;
 text messages
microphone, 27-28, 210, 427
Microsoft Word, 285, 301
MindNode, 443
mirroring, AirPlay, 470-471
missing iPads, 510-512
mistakes, undoing, 291
MLB At the Ballpark, 387
Mocha VNC Lite, 444
model numbers (iPad),
 3-4, 60
modems, 64
Momento, 443
Moments level (Photos),
 236-239, 243
Month view (Calendar),
 146-147
Monument Valley, 457
Move button (Mail), 199
movement detection, 8
movies. *See also* iMovie;
 video
 AirPlay Mirroring, 470-471
 Amazon Instant
  Video, 456
 collecting, 114-115

copy protection, 114
Family Sharing, 98-100
HBO Go, 456
HBO Now, 456
home movies, 112
Hulu Plus, 456
importing from DVD, 112
Netflix, 454-455
orientation of, 112
playing, 111
purchasing from iTunes,
 95-97, 114
renting, 114-115, 455
sharing, 98-100
syncing, 79
YouTube, 450-452
moving
 apps
  on Home screen,
   364-365
  to/from Dock, 366-367
 email, 199
 files
  between apps, 371
  between machines, 83
  images, 42
Multi-Passes (iTunes), 115
multiple apps, using
 simultaneously, 372-373
multitasking
 dragging/dropping
  between apps, 376-381
 Picture-in-Picture feature,
  374-375
 simultaneous apps,
  372-373
music, 89
 adding to video, 276
 AirPlay, 472
 Apple Music, 76, 79,
  97, 100
  cancelling, 102
  discovering new music
   with, 105-106
  playing music with,
   102-104
  radio stations, 106
  subscriptions to,
   101-102
 EarPods, 481-482
 Family Sharing, 98-100
 GarageBand, 447-450
 pausing, 91

playing, 90-92,
 102-104, 115
playlists, 91-95
purchasing from iTunes,
 95-97
searching for, 92
sharing, 98-100
syncing, 75-76, 79, 95
volume of, 91
My Books (Books), 128
My Info (AutoFill), 184
My Music (Music), 90
My Podcasts button
 (Podcasts), 109
MyScript Calculator app, 434
MyScript Memo app, 430

N

naming folders, 368
Netflix, 454-455
networks
 syncing with iCloud,
  66-71
 transferring photos over
  networks, 234
 Wi-Fi network
  connections, 60
  security, 65
  setting up, 63-64
  turning on/off, 66
New Contact form, 136
New Message button
 (Messages), 209
news
 Feedly, 418
 Flipboard, 418
 local, 418
 News app, 70, 413-417
 USA Today, 418
News app, 70, 413-417
nicknames, adding to
 contacts, 138
Nook app, 132
Note button (Books), 126
Notes
 adding to books, 125-126
 checklists in, 151
 creating, 149-158
 in text messages, 217
 MyScript Memo, 430
 photos/sketches in,
  152-158

reminders compared to, 151
syncing, 66-71, 150
taking, 149-151
web page text in, 378-379
WritePad, 427-428
Notes setting (iCloud), 70
Notification Grouping setting, 390
notifications, 17
alerts, 43
Do Not Disturb, 52-53
settings, 389-390
silencing, 36
numbered lists, creating, 293
Numbers, 303
cell styles, 311-312
charts, 318-320
columns, 307-311
forms, 313
sheets, 304
spreadsheets, 303-306
tables
definition of, 304
multiple tables, 315-317
selecting, 315
styles, 311-312
terminology, 304
numbers and punctuation mode (keyboard), 21

O

object transitions, 334-336
Offload App button, 366
offloading apps, 366, 384
Offload Unused Apps setting, 366
On/Off button.
See Wake/Sleep button
on-screen keyboard.
See keyboard (on-screen)
Open in Books option, 120
Open in New Tab option (Safari), 171
Open iTunes When This iPad Is Connected option, 73
options lists, 18
organizing
apps
on Dock, 366-367
on Home screen, 364-365

with folders, 368-369
books in Books, 127-130
files, 83
on iCloud Drive, 83-85
on other cloud services, 86-87
project organization with MindNode app, 443
slides, 336-338
orientation
Books, 124
detection, 8
locking, 35
photos, 226-228
video, 112, 451

P

Pages documents
charts, 298
creating, 286-288
document setup, 298-299
images, 295-298
lists, 292-294
paragraph styles, 292
printing, 300-301
scanning, 154
shapes, 298
sharing, 300-301
syncing, 66-71
tables, 298
text formatting, 288-292
undoing mistakes, 291
paid apps, 361
Pano mode (Camera), 224, 230-231
panoramic photos, 230-231
Paper by FiftyThree, 430-431
paragraph styles, 292
parental guidance (Family Sharing), 100
parental restrictions, 53, 56
passcodes, 508
changing, 46
forgotten, 47
setting, 45-46, 185, 44
passwords, 44-47, 508
1Password app, 443
Apple ID, 68
Password & Security section (Apple ID), 68
Pause button (Voice Memos), 422

pausing
music, 91
video, 452
Payment & Shipping section (Apple ID), 68
PCalc Lite, 432-433
PDFs, opening in Books, 120
Pencil (Apple), 485
People section (Photos), 238
permissions, 388
Personal Hotspot option (Settings), 65
Perspective Zoom, 42
Photo mode (Camera), 224
photos
albums, 246-247
creating, 249
deleting photos from, 247
iCloud Photo Library, 249
iCloud Photo Sharing, 245-246
public, 246
shared, 246
apps, 234, 361
browsing, 235-239
Camera Roll, 225
color adjustments, 229
commenting on, 245
cropping, 227-228
deleting, 227, 247
duplicating, 78
editing, 226-233, 243
enhancing, 227
exporting
from SD cards/USB adapters, 477-479
to files, 379-381
to iCloud Drive, 244
filtering, 229, 232-233
flash, 233
For You section, 252
HDR, 225
iCloud Photo Library, 234-235
iCloud Photo Sharing, 235, 244-245
iCloud Photo Stream, 235
inserting
into contacts, 137
into documents, 295-298

into email, *376-377*
into Keynote
    presentations, *326*
into notes, *152-158*
into slides, *327-330*
into video, *273-274*
Instagram, 413
location information, 239
marking as favorite, 227
Memories slideshow, 253
moving, 42
orientation, 226-228
panoramic, 230-231
Photo Booth, 232-233
Photo Stream, 235
posting to social media,
    244-246
resetting, 228
rotating, 228
screen captures,
    257-258, 470
SD cards, 477-479
searching, 240-242
sharing, 227, 235, 243-246
slideshows, 250-253, 275
sources of, 234-235
syncing, 77-80, 234
taking, 224-225, 234
    Camera app
        modes, 224
    Camera Roll, 225
    exposure, 225
    flash, 233
    focus, 225
    from Lock screen, 224
    front/rear cameras, 225
    HDR, 225
    orientation, 226-228
    Photo Booth, 232-233
    time delay, 225
transferring over
    networks, 234
viewing, 242-244
wallpaper, 40-42
zooming in/out, 42, 228,
    242-243
Picture-in-Picture feature,
    374-375
pictures. *See* photos
pinching (gestures), 42
Pinterest, 413

planning/organizing
    apps, 443
Plants vs. Zombies HD, 461
Play button
    Keynote, 338
    Voice Memos, 422
playing
    games. *See* games
    Keynote presentations,
        338-340
    movies, 111
    music, 90-92, 102-104,
        115
    podcasts, 108
    TV shows, 111
    video, 111, 263
        AirPlay, 115
        Amazon Instant
            Video, 456
        HBO Go, 456
        HBO Now, 456
        Hulu Plus, 456
        Netflix, 454-455
        YouTube, 450-452
playlists
    music, 91-95
    YouTube, 452
podcasts
    playing, 108
    subscribing to, 108-109
    syncing with iTunes, 79
police, reporting stolen iPads
    to, 513
ports, USB, 480
posting to social media
    photos, 244-246
    videos, 263, 270
power accessories, 479-480
power adapters, 480
Power button.
    See Wake/Sleep button
predictive text, 26, 50
presentations (Keynote), 323
    building, 323-326
    playing, 338-340
    presenting on external
        display, 340-341
    slides
        building, 327-330
        charts, 329
        deleting, 338
        grouping, 337

images, *327-330*
organizing, *336-338*
selecting, *338*
shapes, *329*
skipping, *338*
tables, *329*
transitions, 331-336
previewing
    email, 205
    wallpaper, 42
Preview settings (Mail), 205
printing
    AirPrint, 301, 467, 470
    documents, 300-301
    notes, 468-469
    Pages documents, 469
    Printer Center, 469
    screen captures, 470
    third-party printing
        software, 470
Privacy settings
    Location Services,
        386-387
    Safari, 172
Private button (Safari), 172
processors, 4
public albums, 246
public transit directions,
    348-349
purchasing items. *See* buying
    items
push delivery (email), 202

Q

questions, asking
    Apple discussion forums,
        503-504
    Siri, 31-32
    Wolfram Alpha, 443
quick replies, 213
Quit button. *See* Home
    button
quitting apps, 6
QWERTY keyboard, 50

R

radio stations (Apple
    Music), 106
ratings (App Store), 359, 362
Reader button (Safari), 173

reading
books
in Books, 122-127
in Kindle app, 130-131
with Google Play
Books, 132
with Nook app, 132
with iTunes, 79
email, 195, 203
news, 418
text, 56-57
Trash, 197
reading lists (Safari), 179-180
rearranging document
images, 297
receiving
email, 202
text messages, 209-210
recipe apps
All Recipes Video
Cookbook, 437
Epicurious, 434
Food Network In the
Kitchen, 437
Yummly, 437
recommended apps, 364
Record button (Voice
Memos), 421
recording
Siri Shortcuts, 399
video, 262
voice memos, 421-423
recovering email, 200
redeeming Apple Store
codes, 358
redownloading apps,
359-360
Related section (Photos), 239
Reminders
compared to notes, 151
setting, 158-160
syncing with iCloud,
66-71, 160
Reminders setting
(iCloud), 69
remote images in email,
205-207
removing apps from
folders, 369
renaming folders, 368
renting video, 114-115, 455
Repeat Alerts setting, 390

replying to
email, 197, 206
text messages, 213
Request Desktop Site option
(Safari), 168
Reset button (Photos), 228
Reset settings, 60
resetting your iPad, 60
restarting apps, 371
Restrictions settings, 54
Resume button
Books, 123
Voice Memos, 422
Retina displays, 225
reviews (App Store), 359, 362
ringtones, 44, 283
roaming charges (cellular
data plans), 66
The Room, 463
Rotate button (Photos), 228
rotating photos, 228

S

Safari
bookmarks
creating, 174-176
Home screen, 178
syncing, 177
extensions, 188
favorites, 174-176
History, 176-177
keyboard shortcuts, 25
reading lists, 179-180
Safari Reader, 173
syncing with iCloud,
66-71
web pages
browsing, 166-169
opening multiple,
171-172
private browsing, 172
searching, 166-169
viewing, 169-170
web forms
AutoFill, 183-188
filling in manually,
182-183
zooming in/out, 170
Sample button (Books), 121
Satellite view (Maps), 350
Save button (Clock), 162

Saved Credit Cards
(AutoFill), 185
Save Password option
(AutoFill), 186
Scan Credit Card button, 181
scanning credit cards, 181
scenes (Home), 491
Scrabble for iPad, 462
screen captures, 257-258, 470
screen gestures. See gestures
screen sharing apps, 444
screen time
limiting, 394-397
Screen Time widget, 393
shared, 393
viewing, 391-393
Scripting actions, 407
Scrolling View (Books), 124
SD cards, exporting photos
from, 477-479
Search button (Kindle), 131
Search field (Mail), 201
searching
App Store, 357
apps, 362-364
contacts, 138-139
email, 201
Find My iPad, 70
locations
with Map app, 344-346
with Siri, 347
music, 92
Netflix, 454
News app, 415
photos, 240-242
Search screen, 13-14
Siri search suggestions, 13
Spotlight Search, 60
web, 166-169
Widgets screen, 16
YouTube, 451
season passes (iTunes), 115
security
Activation Lock, 512
alerts, 43
Apple ID, 508
AutoFill, 185-186
backups, 508
Find My iPad, 508-512
iCloud accounts, 508
parental restrictions,
53, 56

passcodes, 508
  changing, 46
  forgotten, 47
  setting, 45-46, 185, 44
passwords, 44-47, 508
  1Password app, 443
  Apple ID, 68
Touch ID, 48-49
two-factor
  verification, 508
Wi-Fi network
  connections, 65
Select All command, 328
selecting
  all objects, 328
  slides, 338
  tables, 315
Send button (Mail), 198
sending
  email, 198-199
  text messages, 209-210
Settings
  Apple ID, 68
  Apple Music, 101-102
  AutoFill, 184-186
  Battery, 385-386
  Cellular Data, 58, 65-66
  Data Roaming, 66
  Display & Brightness, 56
  Do Not Disturb, 52-53
  Family Sharing, 98-100
  Find My iPad
    locating missing iPads,
    510-512
    setting up, 509
  General, 28, 49-54, 60-61
  iCloud, 67-70, 98-100
    Calendars, 69
    Contacts, 69
    Find My iPad, 70
    iCloud Backup, 70
    iCloud Drive, 71
    Keychain, 70
    Manage Storage, 69
    Notes, 70
    Reminders, 69
  iPad Storage, 383-385
  Location Services,
    386-387
  Mail, 192, 202, 205
  Messages, 207
  miscellaneous settings, 60
  Notifications, 389-390

Offload Unused Apps, 366
parental restrictions,
  53, 56
password protection,
  44-47
Personal Hotspot, 65
Privacy, 386-388
Safari, 184-186
Screen Time, 391
  limiting, 394-397
  shared time, 393
  time usage, viewing,
  391-393
  widget for, 393
Sounds, 43
Touch ID & Passcode, 45,
  48, 49
Wallpaper, 40-42
Wi-Fi, 64
setting up iPad.
  See also Settings
  AirDrop, 80
  alarms, 161-163
  alerts, 43
  AutoFill, 184-186
  automatic downloads,
    57-58
  Books, 123-124
  brightness, 56-57
  cellular data connections,
    65-66
  Display, 56-57
  Do Not Disturb, 52-53
  documents, 298-299
  email, 192-193, 202-205
  Face ID, 49
  FaceTime, 277-278
  Family Sharing, 98-100
  Find My iPad, 509
  iMessage, 207
  keyboard, 49-52
  messages, 207
  parental restrictions,
    53, 56
  password protection,
    44-47
  personal hotspots, 65
  reminders, 158
  ringtones, 283
  text, 56-57
  Touch ID, 48-49
  wallpaper, 40-42

Wi-Fi network
  connections, 63-64
Set Up Family Sharing
  setting, 98
shaking (gestures), 9
shapes, inserting
  into documents, 298
  into presentations, 329
Share button
  Books, 125
  Notes, 150
  Pages, 300
  Voice Memos, 422
sharing. *See also* syncing
  with AirDrop, 80-81
  apps, 360, 382
  Books, 125
  calendars, 149
  contacts, 140
  directions, 349
  documents, 300-301
  Family Sharing, 382
  from iCloud Drive, 85
  media, 98, 100
  permissions for, 388
  photos, 227, 235, 243-246
  screen, 444
  screen time, 393
  video, 263, 270
sheets, 304
shooting photo/video.
  See Camera
shortcuts, keyboard, 24-25,
  51, 477
Shortcuts, Siri
  creating, 401, 404-407
  prebuilt, 398-399
Show Completed option
  (Reminders), 160
Show Previews setting, 390
Show To/Cc Label option
  (Mail), 205
Show Traffic button
  (Maps), 352
shuffling music, 91-92
signatures, email
  case-by-case
    signatures, 204
  creating, 204
  customizing, 204
  images in, 204
  styling, 204

signing in
to iCloud, 67
to iCloud account, 67-68
silencing
clock alarms, 163
notifications, 36
Siri
calculator feature, 434
calendar events,
creating, 142
clock alarms, creating, 163
contacts, finding, 139
dictionary feature, 425
directions, 349
EarPods with, 482
email
reading out loud, 203
sending, 199
Hey Siri feature, 33
home controls, 491
map locations,
finding, 347
music, playing, 92
nicknames, adding, 138
questioning, 31-32
reminders, creating, 159
schedule, checking, 147
search suggestions, 13
Shortcuts
Coding
creating, 401, 404-407
prebuilt, 398-399
text messages, 211
traffic reports, 352
turning on, 31-33
web searches, 168
Siri App Suggestions
widget, 15
sizing text, 56
sketches
in notes, 152-158
in text messages, 217
sketching apps, 430-432
Skip Back button (Voice
Memos), 422
Skip button (Keynote), 338
skipping slides, 338
Skype, 425-427
Slam effect, 215
sleep mode, 6-7

slides
adding to Keynote
presentations, 326
building, 327-330
charts, 329
deleting, 338
grouping, 337
images, 327-330
organizing, 336-338
selecting, 338
shapes, 329
skipping, 338
tables, 329
slideshows
creating, 250
Memories, 253
stopping, 251
video, 275
slide transitions (video), 272
Slip Ahead button (Voice
Memos), 422
slow-mo video, 264
Smart Cover, 7, 483
Smart Keyboard, 7
SMS (Short Message
Service), 211
snooze, 163
Snooze (Clock), 162
social media
Facebook, 410-412
Google+, 413
Instagram, 413
LinkedIn, 413
Pinterest, 413
posting to
photos, 244-246
video, 263, 270
Twitter, 413
songs. *See* music
sound. *See also* music
AirPlay, 115
alerts, 43
Apple Music, 97, 100
cancelling, 102
discovering new music
with, 105-106
playing music with,
102-104
radio stations, 106
subscribing to, 101-102
clock alarms, 161-163
EarPods, 481-482

Keyboard Clicks, 44
Lock Sounds setting, 44
podcasts, 108-109
ringtones, 44, 283
speaker systems, 472
text messages, 208
volume control, 8
S&P 500 index, tracking, 420
spam filters, 200
speaker systems, 472
speech. *See also* Siri
dictation, 27-28, 430
Merriam-Webster
Dictionary HD app, 424
text messages, 210
turn-by-turn
directions, 349
voiceovers, adding to
video, 276
Split command, 23
splitting keyboard, 22-23, 51
Spotlight Search, 60
Spotlight Search field (Search
screen), 13
spreadsheets (Numbers), 303
cells styles, 311-312
charts, 318-320
columns, 307-311
creating, 303-306
forms, 313
sheets, 304
tables, 304
multiple, 315-317
selecting, 315
styles, 311-312
Square mode (Camera), 224
Starts field (Calendar), 141
StarWalk 2, 443
Stills, 41
stocks apps, 419-420, 444
stolen iPads, 510-513
storage space, checking, 60
storing
apps, 383-385
files, 83
on iCloud Drive, 83-85
on other cloud services,
86-87
streaming music. *See* music
streaming video
Amazon Instant
Video, 456

Apple TV and AirPlay
  Mirroring, 470-471
HBO Go, 456
HBO Now, 456
Hulu Plus, 456
Netflix, 454-455
video output adapters,
  472-474
YouTube, 450-452
styling
  cells, 311-312
  email signatures, 204
  tables, 311-312
  text, 288-292
stylus, Apple Pencil, 485
sublists, creating, 294
subscriptions
  Apple Music, 101-102
  podcasts, 108-109
subtitles, Keynote, 325
Superbrothers: Sword &
  Sworcery EP, 458
surfing the web. *See* web
  surfing
swipe gesture, 197, 205
switches, 18
switching between apps, 371
Swype app, 52
syncing
  with backups, 74
  with Handoff, 81-82
  with iCloud, 66-71
  with iTunes, 72, 97
    Apple Music, 79
    books, 79
    Calendar, 79
    Contacts, 79
    movies, 79
    music, 75-76, 79
    photos, 77-80
    podcasts, 79
    syncing options, 73
    TV shows, 79
  music, 95
  photos, 234
  Reading List, 180
  reminders, 160
  Safari bookmarks, 177
Sync Music command
  (iTunes), 75

T

Table of Contents button
  (Books), 122
tables
  definition of, 304
  inserting
    into documents, 298
    into presentations, 329
  multiple tables, 315-317
  selecting, 315
  styles, 311-312
tabs (Safari), 171-172
tapback quick replies, 213
TED app, 442
Temple Run 2, 462
text. *See also* text messages
  adding to Keynote
    presentations, 330
  auto-correcting, 50
  capitalizing, 21, 50
  copying/pasting, 29
  dictation, 27-28, 430
  dragging to Notes,
    378-379
  editing, 28-29
  entering, 20
    dictating text, 27-28
    predictive text, 26
    with keyboard.
      See keyboard
  formatting, 288-292
  large, 56
  predictive, 26, 50
  reading, 56-57
  sizing, 56
  styling, 288-292
TextExpander 3, 52
text messages
  animations, 216, 219-220
  attachments, 301
  audio, 208
  blocking, 208
  bubble effects, 214-216
  conversations, 209-210
  deleting, 208-219
  digital touch, 219
  emojis, 212-213
  grouping, 208
  handwritten notes in, 217
  receiving, 209-210
  replying to, 213

sending, 209-210
setting up, 207
Siri and, 211
sketches in, 217
SMS (Short Message
  Service), 211
spoken, 210
tapback quick replies, 213
text size in Books, 124
Texture app, 418
themes, Keynote, 324
third-party keyboards, 52
This Computer option
  (backups), 74
time delay (Camera), 225
time-delayed rentals, 115
time-lapse, 224, 264
tip calculators.
  See calculator apps
Tips app, 494
titles
  Keynote
    presentations, 325
  video, 275
To/Cc labels (email), 205
Today screen (News), 414
Today View, 393
toolbars, 19
Top Categories list
  (App Store), 357
Top Free list (App Store), 357
Top Paid list (App Store), 357
Top Stories (News), 414
totaling columns, 307-311
Touch ID, 48-49
TouchPal app, 52
trackpad, keyboard as, 30
Tracks view
  (GarageBand), 449
traffic reports, 352
transferring photos over
  networks, 234
Transition button
  (Keynote), 331
transitions
  Keynote presentations,
    331-336
    Magic Move transition,
      332-334
    object transitions,
      334-336
  video, 271-272

Trash, 150, 197-200
travel, Heyday app, 443
Trending Stories (News), 414
trimming video, 265-267
troubleshooting
   Apple support
      AppleCare, 505
      AppleCare+, 505
      Apple Support app,
         497, 500
      Apple Support website,
         500, 502
      discussion forums,
         503-504
      Genius Bar, 497, 502
   apps, 381-382, 495-496
   AutoFill, 188
   Facebook, 283
   Tips, 494
   video calls, 283
   warranties, 505
   wireless keyboards, 474
turning book pages
   in Books, 122-123
   in Kindle app, 131
turning on/off
   iMessage, 207
   iPad, 7
   parental restrictions,
      53, 56
Turn Passcode On button, 45
tutorial videos, 441
TV shows. *See also* video
   Amazon Instant
      Video, 456
   Apple TV and AirPlay
      Mirroring, 470-471
   collecting, 114-115
   copy protection, 114
   Family Sharing, 98-100
   HBO Go, 456
   HBO Now, 456
   Hulu Plus, 456
   importing from DVD, 112
   Multi-Passes, 115
   Netflix, 454-455
   orientation of, 112
   playing, 111
   purchasing from iTunes,
      95-97, 114
   renting, 114-115, 455
   season passes, 115
   sharing, 98-100

syncing with iTunes, 79
   YouTube, 450-452
Twitter, 244-246, 413
two-factor verification, 508

U

undeleting email, 200
Undo button (Pages), 291
Undock command, 23
undocking keyboards, 22-23
undoing mistakes in
   Pages, 291
Universal Resource Locators.
   See URLs
updating
   apps, 506-507
   backups and, 508
   iOS, 505-506
Urban Dictionary, 424
URLs, 166-169
USA Today app, 418
USB cables/adapters, 477-480
USB ports, 480
Use Contact Info switch
   (AutoFill), 184

V

versions
   iOS, 60
   iPads, 3-5
VGA adapters, 339, 472-473
video, 89. *See also* iMovie
   All Recipes Video
      Cookbook app, 437
   Amazon Instant
      Video, 456
   Apple TV and AirPlay
      Mirroring, 470-471
   collecting, 114-115
   copy protection, 114
   deleting, 263
   editing, 265-269
      music, 276
      photos, 273-274
      titles, 275
      transitions, 271-272
      voiceovers, 276
   emailing, 263
   FaceTime, 482
   Family Sharing, 98-100
   HBO Go, 456

HBO Now, 456
   Hulu Plus, 456
   importing from DVD, 112
   Multi-Passes, 115
   Netflix, 454-455
   orientation of, 112
   pausing, 452
   Picture-in-Picture,
      374-375
   playing, 111, 115, 263
   posting to social media,
      263, 270
   purchasing from iTunes,
      95-97, 114
   recording, 262
   renting, 114-115, 455
   season passes, 115
   sharing, 98-100, 263, 270
   Skype, 427
   slideshows, 275
   slow-mo, 264
   TED app, 442
   time-lapse, 264
   video calls, 277-283
   YouTube, 441, 450-452
video adapters, 339, 472-474
Video mode (Camera), 224
views
   Calendar
      Day view, 143-144
      Month view, 146-147
      Week view, 145
      Year view, 144
   Siri Shortcuts, 401
   Today View, 393
Vimeo, 263, 270
VIP (contacts), 198
virtual buttons, 18-19
VNC Viewer app, 444
voice. *See also* Siri
   dictation, 27-28, 430
   Merriam-Webster
      Dictionary HD, 424
   text messages, 210
   turn-by-turn
      directions, 349
   voice memos, 421-423
   voiceovers, adding to
      video, 276
Voice Memos app, 421-423
VoIP (voice over IP).
   See Skype
volume control, 8, 91

W

Wake/Sleep button, 6-7, 47
walking directions, 348-349
wallpaper
    changing, 40-42
    Dynamic, 41
    Home screen, 42
    Lock screen, 11, 42
    previewing, 42
    Stills, 41
warranties, extending, 505
watching. *See* playing;
    viewing
weather apps, 437-439
web browser. *See* Safari
web forms, 181
    AutoFill, 183-188
    filling in manually,
        182-183
web pages
    Apple Support, 500, 502
    bookmarks, 174-178
    browsing, 166-169
    dragging text from,
        378, 379
    favorites, 174-176
    History, 176-177

opening multiple,
    171-172
private browsing, 172
reading lists, 179-180
searching, 166-169
viewing, 169-170
zooming in/out, 170
Week view (Calendar), 145
Where's My Water, 459
widgets
    Calendar, 15
    default, 15
    defining, 15
    Screen Time, 393
    Siri App Suggestions, 15
    Widgets screen, 15, 16
Wi-Fi
    FaceTime video calls, 277
    finding connections, 386
Wi-Fi network connections
    Ask to Join Networks
        option, 60
    security, 65
    setting up, 63-64
    toggling between
        Wi-Fi and cellular
        connections, 66
Wikipedia Mobile, 424
wipe transitions (video), 272

wireless base stations, 64
wireless keyboards, 474-477
wireless network
    connections, 60
Wolfram Alpha, 443
Word, 285, 301
WordPress, 443
word processing
    alternatives, 285
WritePad, 427-428

X-Y-Z

Yahoo Finance, 444
Yahoo Weather, 437-439
Years level (Photos), 236
Year view (Calendar), 144
YouTube, 450-452
    posting video to, 263, 270
    tutorial videos, 441
Yummly, 437
Zinio, 418
Zoom button, 112
zooming in/out
    Maps app, 351
    Perspective Zoom, 42
    photos, 42, 228, 242-243
    web pages, 170

Answers to Your Technology Questions

The **My...For Seniors Series** is a collection of how-to guide books from AARP and Que that respect your smarts without assuming you are a techie. Each book in the series features:

- Large, full-color photos
- Step-by-step instructions
- Helpful tips and tricks

For more information about these titles, and for more specialized titles, visit informit.com/que

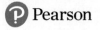